Anonymous

Ancient and Mediaeval India

Vol.2

Anonymous

Ancient and Mediaeval India
Vol.2

ISBN/EAN: 9783337385514

Printed in Europe, USA, Canada, Australia, Japan

Cover: Foto ©ninafisch / pixelio.de

More available books at **www.hansebooks.com**

ANCIENT AND MEDIÆVAL INDIA.

BY

MRS. MANNING.

VOL. II.

LONDON:
WM. H. ALLEN & CO., 13, WATERLOO PLACE,
PALL MALL, S.W.
Publishers to the India Office.
1869.

CONTENTS TO VOL. II.

CHAPTER XXII.

RAMAYANA.

Town of Ayodhyá.—King.—Four sons.—Compelled to banish Ráma.—Grief.—Aged king tells a story of his youth.—Dies.—Ráma, with his wife and brother, go to the woods.—Ráma's wife carried captive to Ceylon.—War.—Conquest.—Return 1

CHAPTER XXIII.

MAHABHARATA.

The Mahábhárata, a storehouse of legends.—Descendants of King Bharata.—Five sons of Pándu, one hundred sons of Kuru.—Education.—Rivalry.—Pándavas banished.—Adventures.—Marriage.—Second Exile.—Adventures. War.—Victory of Pándavas.—Funeral obsequies.—Pándavas' ascent.—Himavat 29

CHAPTER XXIV.

EPISODES OF THE MAHABHARATA.

Allusions to Nágas or Serpent-people.—An ascetic marries to save his ancestors from hell.—Legend of Deluge.—Churning the ocean.—Human sacrifice.—Family of poor Bráhmans.—Story of Sávitrí.—Story of Nala and Damayantí.—Sakuntalá.—Conclusion 68

CHAPTER XXV.

RAGHUVANSA, BY KALIDASA.

Fragments of the Raghuvansa, poem by Kálidása.—Dilípa, father to Raghu.—Homage to the "holy cow."—Child born.—King and Queen retire to the woods.—Raghu reigns.—Story of Aja, son of Raghu.—Marriage.—Combat.—Death.—Ráma and Sítá in flying car.—Ayodhyá described . . 97

b

BIRTH OF THE WAR-GOD.

Umá, daughter of the mountain-king Himálaya, loves Siva.—Siva is an ascetic, and gives no heed.—Earth afflicted by a demon.—Indra intercedes at Brahmá's throne.—A son of Siva alone could conquer the demon.—Anxious manœuvring for Siva's marriage.—Umá's penance.—Siva won.—Marriage. . 115

BHATTIKAVYA 137

CHAPTER XXVI.

INTRODUCTION TO THE DRAMA 141

CHAPTER XXVII.

DRAMA, ENTITLED "THE TOY-CART" 155

CHAPTER XXVIII.

SAKUNTALA.

Drama by Kálidása, translated by Professor Monier Williams . . . 171

CHAPTER XXIX.

VIKRAMA AND URVASI; OR HERO AND NYMPH.

One of the three plays attributed to Kálidása. Translated by H. H. Wilson 191

CHAPTER XXX.

MALATI AND MADHAVA.

Drama by Bhavabhuti 207

CHAPTER XXXI.

MUDRA RAKSHASA, OR THE SIGNET OF THE MINISTER.

Manœuvres and characters of Brahmanical ministers of kings.—Chandragupta, of the Takshaka or Serpent race, supersedes the Nandas. . . . 210

RATNAVALI, OR THE NECKLACE.

A Play, attributed to King Harsha, of Kashmir, who reigned between
A.D. 1113 and 1125 229

CHAPTER XXXIII.

PRABODHA-CHANDRODAYA; OR RISING OF THE MOON OF AWAKENED INTELLECT.

A Theological and Philosophical Drama, by Krishna Misra 241

CHAPTER XXXIV.

LYRIC POETRY.

Messenger-Cloud, and the Seasons, by Kálidása. Gíta-Govinda, by Jayadeva 257

CHAPTER XXXV.

PANCHATANTRA, FABLES IN FIVE SECTIONS 273

CHAPTER XXXVI.

HITOPADESA.

Fables, collected into Four Books 291

CHAPTER XXXVII.

FICTIONS.

Kathá-Sarit-Ságara, "Ocean of the Streams of Narrative;" collected about
A.D. 1088.—Allusion to the grammarians Pánini and Vararuchi . . . 311

CHAPTER XXXVIII.

THE VETALA-PANCHAVINSATI; OR TWENTY-FIVE TALES TOLD BY A VETAL . 319

CHAPTER XXXIX.

DASAKUMARACHARITA, OR STORIES OF TEN PRINCES; AND VASAVADATTA 333

CHAPTER XL.

COMMERCE AND MANUFACTURES.

Ancient Hindus a commercial people.—Products and Manufactures early obtained in Western Countries.—Ancient Hindu Laws treating on Commerce.—Merchants in Old Literature.—Trade with India of present importance to Europe.—Success depends upon knowledge of Hindu Habits and Antecedents.—Indigo, Cotton, Wool, Iron.—Perfection of Hindu Manufacture 347

And Ráma said: "I, with Sítá and Lakshmana, will enter the forest Dandaka."
—Page 18.

CHAPTER XXII.

RAMAYANA.

Town of Ayodhyá.—King.—Four sons.—Compelled to banish Ráma.—Grief.—Aged king tells a story of his youth.—Dies.—Ráma, with his wife and brother, go to the woods.—Ráma's wife carried captive to Ceylon.—War.—Conquest.—Return.

THERE are two large poems in Sanskrit, which, from century to century, have been so loved and valued by the natives of India, that it would not be preposterous to describe Hindustan as the country which possesses the Rámáyana and the Mahábhárata.

Some trumpet-notes were long ago sounded in their praise by Sir William Jones, whose Sanskrit-emblazoned banner was upheld with such energy that the scholars of all Europe rallied around it. But although these Orientalists have, ever since, been giving us, at intervals, interesting outlines and exquisite specimens of portions of the poems, it is only within the last few years that Europe has possessed any complete translation of either work.

The comparative ages of the poems have given rise to much able discussion, from which we gather, that some portions of the Mahâbhârata are probably more ancient than any portion of the Râmâyana; but that, taken as a whole, the Râmâyana is probably the older composition. The Hindu name for a poem of this description, which is complete within itself, and is the work of a single author, is Kâvya, and, judged by this rule, the Râmâyana is a Kâvya; and Vâlmiki is the author, poet, or kavi, who composed the Râmâyana. And because the Râmâyana has unity, and is stamped with the individuality of a single mind, and is pre-eminent for purity of diction, it ranks higher as a work of art than the Mahâbhârata, which is encumbered with foreign accretions, and has been made subservient to practical purposes.

The Râmâyana narrates the deeds of princes who reigned at Ayodhyâ, the town or country now known to us as Oude. Râma, the hero, is the eldest son of Dasaratha, king of Ayodhyâ, which is described as the chief city of the province of Kosala. Râma has three younger brothers, but the poem opens at a period previous to the birth of these sons. The city of Ayodhyâ, in which king Dasaratha dwelt, is thus described:—

"The streets and alleys of this city were admirably disposed, and the principal streets well watered. . . . . . It was beautified with gardens, ... fortified with gates, ... crowded with charioteers and messengers furnished with arms, adorned with banners, filled with dancing girls and dancing men, crowded with elephants, horses and chariots, and with merchants and ambassadors from various countries. It resembled a mine of jewels or the residence of Sri. The walls were variegated with divers sorts of gems, like the divisions of a chess-board;[1] the houses formed one continued row, of equal height, resounding with the music of the tabor, the twang of the bow, and the sacred sound of the Veda. It was perfumed with incense, chaplets of flowers, and articles for sacrifice, by their odour cheering the heart."

"In this city of well-fed, happy people, no one practised a calling not his own. .... None were without relations. .... The men loved their wives; ..... the women were faithful and obedient to their husbands. .... No one was without ear-rings; no one went unperfumed. No Brâhman was without the constant fire, and no man gave less than a thousand rupees to the Brâhmans. This city was guarded by warriors as a mountain-den by lions; filled with horses from Kamboja and other places, and elephants from the Vindhya and Himalaya mountains; and governed as Indra governs his city, by Dasaratha, chief of the race of Ikshwâku."[3]

This king was perfectly skilled in the Vedas and Vedângas, beloved by his people, a great charioteer, and constant in sacrifice. His courtiers were wise, capable of understanding a nod, and constantly devoted to him. Eight Brâhmans are mentioned as chief counsellors—two as *chosen priests,*—and these appear to have been his prime ministers; six others were also in office. "Surrounded by all these counsellors—learned, faithful, eminent, —seeking by wise counsels the good of the kingdom, Dasaratha shone resplendent as the sun irradiating the world."[4]

But even Dasaratha, king of Ayodhyâ, had a grief: he pined because he had no son; and, consulting his Brâhmans, they brought an ascetic or devotee capable of conducting for him the aswamedha, or horse-sacrifice, supposed to ensure the boon de-

---

[1] This expression seems to indicate that in India, as in Assyria, the walls were ornamented with mosaic. See Fergusson.
[2] Carey, vol. i. pp. 96—98.

[3] The above is given nearly verbatim with Carey's translation, only omitting all repetitious and redundancies.
[4] Carey, vol. i. p. 3.

sired by him who performs it with sufficient munificence. The sacrifice succeeded, the divinities were propitiated, and the king's three wives became the mothers of four sons. The first and favourite wife had two sons: Ráma and Lakshmana. Ráma was the eldest of the four, destined by his father to assist him in his advancing years, and to succeed to the throne at his demise.

Nothing is said of the young princes during their infancy; but when they are on the verge of manhood, the celebrated Bráhman, Viswámitra, appears at court, soliciting the king to allow Ráma to go with him to his hermitage in the hills, and clear it from fiends, who destroy his attempts to perform a ten-night sacrifice.[1] The king is distracted by contending feelings, his reverence for Viswámitra, and love for his son, being equally unbounded. After some efforts at remonstrance he yields, but not until Viswámitra's anger was such, that "fear seized even the gods." The king's two sons, Ráma and Lakshmana, are then sent away with their holy guide. Ráma was taken to holy water to render him proof against fatigue, disease, or change of form. On the following day Viswámitra presents him with celestial weapons, and thus prepared, the party proceeded to the hermitage, where, in "dreadful combat," Ráma encountered and destroyed the "night-wandering Rákshasas." On leaving the hermitage, some of the pious anchorites accompanied them as far as "Gangá's sacred bank;" and, pointing out to them "where lay a boat fast moored," bid them embark. No sooner were they in the middle of the stream than

"They heard the heavy, ceaseless sound of mighty waters
    crashing down."

And immediately we find ourselves near to Gangotri and Jam-

---

[1] Viswámitra will be remembered as an important character in the Rig-Veda, apparently a man of decided character, who ever afterwards appears in the chronicles of his country as a representative Bráhman. See remarks to that effect in our Chapter IV.

notri, the sources of the Ganges; only the poet holds the exploded opinion that the Ganges takes its rise in the Mânasa Lake.

> "High on Kailâsa's sacred peaks, hid in its paths of pathless gloom,
> Lies a deep lake, which Brahmâ erst called into being by a thought;
> And from its ever-silent depths, by unknown mountain-clefts, flows forth
> The stately river, which, at last, washes thy fathers' city round."[1]

At the sound of the endless, crashing water, Râma bowed his head in silent, wondering reverence, whilst the boat glided on across the mighty stream, until, on reaching its southern bank, a forest rose before the travellers, hanging like a blackening thunder-cloud upon the lofty cliff.[1] Stories are here introduced of goddesses who are also rivers, tributaries to the Ganges; but these are, I understand, unfit for translation, and they are easily separated from the beautiful descriptions of character and scenery amongst which they are introduced. The point to which the holy guide was conducting his young pupils was Mithilâ, in Tirhut, where a certain king, named Janaka, resided, whose daughters and nieces would, he considered, prove desirable wives for the four young princes.

Janaka, king of Mithilâ, received the travellers with much solemnity. Joining his hands together, he said to Viswâmitra: "O thou, god-like! take a place among the great sages." And having seated the holy man, he drew near with joined palms, saying: "O thou heavenly one! to-day am I blessed with the water of immortality." Then, turning to his young companions, he asked who are "those noble youths, of majestic gait like the elephant, courageous as the tiger and buffalo, ... with eyes like the lotus, of god-like aspect, and armed with daggers?"

[1] Westminster Review, Oct. 1849, p. 40.

Viswâmitra replies, that they are the sons of the king of Ayodhyâ, come to Mithilâ to enquire after king Janaka's great bow. The bow was at once sent for, and brought in an eight-wheeled carriage drawn by eight hundred men.[1] To the man who could draw this bow, the king had promised his most lovely daughter, whose name was Sîtâ. None but Râma could either lift or bend the weighty weapon; but he, with one hand, snapt it asunder,— and the crash was like that of a falling mountain.

And thus Râma won the lovely Sîtâ for his bride, whilst to his brothers were awarded the three other princesses of Mithilâ. Ayodhyâ being only a four days' journey distant from the kingdom of Mithilâ, the old king, Dasaratha, with his counsellors, journeyed thence to attend the celebration of his sons' nuptials. Rare and costly presents of shawls and silks, furs and precious stones,[2] were made upon the occasion; and then the whole party returned to Ayodhyâ, where Dasaratha's wives were eager to embrace the beautiful brides of their sons. And "all these ladies, sumptuously clad in silk, and entertaining each other with agreeable conversation, hastened to the temples of the gods to offer incense."[2]

To the aged monarch, the return of his son Râma appeared as the accomplishment of the one great wish of his life, and he joyfully commenced preparations for his public acknowledgment as vice-king, sharing with himself the honour and fatigues of his throne. But this happiness was prevented by the intrigues of Dasaratha's second wife, who desired that her son Bharata should be the future king. Unfortunately, Dasaratha had once given her the promise that he would grant any two boons she pleased to ask.

Kaikeyî herself seems to have forgotten this promise, and to have been not unfriendly towards Râma, but a crooked waitingmaid, named Mantharâ, who was surveying the town from the

[1] Hindu Theatre, vol. i. p. 280.   [2] Heeren, vol. ii. pp. 273-298.

palace roof, and observed flags and flowers, and scents and music, became aware that preparations were making for the installation of Kausalyâ's son. Rushing down in furious haste to where the queen, Kaikeyî, lay asleep, she worked upon her worst passions, and never rested until she had made her feel more wicked and jealous than herself. She then reminded her mistress of the vow which the king had formerly made to grant two boons, and suggested that she should demand that her own son Bharata be installed as vice-king, and that Râma be banished to the woods for twice seven years. Gradually, hate and jealousy were sufficiently engendered; and then Kaikeyî tore off her jewels and threw herself on the ground in the "chamber of anger."[1]

> "The lady of the glorious eyes
> Rose from her couch, as Manthara bade her rise,
> And sought the mourner's cell, in beauty's pride,
> Sure of his love who gave and ne'er denied.
> There on the ground, obedient to the girl,
> She threw her necklace and each matchless pearl.".

At the accustomed hour, king Dasaratha sought for Kaikeyî in her palace, where

> "Stalked flamingoes, mixt with swans and cranes,
> And gorgeous peacocks spread their jewelled trains.
> There screamed the parrot in his home of wire;
> There breathed the music of the flute and lyre.
> There many a damsel waited in the shade;
> Here sat a dwarf; and there a crook-back maid
> Lay in the shadow of the woven bower,
> Where glowed the champak and asoka flower.
> There many a porch, above the waving wood,
> On ivory columns wrought with silver, stood."

* * * * * *

---

[1] This chamber, called *krodhágára*, is, Mr. Ward tells us, an institution still in vogue in Hindu families, wives resorting to it when discontented or angry with their husbands. See Calcutta Review, No. xlv. p. 183.

"But no Kaikeyî in her bower he found;" and, moved by love and racked by anxious thought, he learns from a trembling damsel that "the queen in anger to the cell has hied;" and, "finding her there in mean attire, while grief consumed her as burning fire," he inquires into the cause of her wrath and woe with the utmost tenderness. She makes her petition; he pleads with her to ask for anything but Râma's banishment. She is inexorable, and presses the irrevocable nature of his vow,[1] threatening to take poison, rather than live to see Râma's mother receive more homage than herself.

The poor old king yields, but is broken-hearted.

> "A mighty monarch but an hour ago, —
> Now a poor mourner, weak and wan with woe;
> Weeping and groaning, mad with 'wildering thought,
> Like the deep wave-crowned sea to frenzy wrought."[2]

When Râma sees his father so changed, he is startled, as if his foot had touched a snake; but when queen Kaikeyî explains her case and urges Râma not to let his father break his vow, he replies: that she need not talk thus to him; for that to do his father's will would be his highest joy; and that he would give his body to the flames, or drink poison, or plunge into the tide, if his father desired it. The queen then desires that a herald, "carried by coursers of the fleetest breed," be dispatched to bring her son Bharata home to Ayodhyâ. Râma bows at the feet of his father, who had fainted, and to the stern Kaikeyî; and, walking once round them, departs, to bid adieu

---

[1] Whilst pressing upon him, that truth and honour alike require that he keep his vow, she records instances of other kings who have sacrificed what was dear to them rather than violate duty.

[2] "His flesh and blood the truthful Sairya gave,
And fed the hawk, a suppliant dove to save."

This story, of giving flesh to a dove, is told at length in the Mahâbhârata.— Bhîshma's speech, Anusâsana Parva, sect. 32. Calcutta edition. vol. iv. p. 72. Pandit, Nov. 1867, vol. ii. No. 18.

[3] Griffith. Pandit, April, 1867, vol. i. No. 11.

to his mother and comfort his wife. After a touching scene with his mother (the queen Kausalyá), he goes to his wife Sítá, who cannot understand what has happened, and asks "why no royal canopy, like foam for its white beauty," is held above him; why no gilded car leads him in triumph with four brave horses, preceded by a favoured elephant. And Ráma tells her of his father's vow, and that he is banished for twice seven years to distant forests, and is come to see her before he departs. His admonitions are: that she be firm and strong, keep well her fasts, rise from her bed when day begins to break, and to the gods her constant offerings make. He also bids her be loving and dutiful to the king, and to the consort queens; and that she cheer his mother, Kausalyá.

Sítá most vehemently and eloquently objects to being left behind. Ráma describes the dangers and hardships she would encounter in forest-life; but she declares that terror, toil and pain, with him, would be but joy: and at length she and Ráma's brother Lakshman obtain leave to go with him.

When they left Ayodhyá, one universal shriek arose; and the whole city,—the old, the young, the strong, the weak,—rushed toward the car. All proceeded together to the river Támasa,[1] where they encamp for the night; and Ráma, hopeless of persuading the citizens to leave him, crosses the river during the night, whilst they still slept. Ráma's chariot next reaches the Gomatí (or Goomtee, xlix. 10), and thence proceeds to Snugroor,[2] on the Ganges, in the neighbourhood of Allahabad. This was the extremity of Dasaratha's dominions; and Ráma here dismissed his charioteer (Sumantra), charging him with loving messages to his father. Professor Monier Williams observes, that every step of this journey is still known, and traversed annually by thousands of pilgrims. "Those," he says, "who have followed the path of Ráma, from the Gogra to Ceylon, stand out

---

[1] Now called the Tonse.   [2] Then called Sringavera.—Indian Epic Poetry, by Monier Williams, p. 68.

as marked men among their countrymen."[1] It is this that gives to the Rámáyana a peculiar interest. "The story still lives;" whilst "no one in any part of the world," concludes the Professor, now "puts faith in the legends of Homer."

When the empty chariot returned to Ayodhyá, the bereaved father could no longer endure his grief. "Six days he sat and mourned and pined for Ráma." In the middle of the seventh night a crime, inadvertently committed in his youth, rose up in his mind. He sought sympathy, but not from the mischievous, ambitious Kaikeyî. He goes to his older wife, Kausalyá, the mother of Ráma, and asks her to listen to "an ancient deed of fear," to which he attributed the present affliction. "Every deed," he says, "whether good or evil, brings in time its proper fruit;" and he then relates, that long ago, when Kausalyá was still in "virgin bloom and he in youth's delicious prime," he went into the woods to shoot. It was a most lovely "day of summer-rain time."

> "Balmy cool the air was breathing, welcome clouds were floating by,
> Humming bees with joyful music swell'd the glad, wild peacock's cry.
> Their wing feathers wet with bathing, birds slow flying to the trees,
> Rested in the topmost branches, fann'd by the soft summer breeze.
> Like the Great Deep, many-twinkling, gold-shot with gay peacock's sheen,
> Gleaming with the fallen rain-drops, sea-bright all the hills were seen.
> Whilst like serpents, winding swiftly, torrents from the mountain side
> Hiss'd along, some bright and flashing, turbid some and ochre dy'd."[2]

[1] R. T. Griffith. Pandit, June, July, and August, 1867.
[2] R. T. Griffith. Specimens of Indian Poetry, p. 11.

The first showers of May and June were giving a reprieve from the intense heat of the previous months, and, with bow in hand, the youthful monarch left the city for the woods, which skirt Sarayû's flood, intending to try his skill as an archer upon the beasts of the forest, who come down to the river to drink in the cool in the evening. Whilst laying in ambush by the river's reedy side, he heard the gurgling sound of a water-cruize being slowly filled: this he mistook for the noise made by an elephant in drinking. It was dark; and, eager to secure the game, he drew forth a glittering shaft; but, scarcely had the arrow flown, when he heard the bitter wail of a human voice, exclaiming, "Ah, me! ah, me!" in dying agony.

"Writhing on the bank in anguish, with a plaintive voice cried he,
 Ah! wherefore has this arrow smitten a poor harmless devotee?'"

The king's arrow had fatally wounded a youth who had come down to the river to draw water for his parents, who were recluses in the forests. The youth is at a loss to imagine why any murderer should seek his life. "Who," he says, "should slay a hermit, living upon roots and fruits? Does he want my vesture? Little will he gain from my deer-skin mantle and coat of bark." But it is not for his death, he says, that he is pained, but for the destitution in which he will leave his aged parents. Horror seized the king, as in the stilly calm of evening he heard this piteous moan; and, rushing through the reeds and bushes, perceived a young ascetic lying transfixed by an arrow, his hair dishevelled, his pitcher cast aside, and the life-blood fast ebbing from his wound. The dying youth fixed his eyes upon Dasaratha, and recognised him as the king; but still wondering what offence he can have given, he adds:—

"Ah! I am not thine only victim: cruel king, thy heedless dart,
Pierces, too, a father's bosom, and an aged mother's heart;
They, my parents, blind and feeble, from this hand alone can drink:
When I come not, thirsting, hoping, sadly to the grave they'll sink."

Fruitless, now, he continues, are his Veda studies, and fruitless his father's ascetic merit; for even were his father present, he would be powerless to save: "as a tree can never rescue from the axe the doomèd tree." But although his father was powerless to save, he knew that he was mighty to curse; and the gentle spirit of the sufferer recoiled from the thought that the king, the son of Raghu, would be blasted by that curse. He bids him therefore hasten to deprecate his father's consuming wrath, by being himself the bearer of the evil tidings; but begs first to have the arrow taken from his side that he may be released from agony. Dasaratha hesitated; and the youth, rightly interpreting his hesitation, assures him, that although withdrawing the shaft will occasion death, he need not fear, for he is not a Brâhman:

> "'Let not thy sad heart be troubled for thy sins, if I should die;
> Lessen'd be thy grief and terror, for no twice-born king am I.
> Fear not! thou may'st do my bidding, guiltless of a Brâhman's death,
> Wedded to a Vaisya father, Sûdra mother gave me breath.'
> Thus he spake, and I, down kneeling, drew the arrow from his side;
> Then the hermit, rich in penance, fix'd his eyes on me, and died."

The punishment which the Code of Manu awards to the slayer of a Brâhman was, to be branded in the forehead with the mark of a headless corpse, and entirely banished from society;[1] this punishment, however, being apparently commutable for a fine. The poem is, therefore, in accordance with the provisions of the Code, regarding the special guilt of killing Brâhmans; but in allowing a hermit who was not a *dwija* (twice-born) to go to heaven, the poem is in advance of the Code. The youth in the poem is allowed to read the Veda, and to accumulate merit by his own as well as by his father's pious acts; whereas the exclusive Code reserves all such privileges for *dwijas*, invested with the sacred cord. Many such inconsistencies are met with, showing that the Code never was in universal practice.

[1] Manu, ix. 237.

The king stood for a time motionless with sorrow, but as soon as he recovered himself he filled the pitcher with water from the stream; and, taking the path which had been directed, he soon reached the lowly cottage of the poor old sightless couple, who were sitting like two birds with clipt wings,—helpless, with none to guide them. The next scene will admit of no abridgment:—

"Sadly, slowly, I approach'd them, by my rash deed left forlorn,
Crush'd with terror was my spirit, and my mind with anguish torn.
At the sound of coming footsteps thus I heard the old man say:
'Dear son, bring me water, quickly—thou hast been too long away!
Bathing in the stream, or playing, thou must stay'd so long from home;
Come, thy mother longeth for thee—come in quickly, dear child, come!
Be not angry, mine own darling—keep not in thy memory
Any hard word from thy mother, any hasty speech from me.
Thou art thy poor parents' succour,—eyes art thou unto the blind.
Speak! on thee our lives are resting; why so silent and unkind?'
Thus I heard; yet deeper grieving, and in fresh augmented woe,
Spake to the bereaved father, with words faltering and slow:
'Not thy child, O noble-minded!—Dasaratha, sage, am I;
By a deed of sinful rashness plunged with thee in misery.'"

The unhappy king then tells his tale, and entreats pardon; and the hermit, who can scarcely speak for weeping, tells him, that had he concealed this sin, its fruits would have fallen upon his head ten thousand-fold; and had it been intentional, the whole race of Raghu would have perished. And before saying more he begs that they may be conducted to the fatal place, and be enabled once more to fold their darling in their arms. The lamentations uttered by the side of the "death-cold clay" are very touching, especially when the father urges the son, no longer living, to speak to his parents.

"Come, dear child, embrace thy father; put thy little hand in mine:
Let me hear thee sweetly prattle some fond, playful word of thine.

Ah! who'll read me now the Vedas, filling my old heart with joy?
Who, when evening rites are over, cheer me, mourning for my boy?
Who will bring me fruits and water, roots and wild herbs from the wood?
Who supply the helpless hermit, like a cherish'd guest, with food?
Can I tend thine agèd mother till her weary life is done?
Can I feed her, soothe her sorrow,—longing for her darling son?"

The father's thoughts then turn to the blissful mansion which his son shall attain in heaven, where he shall be welcomed by those who have fallen nobly in battle, and shall dwell in Indra's paradise with the good who have loved their Achâryas, or spiritual teachers, tended the sacred fire, studied the Veda, and performed penance; but he denounces sorrow on the wretch by whose rash hand his son fell.

Whilst the parents are occupied in sorrow's last duties over the corpse, their son, already glorified, addresses them from a heavenly chariot in the sky; saying, that through filial devotion he has attained the highest bliss, and that they must cease to grieve, and follow him to partake his joy. The old hermit cannot, however, forgive, but curses the humbled king, saying:—
"For this thing that thou hast done, as I mourn for my beloved, thou shalt sorrow for a son."

The agèd pair then ascend the funeral pile of their son, and there expire. This youthful folly it is, Dasaratha says, which has caused his present bereavement: it is the fulfilment of the ancient hermit's curse. The poor old king then bids his affectionate wife farewell, and sinks in anguish. His eyes become darkened and his memory overcast, and he bows to the awful summons of death's messengers. He envies those who will see Râma return in triumph after his exile, and dies, saying, "Ah, Râma! ah, my son!"[1]

[1] This affecting story was published in Paris in 1826, with a poetical translation by M. Chézy, and a literal version in Latin by M. Burnouf. We have also a very pleasing versified translation by Dean Milman. In the abridgment given above, the later rendering of Mr. Griffith has been almost entirely followed.

Bharata, in whose favour Ráma was banished, was at the time living amongst his maternal relations in the Punjab, to the west of the Becas (the river Vipása of the Rig-Veda); and although fleet horses were dispatched for him in haste, his journey occupied seven days. When he arrived Ráma was gone, and his father dead; and Bharata, struck with amazement and horror, instead of praise, "heaped imprecations" on his mother.

On the twelfth day, Bharata performed the *sráddha*,—those prescribed ceremonies by which a son secures rest and happiness to a deceased parent's soul. These rites are minutely described as being performed in Ayodhyá with considerable pomp. The body of the deceased king is wrapped in silk before being committed to the flames. His wives are not burnt; but a passage occurs, in which Kausalyá is said to desire to throw herself upon the burning pile. The probability is, however, that widow-burning is the practice of a later period. In the Mahábhárata, Pándu's favourite wife is said to have been permitted to burn herself with her husband's corpse; but this may be one of the many later additions made to that poem. In the striking scene which occurs at the close of the Mahábhárata, when the queens and other women come to the field of battle to recognise their deceased sons or husbands, there is much lamentation, but not a hint of widow-burning.

King Dasaratha's funeral was the occasion of a great sacrificial feast, at which animals were slaughtered and distributed.[1]

[1] Ancient Hindu customs bear a certain occasional resemblance to customs yet practised amongst the northern pastoral tribes of Asia. Mr. Atkinson describes the funeral of a sultan, on the Amoor, at which he was present. Darma Sriyin died at his pastures, near Nor-Zaraan, within the Chinese frontier. Messengers were immediately sent out on swift horses, and "within the space of a few hours the news of the sultan's death was spread over an area of near two hundred miles in diameter."

The deceased was laid out, dressed in his best attire, the chair of state at his head; his saddle, horse-trappings, arms and clothing, arranged in piles on either side; his wives and daughters knelt, with their faces towards him, chanting. There were no shrieks, tearing of hair, or wailing. We continue, in Mr. Atkinson's own words:—

"In the rear of the sultan's court, men were engaged in slaughtering ten horses and one hundred sheep for the funeral feast. Near these, numerous iron cauldrons were boiling, over fires in the ground, attended by men stripped

A lively description is then given of the poets, panegyrists, parasites, &c., resident at an Indian court; and details concerning court-customs and amusements, which were all abandoned out of respect for the deceased rajah. "At other times the town resounded with the noise and bustle of men and women, like the shout of contending armies; the great men ever going to and fro upon chariots, elephants, and prancing steeds."[1] Now the pleasure-gardens were abandoned, the tables for sacrificial offerings empty, the flower-shops closed, and bankers and merchants absent.[2] The State was without a king; and although the poet is eloquent upon the disasters to which this exposed it, we may doubt whether Brâhman-poets or Brâhman-ministers considered in their hearts this of any practical importance. Vasishtha assumed the conduct of affairs, and assembled the council, and invited Bharata to occupy the vacant throne; but Bharata positively refused the insignia of royalty, which was, according to Hindu law, the heritage of his elder brother.[3]

Under these circumstances, it is resolved that Bharata must go to the forest with a complete army and bring Râma back. He tracked the footsteps of the wanderers, spoke with the king of the Nishâdas, who had been kind to them at Sringavera, saw

naked to the waist, who, with wooden ladles in their hands, were employed skimming the boiling contents.
"When a sufficient portion was cooked the guests assembled, and seated themselves in a circle on the ground. The festival lasted for seven days, during which other sultans and kirghis were constantly arriving. It was supposed that near two thousand people assisted at this funeral. On the eighth day the sultan was interred. .... Two of the sultan's favourite horses formed part of the procession, being led immediately after the body. ... During the march, funeral hymns were chanted. .... On reaching the tomb, the body was placed in the grave, when the mullahs recited prayers and told of the great deeds of the departed. While this was performing, the two horses were killed, and interred on each side of their late master. After which the graves were filled up, and the procession returned to the soul to partake of another grand funeral banquet. One hundred horses and one thousand sheep were slain to do honour to the deceased sultan."—Atkinson's Upper and Lower Amoor. 1860. Page 62.

[1] See Col. Sykes, J. R. A. S., No. xii. May, 1841. At page 269 he gives a note referring to the Râmâyana, book 2, section 61, saying, that a cow and calf were sacrificed at Dasaratha's funeral, and ghee, oil, and flesh, distributed.
[2] Hoeren, vol. ii. p. 267. Râmâyana, iii. 98.
[3] Ibid. vol. ii. pp. 155, 156.

with emotion the inguddi tree[1] under which they had rested[2] and were hospitably entertained by Bharadwâja (near Allahabad), who also had welcomed Râma. The army is feasted on venison and peacocks, whereas in the same poem a feast is described, at which Vasishtha gave the army of Viswâmitra—no flesh,—but "an immense variety of dishes, piled mountain high, containing dainties for sucking, licking, chewing and drinking, together with rice-curries, sweetmeats, pastry, curds and whey."[3] The explanation is, that Viswâmitra and his followers were Brâhmans, whilst Bharata was a Kshattriya, accompanied by warriors, to which caste flesh-meat appears to have been habitual.

Bharata's journey is said to have been impeded by the want of roads; but able carpenters, and diggers, and labourers with carts, accompanied him,—breaking through rocks, building bridges, digging wells, and making canals.[4] As Râma and his two companions had made the same journey without roads, we must suppose that the carts, and carriages and horses, which accompanied Bharata, caused the necessity for the roads. Heeren observes, that great high roads are frequently mentioned in the Râmâyana.[5] After crossing the Jumna, they entered the district of Bandah (in Bundelkand), and advancing into the forest they approached the isolated hill of Chitrakûta,[6] which Professor M. Williams speaks of as "the holiest spot of the worshippers of Râma: it is crowded with temples and shrines of Râma and Lakshmana. Every cavern is connected with their names; the heights swarm with monkeys, and some of the wild-fruits are still called Sitâ-phal."

The meeting of Bharata and Râma was most affectionate. Râma's first enquiry was after his father. Bharata tells the sad

---

[1] Inguddi terminalia calappa—Bombay products.—Birdwood, p. 33.
[2] Monier Williams, Ind. Epic Poetry, p. 70.
[3] Heeren, vol. ii. pp. 274, 275.
[4] Ibid, p. 270, note.
[5] Heeren, vol. ii. p. 278. Râmâyana, iii. 238, and iii. 226.
[6] Monier Williams, Ind. Epic Poetry, p. 69. Chitrakûta is situated on a river called the Pisuni, fifty miles south-west of the town of Bandah.

news of his death, and entreats Ráma to return to Ayodhyá and assume the kingdom. Ráma refuses, and insists upon the duty of fulfilling his father's vow; because, unless he keep his father's vow, he cannot secure his father's happiness in heaven. He, therefore, adjures his brother to return to Ayodhyá, and "console the people and the twice-born: I, with Sítá and Lakshman, will enter the forest of Dandaka. Be thou the king of men: I will be sovereign of wild beasts. Let the umbrella shade thy head: I will take refuge in the shade of the woods."[1] Bharata makes a pathetic remonstrance, but at length Ráma embraced him, "sobbing like a staggering duck," and put an end to the discussion by saying: "Though the rising of the cool moon should cease to be pleasing, though Himavat should abandon its snow,—I will not relinquish my promise: . . . . . the sea may overflow its shore,—but I will never relinquish my father's engagement." In sign of obedience to Ráma's wishes, Bharata then begs him to put on the golden shoes (which he had brought); Ráma does so, and returns them to his brother. Bharata, then bowing to the shoes, says: "For fourteen years I will assume the matted hair and the habit of a devotee, and feed on fruits and roots. Waiting thy return, I will reside without the city, ... committing the kingdom to thy shoes."[2] The brothers embrace; and Ráma's last words are: "Cherish thy mother, Kaikeyí; be not angry with her: to this thou art adjured, by both me and Sítá."[3]

Thus ends the second book, or *Ayodhyá-Kánda*, which, Professor Monier Williams observes, "is certainly the best and most free from exaggerations in the whole poem."[4]

After Bharata's departure, Ráma travelled farther south, living in the Dandaka forest. At a hermitage they found an aged ascetic, who was mounting the funeral pile to anticipate death

---

[1] Carey, vol. iii. p. 429.
[2] "Bowing to the Shoes." See Bas-reliefs, Fergusson.
[3] Carey, vol. iii. pp. 472, 473.
[4] Monier Williams, Ind. Epic Poetry, p. 71.

and beatitude. He hailed Râma as one whom he had expected. When his body was consumed, it re-appeared in a glittering shape. This hermitage is still known as Sarbhang, in Bundelkand. Ten years they passed in this kind of life, going from hermitage to hermitage. During this time, morning and evening devotions were never omitted; and Sîtâ always waited on her husband and brother-in-law at their meals, never eating until they had finished;[1] and when travelling, she followed her husband, whilst Lakshmana brought up the rear.

At length they are advised by an ascetic at Râmagiri to visit the celebrated Agastya, who was said in the Mahâbhârata to have gone to the south of the Vindhya mountains, and there to have remained. Agastya presented Râma with a bow and weapons, and advised him to live for the remainder of his exile in the neighbourhood of Janasthâna, on the Godavery. Unhappily, the travellers' path lay through a district which was inhabited by savage, hostile tribes, called Râkshasas. Amongst these Râkshasas is a woman who falls in love with Râma. He repels her, and says that he is married. She resents his refusal. Lakshmana gets angry, and cuts off her ears and nose. This injury she avenges, by depriving Râma of his beloved Sîtâ. One of this wicked woman's brothers was Râvana, the demon-king of Lankâ (Ceylon). Râvana was a most dreadful personage, with superhuman strength and a bad disposition. He had "ten faces, twenty arms, copper-coloured eyes, white teeth," &c. "The sun, when it passed over his residence, drew in its beams with terror." But because this monster underwent severe austerities for ten thousand years, "standing in the midst of five fires with his feet in the air,"[2] Brahmâ had given him the power of taking what form he pleased.

The aid of this dreadful king Râvana his wily sister secured, by bewitching him into love for Sîtâ, the wife of Râma.[3] Râvana,

[1] Monier Williams, I. E. P., p. 72.
[2] Ibid, p. 73.
[3] H. H. Wilson, Hindu Theatre, vol. i. p. 281.

finding it in vain to hope to gain Sítá without the aid of stratagem, took with him an assistant-sorcerer, disguised as a deer; and as Ráma took great pleasure in the chase, it was not difficult for the deer to lure him from his cottage in pursuit. He did not leave his beloved Sítá without charging his brother Lakshmana to remain on guard; but the pretended deer knew how to defeat this precaution, and when wounded, cried out in the voice of Ráma: "O Lakshmana, save me!" Sítá heard the cry, and entreated Lakshmana to fly to his brother's rescue. He was unwilling, but yielded to her earnestness. Then out came Rávana from his hiding place, disguised as an ascetic, in a red, threadbare garment, with a single tuft of hair on his head, and three sticks and a pitcher in his hand. All creation shuddered at his approach; birds, beasts, and flowers were motionless with dread; the summer wind ceased to breathe, and a shiver passed over the bright waves of the river. Rávana stood awhile looking at his victim, as she sat weeping and musing over the unknown cry, but soon he approached, saying:—[1]

> "'Oh, thou! that shinest like a tree with summer blossoms overspread,
> Wearing that woven *kusa* robe, and lotus garland on thy head;
> Why art thou dwelling here, alone,—here in this dreary forest's shade,—
> Where range at will all beasts of prey, and demons prowl in every glade?
> Wilt thou not leave thy cottage home, and roam the world which stretches wide;
> See the fair cities which men build, and all their gardens and their pride?
> Why longer, fair one, dwell'st thou here, feeding on roots and sylvan fare,
> When thou might'st dwell in palaces, and earth's most costly jewels wear?

[1] Westminster Review, p. 45.

Fearest thou not the forest gloom, which darkens round on
   every side?
Who art thou, say! and whose and whence, and wherefore
   dost thou here abide?'
When first these words of Rávana broke upon sorrowing
   Sitá's ear,
She started up and lost herself in wonderment, and doubt,
   and fear;
But soon her gentle, loving heart, threw off suspicion and
   surmise,
And slept again in confidence, lulled by the mendicant's
   disguise.
'Hail, holy Bráhman!' she exclaimed: and, in her guilt-
   less purity,
She gave a welcome to her guest with courteous hospitality.
Water she brought to wash his feet, and food to satisfy his
   need,—
Full little dreaming in her heart what fearful guest she had
   received."

She even tells him her whole story: how Ráma had won her for his bride, and taken her to his father's home; and how the jealous Kaikeyî had cast them forth to roam the woods; and after dwelling fondly on her husband's praise, she invited her guest to tell his name and lineage, and what had induced him to leave his native land for the wilds of the Dandaka forest, inviting him to aid in her husband's return; for "to him are holy wanderers dear." Suddenly, Rávana declares himself to be the demon-monarch of the earth, " at whose name heaven's armies flee." He has come, he says, to woo Sítá for his queen, and to carry her to his palace in the island of Ceylon. Then burst forth the wrath of Ráma's wife:—

" *Me* would'st thou woo to be thy queen, or dazzle with thine
   empire's shine?
And did'st thou dream that Ráma's wife could stoop to such
   a prayer as thine?

I, who can look on Ráma's face, and know that there my
husband stands;
My Ráma!—whose high chivalry is blazoned through a
hundred lands!
What! shall the jackal think to tempt the lioness to mate
with him?
Or did the king of Lanka's isle build upon such an idle
dream?"

Rávana's only answer was to throw off his disguise, and with brows as dark as the storm-cloud in the sky, he carried off the shrieking Sítâ, as an eagle bears a snake, mounting up aloft and flying with his burden through the sky. The unhappy Sítâ calls loudly upon Ráma, and bids the flowery bowers, and trees, and river, all tell her Ráma that it is Rávana has stolen his Sítâ from his home.[1] Here our attention is again called to the beauty of a river running between groves of trees. On the former occasion, the Sarayû river (or the Gogra), on which Ayodhyâ stands, was frequented by water-fowl, who dipped their wings into its cooling flood, and then flew to the topmost branches of the trees to catch the faintest movement of the breeze; whilst the soothing hum of bees tempered the glad cry of the gay peacock. The river which the unhappy Sítâ loved was a tributary to the Godavery, running through the dense forests and wild districts not yet entirely explored, which lay to the north of Bombay and stretch away towards Orissa. The plash of the water-fowl, bathing in the bright waters of the Godavery, is the most cheerful feature of the scene; but, unlike the Gogra, it is skirted by no "sea-bright hills" with flashing torrents, but hemmed in by the weary woods of "the pathless Dandaka," where twining creeper-plants, hanging and climbing from bough to bough, and the rich blossoms of the lofty trees, alone relieve the forest gloom.

This country appears to be still "the pathless Dandaka;" for

[1] Westminster Review, pp. 47, 48.

a "Friend of India," writes in the *Times* newspaper, Thursday, 27th October, 1853:—"If one-half of the money that has been expended in endeavouring to improve the quality of the cotton of India had been invested in improving the navigation of the Godavery, ... slave-labour would become a drug in America." And Sir A. Cotton states: "There seems no reason why the Godavery may not become the line of a trade of a million tons a year, when once the pent-up treasures of its basin effect a breach in the barriers which have hitherto shut it up. ... Wheat might be manufactured into flour by the abundant water-power of the Godavery, and conveyed to England by hundreds of thousands of tons."

In Râma's time the woods were not haunted by Gonds, Khonds, and Koles, but by Râkshasas and monkeys; and as he did not feel strong enough to recover Sítâ single-handed, he entered into alliance with the apes or monkeys.

Sugriva, king of the apes, had a general, called Hanumat,— son of the wind. This general he sent to discover Sítâ. When he arrived at the sea-shore, opposite Ceylon, several of his companions offered to leap across, but Hanumat alone was equal to so great a leap. Having discovered Sítâ in a grove of asoka trees attached to Râvana's palace, he gave proofs of his supernatural strength, and was then conducted into the presence of the king, where he announces himself as the ambassador of his master, Sugrîva, who demands the restoration of Sítâ, on behalf of Râma. Râvana orders that Hanumat be put to death, but Vibhîshana, Râvana's brother, reminds him that the life of an ambassador is sacred. It is therefore decided that he be punished, by setting his tail on fire. Hanumat jumps on the house-tops with his burning tail, and sets the town on fire. He then escapes by springing from a mountain, which, staggering under the shock, sunk into the earth.[1] Hanumat ultimately rejoins Râma,

---
[1] Monier Williams, Indian Epic Poetry, p. 80.

and conducts the whole army to Mahendra, on the borders of the sea.

On the approach of Ráma and his allies, a council is held in Lanká, the capital of Ceylon. Rávana advises war; Vibhíshana again urges conciliation. Rávana is enraged, and kicks his brother. Vibhíshana then escapes and joins Ráma. But now the difficulty of transporting a great army across the sea occasions delay. By the help of the gods a bridge was formed, by casting huge masses of rock into the water; and vestiges of Ráma's bridge may still be seen, occasioning much inconvenience to navigators, who are obliged to lighten heavy-burdened vessels before they can pass the rocks and sand-banks of the Straits of Manaar. All over India there are scattered isolated blocks, attributed by the natives to Ráma's bridge-builders; and a writer in the Calcutta Review mentions a temple, of Cyclopean workmanship, still standing near the Straits of Manaar. "Thither," he says, "from all parts of India, wander the pilgrims, who are smitten with the wondrous love of travel to sacred shrines. From Chitrakote, near the Jumna, it is roughly calculated to be one hundred stages. We have conversed with some who have accomplished the great feat; but many never return: they either die by the way, or their courage and strength evaporates in some roadside hermitage."[1]

To travellers from Europe, also, in the present day, the Hindu sailor yet points out the remains of Ráma's bridge, across which the army passed into Ceylon. The poem relates that, after a fierce conflict, Rávana was killed, his forces dispersed, and Sitá rescued. Throughout the poem, record continually is made of the extreme fidelity of Sitá, under all the trials to which she is exposed; but although Ráma, on seeing her again, is deeply moved, he will not receive her as his wife until she has proved her purity, by undergoing ordeal by fire. Professor Williams

[1] Monier Williams, I. E. P., note, pp. 81, 82. Calcutta Review, No. xlv.

speaks of the repudiation of Sítá by Ráma as one of the finest scenes in the Rámáyana. It ends by Agni, the god of fire, placing her unhurt in Ráma's arms. He is overjoyed, and forthwith the whole party, including Rávana's brother Vibhíshana, and Ráma's monkey allies (Sugríva and Hanumat), return to Ayodhyá. Bharata hastens to meet them, and in token of delivering over the power which he still holds in trust, places on Ráma's feet the two shoes.[1]

This story most probably refers to a real expedition through the peninsula of India, and to real victories in the south; but the Hindus did not then retain conquests or make settlements in Ceylon; for at a subsequent period, about B.C. 546, the island was still, in poetic phrase, inhabited by Rákshasas, or demons, whom the Hindu warrior Vijaya ultimately conquered.[2] Ráma's expedition left more permanent traces on the "Malabars" of the neighbouring coast, amongst whom "ancient" families bear the name of Ráma's ancestor, Ikshwáku or Okkáku: see "Turnour's Epitome of Ceylon History." We already observed on the occasion of Agastya's making his way to the south of the Vindhya hills, that Brahmanical colonization then began, and the goodness of Vibhíshana, who was brother to the bad Rávana, may have been one of its results. Professor Monier Williams observes, that "Vibhíshana is described by his bad sister Suparnaká as having forsaken the practices of the Rákshasas." And Dr. Muir is referred to as thinking "that he may represent a southern tribe which had been converted to Brahmanism."[3]

Ráma's return to Ayodhyá is solemnized by a formal coronation, and with this the original work is supposed to close. The seventh book, which critics believe to be a comparatively modern addition, describes Ráma as finding no rest in this world. The story it relates is given in the drama entitled Uttara-Ráma-Charitra.

[1] Monier Williams, Indian Epic Poetry, p. 87.   [2] See woodcut, vol. i. p. 399.
[3] Monier Williams, Indian Epic Poetry, p. 9, note.

The Rámáyana is, undoubtedly, one of the greatest treasures of Hindu literature. We especially note in this poem exquisite poetry, fine feeling, tender emotion, and love for the beautiful in scenery. And in matters of fact we also find it rich and instructive. It marks, for instance, the progress of Hindu occupation in India; for in the Rámáyana the more important Hindu kingdoms are all beyond the range of the primitive Vedic locations treated of in our early chapters. The river Sarayû, eastward of the Vedic river Saraswatî, and eastward even of the river Jumna, exhibits the celebrated Aryan race of Ikshwáku reigning at Oude,—the more ancient form of that word being Ayodhyá. And still farther east we read of kings of Mithilá in Tirhut, who are the allies of the kings and princes of Ayodhyá. And again, we observe Hindus migrating into Bundelkand, crossing the Vindhya hills, inhabiting forests in the peninsula, living on the banks of the Godavery, marching down to the southernmost extremity of the country, crossing the sea to Ceylon, and returning again to Ayodhyá, their home.

Before quitting this subject, we feel tempted to call attention to the remarkable similarity which may be traced between customs depicted in the Rámáyana and some of those represented on the bas-reliefs at Sanchi, in central India. The drawings which Colonel Maisey made from the celebrated Tope or monument there discovered, we are now so fortunate as to be able to consult in the valuable lithographs given by Mr. Fergusson, in his "Tree and Serpent Worship."

The objects of religious reverence exhibited at Sanchi are entirely different from those recognised in the Rámáyana. In the poem, Ráma reveres the Vedas and invokes protection from Brahmá, Vishnu, and the sun; whilst religious people in the bas-reliefs make prostrations and offerings to Buddha's Bo-Tree or wheel. But if we keep in our minds that the poem describes the city of Ayodhyá "as beautified with gardens, fortified with gates. . . . . . crowded with charioteers, and with messengers furnished with arms, adorned with banners, filled with dancing girls and dancing men, with elephants, horses, and chariots, with merchants and ambassadors from various countries;" and that in this "city of well-fed, happy people, no one was without car-rings," and "no Brâhman was without the constant fire;" —we may then turn to plates xxxiv. and ff. of Mr. Fergusson's magnificent work, where we see streets full of people, which in most respects answer to the above description. These series of plates show also pleasure gardens,[1] with birds, and flowers, and pavilions—such as those around the queen's palace—supported "on ivory columns wrought with silver;" and "..... trees that aye with fruit and blossom glowed," which, "o'er limpid waters hung their tempting load." And we see seats, probably "seats of silver and of gold;" and such cakes and viands as lured the "dainty taste" of the kings and princes of Ayodhyâ.

The dramatis personæ of the stories recorded in marble on the Sanchi Tope are, undoubtedly, not the individuals whose histories are given in the poem; but the incidents depicted bear sometimes a strange resemblance, as in plate xxxv.

Animals resort to a river in the cool of the evening. A boy stands in the water to fill a cruize, and is transfixed by the arrow of a huntsman. In plate xxvi., fig. 2, two apes or monkeys, answering to Râma's friends, Sugrîva and Hanumat, associate on equal terms with Hindus. And again, in plate xxxv., the Horse of Sacrifice runs loose, followed by a rajah in a chariot,—thus corresponding with the horse which, in the last book of the poem, wandered for a year, attended by princes in preparation for Râma's coronation and aswamedha, after his return to Ayodhyâ.[2]

---

[1] *Ante*, p. 10. Griffith, in Pandit, for May, 1867, p. 179.

[2] We observed at the commencement of this chapter that the Râmâyaṇa is the work of the poet Vâlmîki, and that it bears the impress of being the work of one mind, but that in the course of time it had suffered from alterations and additions. I am assured, however, that we are so fortunate as to possess manu-

scripts which enable critics to distinguish the original work from the later recensions. The older text is that which has been published at Calcutta, and even with greater care it has been also published in Bombay. The later version, which is sometimes called the Bengal recension, is that which M. Gorresio has translated into Italian. It has the disadvantage of containing many interpolations, and indulges, moreover, in considerable prolixity. Another variety in the later edition, is a disposition to smooth down "grammatical peculiarities," which appear in those days to have been esteemed "grammatical difficulties."

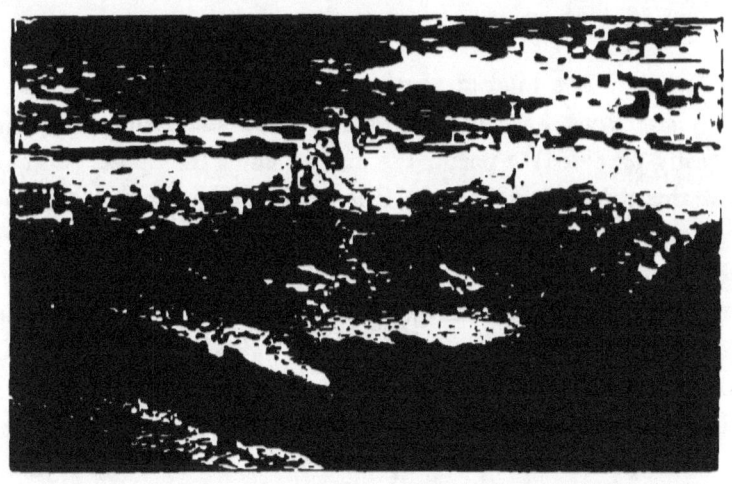

"Then, with their senses subdued, the heroes having reached the north,
Beheld, with their heaven-desiring eyes, the lofty mountain, Himavat;
And, having crossed its height, they beheld the sea of sand,
And next they saw Mount Meru, the king of mountains."

MAHABHARATA.

CHAPTER XXIII.

MAHABHARATA.

The Mahábhárata, a storehouse of legends.—Descendants of King Bharata.—Five sons of Pándu, one hundred sons of Kuru.—Education.—Rivalry.—Pándavas banished.—Adventures.—Marriage.—Second Exile.—Adventures.—War.—Victory of Pándavas.—Funeral obsequies.—Pándavas' ascent.—Himavat.

SIR WILLIAM JONES, with affectionate enthusiasm for the Sanskrit literature, then lately discovered, compared the Mahábhárata and the Rámáyana to the epic poems of Greece and Rome. But more accurate knowledge, and cooler judgment, shows that, according to Hindu rules of criticism, the Mahábhárata is not a poem, but an Akhyána (legend); meaning that it is a storehouse of legends, or a kind of regal or official cyclopædia. A poem, they say, must have had an author; and the Rámáyana is (as already observed) a poem, the author being the poet Válmiki; but this does not make it an *epic* poem, and it does not in fact conform to Aristotle's definition of an epic. On the other hand, the Mahábhárata consists of a series of legends, but gives the impression of a poem, because it has a purpose and a story peculiar to itself. It is said to be the work of Vyása, the arranger,[1] who never loses sight of the main story, amid the countless dissertations and episodes which have been introduced at various epochs.

In its present form it is very voluminous, consisting of eighteen books or cantos, containing, it is said, one hundred thousand stanzas.[2] The word Mahábhárata is formed from *mahat* (changed to mahá—great), and Bhárata; and as the main subject of the work is the contests which took place between the rival families of this descent, the word probably implies, "the great history of the descendants of Bharata." Their adventures and their warlike deeds are chronicled; and of such interest is the chronicle, that Akbar the Great caused these heroic verses to be translated into Persian, omitting, however, all that related to Hindu gods.[3]

The story begins at the time when the Bharatas are represented by the families of the two brothers, Pándu and Kuru, called collectively Pándavas, and Kauravas or Kurus.[4]

The Pándavas, or sons of Pándu, are the heroes of the tale. The combats which took place between the Pándavas and their cousins, the Kurus, are the subject. Their common ancestor,

---

[1] Goldstücker, in Chambers' Cyclopædia, art. "Mahábhárata." From *vi*, implying distribution, diffusion, and *as*, "to throw"; hence Vyása, literally throwing asunder, diffusion, or one who throws asunder, diffuses; the counterpart of *samdos*, literally throwing together, concision: from *sam*, together, and *as*, to throw,—a word kindred to *homerus* (ὁμ—ηρος).

[2] Wilson's Works, vol. iii. pp. 277, 278. Intro. to Mahábhárata, published in Quarterly Oriental Magazine.

[3] Heeren, Hist. Re., vol. ii. p. 159, where he refers to the Ayín Akberí, the editor of which has rendered into English the tables of contents prefixed to each Book of the Persian translation.

[4] Kaurava is the correct form, but custom permits the simpler word.

king Bharata, reigned over a small domain, of which Hastinápura (Elephant Town), on the Ganges, was the capital. Pándu, the father of the five Pándavas, was a successful king, who had renewed the somewhat waning glory of his kingdom; but in middle life he followed a not unusual fashion in India, by abdicating his throne. He then retired with his two wives and five sons to the woods, on the southern slope of the Himalayas, there to indulge his passion for hunting. He died whilst his children were yet young; and they and their mother were taken to their uncle, at Hastinápura. This uncle, named Dhritaráshtra,[1] although blind, had become king when his brother went to live in the woods. He received the young princes graciously, and allowed them to share in all the arrangements made for their hundred cousins.[2] Dhritaráshtra's hundred sons, the Kurus, whilst yet boys, showed themselves to be jealous of the Pándavas, who are in fact children of the elder branch, and have a nearer claim to the succession of the throne than themselves. The eldest of the Kurus is Duryodhana, a name intimating "difficult to be fought with." The others we must leave at present unnamed, it being purposeless to introduce one hundred names at once. The five Pándus are,—Yudhishthira, Bhíma (the "terrible"), Arjuna, and the twins Nakula, and Sahadeva. The three first of these princes were the children of Pándu's first wife, Prithá; but the mother of the twins was Mádri. "The cousins were in the habit of playing together, but even in boyish sports the Pándu princes excelled the sons of Dhritaráshtra. This excited ill feeling; and the spiteful Duryodhana tried to destroy Bhíma, by mixing poison in his food, and throwing him into a pond whilst stupefied from its effect. Bhíma was not, however, killed, but appeared again to play an important part in the struggles of their future lives. Bhíma, the "terrible," is

---

[1] The word Dhritaráshtra means literally, "whose kingdom is upheld."
[2] H. H. Wilson, Quarterly Oriental Magazine, republished in Essays on Sanskrit Literature, vol. i. p. 277.

the strongest of the Pándavas, and is said to have the "stomach of a wolf."[1] When an infant, his mother happened to let him fall on a rock. The rock was shivered, but the child unhurt.

When the king deemed the time to have arrived at which the brave scions of each royal house

> "Of Kuru and of Pándu, should improve
> Their growing years in exercise of arms,
> With sage deliberation, long he scanned
> A suitable preceptor for their youth,
> Who, to meet skill in war, and arms, should join
> Intelligence and learning,—lofty aims,—
> Religious earnestness, and love of truth."[2]

Then we are introduced to a Bráhman, named Drona, who occupies a prominent place throughout the story. Drona was no ascetic; and having in childhood shared the lessons and sports of the royal heir of the neighbouring kingdom of Panchála,[3] he felt inclined to live again at that court, now that his old playfellow had become king. Never doubting of a hearty welcome, he presented himself to king Drupada quite unceremoniously, merely saying: "Behold in me your friend." His reception was, however, totally different to what he anticipated.

> ". . . . . the monarch sternly viewed
> The sage and bent his brows, and with disdain
> His eyeballs reddened: silent awhile he sat,
> Then arrogantly spoke: 'Bráhman, methinks
> Thou showest little wisdom, or the sense
> Of what is fitting, when thou call'st me friend
> What friendship, weak of judgment, can subsist
> Between a luckless pauper and a king?'"

The king of Panchála stares at the idea of friendship between

---

[1] Monier Williams, Ind. Epic Poetry, pp. 90, 97.
[2] Professor Wilson, Oriental Magazine, vol. iii. p. 134.
[3] Panchála was between Delhi and the Punjáb, and apparently descended as low as Ajmeer.—H. H. Wilson, Oriental Magazine, vol. ii. p. 231.

a learned Bráhman and one to whom the Vedas are a mystery, or between a warrior and one who cannot guide a chariot through the ranks of war; and continues—

".....he, to whose high mandate nations bow.
Disdains to stoop to friends beneath the throne.
Hence, then, with idle dreams: dismiss the memory
Of other days and thoughts: I know thee not."

Drona was too much astonished to speak, but he instantly withdrew from Panchála to Hastinápura, where he was most reverentially welcomed, and was at once entrusted with the instruction of the five young Pándu and the hundred young Kuru princes.

The king of Panchála, in the meantime, was in terror to think of the awful calamities to which he had exposed himself, by his contumelious treatment of a Bráhman; and his first anxiety was to secure a son for his protection. He resorted to the usual Hindu plan, of performing an expensive sacrifice, aided and guided by powerful Bráhmans; and he became, in consequence, the parent of one son and one daughter. Of the son, very little is related; whilst the daughter becomes the heroine of the poem. She is of dark complexion, but of exceeding loveliness; and the only wish we have for her is, that we could change her name,— Draupadí; for it is almost beyond the power of art, to invest a heroine with so uncouth an appellation with the poetic charm belonging to her in the Sanskrit.[1] For the present, leaving Draupadí to grow in loveliness at Panchála, we must return to Drona and his numerous pupils at Hastinápura.

Drona had, in youth, been equally instructed in wisdom and in arms; and he taught the young princes "to rein the steed,

---

[1] In the Sanskrit, I am told she is frequently called Rájaputrí, which means "the daughter of a king or a princess." It has been observed, "that though Páṇini knows the word Rájaputra (whence the name of the Rájputs), no rule of his work would justify the formation of the feminine, rájapatrí. It is, however, the object of a special Várttika, by Kátyáyana, a contemporary of Páṇjali, and therefore about b.c. 120. See Goldstücker's Páṇini.

to guide the elephant, to drive the chariot, launch the javelin, hurl the dart, wield the battle-axe, and whirl the mace." The Pándava princes, the favourites of the poet, are always represented as both more amiable and more heroic than their cousins, the Kurus. Yudhishthira, the eldest Pándu, is a calm, inflexible person, who leads and supports his younger brothers; Bhima, the second, as already remarked, noted for his strength,—and Arjuna, the third, is full of enthusiasm and affection, excelling in every martial exercise, and winning all hearts. Nor less conspicuous were his peaceful virtues: "submissive ever to his teacher's will, contented, modest, affable, and mild." Drona already prophesied that he would be an unequalled archer amongst the sons of men.[1]

When these youthful princes had all become expert in the use of arms, their great preceptor proposed to the king that a public trial of their skill should take place. A level plain was consequently chosen, on which the pious Drona reared an altar for an offering to the gods; and a lofty pavilion was prepared, in which were rich seats for the king and his queens, the courtiers and the court ladies. The archery is described with great animation; and from this and other passages we learn, to use Professor Wilson's words, "that the Hindus cultivated archery most assiduously, and were very Parthians in the use of the bow on horseback." The spectators were perfectly dazzled by the fearful shower of arrows which the archers let fly,—sometimes whilst standing on the ground, sometimes whilst "on generous steeds, in rapid circles borne." At the close of the combat, Drona called for Arjuna, who modestly came forward in his radiant armour, "as glorious as a cloud at set of sun;" whilst the gazing crowd uprose and greeted him with "the clang of shells, and trumpets, and loud shouts of admiration." The favourite hero being thus, as it were, *encored*, made further exhibition of his skill. He leapt

---

[1] Professor Wilson, Oriental Magazine, vol. iii. p. 138.

from his chariot and vaulted into it again, whilst it was whirling forward at full speed. He also shot five arrows at once from his chariot into the jaws of a wild boar . . . . . scouring along the plain. A pause then ensued, during which the opposing parties sought repose; but suddenly "a clamour, rending heaven," was heard behind the barrier, and Karna, a new combatant, was announced. His ears shone with gorgeous pendants, and, with bow in hand, he advanced proudly, like a moving mountain. This new hero was anxious to enter the lists with Arjuna, and offered to perform every feat which Arjuna had achieved.[1]

Arjuna and Karna were about to try their strength, when a kinsman of the royal house, named Kripa, who was the brother of the wife of Drona, interposed, saying to Karna: "O young man, are you come hither to measure weapons with Arjuna? Know you that he is the son of Raja Pándu and the Ráni Kunti; and you must now declare the names of your father and mother, that we may know whether you are worthy of being matched with Arjuna?" At these words Karna, believing that his father was a charioteer, hung his head, "as, when surcharged with dew, the blooming lotus bows its sacred blossom."[2] But Duryodhana, who desired to set up Karna against Arjuna, replied thus to Kripa: "Greatness depends not upon birth, but strength; and I hereby appoint Karna to be Raja of the country of Anga." So saying, Duryodhana took Karna by the hand, and led him to a golden seat, and ordered "the umbrella of royalty to be held over his head."[3]

At this moment the father of Karna appeared, trembling with age. His son advanced to show him reverence, and kissed his feet; but the Pándavas looked on with contempt, and Bhima said to Karna: "Is it with such a father as this that you presume to match yourself with Arjuna? You, the son of a cha-

[1] Oriental Quarterly Magazine, vol. iii. p. 140.
[2] Ibid.
[3] Hist. India, by J. Talboys Wheeler, vol. i. p. 89. This is allowed to be "mythical," as also that Karna's father was the sun, and his mother the mother of the three elder Pándavas, Kunti.

rioteer,—what have you to do with a bow and arrows? You had better far take a whip and drive a bullock-cart after your father." Hereupon the sports were suddenly concluded. Darkness came on, Duryodhana led Karna away to his own palace, and the multitude dispersed.[1]

The jealousy and hatred of the Kurus towards the Pándavas increased as they all attained manhood. The father of the Kurus being blind, required a vice-king, or Yuvarája, *i.e.*, "Little Raja." In this office Yudhishthira was installed, he being entitled to it as eldest son of the late king Pándu. But Duryodhana was highly discontented at this arrangement, and at length persuaded his blind father to send away the Pándavas to the city of Váranávata (the modern Allahabad). Here a splendid house was prepared for them; but hemp, resin, and other combustible substances, were secreted within; for the wicked Duryodhana plotted that the house should be set on fire, and the five Pándavas and their mother burnt to death. Warning, however, was given to these intended victims before they left Hastinápura; and, on taking possession of their splendid new habitation, they had an underground passage made, by which, when the expected fire took place, they all escaped.[2]

---

[1] Mr. Wheeler observes that the implication, that Karna was of low birth, by reason of his being the son of a charioteer, is open to question. "The driving of chariots was a favourite and royal amusement with the ancient Kshattriyas. .... But the 'arrangers' of the Mahábhárata were evidently anxious to throw contempt upon charioteers," ... the reason being, apparently, that "the charioteers anciently occupied the same confidential position in relation towards a raja as was subsequently filled by the purohita, or family priest." It may, therefore, be inferred, that the Bráhmans were jealous of the influence exercised by the charioteers; and, Mr. Wheeler continues, " the substitution of a purohita for a charioteer probably marks *the* period in *Hindu* history when the military domination of the Kshattriyas was brought under the ecclesiastical and caste-supremacy of the Bráhmans."—Hist. India, vol. i. pp. 90, 91.

[2] Mr. Wheeler considers this story "totally opposed to ancient Kshattriya ideas," which regarded an attack on a sleeping enemy as a heinous crime; but such proceedings would be "familiar to the Brahmanical compilers of the Mahábhárata, who had recently been engaged in burning down the monasteries and temples of the Buddhists." He thinks, also, that the splendour of Váranávata, the "college of holy men," the feast given to the poor by Kunti, &c., are details which "belong altogether to a later period of Hindu civilisation."—Vol. i. pp. 102, 103.

The under-ground passage is still

Among the poor people whom Kuntí had been feasting was a Bhíl woman, with five sons, who, according to the practice of their tribe, drank deeply of intoxicating liquor, and then lay down and slept heavily. The next morning their bodies were found amid the ruins of the conflagration; and it was believed in Hastinápura that the Pándavas had perished. This report promoted their safety; and, wishing to remain concealed, they proceeded in all haste to the southern jungle, which was inhabited by wild beasts, and Asuras and Rákshasas, who were eaters of men. "And Kuntí and all her sons were very weary, except Bhíma, and he was tall and strong, and carried his mother and elder brother on his back, his younger brethren under each of his arms, whilst Arjuna followed close behind."

The next day they reached a dark and dreadful forest, and all except Bhíma were so overpowered with sleep, that they threw themselves beneath a tree, and slept. Then a terrible Asura, named Hidimba, smelt them out, and an improbable story is narrated about his sister. A fierce battle takes place between the Asura and Bhíma, which ends in Bhíma's dashing out Hidimba's brains. Bhíma is said to have married the handsome sister of his assailant, but no reference is made to such a marriage in the subsequent passages of the poem; and we may pass it over "as a later addition to the main tradition."[1] The sage, Vyâsa, appeared to the Pándavas, whilst yet in this wild forest, and advised them to dwell in the city of Ekachakrá. . . . . . "So they de-

---

pointed out in the fort at Allahabad, through which the Pándavas escaped between thirty and forty centuries ago. This is, of course, considered highly mythical; and indeed Mr. Wheeler thinks the original or authentic tradition of the first exile is "lost in a later fiction;" and that all legends referring to places at a distance from Hastinápura, are mythical.—Vol. i. p. 107. Monier Williams, Indian Epic Poetry, p. 98.

The adventures of the Pándavas during these wanderings represent the early struggles between the Aryan race and the ruder tribes who previously possessed the country: "their encounters with Asúras and Rákshasas are all palpable fictions;" but . . . . . valuable, as traces which have been left in the minds of the people of the primitive wars of the Aryans against the aborigines."

[1] Mr. Wheeler considers that this fiction "should probably be referred to the Buddhist period, when caste distinctions were not generally recognised."—Hist. India, vol. i. p. 108.

parted out of the jungle, and took up their abode in that city, and dwelt there for a long time in the house of a Bráhman. Every day the brothers went out in the disguise of mendicant Bráhmans to collect food as alms; and whatever was given to them they brought home at night to their mother, Kuntí, who thereupon divided the whole into two equal portions, and gave one to the wolf-stomached Bhíma, whilst the remaining half sufficed for all the others."[1]

Ekachakrá is identified as the modern Arrah, a city about two hundred miles from Hastinápura, on the southern bank of the Ganges. They were still in the neighbourhood of the cannibal Asuras, and, one day hearing sounds of weeping from the chamber of their Bráhman hosts, they discovered that an Asura raja, named Vaka, who lived in the adjacent forests, claimed daily a man or woman from Ekachakrá, to be devoured; and the day had arrived on which this family was obliged to supply the victim. The story is told with great pathos, and will be found amongst the Episodes of our next chapter. Bhíma destroys Vaka, but the wise-judging Yudhishthira feels that, after so remarkable an exploit, their disguise will not probably avail; and therefore, in order to avoid being discovered by the Kauravas, they all departed out of Ekachakrá, together with their mother, Kuntí.[2]

Whilst wandering through the country, carefully avoiding courts and capitals, news reached them that the daughter of the king of Panchála was about to hold a Swayamvara. This term denotes, that her father was about to invite company

---

[1] Talboys Wheeler, Hist. India, vol. i. p. 110.
[2] Mr. Wheeler observes, that "the lives which the Pándavas are said to have led in the city of Ekachakrá is precisely that of Buddhist priests carrying round the alms-bowl." He also observes, that "whilst the Aryan out-post at Alla- habad seems to have maintained an ascendancy over the aborigines, or at any rate was apparently secure from their attacks, the city of Arrah, which was two hundred miles farther to the eastward, was compelled to pay a daily tribute of provisions to the Raja of the Asuras."—Hist. India, vol. i. p. 114.

to his court, amongst whom she was to choose her future husband.

It must be remembered, that Drupada, king of Panchála, had insulted Drona, who then left Panchála for Hastinápura, and devoted himself to training the youthful princes of that kingdom in the exercise of arms, under promise that they would aid him in his personal quarrel. Drupada lived meantime in constant dread of vengeance, and was anxious to strengthen his position, by getting his daughter married to a warrior who could defeat Drona and his Kuru allies. Arjuna was such a warrior;—he, who had been Drona's favourite pupil in boyhood. The Pándavas were missing, and Drupada knew not how to find them; but not believing them dead, he resorted to the expedient of announcing a public entertainment, at which his daughter's choice of a husband would be determined by feats of strength. The Pándava brothers happening now to be upon the road which leads to Panchála, observed unusual throngs of people, and learned from some Bráhmans that "princes with throbbing hearts" were hastening to attend the Swayamvara, and encouraged the disguised Pándavas to accompany them.

> "Thither we go, and willingly will guide
> Your steps, to share with us the liberal gifts
> That princely bounty on our tribes bestows;
> Or to behold, if so your youth prefer,
> The joyous revelry that gilds the scene.
> For thither mummers, mimes, and gleemen throng;
> Athletics, who the prize of strength or skill
> Contend, in wrestling or the gauntlet's strife;
> Minstrels, with sounding lutes; and bards, who chant
> Their lord's high lineage and heroic deeds.
> These merry sports beheld, you may return
> With us, or where you list; unless it chance
> The Princess toss the wreath to one of you:—
> For you are goodly, and of God-like bearing."[1]

[1] H. H. Wilson, Oriental Magazine; republished 1864, in Works, vol. i. p. 327.

The brothers accepted the proposal, and travelled with the Bráhman band until

"At length arrived, they made their humble dwelling
A potter's lowly roof; and, daily, forth
They fared to gather alms.
And now the day of festival drew nigh,
When Drupada, whose anxious hopes desired
A son of Pándu for his daughter's lord,—
And who had sent his messengers to search
The banished chiefs, still sought by them in vain,—
Devised a test no other force but their's
He deemed could undergo, to win the bride.
A ponderous bow with magic skill he framed,
Unyielding but to more than mortal strength;
And, for a mark, he hung a metal plate,
Suspended on its axle, swift revolving,
Struck by a shaft that from the centre strayed.
This done, he bade proclaim,—that he, whose hand
Should wing the arrow to its destined aim,
Should win the Princess by his archery.

"Before the day appointed, trooping came
Princes and chiefs innumerous: 'midst the throng
Duryodhana, and all the hundred sons
Of Dhritaráshtra, with the gallant Karna,
In haughty cohort at the court appeared.
With hospitable act the king received
His royal guests, and fitting welcome gave.

"Between the north and east, without the gates,
There lay a spacious plain; a fosse profound;
And lofty walls enclosed its ample circuit;
And towering gates and trophied arches rose;
And tall pavilions glittered round its borders.
Here, ere the day of trial came, the sports
Were held; and, loud as ocean's boisterous waves,
And, thick as stars that gem the dolphin's brow,
The mighty city here her myriads poured.
Around the monarch's throne, on lofty seats
Of gold, with gems emblazoned, sat the kings,

Each lowering stern defiance on the rest.
Without the barriers pressed the countless crowd,
Or, clambering upon scaffolds, clustering hung.
Skirting the distance, multitudes beheld
The field from golden lattices, or thronged
The high house-tops, whose towering summits touched
The clouds, and, like the mountain of the gods,
With sparkling peaks streamed radiant through the air.
A thousand trumpets brayed, and slow the breeze,
With incense laden, wafted perfume round;
Whilst games of strength and skill, the graceful dance,
The strains of music, or dramatic art,
Awoke the gazer's wonder and applause.

"Thus sixteen days were passed, and every chief
Of note was present; and the king no more
Could, with fair plea, his daughter's choice delay.
Then came the Princess forth, in royal garb
Arrayed, and costly ornaments adorned:
A garland, interwove with gems and gold,
Her delicate hands sustained. From the pure bath,
With heightened loveliness she tardy came,
And, blushing, in the princely presence stood.
Next, in the ring the reverend priest appeared,
And strewed the holy grass, and poured the oil,—
An offering to the god of fire,—with prayer
Appropriate, and with pious blessings crowned.
Then bade the king the trumpets' clangor cease,
And hush the buzzing crowd; while his brave son,
The gallant Dhrishtadyumna, on the plain
Descended, and his father's will proclaimed:—
'Princes, this bow behold! You mark—these shafts—
Whoe'er with dexterous hand at once directs
Five arrows to their aim; and be his race,
His person, and his deeds, equivalent
To such exalted union,—He obtains
My sister for his bride. My words are truth.'
Thus said, he to the Princess next described
Each royal suitor by his name, and lineage,
And martial deeds; and bade her give the wreath
To him whose prowess best deserved the boon."

And now the competitors came forward, and each endeavoured to bend the bow; but all in vain. Some made such violent efforts that they fell back on the ground, exciting peals of laughter from the spectators; others freed themselves from their royal robes, and diamond chains, and diadems, and, unfettered, put forth their strength; but it was in vain. And the bow defied them all, until Karna came; and he "the yielding bow-string drew and ponderous shafts applied." Loud shouts of acclamation burst from the multitude. But again the reputation of low birth changed Karna's success into defeat.

> "The timid Draupadi in terror cried,
> 'I wed not with the base-born.' Karna smiled
> In bitterness, and upwards turned his eyes
> To his great sire,—the sun; then cast to earth
> The bow and shafts, and sternly stalked away."[1]

Amazement spread through the crowd at finding all the royal suitors foiled. At this moment Arjuna advanced. The Bráhmans thought him a student of their tribe, and tried to hold him back from certain failure; but in vain. And some, who had observed his strength—like that of an elephant, his carriage—which resembled that of a lion, and his self-collected soul,—augured well for his success.

> "Unheeding praise or censure, Arjuna
> Passed to the field. With reverential steps
> He round the weapon circled; next addressed
> A silent prayer to Mahadeo; and, last,
> With faith inflexible, on Krishna dwelt.
> One hand the bow upbore, the other drew
> The sturdy cord, and placed the pointed shafts.
> They flew; the mark was hit! and sudden shouts
> Burst from the crowd—long silent. Fluttering, waved
> The Bráhman scarfs, and drum and trumpet brayed;
> And bard and herald sung the hero's triumph."[2]

[1] Oriental Mag., vol. iv. p. 144.
[2] This passage is literally translated by Mr. Muir, in the fourth volume of his Sanskrit Texts, published in 1863, as

The king and his daughter liked the appearance of the disguised Arjuna, and were very well contented at his success; but the rage of the princely suitors knew no bounds. "Behold!" they cried, "the king regards us no more than straws, and deigns to wed his daughter to a Bráhman boy, whose craft has humbled royalty." And the lightest punishment they can assign for such an offence, is to kill the king of Panchála and all his race, and to throw the damsel herself into the flames, unless she prefer choosing a royal lord. Their gleaming swords were brandished, and Drupada turned in terror to the Bráhmans. Arjuna rushed to his side, Bhíma tore up a tree and stood ready for the fight; and, for awhile, the kings and warriors were so amazed at this novel daring of the priestly tribe that they stood still, admiring. But soon—

"Like elephants,
With passion maddening, headlong on they rushed:
Like elephants the brothers met their might."

And now Karna and Arjuna really met in fight; but when Karna felt the power of his youthful adversary, he was astonished. He paused, to express his wonder and admiration. "No Bráhman," he says, "could have displayed such skill in arms; nor breathes the man who could my strength defy,—save Arjuna." Arjuna does not, however, at once declare himself. The kings are compelled to retire, believing themselves conquered by a set of Bráhmans, from whose bands shouts of triumph fill the air; whilst the trembling hand of Draupadí now ventures to fling the marriage chaplet round the neck of Arjuna.[1]

follows:—"While the Bráhmans thus uttered various speeches, Arjuna stood firm as a mountain, trying the bow. He then made a circuit round it, bowing down in reverence to the boon-bestowing lord, Isána (Mahádeva); and, having meditated on Krishna, Arjuna seized the bow."

Mr. Muir refers to Lassen, Ind. Alth., vol. i. p. 646, who there states that this reference to Krishna must be regarded as a later interpolation.

Professor Wilson observes in a note, that "walking round a temple, an image, a venerable personage, or any object of veneration, is an act of worship among the Hindus." It was constantly practised by the early Buddhists.

[1] Oriental Magazine, vol. iv. p. 146.

The marriage of Draupadí is an unpleasant subject to Brahmanical commentators. The poem distinctly states that she became the wife of the five brothers, and that each brother had a son by her. But such an arrangement is utterly opposed to modern Brahmanical law and custom, and is not willingly recognised as a fact in their national traditions. And although such marriages are disapproved amongst Aryan or Brahmanical tribes, they are still practised by tribes in the northern mountains, by the Nairs of southern India, and by some of the Buddhists in Thibet.[1]

The legend of the Swayamvara of Draupadí is especially valuable, because it "illustrates to a very suggestive degree the rude civilisation which prevailed amongst the earliest Aryan settlers in India." The Raja of Panchála determined to give his daughter to the best archer who might compete for her hand; but "the main incident in the story, and the one which may have served to perpetuate the memory of the Swayamvara, was not so much the fact that Arjuna won the hand of Draupadí by hitting the mark, as the fact that the people all supposed him to be the son of a Bráhman. The disdain with which the ancient Kshattriyas regarded the mendicant Bráhmans, presents an extraordinary contrast to the superstitious respect with which the modern Bráhman is universally regarded."[2]

Krishna, prince of Dwáraká, is said now to have seen through the disguise of the five brothers, and by his intervention to have persuaded the angry rajahs that Draupadí had been fairly won; and so the Pándavas were permitted to carry off their prize to the house of their mother. She received Draupadí as the betrothed bride of her sons, and bid her distribute the victuals at the evening meal. Now it happened, that not only Drupada had been in trouble at his daughter's becoming the bride of a Bráhman, but his son also felt anxious concerning the men who

---

[1] Strabo mentions a similar custom as prevailing in Arabia, Cæsar remarks it in ancient Britain, and Polybius and Xenophon allude to its legality amongst the Spartans.—Fourcaux, Intro., p. xvi.
[2] Talboys Wheeler, vol. i, pp. 127—9.

had won his sister. And this son of Drupada, named Dhrishtadyumna, had followed them home, and heard their conversation, and so learned that they were not Bráhmans, but Kshattriyas, of the royal house of Hastinápura. Upon this, he hastened back to Kámpilya to acquaint his father with the joyful tidings. Next morning Drupada sent his family priest as envoy, formally to ask the brethren who they were. Yudhishthira replies, bidding them remember "that no one but a man of noble birth could have shot the eye of the golden fish at the Swayamvara." A second envoy presently arrived, inviting them all to the palace in Kámpilya; "and Yudhishthira and his brethren proceeded in one chariot, whilst Kuntí took charge of Draupadí, and went with her in a chariot by themselves." A grand feast is then prepared, served up on dishes of gold. Discussions taking place as to whose wife she was to be, her brother speaks modestly, but says that it seems to him, that according to the rules of the Swayamvara, his sister is already the wife of Arjuna." But this is overruled by the sage Vyása, who had come to the city, and was consulted with much reverence. "The sage Vyása then explained to Raja Drupada, that it was ordained by a divine mystery that his daughter Draupadí should be married to the five brethren; and the raja gave his consent. And Draupadí was arrayed in fine garments, and adorned with five jewels, and married first to the elder brother, Yudhishthira." . . . . "Then the Pándavas were no longer afraid lest they should be discovered by the Kauravas; and they dwelt for many days in much joy and tranquillity in the city of Kámpilya."

When the Kauravas heard that not only the Pándavas were living, but were strong in alliance with the king of Panchála, they held a council, which proved stormy, all the elders being in favour of peace, whilst the young clamoured for war. Then Bhíshma urged that the kingdom should be divided between Kauravas and Pándavas, and his counsel prevailed; and Vidura went forth and brought back the sons of Pându to Hastinâpura; and all the people rejoiced.

The portion of the kingdom allotted to Yudhishthira and his brethren was Khândavaprastha, on the banks of the river Jumna; and there they built a city which resembled the city of Indra, and was called Indraprastha, on the site of which stands the modern city, Delhi.

A myth is here introduced, which relates the burning of the forest of Khândava: this work is performed by the god Agni, who had hitherto been continually baffled by the god Indra. On this occasion Agni seeks aid from Krishna. To Arjuna he gave "the bow, which is called gândîva, together with two quivers, and a chariot, having the monkey-god for its standard. Then Arjuna and Krishna fought Indra, and Agni devoured the forest of Khândava; and all the serpents were devoured likewise, excepting their Raja Takshaka, who escaped from the burning." At present we will not dwell further on this tradition than to observe, that it doubtless points to the first settlement of Aryans on the river Jumna, when they cleared the forest of its trees, and also of its aboriginal denizens (called Nâgas).[1]

The kingdom of Khândavaprastha then became established, and its prosperity is thus described:—

"Now Raja Yudhishthira ruled his râj with great justice, protecting his subjects as he would his own sons;" and his kingdom enjoyed perfect prosperity, reminding one of the description of Ayodhyâ city, in the Râmâyana. "Every subject of the Raja (Yudhishthira) was pious; there were no liars, no thieves, no swindlers; and there were no droughts, no floods, no locusts, no conflagrations, no foreign invaders, and no parrots to eat up the grain."[2]

Raja Yudhishthira, having now triumphed over his enemies, resolved on performing the great royal sacrifice, known as the

---

[1] For a further notice of Nâgas, see p. 68, and Chapter xxi., on Architecture.

[2] Talboys Wheeler, vol. i., chap. vi., pp. 155—162.

Râjasûya, which would constitute him an independent and sovereign raja. The account given of these ceremonies must be received with reservation, as being of the later Brahmanical period, when a great sacrifice was no longer a feast, but a symbol, and when the worship of Krishna was being sedulously promulgated.

The raja (Yudhishthira) begins by calling together a council of his brethren, at which the Brâhmans, and his preceptor Dhaumya, and the sage Vyâsa, were also present. But although this council rejoiced at what he proposed, he was still distrustful, and would not commence the sacrifice without taking the counsel of Krishna. Krishna, therefore, came from Dwârakâ, and took part in all that followed.

Krishna, Arjuna, and Bhima, disguise themselves as Brâhmans, and go to Magadha to conquer king Jarâsandha; but Magadha (the modern Behar) is so distant from Indraprastha, or Delhi, as to make this extremely improbable. So, also, in preparation for the ceremony, Yudhishthira sends his brothers in various directions, to compel princes to acknowledge his pretensions, and pay tribute; but these details are also fabulous.[1] The ceremony itself is essentially the same as the inauguration of a king, described in the Aitareya-Brâhmana, but it more closely resembles the inauguration of Râma in the Râmâyana. Here, as on that occasion, the wife of the king participates in a portion of the ceremonies; and, what is considered a more important deviation, is, that Râma, the king, is sprinkled with the consecrated liquid, not only by the chief priest, but also by seven other eminent Brâhmans, by assistant-priests, attendant

---

[1] The description given of the pavilions provided for each raja who attended is striking. "These pavilions were all very lofty, and of a pure white colour, inlaid with gold, and round about each pavilion were very many beautiful trees, and round about the trees was a lofty wall, covered with garlands of flowers. And the windows in those pavilions were made of golden network, and the doors to the rooms were made of gold and silver. And all the rooms were laid with rich carpets, ... and perfumed with sandal wood and incense; and the stairs .... were so made, that no man found it difficult to go up or down."—Talboys Wheeler, vol. i. p. 165.

damsels, the military chiefs and the citizens.[1] But whilst the king thus received a larger quantity of the consecrated liquid than had been prescribed in the Vedic period, the typical quality of the ingredients had in great measure been lost sight of.

The kinds of wood used are the same, whilst the number of seats required is increased.

" Free from anger and pain, the royal son of Kunti sat down joyfully on the golden throne-seat, his face turned towards the east; in front of him took their seat, on a beautiful golden stool, the valiant Sâtyaki, and Vâsudeva; at either side of him, on fine-shaped jewelled stools, the noble Bhîmasena, with Arjuna; on a sumptuous ivory throne-seat, embellished with gold, Prithâ, with Sahadeva, and Nakula. . . . . . The righteous king, having taken his seat, touched with his fingers white flowers—auspicious emblems—fried grain, the soil, gold, silver, and a pearl; so that all his subjects, headed by the house-priest, became aware that he had thus possessed himself in an auspicious manner of earth, gold, and the various kinds of jewels." The implements used were jars made of gold, udumbara-wood, silver and clay, sacrificial grass, cows' milk, fuel of samî (acacia suma), aswattha (pipal), and palâsa (butea frondosa) wood, honey and clarified butter, a ladle, made of udumbara wood, and a conch, ornamented with gold. The king, and the "dark daughter of Drupada," sat on the "white, solid-legged throne-seat," covered with a tiger-skin, looking to the north-east.[2]

The poem represents, that at this festival Brâhmans were held in great reverence. The celebrated Vyâsa was "chief of the sacrifice." Prime ministers, or their sons, "waited upon the Brâhmans." Kripâ gave the gifts to the Brâhmans;" and, lastly, it tells of the crowning honour bestowed upon their caste, viz., "Krishnâ was appointed to wash the feet of the Brâhmans."[3]

[1] Goldstücker, Sanskrit Dictionary, s.v. Abhisheka.
[2] Ibid, p. 251.
[3] Talboys Wheeler, vol. i. pp. 166—176. Monier Williams, Indian Epic Poetry, p. 103.

The Pándavas were now, apparently, in possession of all that could secure prosperity; but the very splendour of their success would seem to have revived the dark jealousy of Duryodhana; for he and his brother Duhsásana, and one or two others, plot to deprive the newly-inaugurated king of his territories. They first secure the co-operation of a relative, named Sakuni, who was a noted gambler, and then induce the blind old Mahárája to invite the Pándavas to a gambling festival at Hastinápura. Yudhishthira accepts the invitation, with secret misgiving; for "he was not very skilful in throwing the dice," and he knows that "Sakuni is dwelling in Hastinápura." Of Sakuni, it is said that "he is very skilful in throwing dice, and in playing with dice that were loaded; insomuch, that whenever he played he always won the game." Nevertheless, Yudhishthira feels compelled to go; for "no true Kshattriya can refuse a challenge to war or play." The game they played at seems to have resembled backgammon, "pieces on a board being directed by the throwing of dice." Certain seeds or nuts served as dice; and dice of this description were used for the guidance of a portion of the religious sacrifice. So that, to throw dice, was not deemed objectionable; and only when a passion, or the stake immoderate, was it esteemed a vice.

It was, of course, contrived that Yudhishthira should be led on to stake and to lose all that he possessed. "He first lost a very beautiful pearl; next, a thousand bags, each containing a thousand pieces of gold; next, a piece of gold, so pure that it was as soft as wax; next, a chariot set with jewels, and hung all round with golden bells; . . . . . next, all his cattle; and then the whole of his Ráj, excepting only the lands which had been granted to the Bráhmans."[1] At length he stakes himself, and then his wife Draupadí. "And all assembled were greatly troubled, and thought evil of Yudhishthira; and his uncle Vidura put his

[1] Talboys Wheeler, vol. i. p. 178.

hand to his head and fainted away; whilst Bhishma and Drona turned deadly pale." ..... When "Sakuni threw the dice and won Draupadî for Duryodhana," the wicked Duryodhana and Duhsâsana grew savagely triumphant, and desired that Draupadî should be brought into the assembly as a slave, and bid to sweep the rooms. A servant is sent to the lodging of the Pândavas to announce to Draupadî that she, Yudhishthira, and his brothers, had been lost at play, and must obey Duryodhana, having become his slave. She is exceedingly wroth, but seeks protection from a point of law. "Then Draupadî cried out: 'Go you now and inquire whether Raja Yudhishthira lost me first or himself first; for if he played away himself first, he could not stake me.'"[1]

Draupadî objects, and tries to escape; but Duhsâsana pursues, seizes her by her hair, and drags her before the assembled chiefs; for which deed Bhîma vows that he will drink the blood of Duhsâsana. This scene of violence is ended by the arrival of the blind old Dhritarâshtra, who had been fetched by Vidura. All were silent under his rebuke; and the Pândavas and Draupadî are permitted to depart peacefully. But, after a time, Duryodhana persuaded his father, that men with anger in their hearts are dangerous, "and will return within a short time," he says, "and slay us all." Give us leave, then, I pray you, to play another game with the Pândavas, and to let the side which loses go into exile for twelve years; for thus, and thus only, can a war be prevented." "So they sat down again to play, and Sakuni had a set of cheating dice, as before; and with them he won the game." The final scene represents Duhsâsana shouting for joy, whilst Bhîma says: "Be not elated; but remember, the day will come when I will drink your blood,—or I am not the son of Kuntî." "And the Pândavas, seeing that they had lost, threw off their garments, and put on deer-skins, and prepared

[1] Talboys Wheeler, vol. i. pp. 180 f.

to depart into the forest with their wife, and mother, and their priest Dhaumya; but Vidura said to Yudhishthira: 'Your mother is old and unfitted to travel; so leave her under my care:' and the Pándavas did so." Then the brethren departed, hanging down their heads and covering their faces; but Draupadí spread her long hair over her face, wept bitterly, and vowed a vow, saying: "My hair shall remain dishevelled from this day until Bhíma shall have slain Duhsásana and drank his blood; and then he shall tie up my hair again, whilst his hands are dripping with the blood of Duhsásana."[1]

And so "the Pándavas, with their wife Draupadí, and their priest Dhaumya, wandered in the jungle for twelve years; and they fed on such game as the brethren shot on their way. And they made many pilgrimages to holy places, and fasted, and bathed, and performed religious worship. And they met with many holy Bráhmans and sages, who instructed them in pious acts, and beguiled them with stories of ancient times; and promised them, that the day should come when they should be restored to the ráj. Sometimes they came to verdant places, covered with flowers, where the trees were loaded with fruits; and many curious animals presented themselves. But at other times violent winds arose, and blackened the sky with dust, and laid prostrate the largest trees; and then the rain would fall heavily, and the torrents would pour down from the mountains like rivers; and the roads would become so wretched that all the Pándavas, excepting Bhíma, would be unable to move, and the weary Draupadí would faint away. But then the giant Bhíma would carry his fatigued brethren and his afflicted wife upon his back and shoulders, and under his arms; and walk on as before."[2]

Some of the myths or stories above alluded to are beautiful, and some of the religious and metaphysical instruction intro-

---

[1] Talboys Wheeler, vol. i. pp. 184, 188.   [2] Ibid, vol. i. pp. 188, 204, 205.

duced is in itself interesting; but we must, nevertheless, proceed speedily with the main thread of the story.[1]

The stipulated period of twelve years' exile in the forest at length drew to a close; and then the Pándavas sent their priest, Dhaumya, to live with their father-in-law at Panchála, whilst they and Draupadí determined to take up their abode in a city named Viráta. But first they assumed disguises and new names; for the poem states that it had been agreed that, after the twelve years of wandering in the jungle had elapsed, they might take up their abode in any city they pleased for a year; "and if, during that year, the Kauravas failed to discover them, they were to be restored to their ráj; . . . . . but if discovered, the twelve years and the thirteenth year were to be repeated."

Before entering the city, they laid aside their weapons and their garments, and hid them in the branches of a tree, in the place where the people of that city were accustomed to burn their dead; and then, to protect their property, they took a dead body, and hung it also on the tree, crying out in a loud voice, "This is the dead body of our mother, and it is to remain here for a whole year, after which we will take it down and burn it." This was rumoured abroad, and no one would go near the tree,

---

[1] Mr. Talboys Wheeler frequently calls attention to the "Brahmanical bearing of the Mahábhárata," and shows that there is likewise "an underlying effort throughout the poem to ascribe a divine origin to the Pándavas, and to associate them with the gods of the Hindus. In the story of their birth, it is plainly asserted that Pándu was not their real father, but that they were directly begotten by the gods: that Yudhishthira was the son of Dharma, that Bhíma was the son of Váyu, and that Arjuna was the son of Indra, whilst Nakula and Sahadeva were the sons of the two Aswins."

Myths, he observes, have been inserted to confirm these relationships; and of these he gives a few outlines. One of these describes Arjuna's wars against the Daityas of the sea :—"On approaching the coast, in a chariot which flew through the air, Arjuna beheld the sea, rising in vast heaps, and saw ships laden with rubies, and fishes and tortoises as large as mountains. . . . . Thousands of Daityas rushed on him, but he uttered powerful mantras as he discharged his arrows, ... and slew them all. Then the women came out, screaming like cranes, but Arjuna passed them by, and entered the city, where he saw chariots with ten thousand horses, of the colour of peacocks." . . . "After this victory, Arjuna returned to Indra, and was rewarded with great praises, ... and a chain of gold and a diadem, and with a war-shell, which sounded like thunder." —Vol. i. pp. 191, 192.

lest he should "offend the ghost of the dead mother of the strange men."[1]

Their next proceeding was to present themselves to the Raja Virâta, who sat in the gate of his palace, holding council. The account which they gave of themselves, and the grace and majesty of their appearance, induce Virâta to accept their services; and they and Draupadî take up their abode in the palace as servants. But the Kauravas were also aware that the term of exile had expired; and being anxious to learn tidings of the Pândavas, they join the raja of another little State, called Trigarta, and carry away the cattle of Raja Virâta. The Raja quickly collected his troops, and has the sagacity to perceive, that although the Pândavas act as menials, they also must give their aid in the battle. And all the brothers, except Arjuna, go with him, who, being disguised as a eunuch, was left in the women's apartments.

No sooner had Virâta and his troops left the city than the chief of the shepherds drove rapidly to the palace. In haste he descended from his car, uttering wild cries of grief. In place of the king, whom he was seeking, he found his pompous eldest son. To him he poured forth his tale.

Sixty thousand cows driven off by the Trigarta and the Kurus. "Arise!" he said, "O glorious prince! Go, instantly—go yourself—recover this precious booty. Let your white horses be instantly harnessed, and go,—displaying your banner with the golden lion." The pompous prince was amongst the women; but he said he would go if a fitting driver could be found. A month ago his charioteer had been killed in battle. If he could be replaced, said the boastful prince, I alone would face the Kurus; I would quickly frighten them. They would run away; they would say that it was Arjuna himself who put them to flight; and the cattle would be recovered."

When Arjuna, in his woman's robes, heard the son of Virâta

[1] Mr. Wheeler observes, that "a dread of ghosts finds no expression in the traditions of the house of Bharata."—Page 205.

speak thus, he said secretly to Draupadí, "Go quickly, and tell this son of Virâta, that although now in woman's robes, I was, formerly, the favourite charioteer of Arjuna." Draupadí had felt much annoyed at hearing the lazy prince boast of being equal to her husband; but she goes and tells him that the pretended eunuch was a renowned driver, that he had been the charioteer of Arjuna, and that it was owing to his driving that Arjuna had performed his many amazing exploits. The prince then desires that Arjuna may be directed to act as his charioteer. Arjuna answers in his character of eunuch, and says, "How could it be possible for me to drive a chariot in battle? To sing, to dance, to play on musical instruments, is my vocation! How should I know how to drive?" The prince replies: "Be you musician, or be you dancer,—mount, instantly, and take the reins in hand!" Arjuna made a little fun with the women, who laughed prodigiously at seeing him put a cuirass over his white robe; but the prince was impatient, and hurried him off. As they departed, the sister of the prince and her young companions called after them, saying, "Bring us from the battle beautiful tissues of bright colours." Arjuna answered, in a voice which sounded like the roll of thunder: "If this prince conquers the chiefs with whom we fight, I will bring you divine and magnificent tissues."[1]

Animated by the son of Pându, the horses sprung forward as if they were flying; and it was not long before the army of the Kurus came in sight. Immediately the boastful son of Virâta was seized with panic. Arjuna tried to reassure him, but he offered countless treasures if he would but drive him safe home; and then jumped out of the chariot and tried to run away. The Kurus, looking on from afar, wondered at the strange sight of

---

[1] Mr. Wheeler speaks of these disguises "as highly improbable." The stories of this belong to "a period long anterior to the rise of Brahmanical ascendancy," and "comprise graphic pictures of the palace-life of Hindu rajas, in an age when princes were brought up with the women, and when eunuchs taught music and dancing to the young damsels in the zenana."—Page 105.

a man running, pursued by another in long, white robes, with flowing hair. The fugitive was quickly caught, and constrained to return, under promise, that if he would guide the horses he need take no share in the fighting. But first, the heroic son of Pándu went to the acacia tree in the cemetery, amongst the branches of which he and his brothers had concealed their arms; and having selected his own peculiar weapons, he threw aside his bracelets, and his armlets, and his woman's robes. He then strung his famous bow, called gándíva, and, removing the prince's standard, placed his own ape-emblazoned banner in front of the chariot. After fighting eight of the Kuru chiefs in single combat, and defeating each in turn, Arjuna remained in possession of the field. The Kurus and their army retreated, and the cattle were recovered. Arjuna then replaced his arms in the cemetery, re-assumed his disguise, and drove the prince home in triumph. King Viráta and the four Pándavas had also returned successful; and some days were given up to rejoicing.

Several anachronisms occur in these stories of the Pándavas' residence at Viráta. "The battle scenes," Mr. Wheeler says, "are all mythical, especially Arjuna's successive combats with the different Kaurava chieftains;" and a recorded marriage between a son of Arjuna and the daughter of Viráta is referred to the Krishna group of legends. And, indeed, the very kingdom of Viráta seems to be connected with Krishna. Mr. Wheeler believes that it should be placed in Guzerat, which is the especial scene of the later adventures of Krishna; and points out the geographical difficulty of associating it with the history of the Pándavas, whether supposed to be in Guzerat, or Matsya, in eastern Bengal. He also observes, that after this supposed alliance by marriage between the Pándavas and the Raja Viráta, he is no further mentioned; but, in his place, Raja Drupada, of Panchála, becomes the important personage. Raja Drupada sends his family priest as envoy to Hastinápura, and his son, Dhrishtadyumna, is elected commander-in-chief when the great war begins. It seems probable, therefore, that the negotiations and preparations which now took place amongst the Pándavas and their allies were carried on, not at the court of Viráta, but under the protection of Drupada, at Panchála. Messages are interchanged, and Drupada sends his purohita to the Kauravas; but all in vain. Then, as a last resource, Krishna is entreated to go to Hastinápura, to plead the cause of the Pándavas, and put forward their claims.

So "Krishna bathed himself, and performed his religious duty, and then set out for the city of Hastinápura. And when he came nigh to the city, all the Kauravas, small and great, save Duryodhana only, went forth on foot to meet him; and all the men and women, young and old, came out of their apartments to see Krishna, and pay him reverence" (p. 259). The next morning a grand council is held, at which the Mahárája and all the grand chieftains are seated on carpets of gold. They receive Krishna with reverence. When all are arranged, Krishna begins:—"I have come hither, O Mahárája, for the purpose of bringing about a reconciliation between the Pándavas and the Kauravas, and thus saving the lives of many." . . . . . "The family of Bharata," he continues, "has ever been famous for mercy, sincerity, forgiveness, and truth; and it would be an evil thing should they commit an act of injustice whilst you are mahárája. . . . . . War is all-destroying. Consider whether the defeat of either your sons or your nephews will give you any pleasure. . . . . . All the Pándavas are great heroes, and well armed; and all, with the exception of the virtuous Yudhishthira, are eager for war: . . . . . do not permit this family war, in which the Pándavas and the Kauravas will kill each other, and in which nearly all the families will be fighting; . . . . . and the number of the slain will be fearful."[1] . . . . .

When Krishna had finished, the old king begs him to counsel

---

[1] Talboys Wheeler, vol. i. pp. 262—265.

Duryodhana, who is "violent and disobedient, and refuses to listen to the advice of his mother Gândhâri, or to the pious Vidura, or to the wise Bhishma." ..... Then Krishna turned to Duryodhana, but without effect; and Bhishma said: "O Duryodhana! follow the advice of Krishna; it will be good for you in this world and in the next. ..... You are wicked, vicious, cowardly, and the pest of the family of the Kauravas." .... When Duryodhana heard these words of Bhishma, he was exceedingly wroth, and began to breathe very hard; and Drona went up to him and said, that what Krishna and Bhishma had said, was for his good, but that his mind was not in a condition to receive good counsel. ..... And after Drona had spoken, Vidura arose and said: "What has been advised is best for the people of this Ráj: for you, Duryodhana, I care not, excepting that if you are defeated, the Mahârâja and the Râni will become beggars in the house of the Pândavas." ..... Then Bhîshma spoke again, and said:—

"Arjuna and Krishna have not armed themselves as yet; the bow gândîva has not as yet been strung for the affray; the homa, which Dhaumya the priest will offer on the eve of battle, has not as yet been given to the fire. ..... There is yet time to prevent these horrible calamities. Go, then, and bow down at the feet of Yudhishthira; ..... let him behold you with a friendly countenance, and throw his right arm upon your neck, ... and strike you on the back as a reclaimed brother." ....

These speeches merely excited Duryodhana's wrath; and Krishna returned to the Pândavas to bid them prepare for war. The armies on either side ranged themselves on the plain of Kurukshetra, which is generally identified with the field of Panniput, to the north-west of Delhi. Drupada, the king of Panchâla, and Virâta of Matsya, came to support the Pândavas. Salya, king of Madra, allied himself with Drona; and there was no chief in India who did not range himself on one side or the other. The numbers of the Kauravas were incredibly greater than those of the Pândavas; but this advantage was balanced by the presence and aid of the divine Krishna, who was the devoted friend of Arjuna, and drove his chariot.

For eighteen days war raged upon the plains of Kurukshetra. The rival chiefs brought up their forces with monstrous elephants, their rattling chariots and horses, and stood face to face, bearing their iron maces, bows and arrows, horns and kettle drums. Arjuna blew his shell, called "God-given;" Bhima blew a great trumpet, named "Paundra; whilst Yudhishthira sounded his "Eternal Victory!"[1] But now

> "A sudden tumult filled the sky: earth shook:
> Chafed by wild winds, the sands upcurled to heaven,
> And spread a veil before the sun. Blood fell
> In showers; shrill screaming kites and vultures winged
> The darkling air; whilst howling jackals hung
> Around the march,—impatient for their meal.
> And ever and anon the thunder roared;
> And angry lightnings flashed across the gloom;
> Or blazing meteors fearful shot to earth."[2]

These were omens, portending terrible calamities; and just at this juncture, when the war-shells were already sounding, the heart of Arjuna is struck with horror, at the idea of this exterminating battle between kinsmen. The arguments by which Krishna overcomes his unwillingness to fight, form the subject of the beautiful philosophic poem, entitled the Bhagavad-Gîtâ. We have placed it in our section on Hindu philosophy; for it is in fact a lucid and beautiful illustration of Yoga doctrine; whereas it would be wholly out of place amid the noise and rapid movement of a battle-field. The poem is probably a late addition; at any rate, Arjuna did not retire from the battle, but fought on to the very last with the utmost heroism.

[1] Monier Williams, Ind. Epic Poetry, p. 34.

[2] H. H. Wilson's Works, vol. iii. p. 294. Essays, vol. i.

Although thunder roared, the sky was perfectly clear. But—

> "Regardless of these awful signs, the chiefs
> Pressed on to mutual slaughter, and the peal
> Of shouting hosts, commingling, shook the world.
> Contending warriors, emulous for victory,
> And great in arms, wielded the sharp-edged sword,
> And hurled the javelin. Frequent flew the dart;
> And countless arrows filled the air,[1]
> "Before the rest rode Drona on his car,—
> By art immortal framed. The banners stood
> Unwaving, as they rapid met the breeze;
> Swift plunged the bounding steeds amidst the throng;
> And terror hovered o'er the warrior's course."

The martial character of the Bráhman tutor, Drona, is throughout sustained.

> "Forgot his years, the veteran chieftain, fired
> With rage . . . . .
> Fast flew his arrows, with unerring aim;
> And heaven loud echoed to his rattling bow.
> The soil was soddened with the crimson stream
> Of the vast numbers,—men, and steeds, and elephants,
> Whom Drona's shafts to Yama's halls consigned."

Drona had not lost all affection for his former pupils, but he had been insulted by their ally, the king of Panchála, which gives him a personal interest in driving back their troops, like "clouds before the gale." At length, however, he is slain by Abhimanyu, who is the son of Drupada, king of Panchála.

Arjuna fights whenever he is needed, but he much disliked contending against his old tutor. He had not the same scruples in regard to his great uncle, Bhishma, who was the oldest warrior present. Arjuna transfixed him with so many arrows, "that

[1] H. H. Wilson. Essays, vol. i. pp. 294—298.

there was not a space of two fingers' breadth on his whole body unpierced. Then Bhishma fell from his chariot; but his body could not touch the ground, surrounded as it was by countless arrows." Arjuna also fought with Karna a long and varying conflict, ending in Karna's death. Bhíma, unlike Arjuna, delighted in fighting. He had vowed to revenge the insult offered to Draupadí, when the Kaurava, Duhsásana, dragged her by her hair into a public assembly; and, accordingly, he kills Duhsásana and drinks his blood. A single combat, fought with maces, between Bhíma, and Salya, king of Madra, is thus described:—[1]

> "A thousand conchs and trumpets, and a shout,
> Firing each champion's ardour, rent the air.
> From either host, spectators of the fight,
> Burst forth applauding cheers 'The Madra king
> Alone,' they cried, 'can bear the rush of Bhíma;
> None but heroic Bhíma can sustain
> The force of Salya!' Now, like two fierce bulls,
> Sprung they towards each other, mace in hand.
> And first, as cautiously they circled round,
> Whirling their weapons as in sport, the pair
> Seemed matched in equal combat. Salya's club,
> Set with red fillets, glittered as if flame;
> While that of Bhíma gleamed like flashing lightning.
> Anon the clashing iron met, and scattered round
> A fiery shower: then, fierce as elephants
> Or butting bulls, they battered each the other.
> Thick fell the blows, and soon each stalwart frame,
> Spattered with gore, glowed like the kinsuka,[2]
> Bedecked with scarlet blossoms."

The end of it is, that both fell, "mangled and crushed," but not killed; for, after this, Salya fights with Yudhishthira, and

---

[1] Monier Williams, Ind. Epic Poetry, p. 116.
[2] Butea frondosa. Kinsuka is another name for the palása. See woodcut, vol. i. p. 106.

is finally killed. And Bhima also fights again with his club, in single combat, with Duryodhana, the most savage of the Kurus. The heroic spirit of the poet is shown, by the disapprobation bestowed upon Bhima on this occasion. The Pândus are the poet's favourites, and Duryodhana was a malignant fiend, but Bhima struck a blow upon his thighs, and this is at once pronounced "unfair;" it being a rule in club fights that no blow should be given below the waist.[1]

When Drona, and Karna, and Salya are killed, and Duryodhana and Bhishma are dying, and but three warriors of note are all that remain of the Kuru hosts, the fighting ceases. The victorious Pândava troops lie down to sleep upon the field of battle, whilst the five Pându brothers repose beside a neighbouring river. The three Kurus retreat to a distant banyan tree. Two of these discomfited warriors fall fast asleep; but the third, who is the son of Drona, plots vengeance against his slain father's foes. Above him he sees thousands of crows, roosting in the great canopy of the banyan branches. Presently, he observes an owl approach stealthily, seize the sleeping crows, bite off their heads, and strew their mangled remains upon the ground. Thus, says the son of Drona, will I do to the sleeping Pândavas. He roused his comrades, but had some difficulty in persuading them to go with him for so foul a purpose. But they went; and all the sleeping Pândava troops are killed: only the five Pândava brothers, and Draupadî, survive.

Were the Mahâbhârata to be arranged as a musical tragedy, a dirge would now commence. The aged queen and a procession of mourning women appear upon the field of battle. They seek their sons and husbands amongst the dead; they chant their virtue, and utter wails of grief. Mutual affliction effects reconciliation. The old queen becomes friendly towards Yudhishthira, allows that insult towards Draupadî justified redress, and that

[1] Monier Williams, Indian Epic Poetry, p. 120.

Bhíma was not to blame for fighting with Duryodhana; but he was wrong for hitting him below the waist. She laments that those who formerly reposed on couches, with their bodies perfumed by sandal and other odours, should be sleeping in the dust; whilst vultures, jackals, crows, make hideous noises, and scatter their jewelled ornaments.[1]

She celebrates them as lying with their faces to the enemy, holding fast their clubs: once the praises of panegyrists were continually sounded in their ears, but now the terrible cries of lamentation.

When, at length, the laments cease, the funeral obsequies are performed with fire.

The tragedy is over. The Kurus are dead. Yudhishthira and his brothers reign over Hastinápura and Indraprastha and the plains bordering the Jumna without a rival. But no rejoicing follows. They have lost their sons, they have participated in the slaughter of their relatives—and they are miserable. Music, suitable to the closing scenes of the Mahábhárata, would be unutterably grand. In an article on Indian Epic Poetry, in the Westminster Review, of October, 1848, the author observes, in reference to this passage: "We know of no episode, even in the Homeric poems, which can surpass its mournful grandeur, or raise a more solemn dirge over the desolation of the fallen heart of man! Yudhishthira has won the throne, and his enemies are all fallen; and an inferior poet would have concluded the story with a pæan upon his happiness! But the Hindu bard had a far deeper insight into man's nature, and his genius would not content itself with any such commonplace catastrophe; he knew well that the human soul was born for the infinite, and that no finite line could fathom the depths of its longings!" "Yudhishthira resigns his crown, and he and his brothers, and Draupadí, set out on a forlorn journey to Mount Meru, where

---

[1] Fouccaux, p. 334.

Indra's heaven lies amongst the wilds of the Himalayas, there to find that rest which seemed denied to their search upon earth."[1] All the inhabitants of the town are grieved,[2] and the women burst into tears when they see these five brothers set out with Draupadí, who was the sixth, as formerly, after they had been vanquished in the game with dice. But the brothers all rejoiced. . . . . .

"Forthwith, with Draupadí, they issued forth, and after them a dog
Followed. The king himself went out, the seventh from the royal city.
And all the citizens and the court followed them on their way.
But none felt able to say unto him, 'Return!'
And at length the train of citizens went back. . . . . .
Then the high-souled sons of Pándu and the far-famed Draupadí
Pursued their way, fasting, with their faces towards the east,—
Yearning for union with the Infinite; bent on abandonment
Of worldly things. They wandered on to many countries, many a sea
And river. Yudhishthira walked in front, and next to him came Bhima,
And Arjuna came after him." "Then the twin sons of Mádri.
And sixth after them, came Draupadí, with her dark skin and lotus eyes.
And, last of all, followed the dog."[3] . . . . .

Arjuna was still bearing his heavenly bow; but this bow, called gándíva, had been given to him by Agni, god of fire: and this god stood suddenly in their path. The bow, he says, must be thrown into the sea. It was from Varuna that Agni had obtained it for Arjuna; and to Varuna it must be returned. The brothers all besought Arjuna to obey. And he flung the bow into the sea, and the immortal arrows. Then Agni vanished.

"And as they journeyed onwards, and came unto the west,
There they beheld the old city of Krishna,—now washed over by the
ocean tide.
Again they turned to the north, and still they went on in their way,

---

[1] Westminster Review, Oct., 1848, p. 57.
[2] We give the next passage in the words of Professor Monier Williams, Ind. Epic Poetry, p. 29.
[3] E. B. Cowell, Westminster Review, Oct., 1848, p. 58.

Circumambulating round the continent to find separation from earth [1]
. . . . . With souls well disciplined,
They reached the northern region, and beheld, with heaven-aspiring hearts,
The mighty mountain, Himavnt. Beyond its lofty peak they passed,
Towards the sea of sand, and saw at last the rocky Meru,—king
Of mountains. As, with eager steps, they hastened on,—their souls intent
On union with the Eternal,—Draupadi lost hold of her high hope,
And, faltering, fell upon the earth." . . . . .

Seeing her thus fallen, Bhima said:—

"'No act of evil hath she done, that faultless daughter of a king. Wherefore, then, O Conqueror! hath she fallen thus low on the ground?'
And thus to him answered Yudhishthira: 'Too great was her love for Arjuna;
And the fruit thereof, O Bhima! hath she gathered here this day.'"

Having thus spoken, without looking at him, the glorious descendant of Bharata went onwards, gathering his soul within itself. Next, Sahadeva fell, the least froward and wilful of all; and Bhima enquires his fault. Yudhishthira replied: "He thought no one ever equal to himself." Nakula, the twin-brother of Sahadeva, falls from grief at seeing the others fall. His fault is pronounced to have been, thinking himself superior to other men in beauty. Then fell Arjuna, his soul pierced through with grief. He, who had never told a lie, had boasted that in one day he could kill all his enemies. The last to fall was Bhima. And as he fell he asked the cause; and Yudhishthira, still without looking back, said he had made use of his great strength without considering his enemies.

"Thus having spoken, the mighty king, not looking back, went on;
And still, as ever, behind him, went, following, that dog alone!"[2]

[1] E. B. Cowell, West. Review, Oct., 1848, p. 58.   [2] Ibid, pp. 59, 60.

Suddenly, with a cry that rang through heaven and earth,
Indra came riding on his chariot, and he cried to the king, 'Ascend!'
Then, indeed, did the lord of justice look back to his fallen brothers,
And thus unto Indra he spoke, with a sorrowful heart:
'Let my brothers, who yonder lie fallen, go with me;
Not even into thy heaven would I enter, if they were not there.
And yon fair-faced daughter of a king, Draupadi, the all-deserving,
Let her, too, enter with us! O Indra, approve my prayer!'

INDRA.

"In heaven thou shalt find thy brothers; they are already there before
   thee.
There are they all, with Draupadi. Weep not, then, O son of Bharata!
Thither are they entered, prince, having thrown away their mortal
   weeds.
But thou alone shalt enter, still wearing thy body of flesh.

YUDHISHTHIRA.

"O Indra! and what of this dog? It hath faithfully followed me
   through:
Let it go with me into heaven, for my soul is full of compassion.

INDRA.

"Immortality and friendship with me, and the height of joy and
   felicity,
All these hast thou reached to-day; leave, then, the dog behind thee.

YUDHISHTHIRA.

"The good may oft act an evil part, but never a part like this.
Away, then, with that felicity, whose price is to abandon the faithful.

INDRA.

"My heaven hath no place for dogs; they steal away our offerings on
   earth.
Leave, then, thy dog behind thee; nor think in thy heart that it is
   cruel.

2—5.

Yudhishthira.

"To abandon the faithful and devoted, is an endless crime, like the
    murder of a Brahman.
Never, therefore, come weal or woe, will I abandon you faithful dog.
Yon poor creature, in fear and distress, hath trusted in my power to
    save it;
Not, therefore, for e'en life itself, will I break my plighted word.

Indra.

"If a dog but beholds a sacrifice, men esteem it unholy and void:
Forsake, then, the dog, O hero! and heaven is thine own as a reward.
Already thou hast borne to forsake thy fondly-loved brothers, and
    Draupadi.
Why, then, forsakest thou not the dog? Wherefore now fails thy
    heart?

Yudhishthira.

"Mortals, when they are dead, are dead to love or hate: so runs the
    world's belief.
I could not bring them back to life, but while they lived I never left
    them.
To oppress the suppliant, to kill a wife, to spoil a Brahman, and to
    betray one's friends,—
These are the four great crimes; and to forsake a dependant, I count
    equal unto them."

The dog was Yama, king of death, in disguise; and, praising Yudhishthira, he now relieved him from his difficulty, by showing himself in his true character. But there was yet another trial to be encountered; for, upon entering Indra's heaven, Yudhishthira beheld his cousins, the Kurus, but looked in vain for his brothers. He refused to remain without them. A messenger was sent with him to the Indian hell; and there he resolves to share their sorrows, rather than live in heaven. But this scene was *máyá*, or a mere delusion, intended to test his virtue. The hell is quickly changed into heaven; and there the brothers are left, with Indra, enjoying boundless bliss.[1]

And thus a tale of wrangling, feud, and bloody warfare, closes in eternal peace.

[1] E. B. Cowell, Westminster Review, l. l.

CHAPTER XXIV.

EPISODES OF THE MAHABHARATA.

Allusions to Nāgas or Serpent-people.—An ascetic marries to save his ancestors from hell.—Legend of Deluge.—Churning the ocean.—Human sacrifice.—Family of poor Brāhmans.—Story of Sāvitrī.—Story of Nala and Damayantī.—Sakuntalā.—Conclusion.

In addition to the beautiful poetry of which we have just been treating, the Mahābhārata contains episodes concerning which we have hitherto been silent, because unwilling to interrupt the main stream of the narrative. In themselves, these episodes are most interesting, and all the more require to have a chapter to themselves. Some of them are stories which appear to have originated amongst the hill and forest tribes of India; and this may account for the remarkable allusions which they make to people called Nāgas, or Snakes. We will begin with one which has been translated from the Sanskrit into French, by M. Pavie.

A certain king, named Janamejaya, accompanied by his three brothers, performed a great sacrifice on the plains of Kurukshetra. Whilst the ceremonies were proceeding, the mystical dog, Sārameya, ran weeping to his mother, Saramā, and complained that the king's brother had been ill-treating him. Saramā sought redress, and informed the king that he was, in consequence, threatened by an invisible calamity. So soon as the sacrifice was over, the king hastened back to Hastinápura to provide himself with a purohita (family priest), capable of averting the impending danger; and, hunting in the woods, he perceived a hermitage, in which dwelt an ascetic Rishi. The ascetic had a son, and the king says: "Blessed! Let thy son become my purohita." The ascetic replies: "O Janamejaya! my son, whom thou seest, dedicated to austerity, advanced in the study of the Vedas, ... is born of a mother of the Nága or Serpent race; . . . . . he is capable of giving you peace concerning all faults, except such as you may have committed against Mahádeva" (Siva). This son of a Serpent mother is then appointed to the office of purohita, and the king conquers Taxila.

A story follows which is wholly unconnected with the preceding, but which also contains an allusion to Serpents.

A Bráhman teacher has three disciples. The first was from the Punjab. To test his virtue, his teacher (or guru) commanded him to stop a flow of water which issued from a pond or lake. To effect this the pupil laid himself down in the hole, and thus closed the outlet. He is praised for performing the task assigned, and promised that in consequence he will attain supreme felicity and knowledge of the mysteries of the Vedas and the law. The next disciple was sent out to guard the cows of his preceptor. Every evening he returned to his house and respectfully did him homage. "What makes you so fat?" said the preceptor. "I feed upon alms," replied the pupil. "You must accept no alms until they have been presented first to me," said the tutor.

At length the pupil, reduced to starvation, eats the leaves of the caloptropis,[1] and becomes blind. The Aswins (called physicians) come to his assistance and give him a cake; but the pupil refuses to eat until he has first presented the cake to his preceptor. The Aswins praise his pious docility towards his precep-

---

[1] Asclepias gigantea Roxb., the mudar of Bengal, a common shrub in India. The milk of this plant is one of the most deadly poisons in India. See W. C. Ondaatje in Jour. Ceylon Branch R. A. S. for 1865-6.

tor, and say: "His teeth shall be of black iron, but thine shall be of gold; thou shalt recover thy sight, and attain supreme bliss." His guru confirms this, and says: "So it will be as the Aswins have announced to thee." To the third pupil the master says: "My son, you must live for a certain time in my house, listening earnestly to my instruction; after this you will obtain the supreme good."[1] The pupil consents. He lives in his master's house, is attentive to his teaching, carries burthens like a bullock, suffers cold and heat, hunger and thirst,—never complaining; and ends by attaining the supreme good, and knowledge of that which he desired to know. Having attained the state of a pupil whose studies are completed, he left his master, and went to keep house for himself. He now had pupils of his own, but he never oppressed them with servile labour; for he remembered the troubles of pupils in a guru's house.

After a time, this excellent Brâhman went away to officiate as spiritual preceptor of two kings. During his absence, he commissioned a pupil, named Utanka, to act for him. When the master returned, he approved the conduct of this pupil, and offered a boon. The pupil, Utanka, begged leave to be allowed to present the usual offering, in token that his term of tutelage was over. The master is unwilling to agree to this; but, on being repeatedly urged, he says, that Utanka may enquire of his wife what present she desires; and he promises, that whatever that may be, he will accept, and permit Utanka to depart. The guru's wife requires, that Utanka go to king Paushya, and ask him for the ear-rings worn by his wife, because in four days she says "there is to be a festival; and I wish to present myself in the assembly of the Brâhmans adorned by these pendants in my ears."

Utanka starts at once for the abode of king Paushya, and is allowed to see the queen, who admires his piety towards his pre-

---

[1] Th. Pavie, Frag. du Mahâb., p. 8.

ceptor, and is willing to give up her ear-rings; but she admonishes him, that these pendants are eagerly coveted by Takshaka, king of Serpents. A little wrangling then occurs between Utanka and king Paushya. The king wishes his guest to take food. Utanka consents, but says it must be in haste. A dish of cold food is therefore brought. Utanka observes a hair in it, and angrily says to the king: "Because you have presented me with impure food, you shall become blind." The king replies: "Because you call food impure which is not impure, you shall be deprived of posterity." The king perceives, however, that there really was a hair, and reflects: it must be that my wife prepared this food with her hair loose. And he apologises to Utanka, and says it was unconsciously and unintentionally; so he trusts that blindness will not come upon him. Utanka says it cannot now be averted, but it will be temporary; and then he begs to have the curse against himself withdrawn. King Paushya replies: "Neither can I retract my malediction; besides which, my anger is not in fact appeased. The heart of the Bráhman is tender as butter, whilst his word is a sharp and pointed blade; but the Kshattriya's word is tender as butter, whilst his heart is a cutting knife."

We now come to the Serpents. As Utanka was journeying home he was intercepted by Takshaka, king of the Serpent race, who contrived to get possession of the ear-rings, and then changing his form, disappeared as a snake through a hole in the ground. Indra sends his thunderbolt, to make the hole larger enough to admit Utanka, who makes his way to the realms of Serpents, and sees temples, palaces, pavilions, porticoes, in startling and confused abundance. By the help again of Indra, the ear-rings are recovered, and Utanka is carried back by a magical horse to the house of his preceptor, where he only arrives just in time to save being cursed by the expectant wife.

So soon as Utanka was released from tutelage he went to Hastinápura, to induce the king to make war on the Snakes, by whose king he had been insulted. He tells the king of Hastinápura that Takshaka, the vilest of Snakes, ought to be burnt in a fire-sacrifice; and he brings witnesses to show that king Janamejaya's father had been killed by the bite of this very Takshaka, and thus succeeds in inflaming the anger of the king, just as the butter of sacrifice excites the fire into which it is thrown. And the king endeavoured to do what Utanka[1] desired, but being himself of Nága descent, the sacrifice saved all his maternal relations, and caused them to pass into higher states of existence.

On another occasion, a poet comes to entertain a company of Rishis, who had assembled for a twelve years' sacrifice, and is desired to relate stories of the Bhrigus. He tells of a young girl about to be married to a king, named Kuru. Whilst playing in the woods with her companions, she stepped by accident upon a sleeping snake, was bitten, and died. Kuru, enraged by grief, vowed that all serpents should henceforth be killed. It is evident that hatred to snakes, as snakes, is in someway connected with enmity to people who bore their name.

The origin of Serpents is always shrouded in most extravagant legend. On one occasion the mother of the race cursed them, saying: "In the sacrifice of Janamejaya, fire will destroy you."

How, then, was the destruction of the Nágas arrested? asks the audience; whereupon the history of Astíka is related, to the following effect:—The father of Astíka was a Bráhman of great repute; one who practised austerities, bathed in all the holy tanks, and abstained from matrimony. With his body dried up by fasting, and his eyes open, but immoveable, he wandered hither and thither, like a burning fire. Accidentally, he came to a hollow place, in which he perceived men hanging over an abyss. Their heads were downwards, and suspended by a straw, at which a rat was gnawing. Inquiring who they were, he dis-

[1] Fragments du Mahábhárata. Par Th. Pavie, pp. 1—25.

covered that they were his own ancestors. These wretched men tell him that they are thus suspended because their posterity, who should have been the means of ensuring their bliss, had perished; and the one living descendant, whose son might have done so, was entirely given up to austerities, and did not marry. The ascetic tells them that *he* is that one descendant. The ancestors then entreat him to marry, and have a son, who would release them. The ascetic says he will endeavour to do what they desire, but he will only marry a girl whose parents give her to him willingly; "and who," he exclaims, pathetically, "will give a wife to so poor a man?"

But although he felt the difficulty, he commenced his search. First he went into the world; but there he had no success. Next he went into the forest; and there, Vásuki, king of Serpents, offered him his sister,—a young girl of lovely form. This beautiful woman he married, and the child of the marriage was Astika. Of him we are told that he had a noble spirit, was well read in the Vedas and Vedángas, and became powerful through austerity. And thus, when the grand sacrifice for destroying Serpents was celebrated, his personal merits enabled him to rescue his maternal relations from the flames. Astika also fulfilled his obligations to his ancestors, by giving them posterity; and delighted the Rishis, by abandoning himself to religious study.[1]

One of these episodes gives a curious history of the earth being tormented by creatures who, when attacked, take refuge in the great waters. Earth has no peace until a powerful ascetic swallows the waters; but earth is still distressed, for she has no water. Then the mighty Ganges is entreated to descend; and a splendid description of the descent of the Ganges is given here, but more fully in the Rámáyana. Leaving this, we will pass on to the wild legend of the Deluge, first related in the Satapatha-

[1] Fragments du Mahábhárata. Par Th. Pavie. pp. 30—34.

Bráhmana, but related again in the Mahábhárata, "at much greater length, and with considerable variations."[1] Whilst Manu (the progenitor of mankind) was performing austerities on the banks of the Cherini, a fish came to him, soliciting protection. Manu put the fish into a jar. When too large for the jar, he threw the fish into a pond. When too large for the pond, the fish spoke, and requested to be taken to "Gangá, ocean's beloved queen." Manu, accordingly, cast the fish into the Ganges, and when too large for the Ganges, he took it to the ocean. Then first was announced the approaching Deluge:— "Thou shalt build a strong ship, with a cable," said the fish: "in it thou must embark, with the seven Rishis. And take with thee all manner of seeds, as anciently described by the Bráhmans; and then await my arrival." Manu did as he was commanded; and whilst he "floated on the billowy sea in the beautiful ship," the fish arrived, and the cable of the ship was bound to its vast horn.

"The fish being attached by the cable, drew the ship with great rapidity over the briny deep, and transported its crew across the ocean, which seemed to dance with its waves, and thunder with its waters. The ship, tossed by the mighty winds, whirled around, like an unsteady, intoxicated woman. Neither earth nor the eight quarters of the world appeared: everything was water, and firmament, and sky. Amid this perturbation of the universe, the seven Rishis, Manu, and the fish, were perceived. In this manner, the fish, unwearied, drew along the ship for many periods of years amid the mass of waters; and at length brought it to the highest peak of Himavat. Then spake the fish, gently smiling, to the Rishis: "Bind the ship without delay to this peak of Himavat." They fastened the ship accordingly; and that loftiest peak of Himavat is, even to this day, known by the appellation of "Naubandhana" (the binding of the ship).

[1] Muir, Orig. Sanskrit Texts, vol. ii. pp. 329—330.

The fish then revealed himself to the Rishis as Brahmâ,—the supreme lord of creatures; and commanded Manu "to create all living beings,—gods, Asuras, and men; all worlds and all things,—moveable and immoveable: a command which Manu fulfilled."[1]

In commenting upon this passage, Mr. Muir observes, that in the Brâhmana the original abode of Manu is undefined; but he is said to have crossed the northern mountain. In the Mahâbhârata, the scene is laid near the Ganges. Whereas, in a still later version given in the Purânas, southern India is mentioned as the country deluged.[2]

After the Deluge was over, it was discovered that many treasures had been lost in the flood, the most precious of which was "the Amrita, or Drink of Immortality." The gods met in council on Mount Meru, to consider how this loss could be repaired. To this we have already alluded, in treating of medicine; but we now give verses from Mr. Griffith's metrical translations:—

> "Then Vishnu, in his wisdom, cried:
> 'Ye mighty gods, arise!
> Deep hid beneath the whelming tide,
> The heavenly nectar lies.
> Untiringly in ceaseless whirl
> Churn ye the vasty ocean;
> And herbs of power, and jewels, hurl
> Into the wild commotion.
> Vex ye the surges in your strength;
> Stir them with ceaseless toil:
> So shall the troubled sea at length
> Yield back the precious spoil.'"[3]

The heavenly band eagerly act upon Vishnu's advice, and strain every nerve to tear up the mountain-peak, Mandara, and

---

[1] Muir, Orig. Sanskrit Texts, vol. ii. p. 331.
[2] Ibid, vol. ii. p. 332.
[3] R. T. H. Griffith. Specimens of Old Indian Poetry, p. 35.

use it as a churning-stick; but their efforts are vain. And they renew their prayers to Vishnu and to Brahmá.

> "Then Brahmá, of the lotus eyes,
>   And deep, unsearchèd mind,
> And Vishnu, terrible and wise,
>   To their request inclined;
> They bade Ananta, Serpent king,
>   Rise from his ocean home,
> That Hill of Glory down to fling
>   Far in the flashing foam.
>
> Now, woe to Mandara's mountain!
>   His days of pride are o'er;
> In woods, by gurgling fountain,
>   The sweet birds sing no more!
> 'Come, let us churn the ocean,'
>   Thus cried the gods around;
> 'For by the ceaseless motion
>   The Amrit will be found.'"

Thus invited, it appears that Ananta, the king of the Serpents, gave his aid, and "he was strong high Mandara's weight to bear." This peak he used as a churning-stick; the great snake Vásuki he desired to wind himself round it, as a turning-strap. Ananta then stood at his head and helped the gods to pull Vásuki backwards and forwards.

> "Then, from the mouth of Vásuki,
>   Roll'd clouds of smoke and flame:
> Like scorching storm-blasts, furiously
>   The stifling vapours came.
> And, ceaselessly, a rain of flowers
>   From the fair mountain's brow
> Fell softly down in fragrant showers,
>   And veil'd the hosts below.

"Like roaring of a tempest-cloud
 The deafening thunder crash'd;
The sound of ocean was as loud,
 To furious raging lash'd.
Unnumber'd creatures of the deep
 Died in the troubled sea;
And, thundering down from Mandara's steep,
 Fell many a lofty tree.

From branches, against branches dash'd,
 Rose the red flames on high,
And flickering round the mountain, flash'd
 Like lightnings o'er the sky.
The dwellers of the ancient woods
 Felt the remorseless power;
Rush'd, vainly, to the steaming floods,
 Scorch'd by the fiery shower.

Lions and elephants in herds,
 By blinding terror driven;
With scathèd wings the beauteous birds
 No more might soar to heaven.
But Indra on the toil and pain
 Look'd, pitying, from on high,
And bade a cloud of gentle rain
 Come, softly, down the sky."[1]

The fatigue of churning is almost overpowering, even to king Ananta and the gods; and they cry out:—

"Our souls are fainting, and our strength
 Fails in the ceaseless strife."

Brahmâ takes pity on them, and bids Vishnu "help the toiling band." Then—

[1] R. T. H. Griffith. Specimens of Old Indian Poetry, p. 88.

"—with one heart and with one will,
　They lash'd the raging ocean;
And furious, fast, and wilder still,
　Arose the fierce commotion.
Then, lo! the moon, all cold and bright,
　Rose from the troubled sea,
And, following in her robes of light,
　Appeared the beauteous Sri:
The heavenly Horse, and Sura rose,
　And Kaustabha, the gem,
Whose ever-beaming lustre glows
　In Vishnu's diadem."

At length the physician appears with the Amrita, and "a long and joyous sound rings through the startled sky."[1] But, as might be reasonably expected,—

"—from the wondrous churning stream'd
　A poison, fierce and dread,
Burning like fire where'er it streamed,
　Thick noisome mists were spread.
The wasting venom onwards went,
　And fill'd the worlds with fear,
Till Brahmá to their misery bent
　His gracious, pitying ear;
And Siva those destroying streams
　Drank up at Brahmá's beck;—
Still in thy throat the dark flood gleams,
　God of the azure neck!"[2]

The feeling for artistic beauty and variety which strikes one in all Sanskrit poetry, is very conspicuous in this little piece. As in our last chapter, here again we are powerfully reminded of compositions in music by Beethoven. The beginning is grand

---

[1] See ante, "Medicine," vol. i. p. 338.

[2] R. T. H. Griffith. Specimens of Old Indian Poetry, p. 40.

and stately; but the rigidity and severity of the peaks of Mount Meru is tempered by graceful allusions to its "cool and shady bowers, inhabited by birds." The wild efforts of the gods to tear up the mountain, their despairing cries for help, and the Serpent king coming to assist, are very like some of Beethoven's scherzos. A tremendous uproar ensues, which is concluded by a sublime crash, when the mountain is uprooted, and the lions, elephants, and birds, are destroyed. A soothing andante follows, which, as a "cloud of gentle rain," Indra sent "softly down the sky." The last movement begins in turbulent triumph; but joy changes to minor tones and discord, as pestilence arises. And this again yields, finally, to the peaceful happiness of trust in heavenly aid.

These wild raphsodies are the popular poetry of the poem, whilst other passages are especially Brahmanical; such as the trials which Arjuna goes through in the forest, and on Mount Meru, in order to obtain heavenly weapons. These, and also the Bhagavad-Gitâ,[1] belong rather to a fully-developed state of Brahmanism than to the free utterances of courts and camps.

Stories of domestic life we gladly insert, believing them to show the genuine Hindu character at some indefinite period,— rather before that at which the Greeks saw India. The following is called in the original Baka-vadha:—[2]

Within the first year or two of the Pândavas' exile they arrive at a town called Ekachakrâ, in the neighbourhood of which lived a giant,—the same sort of creature as the modern earth-goddess of Orissa; that is, a demon who feeds on human beings. They are kindly received by a family of poor Brâhmans, who prove to be in great affliction, because it is their turn to furnish a victim for the monster. Whilst reposing in an inner apartment the Pândavas overheard the father, the mother, and the daughter, each urging a separate claim to be allowed to suffer for the rest.

The father commences, saying, that never would he be so base

---

[1] *Ante*, vol. i. p. 217 ff.   [2] Monier Williams, Ind. Epic Poetry, p. 33.

as to give a victim from his house and consent himself to live; but still he expresses anxiety at not knowing how to provide a place of refuge for his wife, daughter, and little son, after his removal. He cannot, he says, surrender his faithful wife,—the sweet friend given to him by the gods; nor his daughter,—whom Brahma made to be a bride, and the mother of heroes; nor yet his son: . . . . . but if he offer himself, sorrow will pursue him in the world to come, and his abandoned wife and children will be unable to live without him.

The wife next speaks, and chides her husband for yielding to grief, like one of lowly caste; for, whoever knows the Vedas, must know that—

" Fate, inevitable, orders;—all must yield to death in turn.
Hence the doom, th' irrevocable,—it beseems not thee to mourn.
Man hath wife, and son, and daughter,—for the joy of his own heart;
Wherefore, wisely check thy sorrow,—it is I must hence depart.
'Tis the wife's most holy duty,—law on earth without repeal,—
That her life she offer freely,—when demands her husband's weal."

She goes on to argue, that he can support and guard the children when she is gone, but that she would have no power to guard and support them without him. Deprived of his protection, "rude and reckless men," she says, would come seeking their blameless daughter; and helpless, and beset on every side, she would be unable to check the suit of Sûdra lovers. . . . . . She concludes, by saying, that her honoured husband will find another wife, to whom he will be as gentle and kind as he has been to her.

" Hearing thus his wife, the husband fondly clasp'd her to his breast:
And their tears they pour'd together—by their mutual grief oppress'd."

When the daughter overheard the troubled discourse of her parents, she put in her claim to be the offered victim; for, if they died before her, she would sink to bitterest misery: but, if she died to preserve them, she would "then become immortal, and partake of bliss divine."

Whilst they were all thus weeping, the little son opened wide his eyes, and lisped out in broken accents:

"' Weep not, father, weep not, mother; oh, my sister, weep not so
First to one, and then to th' other,—smiling went he to and fro.
Then a blade of spear-grass lifting, thus in bolder glee he said:
'With this spear grass will I kill him—this man-eating giaut—dead.'
Though o'erpowered with bitterest sorrow, as they heard their prattling
    boy,
Stole into the parents' bosom—mute and inexpressive joy."[1]

Happily, the child's chivalry was not required; for the Pându brothers went forth and conquered the Spirit of Evil, whether in the form of "man-eating giant," or "earth goddess."

The following is one of the most charming photographs of woman given in Sanskrit poetry:—

A king, named Aswapati, sighed for offspring, and after praying in vain for eighteen years, the gods of heaven sent him a daughter, who grew up so "bright in her beauty," that she appeared like a child of the Immortals; and the princes around were so dazzled, that none dared to ask for her as a bride. This distressed her father, and he said that she must go now and make choice herself.

"Meekly bowed the modest maiden, with her eyes upon the ground,
And departed, as he bade her, with attendants troop'd around.
Many a hermitage she travers'd, riding in a gold-bright car;
Many a wilderness and forest, holy places near and far."

When she came back she told of a blind old king, driven from his throne by a ruthless kinsman, living with his beloved wife

[1] Translated by the late H. Milman, Dean of St. Paul's.

in a grove; and his brave son, Satyavat, her heart has chosen. "Satyavat," she says, "has all my love."

At this announcement a Rishi, who happened to be present, exclaims, in distress, that she would choose care and grief, in choosing Satyavat. He is

> "Learned as the gods' own teacher,—glorious as the sun is he:
> With the earth's untiring patience, and great Indra's bravery."

He is noble,

> "True, and great of soul,
> Bountiful is he, and modest,—every sense does he control.
> Gentle, brave, all creatures love him,—keeping in the righteous way,
> Number'd with the holy hermits,—pure and virtuous as they."

But alas! in a year, counting from this day, "Satyavat will die." On hearing this, the king considers a marriage out of the question, and says: "Go, then, my dearest child, and choose again." But his daughter replies:

> "Be he virtuous or worthless,—many be his days, or few,—
> Once for all I choose my husband: to that choice will I be true."

The sage and her father give way to her decided wishes: and in due time the young couple are married, and live in great happiness with the hermits in the grove. Sâvitrî, the bride, put aside her jewels, and wore the coarse raiment usually adopted by hermits; and, by her meekness and affection, won the hearts of all with whom she dwelt.

> "Sadly, sadly as she counted, day by day flew swiftly by,
> And the fated time came nearer when her Satyavat must die.
> Yet three days and he must perish, sadly thought the loving wife:
> And she vowed to fast, unresting, for his last three days of life."

Her husband's father feared that the trial would be too great for her, but she answered: "Firm resolve has made me vow it; firm resolve will give me strength." She kept her vow, and maintained her fast; and when the third day dawned, and the fire of worship was kindled, and the morning rites performed, she reverently saluted the aged Bráhmans and her husband's honoured parents, but still refused food. Presently, her husband takes his axe upon his shoulder to perform his daily task of felling trees. She begs him to let her go also; he replies:

"All unknown to thee the forest; rough the path and weary thou:
How, then, will thy feet support thee, fainting from thy fasting vow?"

"Nay, I sink not from my fasting, and no weakness feel to-day;
I have set my heart on going: oh! forbid me not, I pray!"

Sávitrí has always kept her sad secret from her husband; and he has, therefore, no idea of her real reason for wishing to accompany him. He, however, consents, and calls her attention to the lovely woods, stately peacocks, and flowers of brilliant hue; but she can look only upon him, and mourn for him as one about to die. She gathers cooling fruits, and he makes the woods resound with the strokes of his hatchet. But, soon a thrilling agony shoots through his temple. . . . . . She sits down upon the ground, and he rests his head upon her breast, and sleeps. But,—

"Sudden, lo! before Sávitrí stood a great and awful One;
Red as blood was his apparel, bright and glowing as the sun.
In his hand a noose was hanging; he to Satyaván stood nigh,
And upon the weary sleeper fix'd his fearful, glittering eye."

This awful apparition was Yama, god of Death, come to bind and take the spirit of Satyavat. Having done this, he moved towards the south, Sávitrí closely following. Yama tries to persuade her to go back; but she says, no: wherever her husband goes, there she will go also. Yama praises her sweet speech, and offers her any boon except the life of Satyavat; and she begs that the blind king, her father-in-law, may be restored to sight, but without relinquishing her first request. Yama tries again and again to get rid of her, and says she will faint.

> "Can I faint when near my husband? where he goes my path shall be.
> I will follow where thou leadest;—listen once again to me."

Nothing can induce her to return without Satyavat; and at length "love conquers death." Yama relents; the happy wife hastens to where her husband's dead body lay, and, leaning upon her faithful bosom he awakes again to sense and life. A very touching conversation follows, during which he gradually recovers his recollection; but his wife, avoiding any full explanation of what had been occurring, says:

> "Night's dark shadows round us fall;
> When the morrow's light returneth, dearest! I will tell thee all.
> Up, then, and away, I pray thee,—come unto thy parents, love!
> See! the sun long time has vanish'd, and the night grows black
> above."[1]

And accordingly they return to the hermitage, when Satyavat finds his father no longer blind; and every kind of happiness awaits them.

The poets of the Mahábhárata lived, apparently, almost entirely in our north-west provinces. They were familiar with the places now known as Taxila, Lahore, Lodhiana, Saháranpur, Pannipat, Mirat, Delhi, Hansi, &c. Journeys to Guzerat also occur; and one important branch of the paramount royal family

---

[1] Sávitrí, or the Faithful Wife. Translated from the original Sanskrit into English verse. By E. T. H. Griffith. Oxford.

See also an article in the Westminster Review, October, 1848, on Indian Epic Poetry, which most interesting paper is attributed to Mr. Cowell.

lived at Dwáraká, in Guzerat. That they knew little of the country to the south of Delhi, is rather confirmed by a legend which points to the discovery of the Vindhya Hills, and the Brahmanizing of the Dekhan. The Vindhya Hills, says the legend, were jealous of the Himalayas, the peaks of which were each morning visited by the earliest rays of the rising sun. The sun says it is not in his power to alter his course, for it has been prescribed to him by those who created the world. Immediately the Vindhya Hills swell with rage, and, stretching upwards, intercepted the course of the sun, the moon, and the constellations. The gods, being alarmed, request the Rishi Agastya to go to the Vindhya Hills and arrest this proceeding. Agastya, taking with him his wife, went to the Vindhya Hills, and said:

"O excellent mountain! I desire to travel into the south: make a passage possible, and keep it open, by not increasing in size until I shall have returned." The mountain granted his request; and to this day Agastya has not returned, and the Vindhya Hills have not grown bigger.

In the well-known story of Nala and Damayanti, the geographical area is enlarged; and from this, and some other indications, it may, perhaps, be attributed to a more advanced period of Hindu history than that in which Drona took offence at the king of Panchála, Draupadí married the Pándus, and passages in love and war occurred between the Serpent people of the forests and the highest races, or Aryans, of the land.[1]

The lovely Damayantí was the only daughter of Bhíma, king of Vidarbha (supposed to be the modern province of Berar). Nala was the youthful monarch of Nishadha, at no great distance from Vidarbha; and although the two young people had never met, they fall in love by merely hearing reports of each other's beauty and merit. King Nala imparts his wishes to the sacred birds called Hansa, and a flock of these flamingos take flight in

[1] Th. Pavie. Fragments du Mahâbhârata, p. 232.

consequence for Vidarbha; and, finding the lovely Damayanti
in the garden attached to her father's palace, they allure her to
a little distance from her attendants and then, by judicious discourse, succeed in making her participate in her lover's emotions.
From this moment Damayanti pines; and her father determines
she shall hold her Swayamvara, or choose her husband from
amongst attendant suitors.[1]

So soon as this is announced, Nala contrives to procure a private interview, fearing lest his elected bride might not recognise
him amongst the numerous chiefs and nobles whom such an
invitation would assemble. When the expected day arrived,
elephants, steeds, and chariots, brought all the lords of earth as
suitors. They came, wearing fragrant garlands and rich ear-
rings, and entered the court through the golden columns of the
portal arch.

But amongst the earthly suitors appeared four gods, each of
whom knowing Damayanti's inclination, assumed the form of
Nala. The damsel knew that four out of the five Nalas present
must be gods; and she perfectly appreciated the honour they
intended for her. But her heart was fixed on the real human
Nala; and, instead of rejoicing in celestial homage, she was soon
distracted at finding it impossible to distinguish him. In this
dilemma, she appealed to the gods themselves, entreated their
compassion, and implored their aid. The gods, amazed to find
themselves rejected, but in pity for the maiden's anguish, show
signs of their divinity. Damayanti chooses him she loves, and
Nala becomes the happy bridegroom. After the nuptial ceremony the newly-married pair reside at Nishadha, where they have
two children, and enjoy supreme felicity, until a spell is cast
over Nala by a certain evil spirit. The king is described as a
most virtuous monarch, well read in the four Vedas and the
Purânas, gentle to all living creatures, true in word and strict

[1] Chapter iii. pp. 56, 58.

in vow; but in marrying Damayanti he had excited the jealousy of the demon Kali, who had himself wished for the damsel's love, and Kali in consequence was for ever haunting the palace, and watching for some unguarded moment in which to throw his evil spirit into the unhappy king. Negligence of a trifling prescribed ceremony gave, at length, the wished-for opportunity; and the virtuous Nala, now possessed by a demon, gave himself up to gambling.

For months he continues to throw the dice with ill-success, his wife venturing now and then a sad remonstrance, and his wise counsellors saying that he is no longer himself. But Nala, like other desperate gamblers, will listen to no advice. Damayanti then convenes the council in his name, and gets leave to send the children, with a trusty charioteer, to her father's court at Vidarbha, where alone she feels they will be safe. The infatuated king stakes his jewels, his garments, and even his kingdom; and all are lost. The demon strives hard to make him stake his wife, but does not succeed: even in madness, the king's virtue and affection were proof against that trial. But he was houseless and penniless, for his adversary decreed death to whoever should befriend him, and chased him from his palace. The dethroned monarch went forth into the woods, but not alone; for the faithful Damayanti followed. Too desperate to be soothed, her husband felt her gentle presence as an aggravation of his misery; and, instead of desiring her companionship, he showed where ran the road conducting to her father's home. She understood the sign, but said, that with her afflicted, breaking heart, and sinking limbs, she could not leave him. She wished to soothe his weariness; and said, all physicians owned that, in sorrow, there was no healing herb or balsam equal to a wife: therefore, if she went to Vidarbha, he must go also. But that was an insupportable idea; for he could not endure to be seen by Bhima in this extremity of degradation. At night they seek the refuge of a forest hut. Three times, whilst Damayanti sleeps, he resolves upon escape. He thinks, that if he were away, she would go to her father, mother, and children; but that, whilst he remains, there is only misery for all.

"And, departing, still departing,—he returned again, again;
Dragg'd away by that bad demon,—ever by his love drawn back."

And, after thus oscillating "like a swing," he is torn away by Kali, and flies afar.

When Damayanti wakes, she finds herself deserted, and wanders hither and thither, until she meets a caravan of merchants, which is thus described:

"A caravan of merchants,—elephants, and steeds, and cars;
And, beyond, a pleasant river, with its waters cool and clear.
'Twas a quiet stream, and waveless, girt about with spreading canes:
There the cuckoo, there the osprey, there the red geese, clamouring, stood;
Swarmed the turtles, fish, and serpents; there rose many a stately isle."

The merchants take her for a spirit, and are unwilling to speak; but when she entreats assistance, in her search for her lost husband, the chief says, that hitherto he has encountered only "elephants, ... tigers, ... buffaloes and bears;" but he will permit Damayanti to travel to the next city under his protection. And the caravan proceeds, until

. . . . . "A lake of loveliest beauty, fragrant with the lotus flowers,
Saw those merchants; wide and pleasant, with fresh grass and shady trees;
Flowers and fruit bedeck'd its borders,—where the birds melodious sung.
In its clear, delicious waters,—soul-enchanting, icy, cool,—
With their horses all o'er-wearied, thought they there to plunge and bathe."

The captain gave a signal, and they encamped; but in the dead of night down came a herd of wild elephants to the lake for water. For a moment they stood amazed at the slumbering caravan; but presently, scenting the tame elephants,—

"Forward rush they, fleet and furious; . . . . .
Irresistible the onset of the rushing, ponderous beasts.
  * * * * * * *
Strewn was all the way before them with the boughs and trunks of
 trees.
On they crashed to where the travellers slumbered by the Lotus
 Lake;
Trampled down without a struggle, helpless on the earth they lay.
Woe, oh woe! shrieked out the merchants, wildly some began to fly,
In the forest thickets plunging; some stood gasping, blind with sleep:
And the elephants down beat them with their tusks, their trunks,
 their feet.
Many saw their camels dying, mingling with the men of foot,
And, in frantic tumult rushing, wildly struck each other down.
Many, miserably shrieking, cast them down upon the earth;
Many climbed the trees in terror,—on the rough ground stumbled
 some.
Thus, in various wise, and fatal, by the elephants assailed,
Lay that caravan so wealthy,—scattered all about, or slain.
Such, so fearful was the tumult, the three worlds seemed all appalled.
'Tis a fire amid the encampment; save ye, fly ye for your lives!
Lo! your precious pearls ye trample; take them up, why fly so fast?
Save them,—'tis a common venture!"[1]

Damayanti was suspected of being in some way the cause of the calamity, and threatened with death from clods and bamboos; but, happily, some "Veda-reading Bráhmans" had survived, and they took her in charge, and conducted her to a town called Chedi's city. Here she enters,—disturbed, emaciated,

[1] Poems, by Dean Milman. Vol. iii.

wretched. The boys of the town follow her, amazed at her dishevelled hair and wild appearance. The mother of the king, sitting on a lofty terrace, sees the forlorn wanderer, and sends a servant, called a nurse, to bring her in.

Damayanti yields to the kind desire of this grand lady, that she should rest with her at Chedi. Damayanti, however, stipulates that she shall not eat broken victuals, or "wash feet," which would have been Sûdra service; and that she shall be protected from all suitors. After a time she is discovered by messengers from her father's court. She then returns to Vidarbha, and lives with her father, her mother, and her children. But she has not found Nala; and her anxiety to win her husband back is irrepressible. Tedious was her search, and numerous were the devices resorted to, before that search was successful.

Nala had become charioteer to a king of Ayodhyâ, who initiated him into the secrets of dice, in return for lessons from Nala in the art of managing horses. It seems that Nala was ignorant of dice, and that it was in consequence of his ignorance that he had been defeated; whilst in knowledge of horses he was unsurpassed. As soon as he had fully attained " the science of dice," his adversary, the wicked Kali, was defeated, the spell was broken, and the evil spirit, leaving him, entered a tree, which perished instantly. At this juncture a friendly Nâga king (or king of Snakes) offered to restore Nala to his former appearance; and he might then have returned to his kingdom and his wife. But news arrived at Ayodhyâ that Damayanti was about to hold a second Swayamvara. This was a stratagem contrived by the deserted wife, in order to rouse her missing lord, thereby to bring about their reunion. Damayanti's ceaseless enquiries had led her to suspect that the king of Ayodhyâ's skilful charioteer was no other than king Nala; and to Ayodhyâ, therefore (but to no other place), she sent an intimation that, on the dawn of the succeeding day, Damayanti was about to choose a second lord.

The king of Ayodhyá wishes to attend, and says, literally, to Nala, his charioteer:

> "This woman, having bound us, attracts by her good qualities.
> Who (thus) drawn by a woman (can say) nay?
> The assembly,—such the announcement,—is to morrow:
> Thus, our way by measurement is one hundred yojanas."

One hundred yojanas may be five hundred miles, or it may be regarded as amounting to nine hundred miles; and as Ayodhyá stands for Oude, and Vidarbha is supposed to mean Berar, the latter computation seems to be that required. But whether the day's journey was one of five hundred or nine hundred miles, is immaterial; as, to travel either distance in a day, was of course impossible.

When Rituparna, the king, made this announcement to Nala, his charioteer, poor "Nala's heart was torn with anguish;" but although dismayed at the idea of his wife's proposing to choose another husband, he wished at any rate to be present, and promised, therefore, that king Rituparna should arrive in time. Nala's wonderful proficiency in the science of horses is said to have enabled him to perform the amazing feat. Late in the evening, Damayantí recognised from afar the peculiar tramp of steeds, driven by her husband; and she mounted to the palace roof to behold once more her "Nala, prince of men."

Damayanti's mother was the only person in her secret: her father, king Bhíma, knew nothing of her stratagem. He was, therefore, astonished at the arrival of a guest; and the guest and his charioteer were equally astonished to find no preparation for a marriage festival. All, however, keep their counsel; and Damayantí is left undisturbed to work out her scheme. Nala's persevering incognito causes her much embarrassment; but at length she persuades her mother to allow her to defy all apparent propriety, by holding a secret interview with the charioteer, and then, by working upon his feelings, she forces him to acknowledge himself to be Nala, her husband. Nala is very stiff about the proposed Swayamvara; and she has great difficulty in convincing him, that never for a moment had she intended another marriage, and that the "subtle wile" had been adopted solely for the purpose of luring back her own true husband. The sun, moon, and winds come forward to give testimony to her truth; and on their evidence Nala gives up his jealous doubts, resumes his proper form, and is reunited to his loving wife in perfect happiness.

In this beautiful little poem, we find women far more independent than the laws of the Mánavas would appear to approve. But it is one of the heroic poems, which describes more of the life of the Kshattriya than of the Bráhman class. Damayantí's marriage, at the commencement, is similar to that held in Panchála for Draupadí; but it is only amongst princes and princesses that we read of such marriages. No instance is given of how a marriage was celebrated in the Bráhman caste. The story of Nala is told to Yudhishthira, to divert and console him when banished to the forest, in consequence of losing his kingdom through a game with dice; but neither the one nor the other of these gambling monarchs is blamed by the poet as having acted in disregard of the stringent precepts of the "Code of Manu." This merely shows that the poems are, on these occasions, stories of actual life; whilst the Code represents the ideal of what life should be.[1]

The story of Sakuntalá, also, appears in the Mahábhárata. Kálidása made it the subject of a beautiful drama, of which an account will presently be given: we will, therefore, make but a slight outline of this earlier version of the tale. It opens with the royal cavalcade of King Dushyanta starting for the forest to hunt the wild beasts. Ladies look out from their high balconies

---

[1] But the use of dice was not in itself wrong. It forms part of religious ceremonies, and various superstitions are connected with it.

to see the gay pageant. After killing tigers and deer, &c., the tired hunters sit round a fire, hoping to enjoy their cooked venison; but they are disturbed by a troop of wild elephants, who rush upon them, savage from having been wounded. The king and his attendants seek another forest, and find unexpectedly "a garden of delight," "a grove, to make the spirit swell with rapture." Here were cool breezes, scented flowery shrubs, fresh grass, and the sweet melody of birds. And here Dushyanta discovers the lovely Sakuntalá, who was the daughter of the Rishi Viswâmitra and the heavenly nymph Menaká. Abandoned by her parents, she had been adopted by the Rishi Kanwa, to whom the hermitage belonged. Dushyanta falls desperately in love; the adopted father is absent, and can give no consent; but he persuades Sakuntalá that the right thing is for her to marry him at once in Gandharba wedlock, which is a form of marriage requiring no public ceremony, but which is, nevertheless, recognised in ancient Hindu law as legal for kings and warriors. Soon after the marriage the king returns to his seat of government, promising to send messengers and chariots for his bride.

When Sakuntalá's adopted father returns home, she meets him timidly, but he, being "gifted with all god-like knowledge," already knows her secret; and telling her, that for warriors the Gandharbha marriage was the fittest, he rejoices at her being united to a monarch so famous and so noble-hearted as Dushyanta. Time passes; and no messengers arrive for Sakuntalá. She bears a son; and remains at the hermitage until the boy is six years old. Then the Rishi Kanwa declares that the boy must claim his rights; and that Sakuntalá must take him to his father.

But when arrived in the presence of the king they are entirely disowned: Dushyanta has not the slightest recollection of Sakuntalá, or of being married in the woods. In this emergency, Sakuntalá adjures him, in eloquent words. We give some portions of her speech, from the metrical rendering of Mr. Griffith:

"Scarce she heard the monarch's answer; in unspeakable distress
Stood she, smitten through with anguish, as a column,—motionless;
Close her swelling lips then press'd she; . . . . .
With her heart awhile she communed, then her angry silence broke."

She upbraids the king with lying, and says that the gods see his sin, and also the spirit from within, and continues:

"Husband! should'st thou drive me from thee, thus unheard,
    dishonoured,
Still thy sin will fruit thee sorrow, hundred-fold upon thy head.
Wife a name is, high and holy. . . . . . She that is his children's
    mother,
One half of the man the wife is. . . . . .
Wives console their lords in anguish, whisper hope in their distress;
Fathers they in heavenly duties,—mothers in their tenderness.
    *   *   *   *   *   *   *
She that loveth well, will follow the dear lord she honoureth
Through all changes of existence,—woe, and misery, and death.
Is she reft from his fond bosom? there she waits for him above;
If he dies, her life is hateful,—till she follows to her love."

And after dwelling further on the "refreshing comfort" of a wife, she describes the blessing of children:

"Oh! how blessed is the father, when he sees his new-born son,
As it were his own face mirror'd: he is saved, and heaven is won
When all dusty, crawling slowly, the belovëd, darling boy,
Comes and kisses his own father,—who can tell that father's joy?
Here thy son is looking on thee! monarch, how canst thou despise
This appeal of thine own offspring,—the mute prayer of those dear
    eyes?
Soft the touch of precious raiment, pleasant woman's kisses are;
Pleasant is the touch of water,—but a son's is sweeter far.
Father! touch thine own fair offspring,—kiss that soft, inviting face."

This appeal was strengthened by a voice from the sky; and then the king comforted his poor wife, and ordered the attendants to bring her dainty food, and fitting raiment. His son he embraced "with all a father's joy," and named him Bharata; and "from this Bharata the glories of the Bharat lineage come."

A paper in the Westminster Review for April, 1868, offers important and interesting thoughts on the relative or comparative date of the Mahábhárata. "We take it for granted," says the writer, "that the Mahábhárata is a traditional record of an early period of Hindu history, compiled however by eminent men of Brahmanical caste, and modelled by them to suit a special purpose of their own,—that of imposing their own law on the Kshattriya, or military caste. The fabric of the great epos was not built up at once: different times supplied different materials for it; and with the importance of the object the greatness of the task increased. These materials, as Professor Lassen himself has in several instances shown, sometimes underwent the treatment of various editors; but the chief object of all these editors, arrangers and modellers, always remained the same,— to demonstrate the necessity and the sanctity of the Brahmanical law." We may, therefore, feel confident, that a fact so repugnant to Bráhmans as the marriage of the fair Draupadî with the five Pándu heroes, would have been excluded from the chronicle, had it not been a fact of history too well established to be denied. The father of the damsel objects to the proposal; the eldest of the brothers pleads, "We follow the path which has been trodden by our ancestors in succession," and refers to precedents. The inference is, that the Pándavas must have lived at "such a remote period of antiquity as to leave behind not only Manu, the oldest representative of Hindu law, but even those Vedic writings of Aswaláyana, and others, on which the ancient law of India is based."

Some other facts recorded in the poem are then adduced, as further evidence of the antiquity of the chronicles of the Bharatas. We are reminded that, in the earliest Vedic period, "caste" was unknown; whereas, in the Code of Manu, caste is fully established, and circumscribed with stringent rules. "At the Vedic period, a warrior Viswâmitra, for instance, could aspire to the occupation of a Brâhmana; and a Brâhmana like Vasishtha could be engaged in military pursuits. At the time of Manu such a confusion of occupations, as an orthodox Hindu would say, was no longer allowed: it recurs only at the latest period of Hinduism. Yet, in the history of the great war, we find the Brâhman Drona not only as the military instructor of the Kauravas and Pándavas, but actively engaged in a war against Drupada." ..... After mentioning further instances, the reviewer alludes to "another *class* of passages in the Mahâbhârata," which prove that the "events to which they relate must have been historical, and anterior to the classical state of Hindu society:" these are passages which bear on laws of marriage and inheritance. The conclusion is, that there are portions of the Mahâbhârata which picture a state of Hindu society anterior to the Code of Manu, and differing from that code not only in positive laws, but also in customs and morality. The *oldest* recension of the epos is, therefore, presumed to be anterior to the standard codes of law. Later recensions have obscured the antiquity of the oldest recension, by introducing legends foreign to it. Such "as relate to Siva, whom, like the god, not the hero Krishna, we consider as an intruder into the oldest portions of the Mahâbharata." Buddhism is believed to be posterior to the great poem, although some passages are post-Buddhistic; but no portion is ascribed by the reviewer "to a date subsequent to the rise of Christianity."

"Once, there was music in the pleshing wave,
Where maidens loved their limbs to lave."—Page 23.

CHAPTER XXV

RAGHUVANSA.

KUMARASAMBHAVA,—BIRTH OF THE WAR-GOD.

BHATTIKAVYA.

1. RAGHUVANSA, BY KALIDASA.

Fragments of the Raghuvansa, poem by Kálidása.—Dilipa, father to Raghu.—Homage to the "holy cow."—Child born.—King and Queen retire to the woods.—Raghu reigns.—Story of Aja, son of Raghu.—Marriage.—Combat.—Death.—Ráma and Sítá in flying car.—Ayodhyá described.

THE Raghuvansa, by Kálidása, is a poem of which Mr. Colebrooke speaks in the highest terms; and, happily, Mr. Griffith having this year given us English renderings of various passages, we are enabled to treat of it amongst the larger poems of Sanskrit literature. It contains the history of Ráma, including his predecessors and successors,—from Dilipa, the father of Raghu, to Agnivarna, a slothful prince, who seems to have been unimportant. The fragments relating to Ráma describe his return to Ayodhyá, and the subsequent desertion of that gay and beautiful city, which stood on the banks of the river Sarayû, where once gay bands of ladies used to sing and plash, "whilst peacocks, listening on the shore, rejoice, spread their broad tails, and raise the answering voice." Mr. Colebrooke observes, that the adventures of Ráma are here recounted with far greater spirit than by the sacred poets, not excepting even Válmíki; but Kálidása approaches the subject with great diffidence, or rather with a feeling of awe, saying:

> "How men will mock the humble bard who sings
> The ancient glories of the sun-born kings;
> Like a young child with little hands outspread
> For fruit that glows above a giant's head!"

But "their noble deeds inspire;" and he feels assisted by the "ancient sons of song," who have prepared the way for him,

> "As diamonds pierce the way for silk to string
> Rich pearls, to deck the forehead of a king."

And thus he resolves to sing—

> "Although the hope be vain
> To tell their glories in a worthy strain."

Resemblance to other productions by Kálidása will be traced, and recurrence of favourite images; whilst at the same time purity of sentiment, and the tenderness and fidelity of the characters pourtrayed, will show its alliance with the dramas attributed to Kálidása.

The story of Dilípa, the father of Raghu, of Raghu and his son Aja, occupy the first eight cantos; and of these, Mr. Griffith gives us the first, second, and part of the third.

DILIPA, THE IDEAL OF A KING.

Dilipa is a grand ideal of what a king should be.

> "Matchless in beauty and heroic might,
> He towers like Meru in his lofty height.
> Meet for his god-like form, his noble mind
> To worthy studies in his youth inclined.
> Thence great designs inspired his generous soul,
> And mighty deeds with glory crowned the whole."

This monarch was the delight of his subjects, who followed him as their guide, and thereby obeyed the laws of Manu.

> "And well they knew the tax they gladly paid
> For their advantage, on the realm was laid.
> The bounteous sun delights to drink the lakes,
> But gives ten thousand-fold the wealth he takes."

Just as the earth and water, fire and ether, were given by the good Creator for the benefit of all mankind; so was the king, Dilipa, sent to bless his subjects, and find his own happiness in that of others. Theft was unknown in his dominions, and

> "He ruled the earth, from rival sceptre free,
> Like one vast city girdled by the sea."

But one boon was wanting. He had a lovely queen, but no son.

> "Oh! how he longed, that childless king, to see
> A royal infant smiling on her knee;
> With his dear mother's eyes and face divine,—
> A second self to ornament his line!"

In the hope of attaining this boon he resolves to seek his holy guide, the renowned Vasishtha, who now lived far away in a secluded hermitage. His queen goes forth with him, and they travel in a car, which "tells his coming with the music of its bells."

> "Fresh on their cheeks the soft wind gently blows,
> Wafting the perfume of the woodland rose;
> And, heavy with the dust of rifled flowers,
> Waves the young branches of the mango bowers.
> They hear the peacock's joyous cry; his head
> Lifted in wonder at the courser's tread.
> They watch the cranes in jubilant armies fly,
> Crowning, like flowers, the portals of the sky.
> From shady coverts by the way, the deer
> Throw startled glances when the car is near.
> *　*　*　*　*　*
> Through towns they pass, and many a hamlet fair,
> Founded and cherished by their royal care."

Peasants bring them curds and milk; . . . . . the king calls attention to the varied beauties of the woodland scene; and, lost in delight, they reach the end of their journey quite unexpectedly.

> "Evening is come, and, weary of the road,
> The horses rest before the saints' abode."

The hermitage reminds one of that described in Kálidása's play, Sakuntalá. Hermits from the neighbouring forest have come for grass and fuel; playful fawns are waiting to be fed with rice; young girls are watering the roots of trees, &c.

The king and the queen are most kindly received.

After "food and rest," the sage inquires of the king his wishes, and having heard that

> "Mother earth, whom tears nor prayers have won,
> Is still ungracious, and denies a son,"

and that "the spirits of his fathers pine," seeing no hope of funeral offerings, ... the great Vasishtha falls into profound meditation, and, after a few minutes, announces the cause of the misfortune. The king, Dilipa, had once, thoughtlessly and unconsciously, omitted to pay reverence to "the holy cow," which was lying under a celestial tree near the falls of the Ganges. . . . Therefore, by way of penance, he and his queen must tend a cow, called Nandini, in the sacred woods close by; and when they have gained the love of this descendant of the affronted cow, the curse will be removed. The attendance is given faithfully: the queen worships the cow, by walking round her and scattering grain; and the king cannot be persuaded, even by illusive phantoms, to desert his trust. At length the cow declares that his prayer is granted. He hastens to the queen;

> "And though she read at once his looks aright,
> He told her all again with new delight.
> Then, at the bidding of the saint, he quaffed
> Of Nandini's pure milk a precious draught
> As though, with thirst that rises from the soul,
> He drank eternal glory from the bowl."

At the dawn of day,

> "Swift towards their home the eager horses bound;
> The car makes music o'er the grassy ground.
> They reach the city, where the people wait,
> Longing to meet their monarch, at the gate.
> Dim are his eyes, his cheek is pale, his brow
> Still bears deep traces of his weary vow."

In due time a son was born.

> "There was a glory round the infant's head;
> And e'en the unlit torches seemed to shine
> As in a picture, with that light divine."

And, when all rites had been duly performed,—

> "Still greater glory crowned Dilipa's son."

This son, born under such auspicious circumstances, proved worthy of sharing his father's throne; and Dilipa's days flow by in glory and bliss, until

> "Mindful of duties by the scriptures taught,
> From worldly cares he drew his every thought;
> Resigned the white umbrella to his heir,"

And with his queen sought a tranquil dwelling in the woods.

> "For such, through ages, in their life's decline,
> Is the good custom of the sun-born line."

Our attention is next claimed for Raghu's son, Aja, who has just attained manhood. The day has arrived on which a lovely princess is to hold a Swayamvara in an open plain. All the young princes of the neighbouring kingdoms are to sit on thrones awaiting her inspection. At early dawn, minstrels present themselves at the palace, singing:

> "Wake, Aja, wake! the night has fled.
> Come, rouse thee, while the morn is red."

They remind the young prince that Raghu, his father, divides with him "the world's tremendous weight," and that it is, therefore, incumbent on him to rouse himself, and take his share. The morning breeze is up, they tell him, and is stealing blossoms from the bough.

> "Thine elephants are gone to take
> Their wonted pastime in the lake.
> And as the flush of morn is shed
> Upon each monster's mighty head,
> Bright gleam their tusks, like ribs of gold,
> That river-sides of mountains hold."

The horses are also awake, and many a steed has bent his stately neck to taste the golden grain before him placed.

"Quick from his couch the son of Raghu sprang."

And hastened to the scene of action.

"Now clear-voiced heralds in the midst proclaim
Each prince's title and ancestral fame:
These, from the sun derive their ancient race;
Those, from the moon their rival lineage trace.
From burning aloes rose a fragrant cloud
High o'er the banners."

Meanwhile drums and conch shells made a noise, so like to that of thunder, that—

"The peacocks, glittering on the garden wall,
Danced in wild glee,—obedient to the call."

And now appears the bride, "high on her car." The princes betray their feelings by various gestures:

"One, with quick fingers, twirled a lotus round,
Dropping the fragrant pollen on the ground:
And, as the bees came near, the baffled thieves
Were driven backward by the whirling leaves."

One turned his head aside to replace his wreath; another tore the jasmine bud which graced his ear; whilst another, again, whose "finger was bright with many a gem," feigned to replace his coronet.

A matron, named Sunandâ, who is called "keeper of her palace door," leads the fair maiden on, and describes each suitor in language "that had graced a man."

The princess rejects severally the lords of Magadha, Anga,

Oujein (or Avanti), Anûpa, Lankâ (or Ceylon), and Malaya, on the coast of southern India,—a place in which grow "betel trees, creeping elâs, sandal, and tamâla." But when the fair maiden arrives at the throne of Aja, she is silent, through modest fear. Each quivering limb proclaims her feeling; and, with a radiant look of love and joy, she throws the flowery wreath upon his neck.

"Long and loud rang out the rapture of the gathered throng," excepting, however, "the rival chiefs." As the wedding procession "speeds on along the royal street," every lady runs to catch a sight of Aja. The next sixteen lines are, word for word, the same as those in the "Birth of the War-God," where

> "Careless of all beside, each lady's eye
> Must gaze on Siva as the troop sweeps by."

One dark-eyed beauty waits not to confine her long, black tresses; another tears her foot away, with the dye all wet and streaming, leaving in her haste a crimson foot-print wheresoe'er she stepped; another rushes to the window with but one eye dyed.

The description of the bridal ceremony also resembles that in the poem of the "War-God:" in either case, the bride and bridegroom are compared to—

> "Day and starry midnight, when they meet
> In the broad plains, at holy Meru's feet."

And, in either case, the lady, at the bidding of the priest, throws grain into the flame, and draws towards her the scented smoke, which round her ears in flower-like beauty hangs. And whilst

> "O'er the incense the sweet lady stooped,
> The ear of barley from her tresses drooped."

The ceremony over, the glad king and the matron train sprinkled them with moistened grain. The king then gave orders that honour be shown to the disappointed suitors. But although the chiefs

> "Sought with words of love and joy to hide
> Their burning rage and disappointed pride;
> Gave gifts, the monarch's honours to repay,
> And bade their host farewell, and went their way,—
> They had united in a treacherous plot
> To wait for Aja in a distant spot;
> Watching the moment when their troops might dare
> The tender lady from her lord to tear."

For this Aja was prepared; and, placing a trusted chieftain and a chosen band to guard the lady, he met his foes as the river Sone, with its mounting billows, meets "mighty Gangá, daughter of the sky."

The combat was terrific, and is described with much spirit: horseman met horseman;—footmen on footmen dashed.

> "And car was whirled at car in mad career;
> While rushing wildly with a shriek and roar,
> Opposing elephants their riders bore.
> 'Twas vain to call each bowman's lineage out,
> 'Mid braying trumpets and the battle's shout;
> But every arrow bore inscribed a name,
> To tell the wounded chief his foeman's fame."

The courage, agility and dexterity of Aja, were amazing; yet,

> "Once more their shattered bands the chiefs unite;
> Once more they charge him with redoubled might."

At this juncture, Aja has recourse to his magic bow; that bow which was of old the pride and wonder of heaven's minstrel host. Then suddenly, as though by sleep opprest, the opposing archers lose their strength, their fingers rest upon their bowstrings, and their failing limbs seek support.

Young Aja now takes up his shell and sounds forth a ringing, triumphant note.

> "His soldiers started at the well-known sound,
> And saw him with his prostrate foes around:
> Like the bright moon, victorious in the skies,
> When the sad lotus, drowned in slumber, lies.
> Then Aja seized a dripping shaft, and o'er
> The princes' banners traced these words in gore:
> 'Aja has torn your warlike fame away,
> But spared your forfeit lives to-day.'"

Aja hastens to "his love," his face radiant with delight:

> "Flushed with the triumph of the glorious fight,
> E'en as a mirror, dimmed by breath, and then
> Bright as before, and fair and clear again."

The lady's way of receiving the joyful tidings is very characteristic of ancient Hindu heroines, who are too modest to speak to the men they love:

> "Modest and silent, though her heart beat high,
> She gave her maids a signal to reply.
> Thus, when the rain has made the earth rejoice,
> She thanks the kind clouds in the peacock's voice.
> He spurned the chieftains, as they prostrate lay,
> And proudly led his faultless bride away."

Aja's father, Raghu, being by this time somewhat old and weary of the cares of state, gladly resigned the kingdom to his son:

> "And he, obedient, not like kings who lust
> For power and empire, took the sacred trust,"—

and was duly consecrated with holy water. The people were proud of their youthful lord, and the prince loved his people:

> "As bending trees the steady wind obey,
> So bent his nobles to his mild, firm sway.
> When Raghu sees his son beloved of all,
> No earthly thought must now his soul enthral:
> For all the monarchs of Dilipa's race,
> When blest with worthy sons to fill their place,
> Forsaking worldly cares in life's decline,
> To them the sceptre and the throne resign;
> Assume the garment of the holy sage,
> And spend in thoughts of God their tranquil age."

At the entreaty of his son, however, Raghu consented to remain near him:

> "For his loving heart
> Still clings to Aja, and is loth to part.
> But royal rank he claims not; as the snake
> Cares not again his cast-off skin to take."

Raghu determines, therefore, to live in a humble cottage outside the city. And, whilst devoted to his "hermit vow," his son's wife tends him with a daughter's care:

> "E'en as the sky, what time the moon has set,
> And the new sun has scarcely risen yet,—
> So was that race: the sire in his retreat;
> The heir just placed upon the royal seat."

Aja, in kingly robes arrayed, sat daily in his judgment-seat; whilst Raghu, clad in humble hermit's dress, reclined on sacred grass, gradually vanquishing Nature's triple chain. "He looked on all below with equal eye; and with his thoughts fixed upon the glorious sky, he became united with the Great Spirit in the world of light." Aja shed tears of anguish when his father died, and performed the last sad duties, but without the aid of fire; because his father, as a devotee, had given up the use of fire.

The remainder of Aja's history requires but few words. A gentle infant came to clear him from the "ancient claim;" and in the performance of other duties he was equally faultless. He supported the weak, honoured the wise, succoured the distressed. He was blessed by his subjects; but his happiness was to steal away from the crowded city, and, with his darling wife, and happy child, enjoy the neighbouring shades, until, alas! it was decreed that this beloved wife should die. A chaplet of flowers fell from heaven to recall her to the regions from which she came.

Then, for eight years, the bereaved husband endured his life "without a joy."

> "The sword of anguish cleft his broken heart,
> As the wild fig-tree, bursting through, will part
> The palace pavement."

But so soon as his son could wear armour, and perform the duties which claim a ruler's care,—

> "Then Aja, weary of the light of day,
> Resolved to fast his noble life away.
> Where Sarayú's waves with Gangá's stream unite,
> From the dead clay his spirit winged its flight."

Cantos eight to sixteen, which concern Ráma, contain "An Address to Vishnu," which describes the god upon his serpent-bed, with celestial beings around; but this being purely mythological, is far less interesting than passages which touch on human affections and earthly beauty. In the "Flying Car," from canto thirteen, we have, for instance, a description, given by Ráma to his beloved Sitá, of the country over which they are supposed to be passing. Ráma has just rescued Sitá from his enemy, the king of Ceylon; and he and his wife have mounted the flying car. This journey gives rise to descriptions, which show how close and accurate was Kálidása's poetical observation.

The ocean, as seen at the southern extremity of India, much impressed him. Ráma says, addressing his wife:

" Look, Sitá, look! away to Malaya's side
My causeway parts the ocean's foamy tide.
Thus hast thou seen, on some fair autumn night,
When heaven is loveliest with its starry light,
From north to south a cloudy pathway spread,
Parting the deep, dark firmament o'erhead.
Deep is that sea, but deeper still, they say,
Our glorious fathers dug their eager way;
Following fast where Kapil dared to lead
Away to hell their charge, the hallowed steed.
From the deep sea the sun-god draws the rain,
To pour it down in boundless wealth again."

From the ocean also arose, he says, the silver light of the moon:

" That ocean, whose waves are now at rest;"

but whose might is unknown, and unmeasured, and impossible to tell:

" When, from sky to sky his billows roll;
Boundless as Vishnu,—who pervades the whole."

Where a river runs into the sea, the eager wave of the ocean is said to "drink up the river's lips," and, foaming o'er, to "leap, in a storm of passion, on the shore."

Beasts, birds, fishes, shells, trees and flowers, are all observed by Kálidása:

" Look, Sitá, look! those monsters of the deep
Close by the river's mouth their station keep.

Soon as the waves have reached them, they have quaff'd
Water and fish together at a draught.
Now, see! they shut their mouths, while gushing out.
From openings in their heads, high fountains spout."

The shells, cast upon trees of coral by the "furious swell" of the billows, are also noticed. And so soon as the travellers reach the strand, they see "uncovered pearls" upon the sand, "cast by tempests from their ocean-bed." Here, also, they see "groves of betel trees," . . . . . "hanging the burden of their branches low."

When they travel over the scenes in which they passed their years of banishment, Ráma alludes, in touching words, to his distress at losing Sítá; but we can give but a few lines:

"Look far before us; see the distant gleam,
Through the thick reeds of Pampá's silver stream.
There on the bank I saw two love-birds play,
And feed each other with a lotus spray!
'Ah, happy birds!' I sighed, 'whom cruel fate
Dooms not to sorrow for an absent mate!'
Well I remember, in my wild despair,
I thought a bright asoka glowing there
Was Sítá."

When they reach Panchavati, he sees "gazing deer." On the shore of the Godaveri, he observes "troops of cranes" upward soaring. Farther to the north, he calls Sítá's attention to the mountain called Chitrakúta:

"Now to the left, dear Sítá, turn thine eyes,
Where Chitrakúta's lofty peaks arise.
Like some proud bull he lifts his haughty crest;
See, the dark cave, his mouth, and shaggy breast!
Now like a clod in furious charge uptorn,
A cloud is hanging on his mighty horn.
See, how the river, with its lucid streams,
Like a pearl necklace, round the mountain gleams!"

As they approach the junction of the Jumna with the Ganges, he sees a tree "with leaves of rosy red," from which he had twined a garland for Sitâ, and a fig tree "with leaves of emerald green, and fruit like rubies shining bright between," and continues:

"Dost thou remember how thy prayer was prayed
For me, sweet love, beneath its friendly shade?
Now, see the waves of Jumna's stream divide
The fair-limbed Gangâ's heaven-descended tide!
Distinct, though joined, bright gleaming in the sun,
Like pearls with sapphires mixt, the rivers run.
Thus intertwined, the azure lotus through
Crowns of white lilies pours its shade of blue."

The different colour of the rivers, after their union, seems much to have impressed Kâlidâsa, for he uses six different images in its description. First: the blue lotus flowers, seen amongst the white lilies. Second: "the dark gold-shot glories of the drake," amid the white swans that float on Mânas' lake. Third: a line of ochre crossing a sandal mark. Fourthly and fifthly: the Jumna comes into the Ganges looking like

". . . . . the moon, whose silver radiance steals
Through the dark cloud that half its face conceals;
Or as a row of autumn's clouds, between
Whose shifting ranks the blue of heaven is seen."

And, sixthly: the colours of the two rivers remind him of "Siva's body, white with ashes," around which "a serpent's subtle coils are wound."

The fourteenth canto contains beautiful stanzas on the banishment of Sitâ; but, charming as are these stanzas of Kâlidâsa, translated by Mr. Griffith, we must only allude to the opening scene.

Râma is now again settled in his palace at Ayodhyâ; and at

eve, after the cares of council and state are over, he extremely enjoys being with Sitâ in the "long chambers of his happy home." She is expecting shortly to become a mother; and Râma, gazing with love upon her "melting eye," observes with anxious care her "paling cheek." But Râma's love for his wife does not diminish his anxious thought for the happiness of his people; and

> "It chanced, one evening from a lofty seat
> He viewed Ayodhyâ stretch'd before his feet;
> He look'd with pride upon the royal road,
> Lined with gay shops their glittering stores that showed.
> He looked on Sarjû's silver waves, that bore
> The light barks, flying with the sail and oar:
> He saw the gardens near the town that lay,
> Filled with glad citizens and boys at play.
> Then swelled the monarch's bosom with delight,
> And his heart triumphed at the happy sight.
> He turned to Bhadra standing by his side,
> Upon whose secret news the king relied,
> And bade him say what people said and thought
> Of all the exploits that his arm had wrought."

We cannot, however, follow the story, which is given in the fourteenth canto. After Râma's death, or abdication, his son Kusa succeeds to the throne of Ayodhyâ, but he changed the site of his capital.

The complete desolation of the deserted city which ensued is powerfully described in the sixteenth canto:

> "A hundred palaces lie ruined there;
> Her lofty towers are fallen; and creepers grow
> O'er marble dome and shattered portico.
> * * * * * * *
> Once, with their tinkling zones and painted feet,
> Gay bands of women thronged the royal street.

> Now, through the night the hungry jackal prowls,
> And seeks his scanty prey with angry howls.
> Once, there was music in the plashing wave
> Of lakes, where maidens loved their limbs to lave;
> But now, those waters echo with the blows
> Struck by the horns of savage buffaloes.
> Once, the tame peacock showed his glittering crest
> 'Mid waving branches, where he loved to rest.
> * * * * * * *
> Once, on the marble floor girls loved to place
> The painted foot, and leave its charming trace;
> Now, the fell tigress stains with dripping gore
> Of kids just slaughtered, that neglected floor."

Formerly, "in marble statues lived fair women's form;" but now, the statues are hid by dust and the "cast skins of serpents."

> "Once, in the gardens, lovely girls at play
> Called the bright flowers, and gently touched the spray;
> But now, wild monkeys, in their savage joy,
> Tread down the blossoms, and the plants destroy.
> By night, no torches in the windows gleam;
> By day, no women in their beauty beam.
> The smoke has ceased; the spider there has spread
> His snares in safety; and all else is dead."[1]

It is also in this canto that we find the picture of ladies meeting together in the river, to which the woodcut at the commencement of this chapter alludes. They sing, and chat, and tinkle their zones, until some are subdued by the weight of their wet garments; whilst others,—

> "Bolder grown,
> O'er a friend's head a watery stream have thrown;

[1] Griffith. Idylls from the Sanskrit, p. 124.

And the drenched girl, her long, black hair untied,
Wrings out the water with the sandal dyed.
Still is their dress most lovely, though their play
Has loosed their locks, and washed the dye away.
And though the pearls, that wont their neck to grace,
Have slipped, disordered, from their resting place" [1]

[1] Griffith. Idylls from the Sanskrit, p. 128.

"List! breathing from each cave, Himalaya leads,
The glorious hymn, with all his whispering reeds."—
Page 119.

Umá, daughter of the mountain-king Himálaya, loves Siva.—Siva is an ascetic, and gives no heed.—Earth afflicted by a demon.—Indra intercedes at Brahmá's throne.—A son of Siva alone could conquer the demon.—Anxious manœuvring for Siva's marriage.—Umá's penance.—Siva won.—Marriage.

BIRTH OF THE WAR-GOD.

KUMARA-SAMBHAVA,—Birth of the War-God, is another poem, or kávya, composed by Kálidása, and translated into English verse by Mr. Griffith. In his Preface, he expresses earnest hope that this "poem, now for the first time offered to the general reader, in an English dress, will not diminish" the reputation which translations from Kálidása's dramas have obtained for him in England and Germany. And "yet," he says, "my admiration of the grace and beauty that pervade so much of the work must not allow me to deny that, occasionally, even in the noble Sanskrit, if we judge him by an

European standard, Kálidása is bald and prosaic." We must, however, remember, that Asiatics are not habitually so sparing of time as Europeans; and that Kálidása's Hindu audience possibly preferred "bald and prosaic intervals" to relieve the attention. Nevertheless, the omission of redundancies, repetitions, and long-drawn sentences, assists English readers to perceive and enjoy the "rich, creative imagination," and "tenderness of feeling with which these beautiful poems abound; and we therefore do no wrong in transcribing chosen fragments.

Mr. Griffith regrets the inadequacy of translation to "reproduce the fanciful creation;" and is conscious that numerous beauties, of thought and expression, may have been passed by or marred, and thinks his own versification "harsh as the jarring of a tuneless chord, compared with the melody of Kálidása's rhythm." This poet's language is, indeed, so admirably adapted to the soft repose, and celestial, rosy hue of his pictures, that, to do it justice in English, would "have tried all the fertility of resource, the artistic skill, and the exquisite ear of the author of Lalla Rookh."[1]

The Birth of the War-God, or Kumára-Sambhava, appears to have come down to us in an incomplete condition. Tradition says it once consisted of twenty cantos, but it has at present only seven or, as some think, eight; and whereas it is entitled "The Birth of the War-God," it gives the history of the war-god's grandfather, of his father and his mother, and of their espousals; but finishes before his birth.

The poem opens with a description of Himálaya, who is both king and mountain:

> "Far in the north, Himálaya, lifting high
> His towery summits, till they cleave the sky,
> Spans the wide land from east to western sea:
> Lord of the hills,—instinct with deity."

[1] Birth of the War God,—Kumára-Sambhava. Translated from the Sanskrit, by R. T. H. Griffith. Preface.

The vassal hills contributed gems and gold to decorate Himálaya, whom they loved; and earth, the mother, gave her store, "to fill with herbs and sparkling ores the royal hill." The local tints are in consequence so bright, that

> "Oft, when the gleamings of his mountain brass
> Flash through the clouds and tint them as they pass,
> Those glories mock the hues of closing day.". . . . .

The denizens of the mountain wilds are hinted at as attracting the eager hunter, who "tracks the lion" and "o'er-masters the elephant." And the poet then describes the softer features:

> "Dear to the sylphs are the cool shadows thrown
> By dark clouds wandering round the mountain's zone,
> Till the big rain drops fright them from the plains
> To those high peaks where sunshine ever reigns.
> There birch-trees wave, that lend their friendly aid
> To tell the passion of the love-born maid;
> So quick to learn with metal tints to mark
> Her hopes and fears upon the tender bark."

In the caves and valleys winds resound, which are described as a glorious hymn, led by Himálaya.

> "List! breathing from each cave, Himálaya leads
> The glorious hymn with all his whispering reeds,
> Till heavenly minstrels raise their voice in song,
> And swell his music as it floats along,—
> Where the fierce elephant wounds the scented bough,
> To ease the torment of his burning brow;
> The bleeding pines their odorous gums distil,
> And breathe rare fragrance o'er the sacred hill."

The river Ganges is mentioned, as "loading with dew" the gale which makes the dark pine trees wave in the valley, and breathes freshness o'er the face of "wearied hunters, quitting the chase." Nor are the "tranquil pools" forgotten, where sweetly sleep the lotus flowers, which are awoke each morning by the kisses of the rising sun.

This mighty mountain, the monarch Himálaya, "obedient to the law divine," chose "a consort to prolong his line." She was no child of earth, but a heavenly nymph, named Menâ. "Swiftly the seasons, winged with love, flew on;" and Himálaya became the father, first of a fierce son, and afterwards of a gentle daughter. This daughter is, in this poem, born for the second time. In an earlier life she had acquired fame as the faithful wife of the god Siva. But it would appear that Siva had not then acquired much importance, for the mountain-king, Himálaya, treated his son-in-law with scorn; and the "tender soul" of his daughter was in consequence "so torn with anguish," that her "angered spirit left its mortal cell," or, in other words, she died. And Siva, from that moment, "knew no love."

> "High on that hill, where musky breezes throw
> Their balmy odours o'er eternal snow;
> Where heavenly minstrels pour their notes divine,
> And rippling Gangá laves the mountain pine,—
> Clad in a coat of skin, all rudely wrought,
> He lived,—for prayer and solitary thought.
> The faithful band that served the hermit's will
> Lay in the hollows of the rocky hill,
> Where, from the clefts, the dark bitumen flowed;
> Tinted with mineral dyes, their bodies glowed;
> Their garb, rude mantles of the birch-tree's rind;
> With bright-red garlands was their hair entwined.
> The holy bull before his master's feet
> Shook the hard-frozen earth with echoing feet."

It was whilst Siva was living in this "stern seclusion" that his lovely and lamented wife was born again. She was again the daughter of the mountain Himalaya and the nymph Menâ:

> "Blest was that hour, and all the world was gay,
> When Mena's daughter saw the light of day.
> A rosy glow fill'd all the brightening sky;
> An odorous breeze came sweeping softly by,
> Breathed round the hill a sweet, unearthly strain:
> And the glad heavens poured down their flowery rain."

Looking on her face, her father could never satisfy the thirsty glances of a parent's eye:

> "She was the pride, the glory of her sire;
> Shedding new lustre on his old descent."

But she came as our poet Wordsworth imagines men to come,—trailing recollections of a former existence.

> "As swans in autumn in assembling bands
> Fly back to Gangá's well-remembered sands;
> As herbs beneath the darksome shades of night
> Collect again their scattered rays of light:
> So dawned upon the maiden's waking mind
> The far-off memory of her life resigned;
> And all her former learning in its train,—
> Feelings, and thoughts, and knowledge,—came again."

And these dawnings of her former life gave her an instinctive desire to perform penance, which should win the love of Siva. Her mother thought "stern penance" unsuitable for her lovely child, and cried, "Forbear! forbear!" And the maiden was in consequence called Umá.[1] That Umá was destined to be the bride of Siva, was intimated to her father by the holy saint Nárada; and her father was apparently gratified at the prospect of his child's becoming united to "heaven's supremest king;" . . . . . but at present such a marriage seemed hopeless.

In the second canto, heaven and earth having suffered "wild

---

[1] From u, an interjection, and má, the prohibitur particle. Among the meanings given for the word umá, are "brightness," "glory," "repose."

affright," in consequence of the power of the impious Táraka, Indra leads the mournful deities to Brahmá's throne. They bow low to him, as the "maker, preserver, and destroyer." We quote some passages from their address:

> "Thou countest not thy time by mortals' light;
> With thee there is but one vast day and night.
> When Brahmá slumbers, fainting Nature dies;
> When Brahmá wakens, all again arise.
> "Creator of the world,—thou uncreate!
> Endless! all things from thee their end await.
> Before the world wast thou! Each lord shall fall
> Before thee,—mightiest, highest, lord of all!
> Thy self-taught soul thine own deep spirit knows;
> Made by thyself, thy mighty form arose.
> Into the same, when all things have their end,
> Shall thy great self, absorbed in thee, descend.
> Lord, who may hope thy essence to declare?
> Firm, yet as subtile as the yielding air.
> "Father of fathers, God of gods art thou!
> Creator, highest, bearer of the vow!
> Thou art the sacrifice, and thou the priest;
> Thou, he that eateth,—thou, the holy feast.
> Thou art the knowledge which by thee is taught;
> The mighty thinker, and the highest thought!"

Brahmá is pleased with their address, and in reply, his words welling softly from "four mouths," enquires the cause of their distress.

> "Then Indra turned his thousand glorious eyes,
> Glancing like lilies when the soft wind sighs;
> And, in the gods' behalf, their mighty chief
> Urged the Most Eloquent to tell their grief.
> Then rose the Heavenly Teacher,[1] by whose side
> Dim seemed the glories of the Thousand-eyed,
> And, with his hands outspread, to Brahmá spake,
> Couched on his own dear flower, the daughter of the lake;

[1] Vrihaspati.

TARAKA'S EVIL DEEDS.

> "'O mighty Being! surely thou dost know
> The unceasing fury of our ruthless foe,
> (For thou dost see the secret thoughts that lie
> Deep in the heart, yet open to thine eye;)
> The vengeful Tarak, in resistless might,
> Like some dire comet gleaming wild affright,
> O'er all the worlds an evil influence sheds,
> And, in thy favour strong, destruction spreads.'"

The evil deeds of Táraka are enumerated. Amongst them, it is said that the fiend has taken the golden lotuses of the heavenly Gangá, and has stolen the "steed of heavenly race, great Indra's pride." The gods are all defeated, and seek a chief, that he

> "May lead the hosts of heaven to victory,
> Even as holy men who long to sever
> The immortal spirit from its shell for ever,
> Seek lovely Virtue's aid to free the soul
> From earthly ties, and action's base control."

Brahmá's answer to this petition is said to have been sweet as refreshing rains to the parched earth; but he bids them wait in patience: the fiend must not be destroyed by his hand. Táraka had once received favour from Brahmá, and Táraka in return had stayed his awful penance, which had otherwise hurled flames, death and destruction o'er the world.

No one, Brahmá concludes, can conquer in the deadly strife with Táraka save one of Siva's seed.

> "He is the light,
> Reigning supreme beyond the depths of night,
> Nor I, nor Vishnu, his full power may share,
> Lo, where he dwells in solitude and prayer!
> Go, seek the hermit, in the grove alone,
> And to the god be Umá's beauty shown.
> Perchance, the mountain-child, with magnet's force,
> May turn the iron from its steadfast course."

Brahmá, having spoken, vanished, and the gods went home to their world of light, except Indra, who, intent on Brahmá's words, bent his footsteps towards the dwelling of Káma, the god of love.

> "Swiftly he came,—the yearning of his will
> Made Indra's lightning course more speedy still.
> The love-god, armed with flowers divinely sweet,
> In lowly homage bowed before his feet.
> Around his neck, where bright love-tokens hung,
> Arched like a maiden's brow, his bow was hung;
> And blooming Spring, his constant follower, bore
> The mango twig,—his weapon famed of yore."

Canto three recounts the meeting of Indra with Káma:

> "In eager gaze, the sovereign of the skies
> Looked full on Káma, with his thousand eyes:
> E'en such a gaze as trembling suppliants bend
> When danger threatens on a mighty friend."

Káma enquires at once who has been offending Indra:

> "What mortal being dost thou count thy foe?
> Speak! I will tame him with my darts and bow."

He bids Indra lay aside his threatening bolt:

> "My gentle darts shall tame the haughtiest pride;
> And all that war with heaven and thee shall know
> The magic influence of thy Káma's bow."[1]

---

[1] It is the universal idea of Cupid and his bow,—an idea not yet extinct. "Est-on," says a victim, "dans son bon sens quand cette flèche vous arrive sans qu'on l'ait prévue, sans qu'on ait eu le temps de s'en préserver?.... Oh! le vieux Cupidon avec son carquois et son arc. Je n'avais jamais songé que ses emblèmes fussent l'explication de l'éternel phénomène, de l'événement fatal, aussi vieu que le monde et aussi vrai il y a quatre mille ans qu'il est encore aujourd'hui."—Mdlle. La Quintinie, p. 5.

Indra confesses that his only hope is in Kâma (love); for Siva's mind is fraught with holiest lore, and his every thought is bent upon "the Godhead." Thunderbolts are powerless against so holy a saint:

> "Thy darts, O love, alone can reach him now,
> And lure his spirit from the hermit vow."

What Indra requires is further explained, thus:

> "Hear what the gods, oppressed with woe, would fain
> From mighty Siva through thine aid obtain;
> He may beget, and none in heaven but he,—
> A chief to lead our hosts to victory."

Indra strives still further to encourage Kâma, by saying:

> "Thy task is e'en already done,
> For praise and glory are that instant won,
> When a bold heart dares manfully essay
> The deed which others shrink from in dismay."

Thus urged by Indra, Kâma sets forth, accompanied by Rati, his bride, and his comrade, Spring. The loveliness of Spring, in the groves of the snow-crowned hill, is described at length:

> "Then, from its stem the red asoka threw
> Full buds and flowerets, of celestial hue;
> Nor waited for the maiden's touch the sweet,
> Beloved pressure of her tinkling feet.
> There grew Love's arrow, his dear mango spray,—
> Winged with young leaves to speed its airy way,
> And at the call of Spring the wild bees came,
> Grouping the syllables of Kâma's name."

The palâsa blossoms are described as "curved like the crescent moon," their opening buds being the shape of pea-blossoms:[1]

---

[1] See woodcut, vol. i., chapter vi.

"The cool gale, speeding o'er the shady lawns,
Shook down the sounding leaves, while fawns
Ran wildly at the viewless foe, all blind
With pollen, wafted by the fragrant wind."

When Kâma arrived at the abode of Siva, a servant came to the door, bearing in his left hand a branch of gold. He touched his lip in token of silence, and said, "Peace! be still!" There were no sounds; not even a wild bee murmured. Every bird was hushed, and all life stood unmoved, as in a picture. Kâma instinctively hid himself from Siva's eye, behind the tangled flowers and clustering trailers, which were his canopy. This terrific three-eyed lord was sitting on a tiger's skin, spread on a hill beneath a pine-tree's shade. A very graphic picture is given of the "great penitent." He sat erect, his shoulders drooping, each foot bent under his body:

"With open palms, the hands were firmly pressed
As though a lotus lay upon his breast.
A double rosary in each ear; behind,
With wreathing serpents were his locks entwined.
His coat of hide shone blacker to the view
Against his neck, of brightly beaming blue.
How wild the look! how terrible the frown
Of his dark eyebrows, bending sternly down!
How fiercely glared his eyes' unmoving blaze
Fixed in Devotion's meditating gaze!"

He was as calm as a cloud resting on a hill; as still as a waveless lake: he neither moved nor breathed.

"At all the body's nine-fold gates of sense
He had barred in the pure intelligence
To ponder on the soul, which sages call
Eternal Spirit,—highest,—over all."

At this awful sight Kâma's courage failed, and

> "Unconsciously, his hands in fear and woe
> Dropped the sweet arrows and the flowery bow."

But then appeared Umâ and her maiden train, and Kâma's fainting heart revived.

> "Through Kâma's soul fresh hope and courage flew,
> As that sweet vision blessed his eager view."

Waiting until Siva again moves, Umâ is allowed to approach. Siva receives her graciously. Kâma prepares to aim.

> "Like the moon's influence on the sea at rest
> Came Passion, stealing o'er the hermit's breast;
> While on the maiden's lip, that mocked the dye
> Of ripe red fruit, he bent his melting eye.
> And oh! how showed the lady's love for him
> The heaving bosom and the quivering limb!"

With strong effort Siva quelled the rising storm of passion, and looked round to discover what had occasioned this tempest in his tranquil soul. He sees Kâma in the very act of drawing his bent bow; and his anger is such, that he flashes a glance upon the god of love, which scorches him to ashes.

Then Kâma's bride, Rati, swooned away. Siva withdrew to some place far away from woman; and Umâ, overwhelmed by grief and shame, was carried home by her father.

Canto four gives the lament of Rati for her beloved Kâma. She entreats him to speak to her:

> "Let not my prayer, thy Rati's prayer, be vain;
> Come, as of old, and bless these eyes again!
> Wilt thou not hear me? Think of those sweet hours
> When I would bind thee with my zone of flowers;—

Those soft, gay fetters, fondly o'er thee wreathing :—
Thine only punishment, when gently breathing.
In tones of love, thy heedless sigh betrayed
The name, dear traitor, of some rival maid.
Then would I pluck a floweret from my tress,
And beat thee till I forced thee to confess.
While in my play the falling leaves would cover
The eyes,—the bright eyes,—of my captive lover."[1]

Canto five presents Umá doing penance, she being convinced that only as a penitent can she win the love of Siva. Umá's mother wept at the idea, and entreated her daughter not to expose her frail body to such a trial. But Umá persevered, and begged her mountain-father to grant her a bosky shade, in which she could give all her soul to penance and to prayer; and her father granted her the hill which peacocks love, and which is known to all ages by her name.

Her string of pearls she laid aside, for her garment she wore the hermit's coat of bark, for her zone rough grass.

"Cold earth her couch,—her canopy the skies,—
Pillowed upon her arm, the lady lies.
The maid put off, but only for a while,
Her passioned glances and her witching smile.
She lent the fawn her moving, melting gaze,
And the fond creeper all her winning ways."

The hermits of the wood, and grey-haired elders, came to see this remarkable maiden, whose perfect virtue commanded universal esteem. They found the fires of sacrifice kindled, no rite forgotten, and the grove so pure, that even savage monsters lived together in love and peace. But Umá still feared that her

[1] This passage is from the later translations published by Mr. Griffith, with his "Idylls."

penance was too mild to win the meed she sought, and fain would match in toil the anchoret.

> "Full in the centre of four blazing piles
> Sate the fair lady of the winning smiles;
> While on her head the mighty god of day
> Shot all the fury of his summer ray."

And after spending the summer, scorched by the heat of fire, she was drenched in autumn by the annual rains, and in winter she lay upon

> "The cold, damp ground,
> Though blasts of winter hurled their snows around."

At length her penance exceeded that of the most renowned anchorites, and she earned the glorious title of Aparnâ,—lady of the unbroken fast! Then

> "Came a hermit,—reverend was he,
> As the first rank's embodied sanctity,—
> With coat of skin, with staff, and matted hair;
> His face was radiant, and he spake her fair.
> Up rose the maid the holy man to greet,
> And humbly bowed before the hermit's feet."

He fixed his earnest gaze upon her, and asked in silver speech how her tender frame could bear the toil which her firm spirit imposed upon it. He observes how lovingly she supplies the wants of the plants, the flowers, and the timid fawns; and says:

> "O mountain-lady! it is truly said,
> That heavenly charms to sin have never led;
> For, even penitents may learn of thee,
> How pure, how gentle, Beauty's self may be.
> *   *   *   *   *   *   *   *
> "Purest of motives, Duty leads thy heart:
> Interest and pleasure there may claim no part."

And then he tries to discover what guerdon she proposed to gain by so much penance. What can move one so faultless to dwell in solitude and prayer apart? And at length suggests

> "A husband, lady? Oh, forbear the thought;
> A priceless jewel seeks not, but is sought,
> Maiden, thy deep sighs tell me it is so."

The admiring anchoret is full of tender pity for her sorrow, but cannot understand how one so fair could have loved in vain. He whom she loved must surely have been a vain person, dreaming of himself; but he says, if she will go home and rest in peace, she shall have the benefit of his penances, and gain her secret purpose, without wearing out her tender frame.

> "The holy Bráhman ceased; but Umá's breast
> In silence heaved, by love and fear opprest.
> In mute appeal she turned her languid eye,
> Darkened with weeping,—not with softening dye,—
> To bid her maiden's friendly tongue declare
> The cherished secret of her deep despair."

And then the attendant tells that, as the lotus disdained all gods except the god of day, so Umá had disdained all love except the love of Siva. Love for Siva had caused her sobs and deep-drawn sighs. Love for Siva had given her wakeful and fevered nights; until at length her frenzied grief had brought her to these forest glades.

> "The maiden ceased. His secret joy dissembling,
> The Bráhman turned to Umá pale and trembling:
> 'And is it thus, or doth the maiden jest?
> Is this the darling secret of thy breast?'
> "She clasped the rosary in her quivering hand;
> Scarce could the maid her choking voice command:

" 'O holy sage, learned in the Vedas' lore,
'Tis even thus,—great Siva I adore.
Thus would my steadfast heart his love obtain;
For this I gladly bear the toil and pain.'
   " 'Lady,' cried he, 'that mighty lord I know;
Ever his presence bringeth care and woe.
And would'st thou still, a second time, prepare
The sorrows of his fearful life to share?' "

He asks her how she could clasp her hand in his, when fearful serpents twine around his arm. Even her enemies, he says, would grieve to see her trying to tread Siva's gloomy path amid the tombs. The rich tribute of the sandal trees is alone fit for so gentle a lady; but the breast of Siva is strewed with ashes. The king of elephants would alone be worthy to carry her as a royal bride; but the bride of Siva would be meanly borne upon his bull. And, more entirely to discourage her, he continues:

"Deformed is he,—his ancestry unknown;
By vilest garb his poverty is shown.
 *   *   *   *   *   *   *
Unmeant is he thy faithful heart to share,—
Child of the mountain, maid of beauty rare!
   "Impatient Uma listened; the quick blood
Rushed to her temples in an angry flood;
Her quivering lip, her darkly flashing eye,
Told that the tempest of her wrath was nigh.
Proudly she spoke:—'How could'st *thou* tell aright
Of one like Siva,—perfect, infinite!
'Tis ever thus the mighty and the just
Are scorned by souls that grovel in the dust;
Their lofty goodness, and their motives wise,
Shine all in vain before such blinded eyes.
Say, who is greater,—he who strives for power,
Or he who succours in misfortune's hour?
Refuge of worlds! oh, how should Siva deign
To look on men enslaved to paltry gain?

2—9

"The spring of wealth himself, he careth nought
For the vile treasures that mankind have sought.
His dwelling place amid the tombs may be;
Yet, monarch of the three great worlds is he.
* * * * * * *
Whether around him deadly serpents twine,
Or if his jewelled wreaths more brightly shine;
Whether in rough and wrinkled hide arrayed,
Or silken robe, in glittering folds displayed;
If on his brow the crescent-moon he bear,
Or if a shrunken skull be withering there;—
The funeral ashes, touched by him, acquire
The glowing lustre of eternal fire.
* * * * * * *

The mountain-maid's defence of Siva concludes with these remarkable words:—

"Thy slanderous tongue proclaims thy evil mind;
Yet, in thy speech, *one* word of truth we find.
Unknown thou call'st him;—how should mortal man
Count when the days of Brahma's Lord began?
But cease these idle words; though all be true,—
His failings many and his virtues few,—
Still clings my heart to him, its chosen lord;
Nor fails nor falters at thy treacherous word."

Having spoken, the unhappy Umâ bids her attendant send away the evil-speaking hermit; for, although he is most guilty who begins such faithless speech, yet, those who listen, also sin. She turned away in angry pride; when, suddenly, the hermit changes his form, and,—'tis Siva's self, in all his gentlest majesty.

"She saw, she trembled,—like a river's course,
Checked for a moment in its onward force,
By some huge rock amid the torrent hurled,
Where erst the foaming waters madly curled;

> "One foot uplifted,—shall she turn away?
> Unmoved the other,—shall the maiden stay?
> The silver moon on Siva's forehead shone,
> While softly spake the god in gracious tone:—
> 'O gentle maiden! wise and true of soul,
> Lo! now I bend beneath thy sweet control!
> Won by thy penance and thy holy vows.'"

Canto six relates the espousals. But the remainder of this poem is painfully incongruous. Considered as a narrative of human love, it presents beautiful pictures of father, mother, daughter, husband, and bride; but the pleasure we should take in these details of domestic bliss is marred, when the being of whom they are related is declared to be a manifestation of the Supreme Triune God. It is not, however, difficult to set apart those passages which inculcate *faith* in Siva, and attribute to him divine supremacy; and having done this, we find Kâlidâsa's poem of the War-God a charming, fanciful tale, in which the gloomy, awful Siva is won to love and happiness by the bright daughter of the snow-crowned Himâlaya.

A gorgeous description is given of the royal city on the day of the wedding, when crowds of noble dames were seated under canopies upheld by pillars decked with gems and gold. The bride's hair was graced with feathery grass and wild flowers, amid which a glittering arrow was introduced, and behind each ear was placed an ear of barley. Siva's head-ornament, the "withering skull," became as a "bright coronal;" whilst his "mid-eye" beamed softly, as a mark of glory; and his "twining serpents" changed into ornaments set with blazing gems. At the moment when he is permitted by his chamberlains to behold the bride,—

> ".   .   .   .   . His lotus eyes
> Flashed out the rapture of his proud surprise;
> Then, calm the current of his spirit lay,
> Like the world basking in an autumn day.

> They met; a true love's momentary shame
> O'er the blest bridegroom and his darling came.
> Eye looked to eye,—but, quivering as they met,
> Scarce dared to trust the rapturous gazing yet.
> * * * * * * *
> How grows their beauty, when two lovers stand,—
> Eye fixed on eye,—hand fondly linked in hand!
> * * * * * * *

The nuptial ceremony was performed in accordance with Colebrooke's description of this ceremony:

> "Around the fire in solemn rite they trod.
> * * * * * * *
> Thrice, at the bidding of the priest, they came
> With swimming eyes around the holy flame.
> Then, at his word, the bride in order due
> Into the blazing fire the parched grain threw,
> And toward her face the scented smoke she drew."

The priest pronounced a blessing, saying:

> "'This flame be witness of your wedded life.
> Be just, thou husband; and be true, thou wife.'"

And, lastly:

> "'Look, gentle Umá,' cried her lord; 'afar,
> Seest thou the brightness of yon polar star?
> Like that unchanging ray thy faith must shine!'
> Sobbing, she whispered: 'Yes; for ever thine!'"

Their heads were then sprinkled with moistened grain, and the ceremony was over.[1]

---

[1] See Colebrooke's Miscellaneous Essays, vol. i. p. 203 ff.

THERE are several other poems which are ranked by the Hindus amongst the Mâha-Kâvyas. These appear to European readers more remarkable for verbal ingenuity than for poetic feeling; but they must, nevertheless, be noticed, as forming a portion of recognized Sanskrit literature. Amongst these works, we find the KIRATARJUNIYA, by Bhâravi. The subject is Arjuna's obtaining celestial arms from Siva, Indra, and other gods, as related in the Mahâbhârata. The word Kirâtârjunîya, formed from Kirâta and Arjuna, describes this passage in Arjuna's history. "By a rigid observance of severe austerities in the first instance, and afterwards by his prowess in a conflict with Siva (in the disguise of a mountaineer), Arjuna prevails. This is the whole subject of the poem, which is ranked with the Kumâra and Raghu of Kâlidâsa, the Naishadhîya of Sriharsha, and the Meghadûta of Kâlidâsa, among the six excellent compositions in Sanskrit."[1] Mr. Colebrooke gives some stanzas, as specimens of the variety of measure and the alliteration, for which it is remarkable. The following is Mr. Colebrooke's translation of them:

"Then Arjuna, admiring the mountain in silent astonishment, was respectfully addressed by his conductor, Kuvera's attendant; for even loquacity is becoming in its season.

"This mountain, with its snowy peaks rending the cloudy sky in a thousand places, is, when viewed, able to remove at once the sins of man. An imperceptible something within it, the wise ever demonstrate to exist by proofs difficultly apprehended. But Brahmâ alone thoroughly knows this vast and inaccessible mountain, as he alone knows the supreme

[1] Colebrooke's Misc. Essays, vol. ii. p. 84.

soul. With its lakes overspread by the bloom of the lotus, and overshadowed by arbours of creeping plants, whose foliage and blossoms are enchanting, the pleasing scenery subdues the hearts of women who maintained their steadiness of mind even in the company of a lover. By this happy and well-governed mountain, the earth, filled with gems of easy acquisition and great excellence, delightful to the god of riches, seems to surpass both rival worlds."[1]

SISUPALAVADHA

is the name of another celebrated epic poem. It is commonly attributed to Mágha, " whose designation, with praises of his family, appear in the concluding stanzas of the poem. Yet, if tradition may be trusted," Mr. Colebrooke continues, "Mágha, though expressly named as the author, was the patron, not the poet. As the subject is heroic, and even the unity of action well preserved and the style of composition elevated, this poem is entitled to the name of epic. But the Indian taste for licentious description," disfigures the work, which is otherwise not unworthy its high reputation. The objectionable portion appears to be, the account of Krishna's journey from Dwáraká to Indraprastha, accompanied by damsels. Mr. Colebrooke speaks of this as not only exceptionable in itself, but as unsuitable to the design of the poem.[2]

The subject is the death of Sisupála, slain in war by Krishna; and the argument is as follows:—" In the first canto, Nárada, commissioned by Indra, visits Krishna, and incites him to war with his cousin, but mortal enemy, Sisupála, king of the Chedis. In the second, Krishna consults with his uncle and brother, whether war should be immediately commenced, or he should first assist Yudhishthira in completing a solemn sacrifice which had been appointed by him. The result of the consultation is in favour of the latter measure; and, accordingly, in the third

[1] Colebrooke's Misc. Ess., vol. ii. pp. 85, 86. [2] Ibid. p. 80.

canto, Krishna departs for Yudhishthira's capital," which is Indraprastha, a city which once flourished on nearly the same site as the modern town of Delhi. Krishna's home was in Guzerat, at Dwáraká, on the sea-coast. "In the thirteenth canto, Krishna arrives at the newly-completed city of Indraprastha, and is welcomed by the Pándavas," that is, Yudhishthira and his four brothers, and other relatives. "In the fourteenth canto, the sacrifice is begun; and in the next, Sisupála, impatient of the divine honours paid to Krishna, retires with his partisans from the place of sacrifice. A negociation ensues, which is, however, ineffectual; and both armies prepare for action: this occupies two cantos. In the eighteenth, both armies issue to the field of battle, and the conflict commences. The battle continues in the next canto, which describes the discomfiture and slaughter of Sisupála's army. In the last canto, the king, grown desperate, dares Krishna to the combat. They engage; and, in the Indian manner, fight with supernatural weapons. Sisupála assails his enemy with serpents, which the other destroys by means of gigantic cranes. The king has recourse to igneous arms, which Krishna extinguishes by a Neptunian weapon. The combat is prolonged with other miraculous arms; and, finally, Krishna slays Sisupála with an arrow."

Mr. Colebrooke quotes one passage, and gives a translation as a specimen of what is called the Vaitáliya metre. It is from a speech of Sisupála's ambassador, in reply to a discourse of Sátyaki, brother of Krishna, at an interview immediately preceding the battle. The following is his translation:

"A low man, poor in understanding, does not perceive his own advantage; that he should not comprehend it when shown by others, is surprising. The wise, of themselves, know the approach of danger, or they put trust in others; but a foolish man does not believe information without personal experience. The proposal which I made to thee, Krishna, was truly for thy benefit; the generous are ready to advise even their enemies, bent on their destruction. Peace and war have been offered at the same time by me; judging their respective advantages, thou wilt choose between them. Yet good advice, addressed to those whose understanding is astray, becomes vain,—like the beams of the cold moon directed towards lakes, eager for the warm rays of the sun."

Another specimen, from the twentieth canto, describes Sisupála daring Krishna to single combat:

"Raising his head, and with a countenance terrible by its forked brow and wrinkled forehead, the king of the Chedis, impatient of the prowess thus displayed in battle, banished fear, and challenged the foe of Mura to the fight."

THE NAISHADHIYA, BY SRI HARSHA, is also generally termed a Mahâ-Kâvya. It is a poem in twenty cantos, and is described by Mr. Colebrooke as "a favourite poem on a favourite subject." It is the story of Nala and Damayantî, which we have already seen so beautifully narrated in the Mahâbhârata. Sri Harsha omits all the touching incidents which occur after the marriage. He describes the mutual affection of the lovers continuing, notwithstanding the machinations of the evil spirit, Kali; but ends his poem so soon as they are married. The poet is said to indulge in "glowing descriptions of sensual love;"[1] and Mr. Colebrooke merely quotes a few lines, saying, that to "render the author's meaning intelligible, it may be necessary to premise, that the mere celebrating of Nala and Damayantî is reckoned sufficient to remove the taint of a sinful age; and is so declared in the Mahâbhârata."

Mr. Colebrooke then gives, as a specimen of the Vansastha metre, the following lines from Sri Harsha's Introduction:

"How should a story, which, being remembered, purifies the world in the present age, as it were by an actual ablution, fail of purifying my voice, however faulty, when employed in this narration?"[2]

[1] Colebrooke's Misc. Ess., vol. ii. p. 106.   [2] Ibid, p. 106.

Amongst the larger Sanskrit poems of considerable reputation some also place the BHATTI-KAVYA. It relates the adventures of Ráma, in twenty-two cantos; but verbal ingenuity is its most remarkable quality. Mr. Colebrooke speaks of it as "composed purposely for the practical illustration of grammar," and says it therefore "exhibits a studied variety of diction, in which words anomalously inflected are most frequent. The style, however, is neither obscure nor inelegant; and the poem is reckoned among the classical compositions in the Sanskrit language. The author was Bhartrihari."[1]

A paper on the same subject, by Mr. Griffith, was read before the Royal Asiatic Society in 1851, and afterwards published as an Appendix to "Old Indian Poetry." Mr. Griffith claims but little merit for the Bhatti-Kávya as poetry, but says it is "valuable to a student of the language in which it is written," on account of its copious illustration of the grammatical treatises of Pânini and Vopadeva; and he finds much interest in that portion of it which is called "Art of Poetry," and which teaches by example. The first figure of poetical rhetoric illustrated is called Dípaka, or the Illuminator. This figure throws as it were a "quickening ray of light upon the colouring of the poet's pictures; for its power it is indebted to arrangement in general, especially to the collocation of the single verb, which (to use the expression of the commentator) *lights up the whole description.*"[2] The example given is the journey which Hanumat, the general and envoy of the monkey forces, made to Ceylon in search of Ráma's wife, when carried off by Rávana. The *commencement* of the couplet quoted contains the one emphatic word, which is in this instance the *root* (as the scholiast terms it) from which the succeeding actions spring:

" He *flew:*—the waters wildly dash'd on high,
And shook the trees that droop'd their branches nigh;

[1] Colebrooke's Misc. Ess., vol. ii. pp. 115, 116.
[2] Old Indian Poetry; Appendix, p. 105.

"They pour'd their blossoms down in softest showers,
And wanton sylphs couch'd gladly on the flowers."

The poet expresses the figure of metaphor "by what in Sanskrit is termed the *compound of resemblance*." The following lines are an example:

"A *mountain-monkey* seem'd he to their sight,
Where sharp *snake-weapons* shrink away from light;
Its base, his mighty chest; the flank, his side;
With blood for ochre, and dark metals dyed."

"Metaphor imperfect" is thus illustrated:

"The monkey-moon shone all their care to rest,
And calm'd with light the wild ape-ocean's breast;
Gave forth his moonbeam tidings soft and clear,
And dimm'd each eye with a triumphant tear."

The whole poem is well worthy of study; and although language is allowed to enslave thought, the examples given retain so much of beauty, that the poet must have been a real poet, although in this case he chose to chain his Pegasus to the heavy, weighty burdens of Sanskrit grammar and rhetoric.

THE MEGHADUTA, BY KALIDASA,

concludes the series of what native writers call the Mahá-Kávyas; but as this charming poem properly belongs to lyric poetry, we defer our account of it for Chapter xxxiv.

THE NALODAYA

is not classed by the Hindus among their Mahá-Kávyas; but as it enjoys great celebrity in India, and in some respects at least is kindred to the Mahá-Kávyas, it deserves a short notice here. It treats of the oft-repeated subject of Nala and Damayantí, and it is attributed to Kálidása; but Mr. Griffith, who translates one passage, observes, that "it is at least difficult to believe that the author of Sakuntalá and the Cloud-Messenger should have composed such a work,—a laborious jingling of words,—remarkable, however, for showing the extraordinary powers of the Sanskrit language; and it is impossible not to wonder at the ingenuity of the workman, however misdirected we may think it."[1]

The whole poem was published, with a translation, in 1844, by W. Yates, D.D., at Calcutta.[2] In a Preface, the translator speaks of the great gratification afforded by a perusal of the original; but "in the entire circle of Sanskrit epic poetry," he observes, he "has not found four consecutive books of equal difficulty with these four of the Nalodaya." He trusts, however, that, by the assistance he affords, "they may now be read by any person only just commencing the study of Sanskrit."

We give no extracts; for the translator admits that the translation "will not exhibit the alliterations, which appear to be its chief distinction." Mr. Colebrooke states, in his Essay on Sanskrit and Prakrit Prosody, that, "in this singular poem, rhyme and alliteration are combined in the termination of the verses; for the three or four last syllables of each hemistich within the stanzas are the same in sound, though different in sense. It is a series of puns on a pathetic subject." It contains two hundred and twenty stanzas; but "it is supposed to have been written in emulation of a short poem (of twenty-two stanzas) similarly constructed, but with less repetition of each rhyme, and entitled, from the words of the challenge with which it concludes, Ghatakarpara."[3] Some fifty years since, a prose translation appears to have been made by Mr. Kindersley, of Madras.

[1] Old Indian Poetry.
[2] The Nalodaya, a Sanskrit Poem, by Kálidása; accompanied by a Metrical Translation, and an Essay on Alliteration, &c. By. W. Yates, D.D. Calcutta, 1844.
[3] Colebrooke's Essay, vol. x., Asiatic Researches, reprinted in his Misc. Ess., vol. ii. p. 73.

THE RAGHAVA-PANDAVIYA, BY KAVIRAJA, is rather a curiosity than a poem, but may likewise be noticed in an enumeration of the more prominent Kávyas. Mr. Colebrooke speaks of it as an instance of a complete poem, every canto of which exhibits variety of metre. This extraordinary production exhibits "studied ambiguity;" so that it may, "at the option of the reader, be interpreted as relating the history of Ráma and other descendants of Dasaratha,—or that of Yudhishthira and other sons of Pándu." An example of this style of composition had been set by Subandhu, in the story of Vásavadattá, and Bánabhatta, in his unfinished work, entitled Kádambari. But although these works give continual instances of terms and phrases employed in a double sense, they do not, like the Rághava-Pándavîya, tell two distinct stories in the same words.

Two stanzas are given by Colebrooke, to show the metre used, and also the style of composition; but these would lose all interest, if translated.

[1] Colebrooke's Misc. Ess., vol. ii. pp. 98, 99.

CHAPTER XXVI.

INTRODUCTION TO THE DRAMA.

The Hindu drama is a charming and important feature of old Sanskrit literature, first revealed to Europeans by the works of Sir William Jones. He learned from his Hindu friends that they possessed "conversations in prose and verse, which were held before ancient rajahs;" and, pursuing the subject with persevering zeal, he succeeded at length in procuring a copy of the play entitled "Sakuntalá," which he translated into English. This was published nearly a hundred years ago, and was admired by the German poet Göthe, who wrote:

"Willst du die Blüthe des frühen, die Früchte des späteren Jahres,
Willst du was reizt und entzückt, willst du was sättigt und nährt,
Willst du den Himmel, die Erde mit einem Namen begreifen:
Nenn' ich Sakontala, Dich, und so ist Alles gesagt."

And again, in prose:[1]

"Wir würden höchst undankbar seyn wenn wer nicht indischer Dichtungen gedenken wollten. . . . . . Vor allen wird Sakuntala von uns genannt, in deren Bewunderung wir uns Jahre lang versenkten."

[1] Göthe's Works.

Such words from Göthe stimulated his countrymen to the study of Oriental literature; and amongst those who first entered this new field, we find Augustus Schlegel, who not only translated from Sanskrit, but also wrote and gave lectures upon it. Of Sakuntalá, he says that it presents, "through its Oriental brilliancy of colouring, so striking a resemblance . . . . . to our romantic drama, that it might be suspected that the love of Shakspeare had influenced the translator, were it not that other Orientalists bore testimony to his fidelity."[1]

Alexander von Humboldt, also, bore testimony to the merits of Sakuntalá, noting the masterly mode in which Kâlidâsa described the influence of Nature on the minds of lovers, his tenderness in the expression of feeling, and the richness of his creative fancy.

Early in the present century the mantle of Sir W. Jones may be said to have fallen on the late Professor Horace Hayman Wilson. He also delighted in the Sanskrit language, believed in Hindus, loved their literature, and persevered in his researches; although, like his predecessor, he encountered many difficulties. Works in Sanskrit, which purported to give distinct and accurate information, he met with; but he says: "The brevity and obscurity of the technical definitions, the inconceivable inaccuracy of the manuscripts, and the little knowledge of the subject which the Pundits generally possess, have rendered the task of interpreting them laborious and painful, to an extent of which readers accustomed to typographical facilities can form no adequate conception."[2]

At length two volumes of dramas, translated from the Sanskrit, were published, by the title of "Select Specimens of the Theatre of the Hindus." To "George IV., as patron of Oriental literature, this attempt to familiarize his British subjects with

---

[1] Sakuntalá; edited by Monier Williams. Preface.

[2] H. H. Wilson, Theatre of the Hindus, vol. i. p. xxiii., "On the Dramatic System of the Hindus."

the manners and feelings of their fellow subjects in the East," is dedicated. Calcutta, 15th May, 1827.

As in other departments of Sanskrit literature, so also in the drama, we can only arrive at approximate dates; and even tentative, or conjectural dates, can only be gained by inference. We therefore make observation, that the "Toy Cart," which is the first play in Wilson's volumes, commences by invoking the protection of Siva:—

"That profound meditation .... which is intent on Brahma (neuter) .... as he (Siva) contemplates with the eye of wisdom, spirit, in himself, detached from all material instruments; his senses being restrained by holy knowledge, as he sits ruminating with suspended breath, whilst his serpents coil with the folds of his vesture round his bended knees."

In the course of the drama, Buddhists and Bauddha practices are introduced, and no surprise or disapprobation is expressed at their presence. In other dramas which commence with homage to Siva, we shall again meet with similar respectful allusions to Buddhism; and the inference is, that the plays must have been composed before Buddhists were expelled, and in places where they were not even persecuted. But it must also be noted, that they were composed after Buddhism had lost its ascendancy, and at a time when Brahmans were worshipping Siva, the god of meditation, as the highest type of actual deity, and representing serpents as amongst his emblems. Yoga postures were also in vogue and the practice of magic. These several circumstances are believed to point to the fourth century of our era; and this date is confirmed by the names of certain authors. To some plays no author's name is attached, but several are known to have been written by Kálidása; and this celebrated poet is now believed, on good authority, to have flourished about A.D. 500.

Professor Wilson draws attention to Sanskrit works on the drama which give the Hindu view of the subject. He more especially cites the Dasa-Rúpaka, ten varieties of dramatic performance, and a poem entitled the Kâvya-Prakâsa. The authors of these critical essays give numerous examples, but omit to say from what play or poem they are quoting,—taking it for granted, apparently, that all plays and poems are graven in the memories of their readers.

Glosses are also supplied, and this is the more necessary, because "rules multiplied as art declined;" and "the task of interpreting them became" laborious and painful. This labour was, nevertheless, accomplished by Professor Wilson early in this century. The rules he disclosed, and the intentions and principles pursued, he unfolded.

Three kinds of dramatic composition are distinguished: Nâtya, gesticulation with language; Nritya, gesticulation without language; and Nritta, simple dancing.

What we call a play is a Nâtaka, and the term for dramatic performance in general is Rûpaka. The word *rûpa* means form; and a play gives form to characters, incidents, feelings, passions. Hence Sanskrit writers speak of a play as "a poem that is to be seen."[1]

The poet is said to make certain emotions manifest, to excite certain sentiments, and thus convey instruction through the medium of enjoyment. Poets must, therefore, understand emotions; and, to assist them in acquiring this knowledge, emotions and sentiments are analysed. It is shown that they come from conditions of body and mind, and are affected by previous conditions; and to each description an example is appended.

Perplexity, distraction, not knowing what is to be done or left undone, is a state of mind of which the preliminary is terror, impetuosity, painful recollection. It is exhibited by giddiness, falling on the ground, insensibility.

[1] H. H. Wilson, Hindu Theatre; Introduction, p. xxiii.

Example.

"I know not whether this be pain or pleasure, whether I wake or sleep, whether wine or venom spread through my frame. Thy touch has confounded all my faculties; and now I shake with cold, and now I burn with inward heat."—*Dasa-Rúpaka; from the Uttara-Ráma-Charitra.*[1]

Repose or concentration of mind, fortitude or content, is a condition of which "knowledge, power," is said to be the preliminary, and "calm enjoyment," or "patient suffering," the sign.

Example.

"We are contented here with the bark of trees; you are happy in affluence. Our satisfaction is equal; there is no difference in our conditions. He alone is poor whose desires are insatiable."—*Dasa-Rúpaka.*[2]

The most approved subject for the nátaka, or "poem that is to be seen," is one taken from sacred history or legend.

"The action, or more properly the passion of the piece, should be but one: as, love or heroism." The plot is to be simple, and the working of the play to "spring direct from the story, as a plant from its seed."[3] The circumstance from which the plot arises is called the *víja*, or the seed.[4] The hero of a story, thus developed, should be a monarch or demi-god; but this of course varies, according to whether the subject is sacred or domestic. The time should not be protracted, and the duration of an act should not exceed a day. The number of acts is not absolutely prescribed, but there must not be fewer than five, or more than ten acts. If the story require more time than can elapse on the stage, the intervals must be supposed to pass between the acts.

---

[1] H. H. Wilson, Hindu Theatre, 2nd ed., Intro., p. xlviii.
[2] Ibid, p. liii.

[3] H. H. Wilson, Hindu Theatre, 2nd ed., Intro., p. xxiv.
[4] Ibid, p. xxxviii.

Unity of place is little noted. Stage scenery was not apparently attempted. And "where everything was left to the imagination, one site was as easily conceivable as another; and the scene might be fancied, one while a garden, and another a palace, as well as it could be imagined to be either."[1]

Professor Wilson points out some analogies between the plays of India and those of the Greeks; but one important difference, he observes, is the total absence of the distinction between tragedy and comedy. The Hindu plays are invariably of a mingled web, and blend "seriousness and sorrow with levity and laughter;" but they never end with death. And "although they propose to excite all the emotions of the human breast,—terror and pity included,—they never effect this object by leaving a painful impression upon the mind of the spectator."[2] Hindu ideas of propriety forbid the sight of death upon the stage, and do not even allow the death of the hero or heroine to be announced. Some of the interdictions are peculiar; as, that no biting, scratching, kissing, eating, sleeping, are allowed upon the stage."[3]

Some characteristics are remarkable to us, which Hindus would not themselves observe as in any way peculiar to their theatre. For instance: the plays are written in Sanskrit, although Sanskrit was no longer the vernacular of the country. This appears at first view to be analagous to the Italian opera of London or Paris,—our opera not being arranged with a view to people in general, but adapted to the amusement of the exclusive class, to whom Italian is not unknown. The resemblance, however, is incomplete. Italian is chosen as the language for the opera because best suited to music, and to those who were to perform the music; whereas Sanskrit is chosen as the language of the Hindu drama because the subjects are usually legendary, and the performers of the privileged Sanskrit-speaking race. A somewhat closer analogy may be traced between the plays of

[1] H. H. Wilson, Hindu Theatre, Intro., p. xxv. [2] Ibid, p. xxvi. [3] Ibid, p. xxvii.

India and those which were acted in England in the thirteenth and fourteenth centuries, A.D., when English was the language of the people; but their plays were acted in Norman-French,— the language of the kings, priests, and nobles. The plays to which we refer are the miracle-plays of Coventry. Like their prototypes in India, they were composed at rare intervals, on occasion of a marriage, a coronation, or other great festival; and were not intended to be reproduced. Whether the priestly and religious bearing of the English miracle-plays was the cause of their not being composed in the vernacular, I do not know; but religious feeling undoubtedly dictated the choice of Sanskrit for the plays of India, that being the language of sacred literature, well understood by all who were privileged to possess divine knowledge. But there is another peculiarity in the Hindu drama, which it does not appear to share with the drama of any other country, which is, that whilst men and demi-gods speak Sanskrit, women and common people speak Prâkrit, which appears to have been at one period the language of common life. But although women are not allowed to speak the same language as men of rank, this does not indicate that women were treated as slaves or servants. They were loved, and cared for, and tended with respect and kindness, from birth to death; but in ancient India women are never thought of as independent beings. A woman is a daughter, a wife, a mother; but she seems never to be thought of as herself a person. In the plays, queens and heroines receive outward homage; but still they are but appendages to man. Women are not supposed to have an interest in the progress of civilisation, the cultivation of literature, or even in the general conduct of life: they are treated as pets or babies, kept chiefly in a nursery, and addressed in effeminate tones. It is, therefore, in accordance with this idea, that whilst all serious conversation of a drama is carried on in Sanskrit, women should talk Prâkrit,—a softer dialect, allied to Sanskrit, as Italian is to Latin. Virtuous women were not secluded in ancient India, as they have been since that fashion was brought into the country by the Mahommedans; but, from the principle that women are dependant upon men, as shadow upon substance, they lived monotonous lives, and showed no variety of character. Jews, Greeks, Egyptians, inscribe the names of women on their historical records; but in Brahmanical India women have but one aspect. Nowhere is love expressed with greater force and pathos, than in the poetry of India; but when love has faded, a woman's highest merit consists in giving no trouble. A wife must not feel aggrieved if her husband fall in love with a younger woman, but must welcome such an one as "sister." That these laws and customs did not work altogether well for general morality, is thus expressed by Professor Wilson:—

"The defective education of the virtuous portion of the sex, and their consequent uninteresting character, held out an inducement to the unprincipled members, both of Greek and Hindu society, to rear a class of females who should supply those wants which rendered home cheerless, and should give to men hetæræ, or female friends,"[1] capable of intellectual companionship. An amiable woman, of this Aspasian class, is introduced into the play called the Toy-Cart. But although such cases were not unknown, the habitual aspect of respectable society is one of great propriety.

Brâhmans, Kshattriyas, and other high personages of the twice-born or privileged class, were, as we have seen, the only performers who spoke Sanskrit. The dialects given to the other actors and actresses were considerably varied. The chief ladies and their friends talked a soft and elegant Prâkrit; women of lower rank spoke in a similar tongue, but less refined.[2] Rogues and intriguers, cowherds and foresters, have dialects peculiar to themselves; and even goblins, and imps of mischief, have each an appropriate jargon.

[1] H. H. Wilson, Hindu Theatre, Intro., p. xliv.   [2] Ibid, p. lxiv.

Among the dramatis personæ we often find an anomalous sort of person, called a Vita. He attends the hero, and is a poet, musician, and singer; but he is not introduced as teaching the arts which he practised. This may have been his original profession, but practically he seems to have been retained "about the person of the wealthy and dissipated, as a kind of private instructor as well as entertaining companion." "He is generally represented on familiar and easy, and yet dependant terms, with his associate; and evinces something of the character of the parasite of the Greek comedy, but that he is never rendered contemptible."[1]

The Vidûshaka is another favourite character of the Hindu theatre; he is the buffoon of the piece, although the companion (not the servant) of a prince or man of rank, and is always a Brâhman. The Vidûshaka "bears more affinity to Sancho Panza than to any other character in Western fiction,—imitating him in his combination of shrewdness and simplicity, his fondness of good living, and his love of ease." According to the technical definition, this character was intended to "excite mirth, by being ridiculous in person, age, and attire." But, as we shall see, this did not prevent his being also distinguished, in certain instances, by high morality and faithful friendship.

Each Hindu play opens with a prayer or invocation to a chosen deity, which is in accordance with the religious occasion of the performance. This invocation or benediction is followed by a panegyric on the author, and a dialogue between the manager and one of the actors, in which he gives information concerning himself and his company, or of events which occurred prior to the story of the piece; and this dialogue is so contrived as to lead immediately into the business of the play, ending by an abrupt announcement of the appearance of some of the characters.

The manager of the theatrical corps was a Brâhman, required

---

[1] H. H. Wilson, Hindu Theatre, Intro., p. xlvii.

to "be well versed in light literature,—as narrative, plays, and poetry; familiar with various dialects, acquainted with the customs of different classes and the manners of various people, experienced in dramatic details, and conversant with different mechanical arts."[1]

Whether few plays were written, or whether many plays have perished, is unknown; but the number now extant is singularly small. The first play in Professor Wilson's volumes is one of the most interesting, and is by an unknown author. Others are by Kálidása, who wrote the charming poems on which we have so recently been treating; and others, again, are by a much-admired poet named Bhavabhûti. But only three dramas have been discovered by either of these most popular authors.

[1] H. H. Wilson, Hindu Theatre, Intro., p. xxxv.

[As music is, in the Hindu play, often the accompaniment of dramatic action, this may be a fitting opportunity for appending a few remarks on this subject.]

HINDU music produced its effect by combining voices and instruments with action.

The Sanskrit word *sangíta*, or symphony, expresses this combination; and a Hindu work on *sangíta* is usually, therefore, a treatise on song, instrumental music, and dancing;—the word used for dancing being *nritya*, which includes all descriptions of theatrical action. Ancient Hindu works recognise the gamut of seven sounds, these seven sounds being at unequal distances. The seven sounds perpetually circulate "in a geometrical progression, according to the length of the strings or the number of the vibrations, but two of the seven intervals are shorter than the other five; and from this peculiarity arise various modes."[1]

"The longer intervals we shall call *tones*, the shorter *semitones*, without mentioning their exact rations; and it is evident, that as the places of the semitones admit variations relative to one fundamental sound, there are as many modes which may be called *primary*. But we must not confound them with our modern modes."[2]

Amongst these modes Sir William Jones signalises one which corresponds in character with our "major mode of D;" a key, to which modern musicians have sometimes assigned the popular name of "Lord Mayor's key." This key, he says, "it would be a gross violation of musical decorum in India, to sing at any

[1] Sir William Jones. Works, vol. iv. p. 171. [2] Ibid, vol. i. pp. 174, 180.

time except at the close of the day." This reminds us of the following passage in the Aitareya-Bráhmana:—

"When the sun faces men most (after having passed the meridian), it burns with the greatest force. Thence the Hotri should repeat the Shástras at the third (evening) libation, with an extremely strong voice. He should (only) then (commence to) repeat it so (with the greatest force of his voice), when he should be complete master of his own voice. For the Shástra is speech."[1] . . . . .

The passage concludes by desiring that the same strength of voice be sustained until the whole recitation is concluded.

"The Indian system" is, Sir W. Jones states, "minutely explained in a great number of Sanskrit books, by authors who leave arithmetic and astronomy to their astronomers, and properly discourse on music as an art confined to the pleasures of imagination."[2] A work, called the "Sangíta-Dámodara," he found to be most esteemed by the Pundits of Bengal; but he was unable to procure a good copy, and obliged to content himself with the "Sangíta-Náráyana," a work in which the Dámodara is much quoted. It would appear, however, that a more important work on this subject is named "Rágavibodha, or the Doctrine of Musical Modes;" "and it ought here to be mentioned very particularly," says Sir W. Jones, "because none of the Pandits in our provinces, nor any of those from Casi (Benares) or Cashmere, to whom I have shown it, appear to have known that it was extant." This treatise in the history of the art was brought to light, and probably preserved from destruction, by the zeal of Colonel Polier.

The Rágavibodha is said to be a very ancient composition, but not so old as the Sangíta-Ratnákara, which is more than once mentioned in it. The author of the former work is Soma, a practical musician as well as a great scholar and an elegant poet. The second chapter contains a minute description of different

[1] Haug. Aitareya-Bráhmann, vol. ii. p. 242.
[2] Sir William Jones. Works, vol. iv. pp. 180—183.

vínás, with rules for playing on them. Soma gives a system of his own, and mentions many others; stating, that almost every kingdom and province had its own peculiar style of melody.[1]

With regard to the notation of Indian music, it is observed, that "since every Sanskrit consonant includes by its nature the short vowel *a*, five of the sounds are denoted by single consonants, and the two others have different short vowels taken from their full names. By substituting long vowels, the time of each note is doubled; and other marks are used for a further elongation of them. The octaves above and below the mean scale, the connection and acceleration of notes, the grace of execution, or manners of fingering the instrument, are "expressed very clearly by small circles and ellipses, by little chains, by curves, by straight lines—horizontal or perpendicular, and by crescents,—all in various positions. The close of a strain is distinguished by a lotus flower; but the time and measure are determined by the prosody of the verse, and by the comparative length of each syllable with which every note, or assemblage of notes, respectively corresponds." We understand, moreover, that Hindu musicians have not only the *chromatic* but also the "*enharmonic* genus." But of what use it was, is made doubtful by an apparent admission from Soma,—"that a quarter or third of a tone cannot be separately and distinctly heard from the vínâ."

What is more intelligible is, that in each mode there are three sounds, distinguished as *graha*, *nyása*, *ansa*. The following passage is translated from couplets by the author of the Sangíta-Nárâyana:—

"The note called *graha* is placed at the beginning, and that named *nyása* at the end of a song; whilst that note which displays the peculiar melody, and to which all the others are subordinate,—that which is always of the greatest use,—is like a sovereign, though a mere *ansa* or portion."[2]

[1] Sir William Jones. Works, vol. iv. pp. 183—187.

[2] Sir William Jones. Works, vol. iv. pp. 188—197.

In the poem, entitled Sisupâlavadha, there is a musical simile which may further show that the *ansa* must be tonic, and the two other notes generally its third and fifth, or the mediant and dominant. The verse in question is thus translated:—

"From the greatness, from the transcendant qualities of that Hero, eager for conquest, other kings march in subordination to him, as other notes are subordinate to the *ansa*."

Sir W. Jones gives a great variety of scales, and when treating of minor keys, points out a resemblance between the pathetic airs of Bengal and "the wild but charming melodies of the ancient highlanders of Scotland."

In conclusion, an air from the fifth chapter of Soma's Râgavibodha is presented, with the verses to which it was adapted by the poet Jayadeva.[1]

[1] Sir William Jones. Works, vol. iv. p. 306.

"The asoka tree, with its rich crimson blossoms, shines like a young warrior, bathed with the sanguine shower of the furious fight."—Page 104.

CHAPTER XXVII.

DRAMA, ENTITLED "THE TOY-CART."

THE subject of this drama is domestic. The name is Mrichchhakati,—Toy-Cart. The scenes are laid in Avanti or Ougein. The stream of Hindu civilization had now diverged from the Ganges to penetrate the wild and hilly region to which Sir J. Malcolm gave the name of Central India. It includes Malwa, famous in later days for its production of opium, and is inhabited by Rajputs. The capital of this province is Ougein, anciently written Avanti; a city "sufficiently advanced at the period of this drama to be luxurious and corrupt."[1]

[1] H. H. Wilson, Hindu Theatre, Intro. to Toy-Cart. p. 9.

The author of the Toy-Cart is announced as a king Sûdraka, who lived "a hundred years, and then burnt himself, leaving his kingdom to his son." A benediction, which serves as prelude, recognises Siva as the active, ever-present Power; and Brahma (neuter) as the abstract Power of the Universe.[1]

"May that profound meditation of Sambhu (Siva) protect you! (meaning the audience) which is intent on Brahma, the absorbing end of every effort of abstract vision; as he contemplates with the eye of wisdom, spirit, in himself, detached from all material instruments; his senses being restrained by holy knowledge, as he sits ruminating with suspended breath, whilst his serpents coil with the folds of his vesture round his bended knees."

The representation of Siva as a Yoga ascetic, with his knees coiled round by serpents, is unknown to the Code or the epics. The appellation given in the next sentence to Siva, of "god of the dark-blue throat," refers to the churning of the ocean, in the Mahâbhârata, when Siva swallowed the poison thus generated, and gave his throat a blue stain, which never left him.

The hero of the Toy-Cart is a married Brâhman, who has an affectionate wife and one little son, to whom he is much attached. He is a model of goodness, according to the standard of goodness then accepted. At the opening of the play he is unhappy, because, owing to the munificence of his donations, he is in poverty. "The scene is supposed to represent a street on one side, and on the other the first court of Chârudatta's house."[2] Chârudatta, the impoverished Brâhman, is always accompanied by a friend, named Maitreya, also a Brâhman, described as the "Vidûshaka," or *gracioso* of the piece.

Maitreya enters the court alone, having in his hand a cloth garment. He begins soliloquising:—

---

[1] H. H. Wilson, Hindu Theatre, vol. i. pp. 13, 14.
[2] Professor Lassen attributes this play to the two first centuries after Christ. See Lassen, Indische Alterthumskunde, vol. ii. pp. 1113, 1147.

"Truly, Maitreya, your condition is sad enough, and well qualified to subject you to be picked up in the street and fed by strangers. In the days of Chârudatta's prosperity, I was accustomed to stuff myself, till I could eat no more, on scouted dishes, until I breathed perfume; and sat lolling at yonder gateway, dyeing my fingers like a painter's, by dabbling amongst the coloured comfits, or chewing the cud at leisure, like a high-fed city bull. Now, in the season of his poverty, I wander about from house to house, like a tame pigeon, to pick up such crumbs as I can get."

He then tells us that the garment he holds in his hand is a gift to his master from a dear friend, one Chûrâbuddha; it has lain among jasmine flowers, until it is quite scented by them; and is to be presented to him, so soon as he has finished his devotions. "Here he comes; he is presenting the oblation to the household gods." Chârudatta (with a sigh):

> "Alas, how changed! The offering to the gods,
> That swans and stately storks, in better time
> About my threshold flocking, bore away,
> Now a scant tribute to the insect tribe,
> Falls mid rank grass, by worms to be devoured."

Maitreya approaches, and is kindly greeted as a "friend of all seasons." Maitreya presents the garment. Chârudatta takes it thoughtfully; and being asked on what he meditates, says:

> "My friend,
> The happiness that follows close on sorrow,
> Shows like a lamp that breaks upon the night.
> But he that falls from affluence to poverty
> May wear the human semblance, but exists
> A lifeless form alone."

Being further questioned, Chârudatta declares that he would much prefer death to poverty:

> "To die, is transient suffering; to be poor,
> Interminable anguish."

And he further explains, that he does not grieve for the lost wealth:

> "But that the guest no longer seeks the dwelling
> Whence wealth has vanished.
> * * * * * *
> And then with poverty comes disrespect;
> From disrespect does self-dependence fail:
> Then scorn and sorrow, following, overwhelm
> The intellect; and, when the judgment fails,
> The being perishes. And thus, from poverty
> Each ill that pains humanity proceeds."[1]

He says he would have given up the world and have become an ascetic, but that he did not like to impose such hardship upon his wife. At length he bids Maitreya carry his oblation to "where the four roads meet, and there present it to the great mothers."

Maitreya refuses, asking what the gods have done for him. Chârudatta replies:

> "Speak not profanely. It is our duty; and the gods
> Undoubtedly are pleased with what is offered
> In lowliness of spirit, and with reverence,
> In thought, and deed, and pious self-denial:
> Go, therefore, and present the offering."

But Maitreya won't go; and says that with him every part of the ritual is apt to get out of its place, and, as in the reflection of a mirror, the right becomes left and the left right. Besides, he says, at this time of the evening the royal road is crowded with cut-throats, courtiers, and courtezans.

Whilst he is yet speaking a tumult is heard in the street, to

---

[1] "This passage occurs in the Hitopadeṣa, with a slight variation."—H. H. Wilson. See our chapter on the Hitopadeṣa.

which Chárudatta's house has a side or back entrance, the main entrance being through the court-yard. Vasantasená, the heroine of the play, comes flying down the street, pursued by a dissolute prince and his attendants. Vasantasená belongs to the class of courtezans to which we have already alluded. They are countenanced by the then existing Brahmanical institutions, as is also the custom of plurality of wives. Vasantasená is represented as a lady of great spirit and generosity, and evidently holds a position not esteemed degrading. The prince and his companions all call after her. "Stop, Vasantasená! stop!" says the foremost. "Why, losing your gentleness in your fears, do you ply those feet so fast, that should be nimble only in the dance?" The prince cries the same, and says: "Why do you thus scamper away, stumbling at every step? Be pacified; . . . . . with love alone is my poor heart inflamed; it is burnt, like a piece of meat upon the blazing coals." The servant also cries: "Stop, lady, stop! Why, sister, do you fly? She runs along like a peahen in summer, with a tail in full feather, whilst my master follows her, like the young hound that chases the bird through the thicket." Luckily, at this moment Chárudatta happens to open the side door of his mansion, and in rushes the fugitive, cleverly making her scarf brush out the light of the lamp as she passed; and the night being pitch dark, the whole party are at fault. After much blustering and threatening, the prince and his suit-depart.

Chárudatta re-lights his lamp, and discovers Vasantasená, and he and she forthwith salute each other.

She has seen Chárudatta before, in the gardens of Kamadeva's temple, and "honoured him with her affection" on first sight, in consequence, we are told, of admiration for his goodness. He does not recognise her; but on being told that she has taken refuge from the dissolute prince, who sends him a message,—threatening litigation and eternal enmity if she is not put forth, but reward in case she is delivered up,—Chárudatta says, with disdain, "He is a fool;" and then falls into admiration of Vasantasená. He says to himself:

> "The pride of wealth
> Presents no charm to her, and she disdains
> The palace she is roughly bid to enter;
> Nor makes she harsh reply, but silent leaves
> The man she scorns, to waste his idle words."

He apologizes to her and she to him, until Maitreya says: "Whilst you two stand there, nodding your heads to each other like a field of long grass, permit me to bend mine, although in the style of a young camel's stiff knees, and request that you will be pleased to hold yourselves upright again." As a pretext for further intercourse, Vasantasená begs permission to leave a casket of jewels in Chárudatta's house, saying, that it was for the jewels that the villains were pursuing her.

In the next scene of interest a robber is "creeping along the ground, like a snake crawling out of his old skin." He feels the wall until he discovers a rat-hole. This he hails as an omen of success. He then considers how he is to proceed, saying: "The god of the golden spear teaches four modes of breaking into a house: first, picking out burnt bricks; cutting through unbaked ones; throwing water on a mud wall; and boring through one of wood." And as Chárudatta's wall was of baked bricks, he picks them out, doubting whether to make the aperture in the shape of a *swastika*, or in that of a water-jar; and, feeling at a loss for a measuring-line, he makes use of his Brahmanical thread, which, he observes, is a most useful appendage to a Bráhman *of his complexion*, serving as it does to measure the depth and height of walls, to withdraw ornaments, to open a latch, or to make a ligature for the bite of a snake.

Having entered through the breach, he contrives to abstract the casket from beneath the head of Maitreya; then lets fly what he calls the "fire-flapping insect," which hovers round the light which the insect puts out with his wings; and, finally, the thief escapes. The household wake up just as he departs, and are in a terrible consternation at the loss of the jewels. Chârudatta feels that, now, a foul blight will for ever rest upon his fame; but his wife in the inner apartment, whilst expressing joy that he is himself unhurt, takes a string of jewels, "given to her in her maternal mansion, and over which she alone had control;" and fearing that her husband's lofty spirit "would not accept them from her," sends for Maitreya, pretends that she gives them to him because he is a Brâhman, and feels sure that they will be used for the relief of her husband. Her confidence is not abused: Maitreya presents the jewels to Chârudatta, and after some reluctance and hesitation, Chârudatta bids Maitreya take them to Vasantasenâ; tell her that he had, unhappily, lost her casket at play, and entreat her to accept this offering in its place. When Maitreya reaches the dwelling of Vasantasenâ, he gives graphic descriptions of the place.

Mait. "A very pretty entrance, indeed. The threshold is very neatly coloured, well swept, and watered; the floor adorned with strings of sweet flowers; the top of the gate lofty, and gives one the pleasure of looking up to the clouds; whilst the jasmine festoon hangs tremblingly down, as if it were now tossing on the trunk of Indra's elephant. Over the door-way is a lofty arch of ivory; above it, again, wave flags, dyed with safflower, their fringes curling in the wind, like fingers that beckon me. . . . . . The capitals of the door-posts support crystal flower-pots, in which young mango trees are springing up. . . . . . The whole cries, 'Away!' to a poor man."

Entering the court, he finds what he calls a line of palaces.

"Golden steps, embellished with stones, lead to the upper apartments, whence the crystal windows, festooned with pearls, ... look down upon Ougein. The porter dozes upon an easy chair, as stately as a Brâhman deep in the Vedas; and the crows, crammed with rice and curds, disdain the fragments of the sacrifice."

When Maitreya is conducted to the second court he exclaims:

"Oh, here are the stables; the carriage oxen are in good case: .... straw and oil-cakes are ready for them; ..... their horns bright with grease. .... Here is a buffalo, snorting like a Brâhman of high caste, whom somebody has offended; here stands a ram to have his neck rubbed, like a wrestler after a match;[1] .... here is a monkey, tied as fast as a thief; ..... and here are the Mahuts, plying the elephants with balls of rice and ghee."

On going through a third gateway the public court is entered, "where the young bucks of Ougein assemble;" ...... "the half-read book lies on the gaming-table, the pieces, or men, of which are made of jewels." In the fourth court, drums "emit, like clouds, a murmuring sound," and cymbals flash, like stars that fall from heaven. Some damsels are singing, others are practising the graceful dance. The place is hung with water-jars, to catch the cooling breeze. The fifth court is very exciting to Maitreya, who says:

Mait. "Ah, how my mouth waters! what a savoury scent of oil and assafœtida! The kitchen sighs softly forth its fragrant and abundant smoke; the odours are delicious. The butcher's boy is washing the skin of an animal just slain; the cook is surrounded with dishes. The sweetmeats are mixing; the cakes are baking. (Apart.) Oh! that I could meet with some one who would wash my feet, and say, 'Eat, sir; eat.'"

The arched gateway of the sixth court is "of gold and many-coloured gems, on a ground of sapphire." ...... "It is the jeweller's court. Skilful artists are examining pearls, topazes, sapphires, emeralds, rubies, the lapis-lazuli, coral, and other jewels. Some set rubies in gold, some work gold ornaments on coloured thread, some string pearls, some grind the lapis-lazuli,

[1] Rams in India are commonly trained to fight.—H. H. Wilson.

some pierce shells, and some cut coral." Others, again, are compounding perfumes. Maitreya disapproves the company who loiter about in the court, saying:

"Whom have we here? Fair damsels and their gallants,—laughing, talking, chewing musk and betel, and drinking wine. Here are the male and female attendants, and here are miserable hangers-on,—men that neglected their own families and spent their all upon the harlot, and are now glad to quaff the drainings of her wine-cup."

The description of the seventh court is amusing, and enumerates the birds which, to this day, are tamed and petted by Hindus.

"This is the aviary. The doves bill, and coo, in comfort; the pampered parrot croaks, like a Bráhman *pundit* stuffed with curds and rice, chanting a hymn from the *Vedas*; the *maina* chatters as glibly as a waiting maid issuing her mistress's command to her fellow-servants; while the *koil*, crammed with juicy fruit, whines like a water-carrier. The quails fight; the partridges cry; the domestic peacock ..... fans the palace with his gem-emblazoned tail; the swans, like balls of moonlight, roll about in pairs; ..... whilst the long-legged cranes stalk about the court, like eunuchs on guard."

The maina is an Indian starling, or grakle, handsomer than the English starling, and easily taught to say a few words, and seem angry or pleased, with dramatic effect. The koil is a cuckoo, laying its eggs in another bird's nest. Its plumage is rich, dark-green, of metallic lustre, and its song like the crescendoes, with which Rossini concludes some of his finest scenes. It gives a longer and more sustained strain than that of our nightingale.

In the eighth court, Maitreya meets with members of the family. "Who is that gentleman," he says, "dressed in silken raiment, glittering with rich ornaments, and rolling about as if his limbs were out of joint?" "That," says the attendant, "is my lady's brother." He next inquires who is the lady dressed in flowered muslin, with her well-oiled feet thrust into slippers; and is answered, "That is my lady's mother." Struck with her size, he says:

"A portly old hag, indeed. How did she contrive to get in here? Oh, I suppose she was first set up here, as they do with an unwieldy *Mahádeva*,[1] and then the walls were built round her."

The attendant reproves his jesting, but, nevertheless, conducts him to Vasantasená, who is in the garden, nearly concealed by an arbour of jessamines,—white and yellow, the large kind and the small. The blossoms of the blue clitoria strew the ground. The tank or basin glows with red lotus flowers; and the asoka tree, "with its rich crimson blossoms, shines like a young warrior bathed with the sanguine shower of the furious fight." Sir William Jones was so struck and delighted with this tree, that he gave it his name; and it is now known to botanists as the Jonesia asoka. We shall meet with it again in other dramas. Vasantasená gives Maitreya a most cordial welcome, and alludes to her admiration of his friend and master in a set speech, which Professor Wilson says is "rather in the style of Persian than Indian writing."

Mait. "Is all well with your ladyship?"
Vas. "Undoubtedly, Maitreya: the birds of affection gladly nestle in the tree which, fruitful in excellence, puts forth the flowers of magnanimity and the leaves of merit, and rises with the trunk of modesty from the root of honour."

Maitreya now tells the story invented by Chárudatta, namely, that he had pledged the golden casket at play; and the keeper of the tables, a servant of the prince, had gone,—no one knew whither. The attendant congratulates her mistress on the grave Chárudatta having turned gambler. She already knew the truth;

---

[1] Siva is often so called.

for the thief was in love with a servant of her own. She is, however, touched by Chárudatta's unwillingness to confess that a casket, entrusted to him, was missing. Maitreya now shows the string of diamonds, and says that his master requests she will accept them in lieu of the casket. Vasantasená smiles, takes the diamonds, and putting them to her heart, playfully bids Maitreya tell that sad gambler, Chárudatta, that she will call upon him. Vasantasená had, in fact, already regained her casket, for the thief had presented it to the girl he loved. The girl recognized it as belonging to her mistress, and had persuaded her lover to restore it, and escape the danger of being a thief. Maitreya departs to announce the proposed visit, but says, aside, that he wishes his master was rid of this precious acquaintance. Maitreya is no sooner gone than Vasantasená says to her attendant:

Vas. " Here, girl, take the jewels, and attend me to Chárudatta."
Att. " But look, madam, look; a sudden storm is gathering."
Vas. " No matter.
Let clouds gather, and dark night descend,
And heavy fall unintermitted showers:
I heed them not, wench, when I haste to seek
His presence, whose loved image warms my heart."

The fifth Act opens with a fine description of a storm, which Chárudatta watches from his garden. He says:

" The gathering gloom
Delights the pea-fowl and distracts the swan,
Not yet prepared for periodic flight.
. . . . The purple cloud
Rolls stately on, girt by the golden lightning,
As by a yellow garb, and bearing high
The long, white line of storks. . . . .
From the dark womb, in rapid fall descend

The silvery drops, and, glittering in the gleam
Shot from the lightning, bright and fitful sparkle,
Like a rich fringe rent from the robe of heaven.
The firmament is filled with scattered clouds;
And, as they fly before the wind, their forms,
As in a picture, image various shapes,
The semblances of storks and soaring swans,
Of dolphins, and the monsters of the deep,
Of dragons vast, and pinnacles and towers."

Maitreya returns, finds Chârudatta in the garden, tells him that the necklace is lost. The lady kept it, and she and her damsels made signs to each other, and laughed. Maitreya is indignant, and remarks, that "a courtesan is like a thorn that has run into your foot,—you cannot even get rid of it without pain." Whilst they are yet talking, Vasantasenâ arrives under cover of an umbrella; but, nevertheless, "her locks are drenched with rain, her gentle nerves shaken by angry tempests, and her delicate feet by cumbering mire and massy anklets wearied."

On approaching Chârudatta as he sits in the arbour, Vasantasenâ feels somewhat nervous; but she enters, throws flowers at him, and says: "Gambler, good evening to you." Playfully, she makes her attendant restore the stolen casket; tells him he should not have sent the jewels. Maitreya thinks she might then go home; but the clouds again collect, the heavy drops descend; . . . . . . and Chârudatta and Vasantasenâ confess mutual affection.

In the sixth Act, Vasantasenâ sends the "string of diamonds" to Chârudatta's wife, saying: "Here, girl, take this to my respected sister, and say from me,—I am Chârudatta's handmaid and your slave; then be this necklace again the ornament of that neck to which it of right belongs." It is returned with these words: "You are favoured by the son of my lord; it is not proper for me to accept this necklace. Know, that the only ornament I value, is my husband."

Presently the child comes in playing with the little cart which gives the drama its name. The servant says:

"Come along, my child, let us ride in your cart."
Child. I do not want this cart; it is only of clay (or earthenware); I want one of gold.
Servant. Where are we to get the gold, my little man? Wait till your father is rich again.
Vas. Whose charming boy is that?
Servant This is Rohasena, the son of Chârudatta.

Vasantasenâ finds him very like his father; and, learning that he grieves because a neighbour's child has a cart of gold, whilst his is made of clay, she says: "Don't cry, my good boy; you shall have one of gold." The child asks, "Who is this?" The lady answers: "A handmaid, purchased by your father's merits." On which the servant says: "This is your lady-mother, child!" because she is richly dressed.

Chârudatta was already gone to the old flower-garden, having left orders that Vasantasenâ should follow him there in his curtained carriage, drawn by oxen. This carriage drew up to the gate, but the driver, having forgotten to put in the leather cushions, took his carriage away again to fetch them. In the meantime the carriage of Vasantasenâ's persecutor,—the terrible, dissolute prince, who was in love with her,—drew up. It was accidentally stopped at Chârudatta's door, owing to the road being blocked up by country carts; and Vasantasenâ, believing it to be the carriage Chârudatta had sent for her, jumped in. The dramatic effect would be better, we think, if the play had concluded with the recognition of Vasantasenâ by the mother and child of Chârudatta. The continuation is tedious; but there are several points in it which must not be overlooked. The dissolute prince meets his carriage, and feels triumphant at finding the lady of his admiration within; but when she resolutely rebuffs him, he strangles her, and leaves her for dead beneath a heap of leaves.

Whilst Vasantasenâ thus lies beneath a heap of dry leaves, a Buddhist devotee appears upon the stage. This introduction of Buddhists into a drama, which commences by invoking the god Siva, is a significant incident. The bad prince was making his way to the court, to enter an accusation against Chârudatta, of having murdered Vasantasenâ, saying to himself: "Chârudatta will be ruined; the virtuous city cannot tolerate even the death of an animal,"—which seems to imply "the wide diffusion of Buddha tenets."[1] Catching sight of the "rascally mendicant," as he calls the Sramana (or Buddhist devotee), the prince says: "I fly as the monkey Hanumat leaped through heaven, over earth and hell, from the mountain-peak to Lankâ." He disappears, leaping from a broken wall.

ENTER THE SRAMANA.

"I have washed my mantle, and will hang it on these boughs to dry. No; here are a number of monkeys,—I'll spread it on the ground. No; there is too much dust. Ha! yonder, the wind has blown together a pile of dry leaves; I'll spread it upon them. (*He spreads out his garment and sits down, saying:*) 'Glory to Buddha.'"

This man had formerly been a bath-man and rubber of joints, but, inveigled by gamblers, he was reduced to the extreme of misery, and about to be sold as a slave; when Vasantasenâ, with her usual generosity, gave him protection, and redeemed his debt. Determined never again to touch dice, he had joined the Buddhists; and now, in virtue of his daily duty of begging his food, he was wandering about. The gambling scenes are given with much spirit in Act two. They conclude by his resolving to be a Buddhist mendicant, because "in bidding adieu to gambling, the hands of men are no longer armed against me;

[1] H. H. Wilson, Hindu Theatre, vol. I. p. 140.

and I can hold up my head boldly as I walk along the public road."¹ Whilst this man is drying his mantle, according to Buddhist prescription, Vasantasenâ comes to life. He recognises her hand as "the hand that was once stretched forth to save" him; and he exclaims: "It is the lady Vasantasenâ,— the devoted worshipper of Buddha." He takes her to a "neighbouring convent, where dwells a holy sister."

The ninth Act gives the court of justice. The bad prince ingeniously contrives to make it appear that Chârudatta had robbed Vasantasenâ of her jewels, and then murdered her. The tenth act represents the road to the place of execution, along which Chârudatta walks, attended by executioners. He wears a garland of *karavîra* blossoms, the sweet-scented oleander, or rose-bay, which grows freely all over India, and is much prized by Hindus. At the last moment comes the man who had driven Vasantasenâ to the garden, and who had witnessed the murder effected by the prince. His master had put him in chains; but he leaps from an upper storey, snaps his chain, and rushes in, crying,— "Chârudatta is innocent!" &c. Finally, Vasantasenâ herself arrives. The plot of this play is further complicated, by a circumstance to which we have not yet alluded. Aryaka, a cowherd, conspires against the weak and unpopular king then upon the throne. This cowherd is described as a man with "arms like elephants' vast tusks, his breast and shoulders brawny as the lion's, his eyes a coppery red." The Government succeeded once in capturing this insurgent; but, escaping from his prison, he had taken refuge in Chârudatta's carriage whilst it was waiting for Vasantasenâ; and the driver, mistaking the clank of his chain for the jingle of a lady's bangles, drove him to the garden. Chârudatta is in great grief at finding the cowherd instead of his beloved; but, too generous not to help a fugitive in distress, he desires Aryaka to go forward in his carriage until safe beyond

¹ H. H. Wilson, Hindu Theatre, vol. i. p. 56.

the frontier. Aryaka is now triumphant. Before the assembly has recovered from their surprise at the reappearance of Vasantasenā, a cry is heard of, "Victory to Aryaka!" The weak king has been slain and the cowherd seated on his throne. His first commands are, to "raise the worthy Chârudatta far above calamity and fear;" whilst the bad prince is seized by the mob, and dragged along, with his arms tied behind him. He is, however, released, at the entreaty of the merciful Chârudatta. The wife of Chârudatta, believing her husband dead, is anxious to be burnt, but is told that "the holy laws declare it sinful for a Bráhman's wife to mount a separate pile." Finding her husband alive, she and he greet each other with affection. Then the wife, turning to Vasantasenā, says : "Welcome, happy sister!" and is answered by : "I now, indeed, am happy ;" and they embrace, and a veil is thrown over the "new wife" to mark that she is no longer a public character. To reward the Sramana, they make him "chief of the monasteries of the Bauddhas;" and, after some grateful and pious reflections from Chârudatta, *exeunt omnes*.

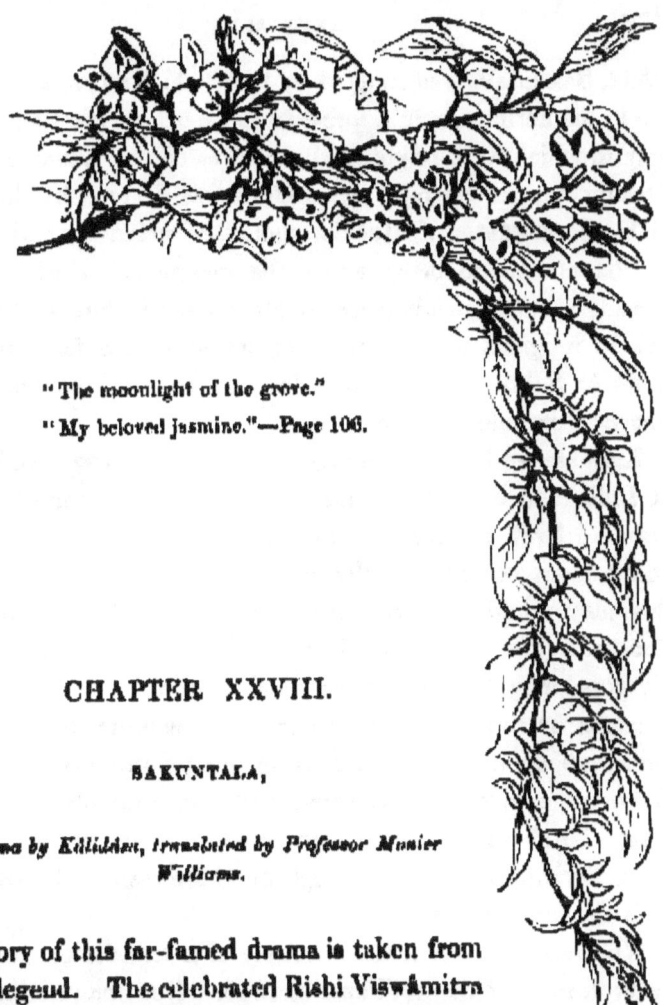

"The moonlight of the grove."
"My beloved jasmine."—Page 106.

CHAPTER XXVIII.

SAKUNTALA;

Drama by Kálidása, translated by Professor Monier Williams.

THE story of this far-famed drama is taken from sacred legend. The celebrated Rishi Viswâmitra is reputed to have gone through a love-passage in the course of his eventful life. It is said that the great god, Indra, feared the power which Viswâmitra was acquiring by severe and prolonged austerity; and, therefore, sent the lovely Menakâ, a nymph of heaven, to allure him from his solitary penance. Viswâmitra yielded, and lived with Menakâ in connubial bliss for some years. Then Viswâmitra returned to his ambitious austerities, Menakâ went back to heaven, and their child, Sakuntalá, was adopted by the Rishi Kanwa, and brought up at his hermitage, in a forest to the south of Hastinâpura, the city in which were reigning the princes of the Lunar line. To Dushyanta, the reigning monarch, it was decreed by the Celestials, the daughter of Menaká should be married; and the plot of the play is to bring about the marriage. Dushyanta has already a queen in his court at Hastinâpura; but, according to Hindu religious notions, this did not unfit him for being husband to Sakuntalá, who was destined to continue the line of heaven-descended Lunar princes.

Kálidása we have already recognised as the most popular poet of India, and Sakuntalá appears to have been his most popular drama. Even so lately as the 3rd of February, 1855, an announcement occurred in the *Bombay Times*, that an outline of this play would be performed that night at the Grand Road Theatre. This is noteworthy; for Kálidása has not obtained his popularity by being sensational or coarse, or by flattering religious or national peculiarities. He delights in delineating tender affection, faithful friendship, gentle sadness, comic and humorous scenes, flowers, trees, birds and animals attached to man. He also loves rich and varied scenic effect, and propitiates his readers in favour of the people of whose taste and civilisation he is the representative.

We avail ourselves almost entirely of a translation published by Professor Monier Williams in 1856. New manuscripts have been brought to light since first this drama was discovered by Sir William Jones. The text now made use of appears to be older and more genuine than that of which he obtained possession. This being the case, we venture to displace the prose translation, made nearly one hundred years ago, for the very attractive metrical version of Professor Monier Williams.

In the Introduction, it is observed that "no directions as to changes of scene are given in the original text of the play;" and "this is the more curious, as there are numerous stage-directions, which prove that, in respect of dresses and decorations, the resources of the Indian theatre were sufficiently ample." Professor Williams thinks it probable, therefore, that a curtain was suspended across the stage, divided in the centre. "Behind the curtain was the space, or room, called *nepathya*, where the decorations were kept, where the actors attired themselves, and remained in readiness before entering the stage, and whither they withdrew on leaving it. When an actor was to enter hurriedly, he was directed to do so "with a toss of the curtain."[1]

The play opens with an invocation to the god Isa, "who is revealed in eight forms,"—Isa being a name of the god Siva. The manager calls an actress, and whilst talking with her, an antelope bounds across the stage. The scene is a forest. King Dushyanta, in a chariot, appears, chasing the deer. He observes to his charioteer, that the fleet antelope has drawn him far away from his attendants:

> "See! there he runs!
> Aye and anon his graceful neck he bends,
> To cast a glance at the pursuing car;
> And, dreading now the swift-descending shaft,
> Contracts into itself his slender frame.
> About his path, in scattered fragments strewn,
> The half-chewed grass falls from his panting mouth.
> See! in his airy bounds he seems to fly,
> And leaves no trace upon th' elastic turf."

After passing carefully over some hollow places they come to a level plain, and proceed again at full speed, with the deer in sight, until some hermits appear and entreat the king not to kill the deer, which is one belonging to their hermitage. The king stops the chariot, takes the arrow from the bow, and enters into conversation. He learns that he is near the hermitage of

---

[1] Sakuntala, or the Lost Ring. Translated into English prose and verse, by Monier Williams. Introduction, p. xxvi.

the great sage, Kanwa, and that the hermits with whom he speaks have come into the forest to collect wood for sacrificial rites. The king inquires whether Kanwa is himself at home, and is told that he is gone to Soma-tîrtha, but has commissioned his daughter Sakuntalá to give hospitality to guests during his absence. As they advance, the king feels that he is within the precincts of a grove consecrated to penitential rites.

> " Beneath the trees, whose hollow trunks afford
> Secure retreat to many a nestling brood
> Of parrots, scattered grains of rice lie strewn.
> Lo, here there are seen the polished slabs
> That serve to bruise the fruit of ingudi.[1]
> The gentle roe-deer, taught to trust in man,
> Unstartled, hear our voices. On the paths
> Appear the traces of bark-woven vests,
> Borne, dripping, from the limpid fount of waters."

And presently he further observes " dusky wreaths of upward curling smoke from burnt oblations." The king feels that this sacred retreat must not be disturbed, and should be entered in humble attitude. He sends away his chariot, giving his driver charge of his ornaments and his bow. He walks around, looks, listens; and, whilst concealed amongst the trees, sees the maidens of the hermitage carrying watering-pots and tending their favourite plants. The king is struck with the loveliness of Sakuntalá, bending over the kesara tree,[2] and the young jasmine, which she had named " the moonlight of the grove." After watching the maidens with admiration, and listening awhile to their prattle, the king shows himself, and is greeted by them with the usual rites of hospitality.

[1] In a note, this tree is said to be commonly called ingua or jiyaputa. Oil from the fruit was used by devotees for their lamps.—Sakuntalá; translated by Professor Monier Williams, notes, p. 4. Terminalia catappa, one of the myrobalans. See Birdwood's Economic Products: Bombay, 1862.

[2] Mimusops elongi, commonly called bakul or vakula, much cultivated on account of its sweet scent.

He inquires into the pedigree of the lovely Sakuntalà, and is told by her attendants that she is in truth the daughter of the Rishi Viswámitra, whose family name is Kausika; that her mother was a heavenly nymph, named Menaká, sent purposely by jealous gods to interrupt and defeat a severe penance, which Viswámitra was then performing in the south, on the banks of the river Godavery; and that, being abandoned by her heaven-born mother, she had been adopted by Kanwa. The king now inquires whether she is bound by vows of celibacy, and doomed ever to dwell amongst her cherished fawns. The answer is, that hitherto she had been engaged in religious duties, and had lived in subjection to her foster-father; but that now it was his fixed intention to give her away in marriage to a husband worthy of her. Sakuntalá, who had been present at these explanations, thinks it time to seek the protection and countenance of Gautamí, the Superior of the female inmates of the hermitage.

Whilst the king strives to detain her, a cry is heard behind the scenes, that the hunting forces of king Dushyanta are near at hand.

"Lo! by the feet of prancing horses raised,
Thick clouds of moving dust, like glittering swarms
Of locusts in the glow of eventide,
Fall on the branches of our sacred trees;
Where hang the dripping vests of woven bark,
Bleached by the waters of the cleansing fountain."

And see!

"Scared by the royal chariot in its course,
With headlong haste an elephant invades
The hallowed precincts of our sacred grove;
Himself the terror of the startled deer,
And an embodied hindrance to our rites.
The hedge of creepers, clinging to his feet
(Feeble obstruction to his mad career),
Is dragged behind him in a tangled chain."

The king is vexed at the interruption, but he exerts himself to protect the hermitage from the wild elephant, and then feels that he must rejoin his attendants, and make them encamp at some little distance. He goes; but says,—

"My limbs, drawn onward, leave my heart behind,
Like silken pennon borne against the wind."

The second Act shows us the plain in which the king and his followers have encamped. His friend, the Bráhman Máthavya, wanders, in a melancholy mood, lamenting the king's love of hunting, which he declares wears him to a shadow.

"'Here is a deer!' 'There goes a boar.' 'Yonder's a tiger!' This is the only burden of our talk, while, in the heat of the meridian sun, we toil on from jungle to jungle, wandering about in the paths of the woods, where the trees afford us no shelter. Are we thirsty? We have nothing to drink but the foul water of some mountain-stream, filled with dry leaves, which give it a most pungent flavour. Are we hungry? We have nothing to eat but roast game, which we must swallow down at odd times as best we can."

But, worse than all former troubles, his royal master has seen the beautiful Sakuntalá.

"From that moment, not another thought of returning to the city! And all last night not a wink of sleep did he get, for thinking of the damsel." . . . . .

Presently the king, having finished his toilet, is seen approaching, "attended by the Yavana women, with bows in their hands, and bearing garlands of wild flowers."

Máthavya leans on his staff, and makes himself appear lame; and when the king asks the cause, he tells the king that he is the cause, and says:

"Here are you living the life of a wild man of the woods, in a savage, unfrequented region, while your State affairs are left to shift for themselves. And as for poor me, I am no longer master of my own limbs, but have to follow you about, day after day, in your chases after wild animals, till my bones are all crippled and out of joint." . . . . .

Whilst this kind of conversation is going on between the king and his confidential Brâhman-jester, the General of the king's forces is announced. He tries to tempt the king to his usual sport; but the king observes that hunting is not fitting in the neighbourhood of a sacred grove, and says, that for the present,—

"All undisturbed, the buffaloes shall sport
In yonder pool, and with their ponderous horns
Scatter its tranquil waters; while the deer,
Couched here and there in groups beneath the shade
Of spreading branches, ruminate in peace.
And all securely shall the herd of boars
Feed on the marshy sedge; and thou, my bow,
With slackened string, enjoy a long repose."

Having come to this decision, he gives his hunting dress into the women's care, and bids his General keep guard outside. "And now that you have got rid of these plagues, who have been buzzing about us like so many flies," says Mâthavya, "sit down,—do." So they sit; and the king tells of Sakuntalâ, and his friend replies:

"This passion of yours for a rustic maiden, when you have so many gems of women at home in your palace, seems to me very like the fancy of a man who is tired of sweet dates, and longs for sour tamarinds as a variety."

The king talks like a man in love, describing the looks, gestures, and words of his beloved, dwelling on his hopes, fears, &c.

Mâthavya interrupts his eloquence, by saying:

"I trust you have laid in a good stock of provisions, for I see you intend making this consecrated grove your game-preserve, and will be roaming about here in quest of sport for some time to come."

The king confesses that he is trying to devise excuses for going again to the hermitage. Mâthavya suggests, that he, as the king, may say that he has come for "the sixth part of their grain," which the inmates owe as tribute. The king rebukes his flippant friend, and says, that hermits pay tribute in prayers and penitential services. The difficulty is removed by the arrival of two young hermits, who have come as a deputation, requesting help from the king. During the absence of the great Rishi Kanwa, evil demons have been disturbing their sacrificial rites; and they petition the king to take up his abode for a few days within the hermitage. Dushyanta immediately orders that his chariot and his bow be brought; and the hermits retire, praising his grace and courtesy.

Very quickly the king's chariot is ready, but at the same time he is told that a messenger has arrived from the seat of government. The queen-mother desires that her son should return, and preside at a solemn ceremony to be held in four days' time. The king resolves this perplexity, by telling his friend Mâthayva to go in his place, tell the queen-mother of his engagement to assist the holy men of the hermitage, and act the part of son to her majesty. This arrangement delights Mâthavya, who departs, well-cautioned by the king not to let out the truth about his present pursuit, to the women of the palace.

All hindrances being thus removed, the king gives himself up to love. Sakuntalâ is suffering from fever; her attendants apply ointment made from the usîra-root,[1] and the cooling leaves and fibres of the lotus. The king is not less tormented by what he

[1] Andropogon muriaticus.—Birdwood, L.L, p. 346.

calls "the god of the flowery arrows." "Foolish those," he says,

> "Who call'd thee thus: they never felt thy wounds!
> And senseless they who say the fair moon's cold.
> Alas! in love, we feel too well thy darts
> Are diamond-pointed: and the treacherous moon
> Sheds fire upon us from those dewy beams."

He seeks for her "footsteps printed in the sand," and sees the "well-known outline faintly marked in front, more deeply towards the heel." He stands concealed behind some branches, and perceives the beloved of his heart reclining on a rock strewn with flowers, and attended by her two friends. They look sorrowful, whilst fanning her with broad lotus leaves. The king flatters himself that it is not merely the intensity of the heat which has affected her.

> "On her slender arm
> Her only bracelet, twined with lotus-stalks,
> Hangs loose and withered: her recumbent form
> Expresses languor. Ne'er could noon-day sun
> Inflict such fair disorder on a maid;—
> No: love, and love alone is here to blame."

The king hears Sakuntalá confess to her friends that she is in love with him, but still remains concealed, rapturous with delight. His very eyes, he says, forget to wink, jealous of losing, even for an instant, a sight so charming.

> "How beautiful the movement of her brow,
> As through her mind love's tender fancies flow!
> And, as she weighs her thoughts, how sweet to trace
> The ardent passion mantling in her face!"

In a prelude to the fourth Act, we are informed that Sakuntalá was married to the king, "by the form of marriage prevalent among Indra's nymphs"—that he chased away the demons, was gratefully dismissed by the hermits, and returned to his seat of government, leaving Sakuntalá with her friends at the hermitage. The next event is the arrival of the irascible and powerful Rishi Durvásas. Sakuntalá is so absent in mind, that she pays him no attention, and he, "a very mine of penitential merit," punishes the unpardonable offence by a curse, saying—"Thus I curse thee;" "he, even he, of whom thou thinkest, he shall think no more of thee, nor in his heart retain thine image."

The curse takes effect. King Dushyanta does not even send a letter. The Rishi Kanwa returns, and, after waiting some months, determines that his daughter, Sakuntalá, must be sent to her husband's palace at Hastinápura. "This very day," Kanwa says, "I purpose sending thee under the charge of trusty hermits, who shall deliver thee into the hands of thy husband." Preparations are quickly made; unguents and perfumes are compounded, and the holy women invoke blessings on her head.

First Woman. "My child, mayst thou receive the title of 'Chief-queen,' and may thy husband delight to honour thee above all others."

Second Woman. "My child, mayst thou be the mother of a hero."

Third Woman. "My child, mayst thou be highly honoured by thy lord."[1]

Whilst the attendants rub Sakuntalá with unguents, and arrange her bridal dress and decorations, she weeps sad to think that perhaps she may never again be dressed by these dear friends. Her father, Kanwa, is not less grieved at the necessary parting, and says—

"This day my loved one leaves me, and my heart
Is heavy with its grief: the streams of sorrow,

[1] Monier Williams, p. 87.

Choked at the source, repress my faltering voice.
I have no words to speak: mine eyes are dimmed
By the dark shadow of the thoughts that rise
Within my soul. If such the force of grief
In an old hermit parted from his nursling,
What anguish must the stricken parent feel—
Bereft for ever of an only daughter?

He gives his blessing, and then bids her walk reverently round the sacrificial fires, whilst he repeats a prayer in the metre of the Rig-Veda.

> "Holy flames, that gleam around
> Every altar's hallowed ground;
> Holy flames, whose frequent food
> Is the consecrated wood,
> And for whose encircling bed
> Sacred Kusa-grass is spread;
> Holy flames, that waft to heaven
> Sweet oblations daily given,
> Mortal guilt to purge away;—
> Hear, oh hear me, when I pray—
> Purify my child this day."

Whilst Kanwa is alluding to her love for the trees and flowers, the note of a Koil[1] is heard, as if in loving reply.

Sakuntalá says aside to her friend—

"Eager as I am to see my husband once more, my feet refuse to move, now that I am quitting for ever the home of my childhood."

Her friend replies that such bitterness at parting is felt throughout the grove.

> "In sorrow for thy loss, the herd of deer
> Forget to browse; the peacock on the lawn
> Ceases its dance: the very trees
> Shed their pale beams, like tears, upon the ground."

[1] Indian cuckoo, gifted with great compass of voice.

Kanwa says, on seeing her take leave of her jasmine,

> "Daughter, the cherished purpose of my heart,
> Has ever been to wed thee to a spouse
> That should be worthy of thee; such a spouse
> Hast thou thyself, by thy own merits, won.
> To him thou goest, and about his neck
> Soon shalt thou cling confidingly, as now
> Thy favourite jasmine twines its loving arms
> Around the sturdy mango. Leave thou it
> To its protector—e'en as I consign
> Thee to thy lord, and henceforth from my mind
> Banish all anxious thought on thy behalf."

Still lingering, unwilling to proceed, Sakuntalá says

"My father, see you there my pet deer, grazing close to the hermitage? She expects soon to fawn, and even now the weight of the little one she carries hinders her movements. Do not forget to send me word when she becomes a mother."

Kanwa says he will not forget; and Sakuntalá, feeling herself drawn back, wonders what can be fastened to her dress. Kanwa replies:

> "It is the little fawn, thy foster child.
> Poor helpless orphan! it remembers well,
> How, with a mother's tenderness and love,
> Thou didst protect it, and with grains of rice
> From thine own hand didst daily nourish it."

Sakuntalá is much affected by the desire of the fawn to go with her. She weeps; and Kanwa says,

> "Weep not, my daughter, check the gathering tear
> That lurks beneath thine eyelid, ere it flow,
> And weaken thy resolve; be firm and true—
> True to thyself and me; the path of life
> Will lead o'er hill and plain—o'er rough and smooth,
> And all must feel the steepness of the way;
> Though rugged be thy course, press boldly on."

The hermit, into whose charge Sakuntalá was committed, next observes, that the sacred precept is to accompany thy friend as far as the margin of the first stream; and as they have now arrived at the margin of a lake, the moment for parting has arrived. Kanwa agrees, but says they must tarry for a moment under the shade of a fig-tree. He then sends a grave message to the king, exhorting him to be just and true to Sakuntalá, and to receive her as his wife, and enthrone her as his queen. His parting advice to Sakuntalá is as follows:—

> "Honour thy betters; ever be respectful
> To those above thee; and, should others share
> Thy husband's love, ne'er yield thyself a prey
> To jealousy; but ever be a friend,
> A loving friend, to those who rival thee
> In his affections. Should thy wedded lord
> Treat thee with harshness, thou must never be
> Harsh in return, but patient and submissive.
> Be to thy menials courteous; and to all
> Placed under thee, considerate and kind.
> Be never self-indulgent, but avoid
> Excess in pleasure; and, when fortune smiles,
> Be not puffed up. Thus to thy husband's house
> Wilt thou a blessing prove, and not a curse."

Sakuntalá still grieves at parting from her foster-father and her young companions; she is, she says, "like a tendril of the sandal-tree, torn from its home in the Western Mountains."[1]

Her maidens embrace her, bidding her remember that if the king should by any chance be slow to recognise her, she has but to show the ring he gave her, on which his own name is engraved. Sakuntalá, still looking back, asks Kanwa when she will see the hallowed grove again; and Kanwa looks forward, in Hindu fashion, to the time when, as Dushyanta's

---

[1] Monier Williams, p. 114.

queen, she shall have seen her son grown to manhood, and united in wedlock, and able to relieve his Sire of the helm of state and the care of the earth.

> "Then, weary of the world,
> Together with Dushyanta thou shalt seek
> The calm seclusion of thy former home :
> There amid holy scenes to be at peace,
> Till thy pure spirit gain its last release."

This farewell scene is really touching, although a little too prolonged. Sakuntalá wanted her young companions to go with her; but Kanwa considers them too young to be introduced to so public a place as the king's palace, and he sends the matron, Gautamí.

The fifth Act changes the scene to Hastinápura. The king, and his jesting friend, Máthavya, are sitting together in the palace. Music is heard. Máthavya says it is the queen, Hansapadiká, practising a new song, wherewith to greet the king. They listen.

> "How often hither didst thou rove,
> Sweet bee, to kiss the mango's cheek :
> Oh! leave not, then, thy early love,
> The lily's honeyed lip to seek."

Máthavya asks the king if he understands the meaning of the words, and he smiles and says, she is reproving him because he has lately deserted her for the queen Vasumatí; and he wishes Máthavya to go and tell Hansapadiká that he takes her delicate reproof as intended. Máthavya thinks the chances are she will have him seized by the hair of the head, and beaten to a jelly; but he goes; and then the king, left alone, says,

"Strange, that song has filled me with a most peculiar sensation. A melancholy feeling has come over me, and I seem to yearn after some long-forgotten object of affection."

"Not seldom in our hours of ease,
When thought is still, the sight of some fair form,
Or mournful fall of music breathing low,
Will stir strange fancies, thrilling all the soul
With a mysterious sadness, and a sense
Of vague, yet earnest, longing. Can it be
That the dim memory of events long past,
Or friendships formed in other states of being,
Flits like a passing shadow o'er the spirit?"

A chamberlain enters, supporting his tottering steps on a staff, which was in youthful days, he says, a mere "useless badge." He wants to tell the king that a deputation of hermits has arrived from the sage, Kanwa, but he is unwilling to trouble him, when but just risen from the judgment-seat; but as "a monarch's business is to sustain the world, he must not expect much repose."

"Onward, for ever onward, in his car,
The unwearied sun pursues his daily course,
Nor tarries to unyoke his glittering steeds:
And ever moving, speeds the rushing wind
Through boundless space, filling the universe
With his life-giving breezes. Day and night,
The king of Serpents on his thousand heads
Upholds the incumbent earth; and even so,
Unceasing toil is aye the lot of kings,
Who, in return, draw nurture from their subjects."

As he gets nearer to the king, he says, that after a monarch has worked for his subjects through the day, he becomes wearied, and seeks seclusion and repose; as the prince of elephants leads the fainting herd to cooling shades before he yields to his own desire for rest. But he determines to deliver his message, and says, " Victory to the king ! So please your majesty, some hermits living in a forest near the Snowy Mountains have arrived here, bringing certain women with them. They have a message to deliver from the sage, Kanwa." Dushyanta, still under the influence of the curse pronounced upon Sakuntalá, has not the slightest recollection of her, or of the hermitage. He, therefore, gives orders that his domestic priest shall receive the hermits with due honour, and that he will await them in the chamber of the consecrated fire. Dushyanta does not hesitate about the duty of attending to this demand upon his leisure moments; but he "walks on with the air of one oppressed with the cares of government," and says to himself:

" People are generally contented and happy when they have gained their desires ; but kings no sooner attain the object of their aspiration, than all their troubles begin."

> " 'Tis a fond thought, that to attain the end
> And object of ambition is to rest :
> Success doth only mitigate the fever
> Of anxious expectation ; soon the fear
> Of losing what we have, the constant care
> Of guarding it doth weary. Ceaseless toil
> Must be the lot of him, who, with his hands,
> Supports the canopy that shields his subjects."

Heralds recite laudatory verses as the king passes on. A warder then says,

" Here is the terrace of the hallowed fire chamber, and yonder stands the cow that yields the milk for the oblations. The sacred enclosure has been recently purified, and looks clean and beautiful. Ascend, sire."

The king ascends, troubled in his mind to think what can have brought the hermits.

The hermits enter, leading Sakuntalá, attended by Gautami;

and, in advance of them, walk the chamberlain and the domestic priest.

The scene is rather tedious. The king does not remember Sakuntalá, but feels attracted towards her. Believing her to be the wife of another, he will not yield to the attraction, and thinks her honeyed words are false. Gautamí interposes, and observes that, brought up in a hermitage, Sakuntalá had never learned deceit; but the king says that,

> "E'en in untutored brutes, the female sex
> Is marked by inborn subtlety: much more
> In beings gifted by intelligence.
> The wily koil, ere towards the sky
> She wings her sportive flight, commits her eggs
> To other nests, and artfully consigns
> The rearing of her little ones to strangers."

Sakuntalá, after expressing indignation, burst into tears; and the hermit who had brought her says, burning remorse must ever follow rash actions; and that marriage should not be contracted hastily, "specially in secret."[1] Sakuntalá thought she could have convinced Dushyanta by showing him his ring; but the ring was gone; and her companions remembered that it might have slipped from her finger when worshipping at "Sachi's sacred pool." The king considers this just another instance of the readiness of woman's invention. He is, however, affected by Sakuntalá's grief, and asks counsel of his domestic priest. He is told to take an intermediate course, and to provide an asylum for Sakuntalá until the birth of her child,—the reason for this being, that it has been predicted that Dushyanta's firstborn shall bear on his hand marks of the discus,—the sign of universal dominion. If, therefore, the coming infant has these marks, the mother must be immediately admitted to the royal

[1] Monier Williams, p. 141.

apartments, with great rejoicings. The king bows to the decision; Sakuntalá calls upon the earth to open and receive her into its bosom, and goes out weeping with the priests and the hermits.

They are no sooner out of sight than a noise is heard behind the scenes, and cries of—" A miracle! a miracle!" The priest comes rushing back, announcing that a shining apparition, in female shape, had descended from the skies, and carried the weeping Sakuntalá up to heaven.

In the sixth Act a poor fisherman is brought forward and treated as a thief, because he has the king's signet-ring. He was cutting open a large carp, and found the ring in the fish's maw. The constables abuse the fisherman, but the superintendent of police brings him money from the king. The play becomes tedious, as usual with the final Acts of Hindu dramas. When the king recovered his ring, his memory was restored. He became a prey to remorse; he forbad the celebration of the Vernal Festival; tossed to and fro upon his couch, " courting repose in vain;" forgot the names of the ladies of his palace, or called them "Sakuntalá;" and was "straightway silent and abashed with shame." He is unable to attend to business, and sends to his prime minister to say that he is too much exhausted, by want of sleep, to be able to sit on the judgment-seat; and that if any case of importance occurs, the minister must attend to it. The king suffers grievously, and gives way to sad memories of the hermitage and its scenery, and of the river Málinî,

> " Its tranquil course by banks of sand impeded.
> Upon the brink a pair of swans; beyond,
> The hills adjacent to Himalaya,
> Studded with deer; and near, the spreading shade
> Of some large tree, where, 'mid the branches, hang
> The hermits' vests of bark; a tender doe,
> Rubbing its downy forehead on the horn
> Of a black antelope, should be depicted."

His reverie is disturbed by hearing that his queen, Vasumatí, is coming. His friend Máthavya makes off, saying that the queen has a bitter draught in store for the king, which he will have to swallow, as Siva did the poison at the Deluge. The queen, however, turns back, having met the female door-keeper with a despatch in her hand. The prime minister refers the following case to the king:

"A merchant, named Dhanamitra, trading by sea, was lost in a late shipwreck. Though a wealthy trader, he was childless; and the whole of his immense property becomes, by law, forfeited to the king."

The king, after reading the case, desires that inquiry be made as to whether he had left any wife expecting to give birth to a child. The answer is, that his wife, the daughter of the foreman of a guild belonging to Ayodhyá, had just completed the ceremonies usual upon such expectations. Whereupon the king declares that the unborn child has a title to his father's property. This proclamation is received with acclamations of joy. The king then falls deeper than ever into grief, at having lost his beloved Sakuntalá, and "his second self,—the child unborn,—hope of his race."

"Alas! (he sighs) the shades of my forefathers are even now beginning to be alarmed, lest at my death they may be deprived of their funeral libations.

> No son remains in king Dushyanta's place
> To offer sacred homage to the dead
> Of Puru's noble line. My ancestors
> Must drink these glistening tears,—the last libation
> A childless man can ever hope to make them."
>
> (*He falls down in an agony of grief*)

To rouse Dushyanta from the torpor of grief, Indra's charioteer comes to the rescue, saying that his friend Máthavya, attacked by a demon, is screaming out in agony; and that Indra has sent him to bring Dushyanta to the celestial regions to assist in subduing evil spirits. Dushyanta obeys, and mounts the car; and their journey through space is described. The king looks down in wonder at the appearance of the earth.

> "Stupendous prospect! Yonder lofty hills
> Do suddenly uprear their towering heads
> Amid the plain; while from beneath their crests
> The ground, receding, sinks. The trees, whose stems
> Seemed lately hid within their leafy tresses,
> Rise into elevation, and display
> Their branching shoulders. Yonder streams, whose waters,
> Like silver threads, but now were scarcely seen,
> Grow into mighty rivers. Lo! the earth
> Seems upward hurled by some gigantic power."

They conclude their journey by visiting the sacred grove of the holy Kasyapa, on "a range of mountains which, like a bank of clouds, illumined by the setting sun, pours down a stream of gold." In this heavenly abode, Dushyanta discovers his son playing with a young lion, and Sakuntalá in widow's garb. Recognition is followed by explanation. Kasyapa (the reputed father of Indra) bestows his blessing, and advises "frequent offerings to preserve the Thunderer's friendship." Finally, he bids Dushyanta re-ascend the car of Indra, and return with his wife and child to his imperial capital. In the last words of the drama, Dushyanta prays that "the words of Bharata be fulfilled."

> "May kings reign only for their subjects' weal!
> May the divine Saraswati, the source
> Of speech, and goddess of dramatic art,
> Be honoured by the great and wise!
> And may the purple, self-existent god,
> Whose vital energy pervades all space,
> From future transmigrations save my soul!"

"The graceful Urvasi, the nymph whose charms defeated Indra's stratagems."—
Act I., scene 1.

CHAPTER XXIX.

VIKRAMA AND URVASI; OR HERO AND NYMPH.

One of the three plays attributed to Kálidása. Translated by H. H. Wilson.

A SECOND drama, by Kálidása, is entitled the Hero and the Nymph,[1] or Vikramorvasi, which means Vikrama and Urvasi,— Vikrama being a king, and Urvasi a nymph of heaven. The story is founded on a legend related in the Satapatha-Bráhmana. Vikrama loves Urvasî, and his love is not rejected; but he is warned that if he is ever seen by her, naked or unveiled, she will vanish. Explanations of this myth are given by Max Müller,

---

[1] The nymph, represented above, is from a drawing by Ghasi, in the collection of drawings presented by the late Col. Tod to the Royal Asiatic Society. She and other nymphs are standing against pillars, outside a temple at Barolli, in Rajputana. This drawing does not appear to have been engraved.

in his "Comp. Mythology," and by Kuhn, in his essay, "Die Herabkunft des Feuers;" in which he alludes also to the ideas of Weber: each of these works should be consulted. Another explanation is, that Purûravas (or Vikrama) personifies the sun; whilst Urvasî is the morning mist.[1] Urvasî is an Apsaras; and we find in Goldstücker's dictionary that the Apsarasas "are personifications of the vapours which are attracted by the sun, and form into mists or clouds." Dr. Goldstücker holds, therefore, that the legend represents the absorption, by the sun, of the vapour floating in the air. When Purûravas becomes distinctly visible, Urvasî vanishes; because, when the sun shines forth, the mist is absorbed. In Kâlidâsa's play, the nymph is changed into a climbing plant; and this is either the invention of the poet, or was a view of the legend, current at the time at which he wrote;—meaning, that sunshine not only renders mist invisible, but shows earthly objects in its place. Thus, Urvasî was apparently transformed into one of those beautiful twining plants for which the gardens and woods of India are celebrated. In Greece, Daphne becomes a laurel, because the country abounds in laurels,—which are manifest so soon as the sun has absorbed the mist; whilst in India, Urvasî becomes a swan, according to the Satapatha-Brâhmana,—or, as Kâlidâsa represents, a beautiful plant. Professor Max Müller's identification of Urvasi with the Dawn should also be considered; but, even apart from etymological considerations, the explanation given above will probably be considered as complete and satisfactory.

In an Introduction, Professor Wilson praises "the richness of the *Prâkrit* in this play," as remarkable both in structure and metre. A great portion, especially of the fourth Act, is in this language, and a considerable variety is introduced; and he concludes "that this form of Sanskrit must have been highly cultivated long before the play was written." But, on the other

---

[1] Chambers' Encyc., s.v. Purûravas.   [2] *Ante*, p. 147.

hand, the play tells the story quite differently, and much better and more simply, than the Puránas; "therefore, we may suppose that the play preceded those works." Comparing this work with Sakuntalá, the Professor says, "there is the same vivacity of description and tenderness of feeling," the same delicate beauty in the thoughts, and elegance in the style. But whilst "the story of the present play is, perhaps, more skilfully woven, and the incidents rise out of each other more naturally," there is, "perhaps, no one personage in it so interesting as the heroine of that drama." The heroine of the present drama is, we have observed, an *Apsaras*,—a word derived from *ap*, "water," and *saras*, "who moves." Their origin is referred to the first book of the Rámáyana.

> "Then, from the agitated deep, upsprung
> The legion of Apsarasas; so named,
> That to the watery element they owed
> Their being. Myriads were they born, and all
> In vesture heavenly clad."[1] . . . . .

The hero, king Vikrama, or Purúravas, reigns at Prayága, at the junction of the Jumna and the Ganges, Prayága standing on the left bank of the Jumna, and nearly opposite to the modern city of Allahabad.

The drama commences with what is called a prelude. The manager enters, and pronounces an address or benediction, which, like Kálidása's other preludes, indicates that the author belongs to "that modification of the Hindu faith in which the abstract deism of the Vedánta is qualified by identifying the supreme, invisible, and inappreciable spirit with a delusive form, which was the person of Rudra or Siva."[2]

"May that Siva, who is attainable by devotion and faith; to whom

[1] H. H. Wilson, Hindu Theatre, vol. i. p. 193.   [2] Hero Nymph, p. 195.

alone the name of Lord (Iswara) is applicable, and who is sought with suppressed breath by those who covet final emancipation, bestow upon you final felicity."

Then addressing the actors, he says,

"Many assemblies have witnessed the composition of former dramatic bards; I, therefore, propose to exhibit one not hitherto represented, the drama of Vikrama and Urvasi. Desire the company to be ready to do justice to their respective parts."

Actor. "I shall, sir."
Manager. "I have now only to request the audience that they will listen to this work of Kálidása with attention and kindness."

Whilst he is yet speaking, a cry is heard behind the scenes of "Help, help!" and a troop of Apsarasas, or nymphs of heaven, enter in the air.

Although the king was a mortal, he was fond of straying amid the heavenly precincts on the peaks of the Himalaya.

The scene represents part of this range of hills. The nymphs cry—

"Help, help! if any friend be nigh,
To aid the daughters of the sky."

The king appears in his chariot, driven by a charioteer. He learns that the most lovely of the nymphs has been torn from her companions, and carried off by a *Dánava*. He hastens to the rescue, and so swift is his progress, that the waving chowry[1] on the steeds' broad brow points backward, motionless; and backwards streams the banner from the breeze.

---

[1] "The white bushy tail of the Tibet cow, fixed on a gold or ornamented shaft, rose from between the ears of the horse, like the plume of the war horse of chivalry; the banner, or banneret, with the device of the chief, rose at the back of the car; sometimes several little triangular flags were mounted on its sides."—H. H. Wilson, Hindu Theatre, vol. i., p. 200, *note*.

The nymphs await his return on a mountain peak. Soon they cry—

> "Joy, sisters, joy; the king advances.
> High o'er yonder ridgy rampart dances
> The deer-emblazoned banner. See!
> The heavenly car rolls on.

Slowly the king returns, bearing in his car the fainting Urvasî, and making his way with difficulty up a rocky ascent. He restores the damsel to her companions. Their congratulations and embraces, with which they greet her, are interrupted by a noise, which is accounted by the charioteers exclaiming—

> "Sire, from the east the rushing sound is heard
> Of mighty chariots; yonder, like clouds, they roll
> Along the mountain cliffs; now there alights
> A chief in gorgeous raiment, like the blaze
> Of lightning playing on the tow'ring precipice."

This newly arrived personage is the king of the Gandharbas, come to deliver Urvasî from the *Dánava* or *Dasyu*. He is very polite to the king, and does not object to his admiration of the nymph. For the present, however, the nymphs or Apsarasas must all return to their heavenly home.

King Purûravas gazes after their vanishing forms, with his heart "full of idle dreams, inspired by idle love."

The scene of the second Act is on earth, at the city of Prayâga. Mânava, the confidential companion of the king, is in the palace garden, lamenting the trouble of having a king's secret to keep.

"Going so much into company as I do, I shall never be able to set a guard upon my tongue. I must be prudent, and will stay here by myself in this retired temple, until my royal friend comes forth from the council chamber. (*Sits down and covers his face with his hands*).

The queen's confidential attendant enters, saying to herself that her mistress, the daughter of the king of Benares, is sure that her husband is changed since his return from the regions of the sun. She perceives Mânava, and says, "if that crafty Brâhman be in the secret, I shall easily get at it. A secret can rest no longer in his breast, than morning dew on the grass."

"There he sits," she continues, "deep in thought, like a monkey in a picture."

Artfully she makes him think that the king has already betrayed his secret, and so he is led to allow that ever since the king saw the Apsaras, Urvasi, he has been out of his senses, "he not only neglects her grace, but annoys me, and spoils my dinner."

The attendant goes back to her royal mistress, and the king arrives, very dull and very silent. He says to Mânava, "What shall we do for recreation?" Mânava replies,

"Pay a visit to the kitchen."
King. "With what intent?"
Mân. "Why, the very sight of the savoury dishes in course of preparation will be sufficient to dissipate all melancholy ideas."

This proposal not being agreeable to the king, Mânava tries to make him observe the beauty of the garden, "heralding, as it were, the presence of the spring." The king replies,

"I mark it well. In the *kurureka*[1]
Behold the painted fingers of the fair
Red-tinted on the tip and edged with ebony;
Here the asoka[2] puts forth nascent buds,
Just bursting into flowers; and here the mango
Is brown with blossoms, on whose tender crests
Scant lies the fragrant down."[3]

Mânava proposes that they should repose in a "bower of

---

[1] Oleander.
[2] *Antv.* p. 164.
[3] H. H. Wilson, Hindu Theatre, vol. i., pp. 210—212.

jasmines, with its slab of black marble." Whilst enjoying this luxurious retreat, Urvasî and a companion hover around them in the air. Being themselves invisible, they overhear the king lamenting for Urvasî, longing for her presence, and calling her cold and unfeeling. Hereupon, Urvasî takes a *leaf*, and inscribing her thoughts upon it, lets it fall near Mânava, who quickly picks it up. The king only longs the more to meet "face to face, eye encountering eye." He bids Mânava take care of the leaf, which he does not; for shortly after, Urvasî became visible, and he was so fascinated, that the leaf dropped from his hands. The interview is hastily ended by a summons from above, requiring the presence of Urvasî and her companion at the palace of the Lord of air.

At this moment, the queen and her attendant enter the garden. They find the leaf, and understand the lines inscribed upon it. Going to the arbour, they hear the king saying that he is in every way unhappy. The queen steps forward and bids him be consoled, if, as she thinks, the loss of the leaf which she presents, is the cause of his distress. The king is shamefaced, and denies his interest in the leaf. The queen objects to his want of truth, and the Brâhman wag, Mânava, says to her—

"Your grace had better order dinner; that will be the most effectual remedy for his majesty's bile."

The king falls at her feet; the queen calls him an awkward penitent, and not to be trusted, and then goes off. Mânava remarks, that "her majesty has gone off in a hurry, like a river in the rains;" and, after a little talk, he says that "it is high time to bathe and eat," and the king assents, saying

" 'Tis past mid-day. Exhausted by the heat,
The peacock plunges in the scanty pool
That feeds the tall tree's root; the drowsy bee
Sleeps in the hollow chamber of the lotus,

Darkened with closing petals; on the brink
Of the now tepid lake the wild duck lurks
Amongst the sedgy shade; and even here
The parrot from his wiry bower complains,
And calls for water to allay his thirst."

And this closes the second Act.

In the third Act, the manner in which the discarded queen faced adversity, is represented. She makes a vow to forego her ornaments, and to hold a rigid fast until the moon enters the asterism Rohiní; and then on the night on which this event is expected, she sends the chamberlain to tell the king that having dismissed all anger and resentment, she is desirous of seeing him for the completion of a rite in which she is engaged. The chamberlain appears on the stage, waiting for the king, who is expected to pass that way. He declares himself thankful for the close of the day, when the "peacocks nod upon their perches, and the doves flock to the turret tops, scarcely distinguishable from the incense that flows through the lattices of the lofty chambers." The venerable servants of the inner apartments now substitute lamps for the offerings of flowers. "Ah! here comes the prince, attended by the damsel train, with flambeaux in their delicate hands." The chamberlain advances to the king, saying that the queen has expressed a wish to be honoured with his presence on the terrace of the pavilion of gems, to witness from it the entrance of the moon into the asterism Rohiní.

The king assents; and his companion, Mánava, observes the pavilion of gems is particularly lovely in the evening. "The moon is just about to rise. The east is tinged with red." When the moon appears, Mánava cries out that it is "as beautiful as a ball of almonds and sugar." The king reproves him for having thoughts, prompted by his stomach; and himself addresses the moon, as "Glorious lord of night, whose tempered fires are gleaned from solar fountains, to light the flame of holy sacrifice." . . . . . Mánava says, "Enough, sir! your grandfather bids you by me his interpreter sit, that he may repose himself." They both sit, and the train and torches are dismissed. Urvasî and her companion enter above in a celestial car, and whilst invisible to mortals, witness the ensuing scene.

The queen enters, dressed in white; flowers are her only ornaments; in her hands she bears offerings. Mânava observes, that her majesty looks very charming. The king replies: "In truth she pleases me. Thus chastely robed in modest white; her clustering tresses, decked with sacred flowers alone; her haughty mien exchanged for meek devotion." She and the king greet each other. Urvasî remarks to her aerial companion that "he pays her mighty deference."

The queen goes through the usual form of presenting the oblation of fruits, perfumes, flowers; and then paying homage to the king, says: "Hear and attest the sacred promise that I make my husband. Whatever nymph attract my lord's regard, and share with him the mutual bonds of love, I henceforth treat with kindness and complacency."

These words greatly relieve the invisible Urvasî; but the imprudent Mânava asks whether the queen has become indifferent to his majesty; and then she says, emphatically: "To promote his happiness, I have resigned my own. Does such a purpose prove him no longer dear to me?" The queen then departs, and is neither seen nor heard of more, until the close of the drama. Urvasî now becomes visible, and says playfully to the king, that he has been presented to her by the queen; and, from this time, she is looked upon as his wife and his queen.

In the fourth Act, this newly-married pair are in trouble. Urvasî had persuaded her husband to resign the cares of government, and go with her into a heavenly grove, somewhere amid the mountains. But, unhappily, whilst in each other's company, the king looked for a moment at a nymph of air, who was gambolling on the sandy shore of a river. This aroused the jealous wrath of Urvasî, and, repelling her lord, she heedlessly rushed into a "hateful grove," forbidden to females. As the penalty of this transgression, she was changed into a slender vine tree; and the frantic king thenceforward wandered about both by day and by night in searching his lost bride throughout the forest. He comes on to the stage, which represents a part of the forest, with his dress disordered, and his general appearance indicative of insanity; he sings,

> "The lonely cygnet breasts the flood
> Without his mate, in mournful mood.
> His ruffled plumage drooping lies,
> And trickling tears suffuse his eyes."

For a moment, he mistakes a cloud for a demon; then cooling raindrops fall, he faints, revives, and sings again,

> "I madly thought a fiend conveyed
> Away from me my fawn-eyed maid:
> 'Twas but a cloud that rained above,
> With the young lightning for its love."

He entreats the clouds to help him; then suddenly determines to assert his kingly power, and to bid the seasons stay their course. (Sings).

> "The tree of heaven invites the breeze,
> And all its countless blossoms glow.
> They dance upon the gale; the bees
> With sweets inebriate, murmuring low
> Soft music lend, and gushes strong
> The koil's deep, thick, warbling song."

Then feeling that all nature attests his kingly state, for a moment he exults. But this mood is quickly succeeded by despondency, and he exclaims, "What have I to do with pomp and kingly pride? My sole sad business to thread the woods in search of my beloved." (He sings).

"'The monarch of the woods,
With slow desponding gait,
Wanders through vales and floods,
And rocks and forest bowers,
Gemmed with new springing flowers,
And mourns heart-broken for his absent mate."

In his anxiety to obtain tidings, he determines to enquire of a peacock, which he sees perched on a jutting crag.

"Bird of the dark-blue throat, and eye of jet,
Oh! tell me have you seen the lovely face
Of my fair bride? lost in this dreary wilderness."[1]

The peacock shows no sympathy, and the king proceeds. (Music is heard continually).

"Yonder (sings the king) amid the thick and shady branches
Of the broad *jambu*,[2] cowers the koïl: faint
Her flame of passion in the hotter breath
Of noon. She of the birds is wisest famed—
I will address her.

"Say, nursling of a stranger nest—
Say, hast thou chanced my love to see,
Amidst these gardens of the blest,
Wandering at liberty;
Or, warbling with a voice divine,
Melodious strains more sweet than thine."

He entreats this bird, "whom lovers deem love's messenger," to lead his steps to where she strays. And then, as if the koïl had spoken, he turns to his left, saying:

---

[1] H. H. Wilson, Hindu Theatre, vol. i., p. 246.

[2] Rose-apple, with flowers similar to the myrtle.

"Why did she leave
One so devoted to her will? In wrath
She left me? but the cause of anger lives not
In my imagination. The fond tyranny
That women exercise o'er those who love them,
Brooks not the slightest shew of disregard.
How, now; the bird has flown. 'Tis even thus—
All coldly listen to another's sorrows."

For a moment he thinks he hears the sweet chime of his "fair one's anklets." But it is merely the cry of the swan, preparing for periodic flight. To the chief of the troop of swans he addresses the same enquiry. The walk of the swan is much admired by Hindu poets, and the king means nothing ludicrous when he says to the swan—

"Why seek to veil the truth? If my beloved
Was never seen by thee, as graceful straying
Along the flowery borders of the lake,
Then whence this elegant gait? 'Tis hers; and thou
Hast stolen it from her; in whose every step
Love sports. Thy walk betrays thee; own thy crime,
And lead me quickly to her (*laughs*). Nay, he fears
Our royal power—the plunderer flies the king."

Other birds, and bees, and lotus flowers attract his attention. "I will hence," he cries.

"Beneath the shade of yon kadamba tree
The royal elephant reclines, and with him
His tender mate. I will approach; yet, hold!
From his companion he accepts the bough
Her trunk has snapp'd from the balm-breathing tree,
Now rich with teeming shoots and juicy fragrance."

At length he perceives a gem, "more roseate than the blush

of the asoka blossom." He is unwilling to take the jewel, because she whose brow it should have adorned is far away. A voice in the air bids him take up the gem,—for it has wondrous virtue. Let it adorn his hand, and he will shortly cease to mourn his absent bride. He obeys; and immediately he feels a strange emotion, as he gazes on a vine;—no blossoms deck the boughs. "No bees regale her with their songs; silent and sad, she lonely shows the image of his repentant love, who now laments her causeless indignation." He presses the "melancholy likeness to his heart,"—and the vine changes into Urvasî. After affectionate explanations and expressions of delight at their reunion, they return to the city which "mourns its absent lord," making "a cloud their downy car, to waft them swiftly on their way." Music is heard, and the invisible voice, or chorus, sings:

> "The ardent swan his mate recovers,
> And all his spirit is delight;
> With her aloft in air he hovers,
> And homeward wings his joyous flight."

And then, on an English stage, no more would be expected. The finale has been brilliant; and the future life of the chief actors may be imagined. But the Sanskrit dramatist gives another Act, in which it is explained rather lengthily, that when the king, and his queen Urvasî, return to Prayâga, his old friend Mânava rejoices, because he finds the king "once more attentive to his royal duties and the cares of State," but, he thinks, out of spirits,—and wonders what should be the cause; for, "except the want of children, he has nothing to grieve for." "This," he observes, "is a bustling day. The king and the queen have just performed their royal ablutions, where the Yamunâ (Jumna) and the Ganges meet: he must be at his toilet by this time, and by joining him I shall secure a share of the flowers and perfumes prepared for him." A noise is heard behind the scenes, with cries of, "the ruby! the ruby!" It appears that a hawk had carried off the ruby of reunion. The king, in haste, demands his bow; but the bird has already flown too far away. He commands that it be tracked to its perch; and, whilst all are in excitement and confusion, the chamberlain enters with an arrow and the jewel: the shaft of a forester had performed the king's bidding. The king looks eagerly at the arrow to see the name inscribed on it. Mânava says: "What does your Majesty study so earnestly?" The king replies: "Listen to the words inscribed: 'The arrow of the all-subduing Ayus, the son of Urvasi and Purûravas.'" The king is in amazement, because, excepting for the period of the Naimisha sacrificial rite, Urvasi has always been with him. He does, however, remember that, for a transient period, "her soft cheek was paler than the leaf, cold-nipped, and shrivelled." Mânava tells him that he must not suppose that nymphs of heaven manage these matters in the fashion of those on earth; and then, whilst yet they are talking, a saintly dame and a young lad from the hermitage of the Rishi Chyavana are announced. The likeness of the lad to the king at once identifies him. The saintly dame addresses the king, saying: "This princely youth, the son of Urvasi, was for some cause confided, without your knowledge, to my secret care. The ceremonies suited to his martial birth have been duly performed by the pious Chyavana, who has given him the knowledge fitted to his station, and has trained him to the use of arms." But now, she adds, "my charge expires; for an act, this day achieved, unfits him to remain one of the peaceful hermitage: this act was,—shooting the hawk, which 'deed of blood excludes him from our haunts:'" therefore, by the sage's order she has now conducted him to Urvasi. The king sends for his queen, Urvasi, who recognises her boy; and they are all too much affected to think of explanations, until the "saintly dame" is gone. Then Urvasi weeps violently, remembering, that when love for the king induced her to leave the courts of heaven, she had been warned, that so soon as the king should see a son of hers, she must return. From fear of this, she had kept her infant's birth concealed. If, indeed, Urvasî must again be torn from him, the king says he will live in the woods, and resign the throne to his son. All present express grief, when, suddenly, the divine Nârada descends upon the stage, and announces that Indra commands him to forego his purpose of ascetic sorrow. Hostilities in heaven are predicted, when the gods will need his prowess; but he promises—

"Urvasî shall be through life united
With thee in heavenly bonds."

Nârada now assists at the inauguration of Ayus, as vice-king. Nymphs descend from heaven, with a golden vase of water from the Ganges, a throne, and other paraphernalia. The rite being concluded, a chorus is heard without, invoking blessings upon Ayus:

"Son of the monarch the universe filling,
Son of the god of the mist-shedding night,
Son of the sage, whom the great Brahma, willing,
Called, with creation, to life and to light."

A second chorus follows, celebrating the sceptre and sway which the father has won:

"And brighter than ever the radiance is streaming,
Enhanced and confirmed by the fame of the son:
So Ganga descends from the peaks of the mountain,
That shine with the light of unperishing snows;
And mighty,—meandering far from their fountain,—
In the breast of the ocean the waters repose."

Urvasî bids her child come and offer to the queen, his elder mother, filial homage. No other allusion is made to the first wife. The last words of the drama are the following curious benediction from the king:

> "May learning and prosperity oppose
> No more each other, as their wont, as foes;
> But, in a friendly bond together twined,
> Ensure the real welfare of mankind."

Bodhisattwas, or Yoginis.—Page 215.
From a picture in the caves at Ajanta.

CHAPTER XXX.

(DRAMA, CONTINUED.)

MALATI and Mâdhava is the title of the play of which we now propose to give a short account. It is written by Bhavabhûti, a dramatist whose popularity rivalled that of Kâlidâsa. He was born in Berar, to the south of the Vindhya Hills, and was a member of the tribe of Brâhmans who pretend to trace their descent from the sage Kasyapa, some of whom are said still to be found in the vicinity of Condavir.[1] The name Srikantha, meaning, "he, in whose throat eloquence resides," was bestowed

[1] H. H. Wilson, Hindu Theatre, vol. ii., Introduction, p. 8.

upon him by his countrymen. Professor Wilson also bears testimony to the "extraordinary beauty and power of his language," and attributes his peculiar talent for describing "Nature in her magnificence" to his "early familiarity with the eternal mountains and forests of Gondwana."

The play of Mâlatî and Mâdhava is one of the few which shares with Sakuntalâ the honour of being still occasionally read by Pandits. It represents a time at which the temples of Siva and Kâma were generally frequented, although Buddhists and Buddhist schools and convents were still powerful. The story is, that two school companions of high rank pledged each other that, so soon as their respective children should be of the right age, they should be married. The father of the girl is prime minister to the king of Padmâvatî, supposed to be Ougein, at which place the scene of the play is laid. The father of the boy is the prime minister of a neighbouring kingdom, to the south of Ougein. In preparation for the intended marriage, the boy, or young man, is sent to study logic in a Buddhist college at Padmâvatî, or Ougein, the city in which resided the future bride and her father, then its prime minister.

The head of the college, or convent, is a woman who had been nurse to the lovely Mâlatî. She is, of course, a Buddhist,—good and conscientious, clever and scheming; and by her the whole plot of the drama is worked out. This woman is ardently attached to both hero and heroine. She loves Mâlatî because she nursed her, and Mâdhava because he is her pupil; and the two fathers having confided to her their intentions, she promotes the love-making, and removes all obstacles with the utmost zeal and ingenuity.

When the play opens, Mâlatî is already in love with Mâdhava. He had been purposely pointed out to her by her maidens, as he passed frequently along the road beside her father's palace. But Mâdhava had not yet seen Mâlatî. She sat above, concealed by curtains, or blinds, or the shade of a balcony. It is now contrived that Mádhava shall go to a festival, to be held at early dawn in the Garden of Love, at which Málati and her train are to attend. Mádhava gives an account of what happens to a friend. "So advised," he says, "I went to Kámadeva's temple, where I strayed, till weary. I reclined beside a fountain that laves the roots of a stately tree, whose clustering blossoms wooed the wanton bees." ..... Presently, a beautiful damsel issued from the temple, and, drawing near to the tree under which the youth reclined, began to collect its fragrant blossoms. After the lady and her train had retired, Mádhava was found by his constant friend Makaranda, all disarrayed, and heaving frequent sighs. "'Tis strange," he says; "my vagrant thoughts no more return to me: deserting shame, or self-respect, or fortitude, or judgment, they dwell perverse upon one idea,—the lovely image of the moon-faced maid." His friend quickly understands his condition, and persuades him to confess.

Amongst other remarks, he says that the damsel drew his heart "like a rod of the iron-stone gem;" making it "seem possible," says Professor H. H. Wilson, "that artificial magnets, as well as the properties of the loadstone, were known to the Hindus." Mádhava felt certain that he was an object of interest to the young lady; and, from the expression of her lotus eyes, "half-averted from his answering gaze," he hoped that she might be in love with him.

> "Incredulous of my happiness, I sought
> To mark her passion, nor display my own,
> Though every limb partook the fond emotion.
> Thence I resumed my task, and wove my wreath,
> Seeming intent, till she at length withdrew,
> Attended by her maidens and a guard
> Of eunuchs, armed with staves and javelins.
> A stately elephant received the princess,
> And bore her towards the city."

Before she had departed, one of her maidens came back, and

under the pretence of gathering more flowers, prevailed upon him to give her the wreath he was weaving, telling him for whom she wanted it,—thus making him acquainted with the rank of the lovely lady, of whom he continues conversing until noon, when his friend observes, the "monarch of a thousand beams" now darts his hottest rays; 'tis noon, let us go home. Mádhava assents, saying:

> "The day's warm influence surely washes off
> The careful labours of the morning toilet
> And steals those sandal marks, so neatly laid
> In graceful lines across the flowery cheek.
> Play o'er my limbs, ye soft, refreshing breezes!
> Whose previous homage has been paid to beauty,
> And wrap in soft embrace my fair one's charms,—
> Diffusing o'er her form the honeyed fragrance
> Shook from the jasmine's scarce-unfolded blossom."

The friend deplores the change which the god of love is working on Mádhava, looking already like a young elephant when a prey to fever. The only hope for his friend is, Kámandakí, the Buddhist priestess, already mentioned. Mádhava sighs, and cries:

> "Where'er I turn, the same loved charms appear;
> Bright as the golden bud of the young lotus gleams her
>   beauteous face,
> Though oft averted from my fond regards."

> "Alas! my friend" (he continues), "this fascination spreads
> O'er all my senses, and a feverish flame
> Consumes my strength; my heart is all on fire;
> My mind is toss'd with doubt, and every faculty
> In one fond thought absorbed; I cease to be
> Myself, or conscious of the thing I am."

And so concludes the first Act. The second Act is occupied

with tender sentiments, and the grief of Mâlatî, because the king wishes her to marry a worthless favourite of his, named Nandana, and Mâlatî's father prefers ambition to his daughter's happiness. The third Act continues the same strain. The Buddhist Kâmandakî, who had been Mâlatî's nurse, says:

> "Poor girl! . . . . . she seeks
> To win me to her; mournfully she pines
> When I am absent; brightens in my presence;
> Whispers her secret thoughts to me; presents me
> With costly gifts. When I depart, she clings
> Around my neck, and only lets me leave her
> When I have vowed repeatedly return.
> Then on my knee she sits, and bids me tell her
> Again the stories of the nymphs that loved:
> And questions o'er and o'er, with flimsy plea,
> Their fate and conduct; then she silent pauses,
> As lost in meditation." . . . . .

Mâlatî herself comes in saying (apart):

> "Alas! my father loves his child no more,
> But offers her a victim to ambition."

A friend tries to comfort her, bidding her taste

> "The freshness of the breeze that sweeps the blossoms,
> And wafts around the champaka's perfume,
> Breathing melodious with the buzz of bees
> That cluster in the buds; and with the song
> The koil warbles thick and hurried forth,
> As on the flow'ry mango's top he sits,
> And, all inebriate with its nectar, sings.
> The garden gale comes wooingly, to sip
> The drops ambrosial from thy moonlike face.
> Come on, those shades invite us."

Mâdhava enters the garden unobserved. On perceiving the

"pious dame," the Buddhist Kámandakí, his heart is filled with such joy as that with which "the pea-fowl hails the flash that heralds the approaching shower." But on discovering that his beloved Málatí is also present, he exclaims, "'Tis she!"

> "'Tis Málatí! Ah, me! a sudden chill
> Pervades my heart and freezes every faculty,
> To marble turned by her moon-beaming countenance,
> Like mountains ice-bound by the gelid ray
> Shot on their summits from the lunar gem.
> How lovely she appears, as o'er her frame,
> Like a fast-fading wreath, soft languor steals."[1]

In the fourth Act it is publicly announced that the king gives Málatí as a bride to his friend Nandana. In the fifth Act we are introduced to Saiva-worship, in its terrific form. A dreadful priest of the goddess Chámundá kidnaps Málatí as a victim to the goddess. She is carried to the temple; but it so happened that Mádhava, in despair at the king's opposition to his marriage, had resorted to this temple, in the hope of obtaining his bride by the help of "horrid mysteries." He hears the plaintive voice of Málatí, and sees the priest running round quickly, as in worship. The priest thus addresses Chámundá, as the consort of Siva:

> "Hail! hail, Chámundá, mighty goddess, hail!
> I glorify thy sport, when in the dance
> That fills the court of Siva with delight,
> Thy foot, descending, fills the earthly globe;
> Beneath the weight the broad-backed tortoise reels;
> The egg of Brahmá trembles at the shock;
> And in a yawning chasm, that gapes like hell,
> The sevenfold main tumultuously rushes.
> The elephant hide that robes thee, to thy steps

[1] H. H. Wilson, Hindu Theatre, vol. ii. pp. 39, 40.

Swings to and fro; the whirling talons rend
The crescent on thy brow; from the torn orb
The trickling nectar falls; and every skull
That gems thy necklace laughs with horrid life."[1]

Just as the priest raises his sword to sacrifice Málatí, Mádhava rushes forward and snatches her up in his arms. Whilst he parleys with the guests, a noise is heard behind the scenes,—the watchful Makaranda had raised an alarm and sent help. Málatí is carried away, whilst Mádhava fights with the terrible chief, and kills him.

The sixth Act opens with preparations for the marriage, which the king still commands, of Málatí to his friend, the odious Nandana.

A hollow murmur comes on the ear, like that of rushing clouds; and, as the procession comes nearer, drums that peal in joy, drown every other sound. "White umbrellas float like trembling lotuses in the lake of the atmosphere." "Banners undulate like waves, as they play before the wind of the Chowris, which hover about like swans. The elephants advance, their golden bells tinkling as they stride. They are mounted by merry bevies of damsels, singing songs of rejoicing, uttered indistinctly, as interrupted by the betel, which perfumes their mouths, and blazing like rays of light with glittering jewels." And these jewels, the author further remarks, were of variegated tints, as if they were portions of Indra's bow. As Málatí herself draws near, we are told that the throng of attendants fall off to a respectful distance, and keep back the crowd with staves, covered with silver and gold. Her elephant, painted with vermilion, resembles the ruddy dawn, or with the twenty-seven pearls on her brow, looks like the brilliant night; whilst Málatí herself,

---

[1] Professor Wilson observes, that the bride of Siva is here invested with a garb, ornaments and attributes, similar to those of Siva himself, or to those of Káli.

in her deep grief, appears like "some fair plant just budding into flower, but withered at the core."

Having arrived at the temple of Srí, the elephant kneels, and Málatí, with the priestess and her friend, Lavangiká, descends. When they are all hidden within the temple, and Mádhava and his friend Makaranda had joined them by appointment, she explains her scheme, and bids Mádhava's friend disguise himself in the bridal costume sent for Málatí. The corset of white silk, the red muslin mantle, the necklace, the sandal, and the chaplet of flowers are placed upon him, whilst the priestess sends her dear children, Mádhava and Málatí, to the pavilion in her convent garden.

The scene of the seventh Act is the palace of Nandana, to which the pretended bride had been brought. Nandana does not discover the trick; but finding that the bride cannot be propitiated by coaxing, he handles her roughly, and gets such treatment in return, that tears of pain and vexation starts from his eyes, and with speech inarticulate from fury, he leaves the apartments, vowing that he would have nothing more to say to so ill-mannered a girl.

In the seventh Act, we find Málatí and Mádhava sitting together in the grove, to which their Buddhist mother, the priestess, Kámandakí, had sent them. Mádhava praises the gentle moonlight gleams, "pale as the palm's sear leaf," and "the grateful fragrance of the *Ketaki*."[1] He sees that Málatí is frightened, and tries to win her confidence. But her ideas of propriety are such, that she will not even speak to him, and so she sits in loving coy reserve, until news is brought that the city guard is in pursuit of the audacious make-believe bride, Makaranda. Mádhava rushes off to help his friend, and immediately a priest from the dreadful temple of Chámundá captures Málatí. In the next, the eighth Act, we are told that Makaranda, aided by Mádhava, performed prodigies of valour; and that the conflict was only ended by the interposition of the king's attendants,

[1] The Sanskrit name for the strongly-scented Pandamus odoratissimus.

who took the two young heroes into his majesty's presence. As they stood before him on his terrace, his eye dwelt with complacency on their lovely countenances; and, turning to his minister and Nandana, who stood nigh, their faces as black as ink with rage and disappointment, he asked them very condescendingly whether they could not be contented with such kinsmen, "ornaments of the world, eminent in worth and descent, and handsome as the new moon."[1] So saying, the king withdrew, and Mâdhava and Makaranda were dismissed, and went back with all speed to the convent garden, in which they had left the objects of their affections. But the garden was deserted; Mâlatî was gone, no one knew whither; and the good Kâmandakî was away seeking her. This trial was too great for Mâdhava, and "unable to endure the scenes where late his Mâlatî was lost," he wandered forth, attended by his ever faithful friend, and roamed amid the rugged paths and rocky valleys of the Vindhya Mountains.

The ninth Act introduces us to the scenery of these hills. A Buddhist Yoginî comes upon the stage, flying through the air. In Buddhist works, we learn that a certain proficiency in asceticism conferred upon the proficient this power; and we are now introduced to a disciple of the good priestess, Kâmandakî, who had, by long continued austerities, obtained this privilege. Her name is Saudâminî; she has been flying to the royal city, Padmâvatî; and, after learning the state of affairs amongst those in whom she was interested, she is now pursuing the steps of the unhappy Mâdhava. She alights upon the mountain, and describes the scene in view.

"How wide the prospect spreads. Mountain and rock,
Town, villages and woods, and glittering streams.
There, where the Pârâ and the Sindhu wind,
The towers and temples, pinnacles and gates.

[1] H. H. Wilson, Hindu Theatre, vol. ii., p. 91.

And spires of Padmavati, like a city
Precipitated from the skies, appear,
Inverted in the pure translucent wave.
There flows Lavana's frolic stream, whose groves,
By early rains refreshed, afford the youth
Of Padmávati pleasant haunts, and where
Upon the herbage brightening in the shower,
The heavy-uddered kine contented browze.
Hark! how the banks of the broad Sindhu fall,
Crashing, in the undermining current,
Like the loud voice of thunder-laden clouds.
The sound extends; and, like Heramba's roar,
As deepened by the hollow-echoing caverns,
It floats, reverberating round the hills.
These mountains, coated by thick clustering woods
Of fragrant sandal and the ripe mílûra,
Recall to memory the lofty mountains
That southward stretch, where the Godaveri
Impetuous flashes through the dark, deep shade
Of skirting forests, echoing to her fury,
Where meets the Sindhu and the Madhumati,
The holy fane of Swarnavindu rises,
Lord of Bhaváni, whose illustrious image
Is not of mortal fabric. *(Bowing)*. Hail! all hail!
Creator of the universal world. Bestower
Of all good gifts. Source of the sacred Vedas;
God of the crescent-crested diadem. Destroyer
Of love's presumptuous power. Eldest lord,
And teacher of mankind, all glory be to thee!"[1]

Saudáminí was not only a pupil of the Buddhist, Kámandakí, but is praised for "exceeding a Bodhisatwa,"[2]—a person endowed with miraculous powers. That she should invoke Siva as creator of the world, and offer homage at a Sivaite temple, is therefore noteworthy, but quite in accordance with evidence from other

---

[1] H. H. Wilson, Hindu Theatre, vol. ii. pp. 95 ff., and *note*, p. 107.

[2] H. H. Wilson, Hindu Theatre, vol. ii., p. 117, *note*.

sources, that belief in Siva was adopted by Buddhists before their expulsion from India.[1]

Before quitting her perch upon the mountain, Saudáminí further describes the objects immediately around her.

> "The mountain is, in truth, a grateful scene.
> The peaks are blackened with new dropping clouds,
> And pleased the pea-fowl shriek along the groves.
> The ponderous rocks upbear the tangled bowers,
> Where countless nests give brightness to the gloom.
> The inarticulate whine of the young bears
> Hisses and mutters through the caverned hills;
> And cool, and sharp, and sweet, the incense spreads,
> Shed from the boughs the elephant's tusk has sundered."

It is noon. Birds cease to feed on acid fruit, and seek for shade or water, whilst lower down,

> "Amidst the woods, the wild fowl make reply
> To the soft murmuring of the mournful dove."

She goes off to find the unhappy youths, assures Mádhava that Málatí is living; and, by a continued exertion of the "powerful knowledge," with which "mystic rites and prayers, devout observance, and a sainted teacher," have endowed her, all things end happily; and, the actors being all assembled, the play concludes with the following speech from Mádhava, addressed to his preceptress, the Buddhist, Kámandakí.

Mad. (*bowing*). "My happiness henceforth is perfect: all
   The wish I cherish more, is this; and may
   Your favour, holy dame, grant it fruition.

---

[1] Professor Wilson cannot determine the site of Padmávatí. At one time, he inclined to identify it with Ougein; but it is placed too near the mountains, whilst the confluence of streams near Ougein is five miles distant. He thinks it probable that the Padmávatí described, may lie further south in the modern Arungabad or Berar, and that the poet may have intended it for Padmanagara, his own birth-place.

"Still may the virtuous be exempt from error,
And fast to virtue cling. May monarchs, merciful
And firm in equity, protect the earth;
May, in due season, from the labouring clouds
The fertile showers descend:—and may the people,
Blest in their friends, their kindred, and their children,
Unknowing want, live cheerful and content."

Professor Wilson observes, that the language of this drama is in general of extraordinary beauty, and that it is "free from the verbal quibbling and extravagance of combination which the compositions of the time of Bhoja offer," although he thinks that it only just escapes these faults. It has undoubtedly many merits, but we do not find in it the beauty, grace, or humour, which characterize the plays of an earlier period.

"Those who are skilled in charms and potent signs, may handle fearlessly the fiercest snakes."—Page 222.

CHAPTER XXXI.

Manœuvres and characters of Brahmanical ministers of kings.—Chandragupta, of the Takshaka or Serpent race, supersedes the Nandas.

THE drama, entitled Mudrâ-Râkshasa, is attributed to Visâ-khadatta, about whom nothing appears to be known. The time chosen is that at which Chandragupta has just succeeded in obtaining the throne of Pâtaliputra, or Patna. Chandragupta has been identified with the Sandracottus who visited the camp of Alexander the Great,—a circumstance of material moment to the chronology of India. He was at that time, apparently, a wandering adventurer. Nine brothers, called the nine Nandas, reigned at Patna. Chandragupta was looked upon as their half-brother by a Sûdra mother. He is called a Takshaka, or descendant of the great Snake Seshanâga. Feeling unsafe amongst his relatives in Behar, he had wandered forth to seek his fortune elsewhere. It so happened that he met with a clever, ambitious, intriguing Bráhman, named Chánakya, who became his ardent friend, and promised to open for him a pathway to the throne of Patna. In pursuance of this intention, Chánakya contrived to give dire offence to the nine Nandas. He entered their dining hall unannounced, and with the cool assumption of a powerful Bráhman, took possession of the place of honour. The kings, having "their understanding bewildered by fate," regarded him as a mere wild scholar; and, not heeding the remonstrances of their wise minister, they dragged him from his seat with scorn.

Then Chánakya, blind with indignation, stood up in the centre of the hall, loosened the knot of hair on the top of his head, and thus vowed the destruction of the Nanda race.[1]

"Until I have exterminated these haughty and ignorant Nandas, who have not known my worth, I will not again tie up these hairs"

Having thus declared war, he sought out the discontented wanderer, Chandragupta.

In the meantime, Rákshasa, who was the prime minister of the Nandas, did all for his princes that could be done, either by valour or sagacity. But all in vain, the Nandas "perished like moths in the flame of Chánakya's revenge."

This play differs from those by Kálidása and Bhavabhúti. It gives no love passages or pious reflections, and it describes neither flowers nor scenery. But it has the stir and action of city life; the endless ingenuity of political and court intrigue, and the staunch "fidelity which appears as the uniform characteristic of servants, emissaries and friends, a singular feature in the Hindu character," which, Professor Wilson remarks, "it has not yet wholly lost."

In the prelude, the manager enters his house, saying, "How

---

[1] H. H. Wilson, Hindu Theatre, vol. ii., p. 145.

now! what festival have we here to-day, that all the domestics are so busy? One is bringing water, another grinding perfumes, a third weaves a chaplet of many colours, and a fourth is sighing over a pestle. I must call one of them, and ask the meaning of all this. Here, you clever, sharp, sensible, hussey, come hither; you sum of all wishes and decorum, come hither." An actress comes forward and tells him that there is an eclipse of the moon, and that Brâhmans have been invited. He doubts the eclipse, and whilst they are talking, angry tones behind the scenes betoken that Chânakya or "*Kautilya*, crooked in nature as in name," is coming, and they escape.

Chânakya enters with his top-knot untied, in sign of wrath. Gradually the angry man opens his mind to the audience.

> " 'Tis known to all the world,
> I vowed the death of Nanda, and I slew him.
> The current of a vow will work its way,
> And cannot be resisted. What is done
> Is spread abroad, and I no more have power
> To stop the tale. Why should I? Be it known,
> The fires of my wrath alone expire,
> Like the fierce conflagration of a forest,
> From lack of fuel—not from weariness "

But although he has rooted out the stem of Nanda, his work is incomplete, so long as the faithful minister, Râkshasa, remains. He then reveals some of his manœuvres.

> " I have my spies abroad—they roam the realm,
> In various garb disguised; in various tongues
> And manners skilled, and prompt to wear the shew
> Of zeal to either party, as need serves."

Some of his agents "keep unwearied watch to baffle those who would administer envenomed drafts and viands to the king." One disguised as a Bauddha mendicant, has obtained the confidence of Rákshasa. Chânakya retires, and one of his agents comes upon the stage, carrying a kind of raree-show. This man's entrance is objected to by the attendants; but Chânakya overhears his discourse and comes forward, with a welcome recognition, asking for news of what the citizens say, and how they stand affected. The answer is, that all grievances are removed, and that men in general, are well affected towards the new king, but that three yet remain who are personally attached to Rákshasa. The first is the Bauddha mendicant, the foe in disguise. The second, Sakata Dâsa, a scribe. The third a jeweller, Chandana Dâsa, with whom Rákshasa left his wife and child, whilst obliged himself to fly from the city.

The second Act opens with an amusing scene in the street, in front of Rákshasa's house, where we find Virâdha, an agent of Rákshasa, disguised as a snake-catcher.

Virâdha. "Those who are skilled in charms and potent signs, may handle fearlessly the fiercest snakes."
Passenger. "Hola! what and who are you?"
Virâdha. "A snake-catcher, your honour; my name is *Jirnarisha*. What say you, you would touch my snakes? What may your profession be, pray? Oh! I see, a servant of the prince,—you had better not meddle with snakes. A snake-catcher, unskilled in charms and antidotes, a man mounted on a furious elephant without a goad, and a servant of the king appointed to a high station, and proud of his success, these three are on the eve of destruction. Oh! he is off."
Second Passenger. "What have you got in your basket, fellow."
Virâdha. "Tame snakes, your honour, by which I get my living. Would you wish to see them? I will exhibit them here, in the court of this house, as this is not a convenient spot."
Second Passenger. "This, you blockhead, is the house of Rákshasa, the prince's minister; there is no admittance for us here."
Virâdha. "Then go your way, sir: by the authority of my occupation, I shall make bold to enter. So, I have got rid of him."

Virâdha then changes his language from the Prâkrit vernacular to Sanskrit, and makes a soliloquy. He thinks it strange that all the efforts of his master, Rákshasa, to shake the power of Chandragupta fail, defeated by Chánakya's foresight, *and so forth*.

The next scene shews us Rákshasa in an apartment, with attendants, sighing that his "anxious days and sleepless nights are all of no avail." After a time, he is informed that a snake-catcher wishes to see him. He feels his left eye throb,—an unlucky omen,—and says:

"I have no pleasure in the exhibition;
Give him a donation, and let him go."

Attendant. Here is for your pains; for not seeing—not for seeing.

Virádha. Inform the minister, I beg of you, that besides exhibiting snakes, I am a bit of a poet in the vulgar tongue. If I cannot have the honour of seeing him, request he will favour me by perusing this."

The verses he presents show that he is the bearer of news, and procure him an immediate audience. The pretended snake-charmer then gives a history of various schemes intended for the destruction of the usurping king, Chandragupta; but the wily Chánakya, he adds, had been ever on the alert, and each scheme of destruction had recoiled upon Rákshasa. The last plot, he says, was to conceal brave men in an underground passage, which led to the king's sleeping apartment, intending that they should kill him whilst he slept; but the watchful minister observed a line of ants come through the crevice in the wall, and noticed that they bore the fragments of a recent meal, and inferring the presence of men in concealment, he commanded the pavilion to be set on fire, and "our brave friends were all destroyed."

Rákshasa. " 'Tis ever thus. Fortune in all befriends
The cruel Chandragupta. When I send
A messenger of certain death to slay him,
She wields the instrument against his rival." . . .

Vir. "Yet let us on, Sir. What is once begun
Is not to be abandoned. Obstacles foreseen
Deter the poor of spirit from an enterprise.
Some, more adventurous, but not all resolved,
Commence, and stop midway; but noble minds
Like thine, by difficulties warned, defy
Repeated checks, and in the end prevail.
A weary burden is the cumbrous earth
On Sesha's head, but still he bears the load.
Day after day the same fatiguing course
The sun pursues, yet still he travels on."

At the end of the second Act, Rákshasa sends to a minstrel, living at Pushpapura (Patna), bidding him sing verses at the palace, tending to make the king believe that Chânakya has been shewing contempt to his authority.

The third Act represents the palace. The king appears lamenting his fate.

Chand. "Fortune makes kings her sport, and vain the hope
To fix the fickle wanton in her faith.
She flies the violent, disdains the mild,
Despises fools, the wise she disregards;
Derides the cowardly, and dreads the brave.
My honoured minister and friend commands me
To wear the semblance of displeasure towards him,
And rule awhile without his guiding aid."

Having finished his remarks, he mounts the terrace, and discourses on the beauty of the night.

Chand. "How beauteous are the skies at this soft season!
Midst fleecy clouds, like scattered isles of sand,
Upon whose breast the white heron hovers, flows
In dark blue tides the many-channelled stream;
And like the lotus blossoms, that unfold
Their petals to the night, the stars expand.
Below is *Gangá* by the autumn led,

> Fondly impatient, to her ocean lord,
> Tossing her waves as if offended pride,
> And pining fretful at the lengthened way.
> But how is this? as city-wards I gaze,
> I mark no note of preparation
> That speaks the festive time." . . . . .

The king is told that Chânakya has countermanded his sovereign's orders, and forbidden festivities. The king sends for him.

Chânakya replies,

> "'Tis craft that snares the monarch of the woods,
> And stratagem alone must win us Râkshasa."[1]

Chandragupta goes on taunting Chânakya with every scheme that had failed, until the irascible Brâhman cries out

> " I understand you;—you would seek
> To trample on me as a slave. My hand
> Hurries to set my braided locks at liberty,
> And my impatient foot again would stamp
> The confirmation of a second vow.
> Beware how you arouse those slumbering flames
> That Nanda's fall has scarcely yet appeased."

Although this scene had been in a measure pre-arranged, the king feels frightened, wondering whether Chânakya's anger is real. He observes, that his eye is "embrowned with lowering wrath," and "the brows above are curved into a withering frown." Chânakya throws down his ministerial sword, telling the king that if Râkshasa is better worthy trust, it is to him he should give the sign of office.

The next scene shews us Chânakya seated in his own house,

---

[1] H. H. Wilson, Hindu Theatre, vol. ii., p. 303.

saying to himself, that however Rákshasa may persist in striving to thwart his schemes, it will be in vain. He forgets, he says, that Chandragupta is not Nanda, cursed with evil counsellors, and that Rákshasa is far from being Chánakya's equal!" Being summoned to the palace, he ascends the terrace, and king Chandragupta throws himself at the feet of the minister, Chánakya.

The manner in which the Bráhman minister accepts this homage, is quite oriental.

> *Chán.* "Arise, my son,
> And may thy regal feet absorb the beams
> Shot from a thousand diadems, as bend
> Before thee in subjection and humility
> The crowned brows of tributary kings—
> Whether they sway the shores of southern seas,
> Whose depths are rich with many coloured gems,
> Or rule the realms where Ganga falls in showers,
> Cold on Himala's ice-encrusted brow."

The bards come and sing verses, as arranged, tending to incite the king's jealousy against Chánakya. The king reproaches him for not having succeeded in every point, and especially because he had allowed Rákshasa to remain at large in the capital.

In the fourth Act, we see Rákshasa lying on his couch, tormented by headache.

> *Rák.* "It will not be—sleep flies me—nor the change
> Of night or day, short intermission brings
> From watchful care; whilst fate continues adverse,
> And aids the crooked projects of Chánakya.
> Such task is mine, as on dramatic bard
> Devolves, to fix the object of the action,
> Develope fitting incidents, uprear
> Fruit unexpected from self-pregnant seeds,
> Dilate, condense, perplex, and last reduce
> The various acts to one auspicious close."

From which reflections we infer that Rákshasa was probably more fitted for literary than for political life. The plots drag on rather wearily, until Rákshasa is subdued, and offers his own life in lieu of that of a friend. This was the point at which Chánakya had been aiming. Rákshasa yields to the "vile Chánakya." "Rather," he says aside, "to the *wise* Chánakya— an exhaustless mine of learning—a deep ocean, stored with gems of richest excellence." This accomplished Chánakya offers homage to Rákshasa. The king enters, and expresses admiration of his holy patron Chánakya's genius. Chánakya bids him salute Rákshasa, "hereditary councillor of his imperial house," and offers to his late enemy the ministerial sword. After some hesitation, Rákshasa yields, and takes it. Chánakya says to Chandragupta, "Fate, prince, is now made sure." Rákshasa's defeated allies are pardoned; and his dearest friend, the goldsmith, Chandana Dása, instead of being executed, is made provost of the merchants.

Professor Wilson makes some interesting remarks on the character of the two statesmen, both of whom belong to the depraved school of politics. Each minister is invested with dignity, "an effect produced in a great measure by shewing them wholly unmindful of personal advantages. Chánakya has to fulfil a vow, but, that accomplished, relinquishes rank and power; and Rákshasa, whilst he pursues Chandragupta with hostility, seeks only to revenge the death of his former sovereign, without the thought of acquiring fortune or dignity for himself." The two characters display, however, considerable individuality. Chánakya is violent and inexorable; Rákshasa gentle and relenting. Chánakya's ruling principle is pride of caste; Rákshasa's, attachment to his friends and sovereign. Chánakya revenges wrongs done to himself; Rákshasa, those offered to them he loves. Chánakya, with his impetuous passions, combines deep design; Rákshasa, notwithstanding his greater temperance, is a bungler in contrivance, and a far better soldier than a plotter."

Professor Wilson observes, in conclusion, that "the thoughts are not brilliant or beautiful, but show vigorous perception of character, and a manly strain of sentiment," stamping the author as "the Massinger of the Hindus."

King to Queen. "As rests your hand, my love, on the stem of the asoka, it seems to put forth a new and lovelier blossom."—Page 232.

CHAPTER XXXII.

RATNAVALI, OR THE NECKLACE.

A Play, attributed to king Harsha, of Kashmir, who reigned between A.D. 1113 and 1125.

This is the last play which Professor Wilson gives us in his volumes of translations. He observes that it marks changes in social organization; and he mentions that king Harsha, under whose patronage it was produced, spent so much money on poets, actors and dancers, that he was obliged to sell the gold and silver vessels belonging to the temples, and even made use of the images of the gods,—which led to an insurrection, in which he perished.

A change in the fashion of dramatic composition is noted: intrigue is substituted for passion, and ingenious conceit for poetic inspiration. The structure of the language is, on the other hand, eminently elegant, particularly in the Prâkrit. This dialect appears to equal advantage in no other drama, although much more laboured in the Mâlatî and Mâdhava. The Sanskrit is also very smooth and beautiful, without being painfully elaborate; and this is thought to constitute the chief value of the play. The Ratnâvalî may, in short, be taken "as one of the connecting links between the old and new school, and as a not unpleasing production of that middle region, through which Hindu poetry passed from elevation to extravagance."[1]

To English readers, the chief merit of the Ratnâvalî will be its liveliness. The scenes follow one another with good effect, and the interest and excitement afforded must have been much the same as that of a modern ballet, or a melodramatic opera. The scene is laid in the palace of king Vatsa. This king is a favourite in the fictions of the period, although probably not a historical personage. The palace is at Kausâmbî, which we must suppose to have been near the site of the ancient Hastinâpura, not far from Delhi.

King Vatsa and his queen were a good, loving couple,—in Eastern fashion; but that fashion, it should be remembered, gave no security that another woman would not take the man's fancy, and the first wife be forthwith superseded or deposed. The play opens at the commencement of spring, just as the annual festival is about to be celebrated. This was a kind of carnival, in which all ranks took part, and indulged themselves

[1] H. H. Wilson, Hindu Theatre, vol. II. p. 258.

in playing pranks, and throwing rose-leaves, and squirting coloured water at each other. The king comes out on his terrace to enjoy the sport. Two of the queen's attendants approach, dancing and singing:

1st *Maid*. "Cool, from southern mountains blowing,
Freshly swells the grateful breeze,
Round with lavish bounty throwing
Fragrance from the waving trees:
To men below, and gods above,
The friendly messenger of Love."

2nd *Maid*. "Lightly from the green stem shaken,
Balmy flowerets scent the skies;
Warm from youthful bosoms waken,
Infant passion's ardent sighs." . . . .

And so the queen sends to the king, begging him to meet her in the palace garden at the image of the god of love. The king consents, and finds the queen prepared to offer homage to the flower-armed deity, whose image was placed at the foot of the red asoka tree. As he approaches, his confidential attendant says:

"This is the place. Behold the rich canopy of the pollen of the rich mango blossoms, wafted above our heads by the southern breeze; and the chorus bursts from the *koils* and the bees, to hail your approach."

King. "The garden is now most lovely. The trees partake of the rapturous season; their new leaves glow like coral, their branches wave with animation in the wind, and their foliage resounds with the blythe murmurs of the bee; . . . . . the bees give back in harmony the music of the anklets, ringing melodiously, as the delicate feet are raised against the stem of the asoka tree."[1]

---

[1] "It was in a grove of asoka trees that Káma incurred Siva's wrath, whence the selection of that tree." The hand or foot of a beautiful woman, touching the stem of the *asoka* tree, was supposed to make it blossom.—H. H. Wilson, Theatre of the Hindus, vol. ii. p. 272, and p. 274, note.

"No, no," says his attendant; "it is not the bees,—it is the queen, with her train approaching." And accordingly the queen appears, with a train of attendants, amongst whom is Ságariká, a beautiful princess, who has arrived from Ceylon, sent on purpose to captivate the king; but, instinctively, the queen was endeavouring to keep this visitor out of his sight. Suddenly remembering Ságariká's presence, she is very vexed with herself for having been so incautious, and bids her withdraw, and go to take care of her favourite starling. Ságariká appears to comply, but says, aside, that the bird is safe with her friend, and that she would like to see the ceremony, and know whether it is similar to that performed in her father's mansion. She, therefore, conceals herself amongst the foliage, and only goes far enough to pick flowers for her own offering. The king advances, admiring the queen, saying:

"The queen stands by the side of the god of the fish-emblazoned banner, as slight and graceful as his own bow, and as delicate as the flowers that tip his shafts."

The queen presents the accustomed gifts of sandal, saffron, and flowers; and the king says:

"Whilst thus employed, my love, you resemble a graceful creeper twining round a coral tree;—your robes of the orange dye, your person fresh from the bath. As rests your hand upon the stem of the asoka, it seems to put forth a new and lovelier shoot. The unembodied god to-day will regret his disencumbered essence, and sigh to be material, that he might enjoy the touch of that soft hand."

The worship of the divinity being concluded, custom required that the queen should offer flowers and unguent to the king. Whilst thus occupied, Ságariká returns with her flowers, and supposes that the king must be the god of love come in person to accept the offerings. She gazes at him from her concealment with unchecked admiration, and says: "the sight, though oft repeated, never wearies."

A bard, behind the scenes, is now heard to sing in praise of the flaming radiance of the setting sun, of the moonlight, and the sweetness of the night-flowers. The king tells the queen that the beauty of the moon is eclipsed by her loveliness, &c. &c.; and they and their attendants return to the palace. In the meantime Sâgarikâ fled in fear, lest she should be discovered, but not before she had perceived that the apparent god of love was, in fact, the king,—

"Udayana (she says), to whom my father destined me a bride."

Udayana being another name for Vatsa,—perhaps the name by which he was better known in Ceylon.

The second Act gives us the next day. The scene is again in the garden of the palace. The princess Sâgarikâ has just painted a portrait of the king, with whom she has already fallen in love. In her picture he is the god of love, to whom flowers and perfumes are being presented, as in the scene which she had witnessed. The friend and companion with whom she came from Ceylon discovers her, and says: "Hah! she is here; but so intent upon some painting that she does not notice my approach." The friend, Susangatâ by name, perceiving whose portrait she has pourtrayed, rallies her upon her admiration for this god of love; and, saying she must give the god his bride, she adds the portrait of Sâgarikâ to the picture. This friend was still in charge of the queen's favourite talking bird, called here a *sârika*.[1]

The princess is rather distressed to find that she has revealed

---

[1] The Indian grakle; it is about the size of a starling, and in Bengal called maina.

her secret. The friend says: "Be assured, I will not betray you; it is more likely this prattling bird will repeat our conversation." The princess becomes much agitated; the friend cools her with lotus-leaves and fibres. Nevertheless, the princess faints, until roused by confused voices behind the scenes, which announce that "the monkey has escaped from the stable, and rattling the ends of his broken chain of gold, he clatters along as if a number of female feet, bound with tinkling anklets, were in sportive motion. Chased by the grooms, and frightening the women, he has bounded through the inner gate. The unmanly eunuchs, lost to shame, fly from his path; and the dwarf takes shelter in the jacket of the chamberlain."

The princess and her friend are alarmed, and, crying out that "the wild brute is coming," they hide themselves in a tamala-grove. When the noise is over, Sâgarikâ says: "What has become of the drawing? some one will discover it." Her companion replies: "Never heed the picture, now. The ape has broken the cage to get at the curds and rice; and the bird has escaped;" and, troubled to think that she will repeat their conversation, they go off in pursuit. In the meanwhile, the king walks in another part of the garden, talking to his constant companion, Vasantaka, of a most wonderful magician, lately arrived at court, who boasts that he can make flowers blossom at any season; and now, at the king's desire, has covered his jasmine "with countless buds, as if smiling disdainfully upon the queen's favourite *mâdhavî*."[1] King Vatsa is delighted, and says: "I shall make the queen turn pale with anger; she will look upon the creeper as a rival beauty," &c. Whilst advancing towards this marvellous jasmine they hear strange sounds, and the friend says: "Fly, sir; fly. There is a goblin in yonder bakula tree." The king listens, calls his friend a simpleton, and says the voice is distinct and sweet, like that of a woman,

[1] Gærtnera racemosa.

but from its small, sharp tone, must be that of a starling; and, looking up, cries: "There she sits." The friend is vexed with himself for having taken a bird for a goblin, and says: "Stop a moment, you impertinent bird; and with this crooked staff I will bring you down from the tree, like a ripe wood-apple." "Forbear, forbear," says the king; "how prettily she talks." "Yes; now I listen again," replies his friend, "she says, 'Give this Bráhman something to eat.'" *King.*—"Something to eat is ever the burthen of the glutton's song. Come, say truly what does she utter." They stand still to listen, and make out that somebody is in love with the king, and fears lest her love should not be returned, and that this person has pourtrayed the king as the god of love. The friend is excessively amused, and says: "How the jade chatters to-day; I declare she speaks in measure, like a Bráhman skilled in the four Vedas." And when the king wonders what it means, he laughs out, and says he must know that it means himself;—who else could have been delineated as the god of the flowery bow; and then, clapping his hands in mirth, frightens the bird, which flies away. The king and his friend follow, and enter the plantain bower. They look in vain for the *sárika*; but they find the broken cage and the tell-tale portraits.

The princess and her friend also come to the bower, wishing to recover these portraits; but, hearing the king's voice, they hide behind the plantain leaves, and listen. Satisfied that the king is enchanted with the portrait of Ságariká, her friend at length shows herself. The king believes her to be one of the queen's attendants, and endeavours to conceal the portraits. Susangatá tells him that she knows the secret of the portrait, and some other matters, of which she will apprise her Majesty. The king offers jewels, saying: "This is but a matter of sport, not to be mentioned to the queen." Susangatá refuses the jewels, but says that her friend Ságariká is angry with her for having drawn her portrait; and that he must appease her resentment. The king springs up, desiring to be led to her. And then, as usual in Hindu love-making, the lady frowns, and is said to be angry, whilst the king expresses irrepressible admiration. Presently the queen comes into the garden, and the king and those with him try to hide themselves. The king is, however, seen; and the queen asks him if he has seen the budding jasmine. Whilst they converse, the king's clumsy friend lets the picture fall; and the queen recognises the likeness of Ságariká. The king and the attendants try to explain, but the queen will not accept "prevarications; and, turning to her husband, says: "My lord, excuse me. Looking at this picture has given me a slight headache. I leave you to your amusements."

In the third Act, plots are made for a secret meeting between the king and Ságariká, who is not known to be a princess, but is simply considered as one of the queen's attendants. The queen defeats the plot, and imprisons Ságariká.

In the fourth Act, the unhappy Ságariká contrives to send a diamond necklace to the king's Bráhman friend and companion, intimating that the queen has her imprisoned, and intends sending her, secretly, at midnight, to Ougein. The necklace is of great value, and sets the Bráhman wondering as to where it came from. When the king sees the necklace, he puts it to his heart and ties it round his neck. One of the female guard now enters with a sword, and announces the return of the king's army from a successful campaign in Kosalá. "The enemy's forces came down in great numbers; the points of the horizon were crowded with the array of mighty elephants." They bore down the king's infantry beneath their ponderous masses. "Those who escaped the shock were transpierced by innumerable arrows." But king Vatsa's general slew the king of Kosalá on his furious elephant, and thus gained the victory. King Vatsa says:

"Honour to our gallant foe, the king of Kosala, for glorious is the warrior's death when his enemies applaud his prowess."

He then gives orders that the treasures of his favour be distributed. The warriors retire, and a messenger from the queen announces that a very famous magician from Ougein has arrived, and asks if his majesty will be pleased to see him. The king says, "By all means; I take much pleasure in this cunning." The magician comes waving a bunch of peacock's feathers, laughing, and saying,

"Reverence to Indra, who lends our art his name, and on whom Samvara and Vivara attend! What are your majesty's commands? Would you see the moon brought down upon earth, a mountain in mid air, a fire in the ocean, or night at noon? I will produce them—command."

He promises further, that by the force of his master's spells, he will place before the eyes of the king the person whom in his heart he most wishes to behold. The king then sends to the queen, saying, that he does not wish to witness the performances alone, but in her presence. The queen comes. The magician waves his plume, saying,

"Hari, Hari, Brahmâ, chief of the gods, and thou their mighty monarch, Indra, with the host of heavenly spirits—appear, rejoicing and dancing in the heavens."

The king and the queen look up, and rise from their seats.
Whilst beholding these marvellous sights, a female attendant announces an embassy from Ceylon. The king of that country has sent his councillor, Vasubhûti, in company with a messenger who had been sent from king Vatsa. The queen at once requests the king to suspend the spectacle, and give audience. "Vasubhûti," she says, "is a man of elevated rank," related to

the king of Ceylon, who, again, is her maternal uncle. The magician retires, but says that he has more to exhibit.

The female attendant and the queen go out to bring in the travellers. The Ceylon minister is struck with admiration, and says,

"The avenues of this palace do, in truth, present a splendid scene. The eye is bewildered amongst the stately steeds and mighty elephants of war. The ear is regaled with harmonious sounds, and the heart is gratified by mixing with the throng of attending princes. The state of the king of Sinhala (or Ceylon) is here effaced; and the magnificence of the entrance into every court, betrays me into rustic admiration."

Advancing towards the king, he perceives the splendid necklace which is round his neck, and recognizes it immediately as the necklace which his master had given to his daughter on her departure, but does not at once disclose his thoughts. When introduced to the queen, the Ceylon minister appears much embarrassed, but at length discloses his mission, saying,

"In consequence of the prophecy of the seer, that whoever should wed Ratnávali, my master's daughter, should become the emperor of the world, your majesty's minister, as you are aware, solicited her for your bride: unwilling, however, to be instrumental to the uneasiness of your queen, Vásavadattá, the king of Sinhala (or Ceylon) declined compliance." . . . . .

But at last, the king of Ceylon, having heard that Vatsa's queen was dead, the princess embarked with the two men now arrived, but the ship was wrecked. The company weep; and whilst perplexity still prevails, a cry is heard that the inner apartments of the palace are on fire. The flames reach a roof of gold. The queen exclaims in agitation that Ságariká will be burnt. The king rushes to the rescue. Ságariká is discovered in chains—flames blazing on all sides. The king takes her in his arms—the flames disappear. The Ceylon minister, and the other messenger from Ceylon, are struck with the likeness between Sâgarikâ and the shipwrecked Ratnâvalí. The queen is desired to state from whence Sâgarikâ came. Her account is, that the prime minister brought her, saying that she had been rescued from the sea, and for that reason they called her Sâgarikâ, the ocean maid. This completes the identification; her father's minister does her homage; she remembers him; and then the queen cannot resist the evidence that the Sâgarikâ to whom she had been cruel, is her cousin Ratnâvalí; and she says, "Is this my sister, Ratnâvalí? Is this the daughter of the sovereign of Sinhala?" And wishing to comfort the fainting girl, she takes her to her arms.

The prime minister is then called in to explain, and makes a speech, acknowledging that he feared to face the queen, for that her husband's contracting marriage bonds with another wife, could not fail to be displeasing to her. "Yet," he continues, "I am confident she will forgive me, when she considers my motives, and will be well pleased that the king obtains by these means the sovereignty of the world. However, happen what may, duty to a master must be performed without regard to such considerations." He then confesses that he had sent a report to Ceylon that the queen had perished by fire. He also confesses that he had brought the conjuror, and caused the magic fire, not knowing how otherwise to release Sâgarikâ, and bring her into the presence of her father's minister, and thus establish her identity with the princess, Ratnâvalí. After these explanations, the king says, laughing, to the queen,

"Well, madam, it remains with you to say how we shall dispose of the sister you have acknowledged."

The queen perceives that resistance would be useless, and says,

"Come here, Ratnâvalí, appear as becomes my sister." (Puts on her jewels, takes her by the hand, presents her to the king, and says), "Accept Ratnávalí, my lord."

King (taking her hand). "Who would not prize the favours of the queen?"

Queen. "And remember, my lord, she is far away from her natural relations; so treat her, therefore, that she may never have occasion to regret them."

And, lastly, the queen embraces Ratnávalí, saying,

"Glory to your majesty."

The prime minister says, "What else can we perform to gratify your highness;" and then the king concludes the drama in the following words:—

"What more is necessary? Vikramabáhú is my kinsman. Ságariká, the essence of the world, the source of universal victory, is mine, and Vásavadattá rejoices to obtain a sister. The Kosalas are subdued. What other object does the world present, for which I could entertain a wish? This be alone my prayer:—May Indra, with seasonable showers, render the earth bountiful of grain;—may the presiding Bráhmans secure the favour of the gods by acceptable sacrifices;—may the association of the pious confer delight until the end of time;[1]—and may the appalling blasphemies of the profane be silenced for ever."

---

[1] "Or of the Kalpa, the period of the world's duration."—H. H. Wilson, Hindu Theatre, vol. ii., p. 317.

CHAPTER XXXIII.

PRABODHA-CHANDRODAYA; OR RISING OF THE MOON OF AWAKENED INTELLECT.

A Theological and Philosophical Drama, by Krishna Misra.

THIS curious composition was discovered by Dr. J. Taylor, of Bombay, about the year A.D. 1810.

Dr. Taylor was, at the time, striving to master the Sanskrit systems of philosophy; and finding that this drama had poetic merit, and that it afforded assistance in the study of religious philosophy, he attempted its translation into English. The work became, however, but little known to Europe until the year A.D. 1842; when Professor Rosenkranz, of Königsberg, induced a friend, who was familiar alike with Sanskrit and with Sanskrit philosophies, to make for him a new translation, from Sanskrit into German. This he published, with a preface by himself and a critical notice by the translator. From this valuable critical introduction we learn that the twelfth century was the probable period at which Krishna Misra composed the drama; that his object was the establishment of Vedânta doctrine; and that he belonged, in all probability, to the Vaishnava sect of the Râmânujas. Of this sect we have already treated, as instituted by Râmânuja, who followed the great Sankara Achárya, and who, like his predecessor, spent his life in labouring to reform religious abuses and extravagances. What they assailed by reason and argument, Krishna Misra combats by ridicule. His work is much praised by Professor Lassen,[1] who calls it peculiarly Indian, and unlike anything in the literature of other countries. The allegorical personifications he finds well sustained, and the whole plot constructed with ability.

In choosing a name whereby to designate this drama, we have experienced much difficulty, because our English language affords no exact equivalent to the Sanskrit *prabodha*. Literally, it means "awaking;" and the sense in which the author uses the word is, I understand, "awaking from ignorance." Krishna Misra's subject is, therefore, intellect awakened from ignorance; and this, in the language of the Vedântists, means intellect capable of distinguishing the real from the unreal, the undivided from the divided deity.[2] The machinery used to enforce and elucidate Vedânta doctrine is allegory.

Delusion (moha) is the king and commander of Love, Anger, Avarice, and all other sensuous powers; whilst Hypocrisy, Self-importance, Materialism, and all heresies, are his allies.

On the opposite side is Reason, the king and leader of a whole army of virtues. The struggle between these opposing forces is sharp; but finally Tranquillity enables Reason to harmonize with Revelation. Then, in allegorical language, it becomes possible for Awakened Intellect to appear in this world, or for the Moon of Awakened Intellect to arise and illuminate mortals.

The prologue to this drama commences with an invocation to Brahma, giving as it were the key-note of the composition. "With reverence," it says, "we approach that spotless, heavenly, self-recognising Light which, appearing as a sea in the deceiving beams of the mid-day sun, evolved itself as ether, air, fire, water, earth," &c.

---

[1] Indische Alterthumskunde, vol. iii. p. 790.

[2] For an explanation of Vedânta doctrine, see *ante*, vol. i. p. 205 ff.

This means, that the creation of the world was the effect of Máyá,—Illusion. By the influence of Illusion, the world appears real and distinct from Brahma. When Illusion is exposed or destroyed, Brahma and the universe are one; and the spirit of man discovers itself to be identical with the spirit of Brahma.

"To that highest Light the created soul returns when plunged in deepest stillness;—the Light which prevails when the world is filled with the ascetic followers of the god whose head is adorned with the crescent-moon;—he, the god who is made known by the eye which illumines the centre of his forehead."

Siva is the type of ascetic power.[1] But it is the activity of Vishnu on earth, and the subsequent tranquillity of Vishnu in heaven, which are at present to be held up for the instruction and encouragement of men. The manager, therefore, interrupts the invocation, saying:

"But wherefore many words? The glorious Gopál;—he, whose lotus-feet are irradiated by the diadems of kings," .... desires us this day to evince our joy in the accomplished victories of our prince, king Kírtivarman. For this purpose we propose to perform a drama, in which personified Tranquillity shall be a leading character; and we have chosen that which is entitled

"The Rising of the Moon of Awakened Intellect."

This piece, the manager says further, composed by the much-honoured Krishna Misra, which "the king and the multitude are eager to see, we will at once prepare." He lifts a curtain, and calls.

An actress appears, enquiring what it is that he proposes. The manager replies much as follows:

"You are aware that Gopála, whose fame resounds through every

[1] See "Birth of the War-God," where Siva's ascetic character is powerfully drawn.

region, has, with his sword, conquered opposing kings, and has re-established our Rája Kírtivarman upon his throne. The battle-field on which the demonesses dance, proclaims his praise in far-resounding notes; whilst the little women of the Kobbolds clash together with their nimble fingers the skulls of the dead; and the wind, resounding through the frontal cavities of slain elephants, trumpets forth his fame. This Gopála," he concludes, "having now become tranquil, desires the performance of the 'Rising of the Moon of Awakened Intellect.' Desire the performers to take their parts."

The actress is amazed to hear of Gopála as tranquil, and asks for explanation of so great a prodigy. The manager replies, that it is analagous to other proceedings in the world's history. Periods of violent activity, followed by seasons of absolute repose, are characteristic of Eternal Deity. And thus Gopála, so soon as his duties had been fulfilled, conquered Karman (activity), as Reason conquers Delusion.

A voice is heard behind the scenes, which says,

"You good-for-nothing fellow! how dare you declare that Delusion will be conquered so long as I exist?"

"Ah!" said the manager, "that is Love, or Káma, who, with his rolling eyes, bewitches the world. We have enraged him. Let us be gone."

The first Act then commences. Love enters, accompanied by his beloved Rati, or Pleasure. Love continues his angry protest against the notion that their king, Delusion, could possibly be conquered by his enemy, king Reason. Reason, he says, originates in mere books, and his power is lost even with the wisest, as soon as the lotus-eyed make an assault.

"A lovely palace, youthful maidens, flowers amongst which the bees are humming, winds laden with the scent of jessamine, moonlight nights." Such, he says, being his weapons, how can it be possible for Reason to get the ascendancy, or for the moon of awakened intellect to arise?

Love's beloved Rati, nevertheless, thinks that king Reason must be a formidable opponent. Love accounts for this by observing that fear is natural to the feminine heart, but bids his darling remember, that although sweet sugar-cane forms his bow, and flowers serve him as arrows, he nevertheless subdues the universe, and forbids the presence of Tranquillity, even for an instant. He alludes to the wiles and longings which he makes use of for this purpose, and refers to the powerful aid which his king, Delusion, derives from his friends, Arrogance, Greed, Hypocrisy, Unrighteousness.

We will not attempt to follow the whole argument, which concludes by Love giving a report that a female called Speech or Eloquence (Saraswati), was about to appear on earth, and that she was terrible as the Night-Râkshasa, which comes at the end of each world-period. This dreadful creature is the daughter of Mind, but will destroy father, mother, brother, &c., and will act according to the wilful godless nature which Love attributes to Reason, and all powers which oppose his power. Love is here interrupted by approaching voices, and hears Reason complaining in angry tones that he and his allies should be called godless. "Thou villain," he says, "Right and Wrong are fixed by the over-ruling Lord."

Love takes no notice of this remark, but says to his companion, "Beloved, yonder come the elders of our family,—Reason, with his consort, Understanding. Deprived of joy, he looks like the moon when blackened by a veil of cloud."

Love and Pleasure then depart, and Reason and Understanding come forward, and talk freely. The audacity of Love is, they say, to be regretted; but it is part of a lamentable state of affairs, occasioned by the deceitful Mâyâ (Illusion). Under her influence Arrogance, and other followers of Egotism, have thrown bonds or fetters over the Lord of the World. Over the Passionless— over that One whose existence is Thought and Joy. The self-seeking and the pleasure-loving hold that these bonds are virtues, and by them, Reason and his coadjutors, who labour to remove the bonds, are denounced as godless.

Understanding ventures to enquire how bonds could be thrown upon that Highest One, whose nature is blessedness, and from whom the three worlds receive light.

"Even the Highest," Reason replies, "could not escape the deceitful power inherent in the feminine nature."

"Brahma has been deceived by Máyá" (Illusion). It is to this that the opening invocation alludes, when it states that as earth, water, air, &c., are produced by mirage, so has this world been produced by Máyá or Illusion.

Reason admits that Máyá is incomprehensible. But Máyá is feminine, therefore it is her nature to deceive. On earth, women deceive men. And Máyá being female has deluded even Brahma.

Whilst Illusion maintains this power, Awakened Intellect will be unable to arise; and that which is one will appear as many. But if Tranquillity gain the ascendancy, Reason will become reconciled with Revelation, divisions of Brahma will cease, Illusion will vanish, and the oneness of all will become established.

Having indulged in this blessed anticipation, Reason and Understanding go forth to work for its fulfilment; and so concludes Act one.

The second Act is wholly occupied with the tactics of the opposing party. First appears Hypocrisy, as a Bráhman, who has just received commands from the king of the faction, here called Delusion.

The commands which this king sends to Hypocrisy are much as follows:

"Beloved Hypocrisy! King Reason and his advisers have determined to revive Awakened Intellect, and are, for this purpose, sending Tranquillity into holy places. This threatens destruction to all our kind; and it behoves you to be especially active and zealous. You are aware that no holy place on earth is equal to the city of Benares. Go, then, to Benares, and exert yourself to frustrate the devotions of the pious people there assembled."

Hypocrisy boasts that this he has already done, and so effectually, that those who by day attend holy fires, &c., are by night the greatest sinners.

After a little more of boasting monologue, Hypocrisy catches sight of a traveller, arriving apparently from the southern side of the Ganges. "He looks," he says, "as though he were striving to crush the world by his pride, to humble it by his discourse, and to render it ridiculous by his wisdom." It then occurs to him that the traveller may come from Rádhá, and be acquainted with his grandfather (Egotism).

The stranger comes on the stage, saying to himself, that the world is full of fools, who prattle, and bungle, and fancy themselves learned, because they have had their heads shaved, and have assumed the character of ascetic mendicants. And he proceeds to insinuate that those who teach Vedánta doctrine, in opposition to evidence given by the senses, are as sinful as Buddhists. He also reckons the Naiyáyikas and the Sivait sects as heretics, who must be avoided as you would avoid the road to hell.

Advancing a few steps, he perceives the abode of Hypocrisy, which is a hut close to the waters of the Ganges. He is eloquent on the subject of hypocrites as a class, who make all manner of pretensions, but who are in fact perfectly indifferent as to whether Brahma and the world are one or not.

He wishes to enter the hut and greet the occupant, but Hypocrisy meets him with a scornful and forbidding aspect. Much wrangling ensues, until Hypocrisy discovers that his visitor not only comes from his native place, the beautiful town of Rádhá, in Gaur, but that he is in truth his grandfather, Egotism, of whom he had been speaking. Thereupon, they embrace; and Egotism inquires affectionately after Deceit, Greed, Avarice, and other relatives. When asked what occasioned the honour of this visit, Egotism replies, that reports were abroad that king Delusion was alarmed by hostile proceedings on the part of king Reason; and he had come, therefore, to ascertain the real state of affairs.

Hypocrisy says he has arrived at the right moment, for that Delusion is on his road from Indra's heaven to the city of Benares. Egotism wonders that Delusion should choose the abode of the Highest for his dwelling. To which Hypocrisy replies, that it is in Benares, the eternal city of Brahma, that Science and Knowledge are about to appear as the allies of king Reason; and in Benares, therefore, must Delusion take up his abode in order to exterminate that race.

A voice behind the scenes is heard, crying:

"Make ready the bejewelled palace of crystal. Sprinkle the floors with sandal-scented water. Let the fountains play. Erect arches of precious stones. Plant waving flags, brilliant as the rainbow, on the palace roof."

King Delusion then enters, surrounded by numerous followers. He talks in a supercilious, mocking tone, of fools who think that soul is distinct from body, and can enjoy reward in future existence. He says, he would as soon believe that trees which grew in the air could produce blossom and fruit, &c. After heaping much scorn and ridicule on such notions, he speaks of the materialist, or Chârvâka doctrine, as that which can be trusted. Earth, water, fire, air, alone are true. Nothing is known of what is beyond. Death is the end. This has been taught by Vâchaspati; and this is the doctrine which the Chârvâkas promulgate.

In the next scene a Chârvâka, or materialist, appears, accompanied by a pupil. These personages explain their vicious doctrine, and when noticed by king Delusion, greet him with flattery, and thank him for giving them and their friend, Vice, comfort and courage.

They warn their king of a dangerous female, a strict devotee of Vishnu, whom they call Devotion. Their warning makes the king look thoughtful, for he is aware that Devotion is his natural enemy, and difficult to vanquish; but he says, aloud, that there can be no need to fear even her superhuman power, so long as she is opposed by Love and Anger. He then issues his commands, that Love, Anger, Greed, Pride, and their brethren, must at once exert themselves, and destroy this dangerous personification of Vishnu worship.

In the fifth scene a messenger appears with a letter. "I come," says the traveller to himself, "from the land of Orissa, where the celebrated temple of Purushottama stands by the shore of the sea. From thence Arrogance and Haughtiness have sent me to the court of king Delusion. This city is Benares, and the royal residence; I will draw near. How confidentially the king is talking with the Chárváka! All hail to king Delusion! whom I entreat to read this letter." The purport of the letter is to warn Delusion that Tranquillity, and Religion, her mother, have become the ambassadors of Reason, and that day and night they urge Revelation, or Upanishad, to join them in this service. The letter further intimates that Dharma, or Virtuous Action, although not wholly unfriendly to Love, yet listens to the whisperings of Passionlessness, and often seeks Tranquillity in retirement.

The king expresses scorn, but sends a confidential messenger with all speed to Love, to bid him put Dharma (Virtuous Action) immediately into bonds.

Anger and Avarice are also called upon to assist in destroying Tranquillity.

It is unnecessary to follow this act throughout. It concludes by a boast from Heresy that he will convince Religion that justice, blessedness, the Vedas, ascetic practices, knowledge of holy books, and the doctrine of rewards in future existence, are all mere follies. And he anticipates that Religion, being thus emancipated from the authority of the Vedas, will perceive the error of seeking blessedness by abstinence from sensuous enjoyment, and will quickly become indifferent to Revelation.

In the third Act Tranquillity enters, weeping for her mother, Religion.

"Mother! mother!" she says, "show me thy fair face! Alas! she, whose delight was in forests where discourse was uninterrupted; in hills, down which the rivers flowed; in holy places, frequented by pious anchorites,—is now in the hands of the godless Chandálas."

Presently a disgusting form appears, which is recognised as a Digambara Jain ascetic. A Buddhist mendicant follows, and then a Kápálika, who is dreadful to behold, but who, by a lavish allusion to the allurements of sense, contrives to enslave both the Buddhist and the Digambara;[1] and the latter gives evidence of his friendship by offering to subject Religion, the daughter of Virtue, to the authority of Delusion. On this, the Kápálika says:

"Only tell me where she is, and I will draw her forth."

But the Digambara cannot tell where she is.

"She is not in the waters, she is not on the mountains, she is not in the woods, she is not in the regions beneath the earth. United with Devotion, she is found only in the hearts of the virtuous."

These words give a death-blow to the hopes of the Kápálika, and he laments the threatened downfall of Delusion, but determines, nevertheless, to stand firm in his service, even though it should cost him his life.

---

[1] These pretenders to holiness hand each other wine-cups, and, getting intoxicated, dance together in drunken fashion.

In the fourth Act Religion enters, trembling like a frightened deer. She had been carried off in the claws of a horrid flying creature, who made a swoop at her like the swoop of a falcon. From this enemy she had been released by Devotion, now called a goddess. By this goddess Religion is entrusted with a message to Reason, commanding him to destroy Delusion. But to do this, Reason must be in alliance with Tranquillity and Revelation, and, under the influence of such alliance, Awakened Intellect will arise; but not until a fierce battle has been fought.

In this Act king Reason holds his court, and enters into conversation with Reason and some other good powers, which are too abstract for our present purpose. At length these discourses are interrupted, by an announcement that the moment has arrived which the astrologers deem auspicious for the departure of the troops.

Commands are forthwith issued to make ready the elephants; to harness horses, fleeter than the wind, to the war-chariots; to push forward the foot-soldiers, whose spears move onward like a forest of lotus-blossoms; and to send forth the cavalry, flourishing their weapons.

As king Reason approaches Benares, his charioteer extols the splendour of buildings, which have stolen their whiteness from the moon; the splashing of the waters, thrown up by fountains; the many-coloured flags, brilliant as lightning on the edges of autumnal clouds; and gardens filled with lofty trees, and flowers of delicious scent.

On seeing the temple of Vishnu, Reason rejoices in Vishnu, as the "Universal Soul, into which all pious souls become absorbed." He descends from his chariot, enters the temple, and prays to Vishnu,—who alone can release the world from that illusory sleep which cause matter and spirit to appear diverse. "Lord of Paradise," he concludes, "grant to the world which implores thee, that Awakened Intellect may arise, and that Delusion may be destroyed."

In the fifth Act Religion enters alone. The battle has been fought, and Reason is victorious; but Religion grieves over the destruction of the forces of Delusion, for amongst the dead are many of her relatives. "Anger," she says, "destroys whole families, as fire destroys whole forests, when hurricanes lash the burning trees the one against the other."

Devotion and Tranquillity coming on the scene, Devotion begs to be told of the battle; and Religion gives a description, of which the following presents the chief points:—

"As you withdrew, and the redness of the sun was fading, the air resounded with the battle-cry of countless combatants. Daylight was obscured by the dust of chariots, horses, and elephants. Then, when all were in thickest conflict, Reason sent to Delusion an envoy, who bore in his hand the books of the Nyáya philosophy. The terms offered were, that Delusion should abandon the altars of Vishnu, the holy places on rivers or in woods; abandon, also, the hearts of the pious, and betake himself and his followers to such peoples as are barbarous." If these terms were not complied with, their heads were to split, and their blood to flow in streams, from miserable wounded faces.

"Delusion answered scornfully, and knitting his brows, desired Heretical Doctrine and Logic to come to the rescue. At this moment Saraswatí (Speech), like a moon, suddenly shone above the heads of our warriors, and revealed herself, invested as she is with the beneficent influences of Vedas, Upavedas, Vedángas, Puránas, law-books, legends, and all holy writ. Immediately the worshippers of Vishnu, Siva, the sun, &c., assembled around the goddess. Also, the Mímánsá, and all the other philosophical works." . . . . .

On hearing this, Tranquillity raises the very reasonable question how the writings of Revelation could unite with the writings of Reason, which are by nature different.

Religion replies, that the origin of all these writings is alike. They all spring from the Vedas; and although they contest some points amongst themselves, all alike are eager to defend the holy writings from unbelievers.

Brahma, or primæval light, is tranquil, endless, unchanging, without beginning. When from this Holy Light qualities are developed, man prays to the qualities,—as Brahmâ, Vishnu, or Siva. And by means of that holy teaching, of which the Veda is the source, and which is diffused by a variety of modes, must the Lord of the Universe be apprehended, as also the ocean is apprehended, amid the multitude of its waters.

A long description of the fierce battle is then given. Some heretics are destroyed by other heretics. And again, some heresies which had not yet taken root, were borne down by floods of holy learning. Buddhists fled to countries tenanted by barbarians,—especially to Sind, Kandahar, Behar, eastern Bengal, the coast of Coromandel, and even further. The Digambaras, the Kâpâlikas, and others, concealed themselves amongst blockheads in Panchâla, Mâlwa, and on the west coast.

Right Discrimination slew Love, Anger destroyed Patience, and all went well, with the exception that Delusion had escaped and had concealed himself, in company with the Magic of the Yoga. Devotion is concerned at hearing that Delusion yet exists, for this will greatly encourage the wicked. When Devotion inquires after Mind, she is told that this power is so distressed at the destruction of his children and grand-children, that he proposes to abandon life. In a subsequent scene Virtue is sent by Devotion to comfort Mind.

"Why, my beloved," he says, "art thou so troubled? Didst thou not know that life was transitory? Hast thou not read the holy legends? Millions of Brahmâs have lived through hundreds of ages. . . . . . Wherefore grieve for bodies which resemble foam, and return to the elements from which they came?" . . . . .

"He, who knows what is eternal and what is transitory, suffers no grief," &c.

It is further intimated, that care for the perishable originates in love of self, or in those affections and fancies which spring from self. "It is commonly observed," says Virtue, "that if the cat eat a man's domestic fowl he is greatly disturbed; but that the death of a sparrow or a mouse gives him no concern, because it does not affect himself. Exert yourself, therefore, to vanquish self-love, which is the root of all evil."

And because to loosen bonds of affection is difficult, man must consider how many millions of parents, husbands, wives, &c., have passed away. The society of friends must, therefore, be enjoyed, as one might enjoy a momentary flash of lightning.

The arguments adduced by Virtuous Action are followed up by Saraswatī (as personified Wisdom), the last words being, that whilst the disturbing influence of the sensuous faculties prevails, the one will appear to be many, as the sun is multiplied when reflected by the waves of ocean. But when the sensuous influences are conquered, the one will be recognised as undivided, as is the sun when reflected by a clear mirror.

The sixth Act is commenced by a discourse between Religion and Tranquillity. Joy is expressed at the defeat of Delusion and the allurements of sense; but it is said that Delusion had reappeared after the great battle, and had so artfully contrived to have these allurements made to appear realities, that Reason had been upon the point of yielding to them. Then came Logic, fixing his angry eye upon the deceivers, and reminding the king that sensuous indulgence would plunge him again into the rivers of fire, from which he had sought escape by embarking in the ship of ascetic self-denial. This discourse prevailed. King Reason bids farewell to the unreal and the misleading, and is now, in consequence, anxious to become united with Revelation. The subsequent scenes bear upon the doctrine previously announced, that not until this union of Reason with Revelation has taken place can Awakened Intellect, or the light of absolute truth, arise upon the world. Much discussion therefore ensues between Tranquillity, Reason, and Revelation,—all tending to show how man can be emancipated from mortal life, and partake in the condition of the spiritual and unchanging.

In the closing scene, the actors appear already to have escaped from earth, for we are introduced to what may be called a transcendental man. This being is Transcendent Spirit, or spirit which is God-man. In Sanskrit he is called Purusha, the being who is supposed to have assisted in the creation of the world. In our German translation, this being is called *Urgeist*. When introduced, he bows with reverence to Reason and to Revelation; and says, that to each of these personages he is under obligations. The troubles to which Revelation has been exposed by doctrines, sects, and practices, are then exposed and discussed, until a voice behind the scenes cries, "Wonderful! most wonderful!" and presently it is announced that the Moon of Awakened Intellect has arisen, that his light has entered into Mind, and that it has, moreover, swallowed up Delusion and his adherents.

Transcendent Spirit, or *Urgeist*, welcomes Awakened Intellect with enthusiastic joy, and says:

"The veil of darkness is lifted. Morning breaks. I scatter from me the blackness of delusion. I cast off the sleep of doubt. Now I am Vishnu, through whom the world becomes filled with religion, reason, understanding, tranquillity, control of the senses, and similar influences. Through the favour of Devotion, or Vishnu-worship, I am emancipated. Now I have no wishes. No wish to see anyone, to ask anything, to seek any doubtful reward, whether here or beyond; but tranquil, and removed from care, and fear-engendering delusions, I will live to myself the life of a pious anchorite."

At this moment the goddess Devotion (or Vishnu-worship) enters, saying joyfully, that all her wishes are fulfilled. Transcendent Spirit (or Purusha) falls at her feet. She raises him; and the drama concludes in the following words from this abstract being:

"Now is Reason contented, now are his enemies overthrown, and I, through the favour of Vishnu-worship, have attained true blessedness. Now, therefore, I pray that seasonable rain may fertilise the earth, that kings may rule in peace, and that the noble-minded, who are delivered from sin by the knowledge of truth, may be safely carried across that ocean of life which is afflicted by the sorrows of egotism."

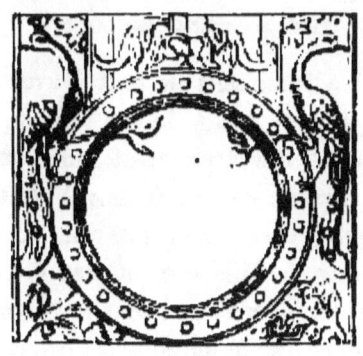

CHAPTER XXXIV.

LYRIC POETRY.

Messenger-Cloud, and the Seasons, by Kálidása.   Gita-Govinda, by Jayadova.

KALIDASA's beautiful "Messenger-Cloud" is the most important of the Sanskrit smaller poems. Its very name identifies it with India, where the clouds which precede the rainy season are so striking and so influential that they are watched and loved, as Ruskin bids us to watch and love the clouds, in his eloquent work entitled Modern Painters. The cloud in the poem, says Professor Wilson, "is one of those masses which seem almost instinct with life, as they traverse a tropical sky in the commencement of the monsoon, and move with slow and solemn progression from the equatorial ocean to the snows of the Himalayas." This cloud is employed as a messenger by a mourning exile, banished from the northern mountains to the south of the

2—17

Vindhya hills. Tradition tells us that Kuvera, god of riches, living in princely state at Alaká, in the Himalaya, had a favourite garden, into which the elephant of Indra broke loose, doing great damage. Kuvera was so incensed that he condemned the servant, through whose negligence this occurred, to twelve months of banishment. This servant was a Yaksha, or minor deity: he is torn from his wife and sent to Nagpore. The poem does not contain above one hundred and thirteen or, according to one recension, one hundred and sixteen stanzas, and is a great favourite, not only in its native land, but also with the Orientalists of Europe. Professor Wilson's first attempt to interest Europeans in the results of his Sanskrit studies, was a very early metrical translation of it into English.[1] In 1842 he republished his work, "correcting some mistakes," but not attempting "verbal approximation." "It is," he says, "recommended to a student of Sanskrit by its style and by its subject. The style is somewhat difficult, but the difficulty arises from no faults of conception or construction. There must, of course, be some unfamiliar imagery, some figures of purely local associations, in every Oriental composition; but with a few possible exceptions, the Megha-Dúta contains no ideas that may not be readily apprehended by European intellect.[2] The language, although remarkable for the richness of its compounds, is not disfigured by their extravagance, and the order of the sentences is in general the natural one. The metre combines melody and dignity in a very extraordinary manner; and will bear an advantageous comparison, in both respects, with the best specimens of uniform verse in the poetry of any language, living or dead."

The time chosen is the commencement of the rainy season, when clouds are packing, and are moved forward by the northwest monsoon.

[1] Another recent translation in English prose, is by Colonel H. A. Ouvry, published in 1868. Our subsequent quotations are made from the metrical translation of R. T. H. Griffith, Principal of Banares College.
[2] Works of H. H. Wilson, vol. iv. p. 310.

THE YAKSHA ADDRESSING THE CLOUD.

The poem opens by describing the poor exile's loneliness at Râmagiri, a place celebrated as the abode of Ráma and Sîtâ during their banishment. "It is a short distance to the north of Nagpore, and covered with buildings, consecrated to Ráma and his associates."

> "Dark are the shadows of the trees that wave
> Their pendant branches upon Ráma's hill,
> Veiling the stream where Sîtâ loved to lave
> Sweet limbs, that hallowed as they touched the rill.
> There, a sad spirit, whom his master's will,
> Wroth for a service he had rendered ill,
> An exile from his happy home had torn,
> Was sternly doomed for twelve long months to mourn:
> Of all his glories reft, of his dear love forlorn."

His days, weary with weeping and fasting, are "intolerably slow." His arm wastes, and can no longer hold his bracelet; when, looking upward on a day in June, he perceives upon the mountain a glorious cloud, vast as an elephant. He knows that this cloud will be visiting Alakâ; and, checking his tears, he hastens to collect such blossoms as yet linger in the wood, and to make an offering of flowers, trusting that the cloud will convey a message to his wife.

> "'O thou, of ever-changing form!' he cried.
> 'I know thee,—offspring of a glorious race;
> The mighty counsellor; close by the side
> Of royal Indra is thine honoured place.
> *   *   *   *   *   *
> On me, on me, thy tender glances turn,
> Who mourn the anger of the god of gold;
> To distant Alakâ fly, uncontrolled,
> Where dwell my brethren in their stately halls.
> There, let my message to my love be told,
> Mid gilded palaces and marble walls,
> On which the silver light of Siva's crescent falls.'"

The Cloud is the herald, or personification of the rainy season. He is attended by "wreathing cranes," on silver pinions; whilst from many a stream the swans ascend at the "glad thunder," and, wild with joy, bend their eager course to "Mânas' mountain lake." To relieve the fatigue of the journey, the Cloud is advised to seek the summits of the Mango Peak, where rain has often been needed to quench the burning of the trees.

Here the "dark glory" of the Cloud is supposed to rest upon the golden fruit of the mango, amid the green boughs which wave around. Soft rain will soothe the heat of Chitrakûta's hill, and then,—

> "With pinions swifter for the minisht store,
> Soon over Vindhya's mountains thou wilt soar:
> And Revá's rippling stream, whose waters glide
> Beneath their feet, without their rush and roar,
> In many a rock-barred channel, summer-dried,
> Like lines of paint that deck an elephant's huge side."

The coming of the Cloud revives the dried-up streams: each bud grows lovelier; fragrant jasmines become yet more fragrant; and woods, no longer burning, waft sweet odours. Rain-birds flock from distant skies; and, in ever-lengthening chain, crane after crane mounts from the fens and fields.

> "On, on, my herald! as thou sailest nigh,
> A green of richer glory will invest
> Dasárna's groves, where the pale leaf is dry.
> There shall the swans awhile their pinions rest;
> Then the rose-apple, in full beauty dressed,
> Shall show her fruit: then shall the crane prepare,
> Warned of the coming rain, to build her nest:
> And many a tender spray shall rudely tear
> From the old village tree, the peasant's sacred care."

Arriving at a "lowlier hill," the Cloud must for a moment

"on its crest descend," and touch its "faint kadambas," and send new life and rapture through each spray. Drooping jasmine-buds, that pine along the parched beds of the mountain-brooks, will revive at its coming; and so also will the young flower-girl, who, whilst weaving her fragrant wreath, is too languid to replace the drooping lotus, which has fallen from her ear.

On another stream the Cloud is bid to look with pity; for it is pale, with the sere leaves shaken from its trees by the hot summer gale; and its waters have grown thin, like the hair of a woman, bewailing her husband's absence.

Several verses are devoted to the bright, imperial city of Ougein,—the pride of all the earth; famed for its minstrel-band, and for the beauty of its women. We have already observed,[1] that Hindu poets take pleasure in the breeze of morning. And here we find the Cloud invited to rest on the flower-sweet terraces, where women sit at open casements; whilst the air of morning

> "Plays wooingly around the loosened hair
> And fevered cheek.
> Then, as it blows o'er Siprá, fresh and strong,
> Bids all her swans upon the banks prepare
> To hail the sunrise."

The temple to Siva, for which Ougein was celebrated, is not forgotten; nor is "the dancing-girl, with rapture-beaming eye." She is thankful for the soft drops of rain which cool the ground; "while her faint hands the jewelled chowries ply, and her languid feet move to the chimes of the tinkling, silver bells around her waist."

After leaving Ougein we read of dark night, and lightning, which sleeps high up in the tower, where the white dove builds her nest; and then we come again to morning,—

---

[1] In reference to Saramá and Yama, in Rig-Veda Hymns, vol. i. p. 12.

"Charged with the odours of the wakened earth,
Whom thy fresh rain has left so pure and gay,
The wind of early morning, wild with mirth,
Amid the branches of the grove shall stray
And woo each tendril to responsive play."

Passing homage is paid to the famous battle-field of Kurukshetra, where "god-like Arjuna, with arrowy hail, laid low the heads of kings." The river Saraswatí is also noticed, as the Cloud moves on.

"On to the place where infant Gangá leaps
From the dark woods that belt the mountains' king,
Hurling her torrent down the rugged steeps."

The confluence of the Ganges and the Jumna is thus alluded to:

"So, when dark Jumna's tributary tide
With kissing waves to blend with Gangá flows,
The mightier waters, beautifully dyed
With borrowed azure, to the sun disclose,
Mixt with their pearly light, the sapphire's darker glows."

Arriving at the snow-clad peaks of the Himalaya, the Cloud is invited to rest upon the breezy heights, "where herds of musk deer wander wild."

The spontaneous fires which often occur in mountain forests during the hot season are thus described:—

"Hark! the gales whistling through the woods of pine,
Urging to madness all the straining boughs,
That twist, and chafe, and bend, and intertwine,—
The latent flame to wildest fury rouse,
Singeing the long hair of the mountain cows.
Quick! rain a thousand torrents on the crest
Of the vast hill, and cool his burning brows."

At length the Messenger-Cloud arrives at "Alakâ—city of the

Blessed." It is described much in the same fashion as Ougein, only its palaces appear to have been yet more remarkable; for the poet says to the Cloud:

> "And she has charms which nought but thine excels:
> High as thyself her airy turrets soar,
> And from her gilded palaces there swells
> The voice of drums, loud as thy thunder's roar:
> Thy pearls are mocked by many a jewelled floor."

Whilst the varied tints on arch and corridor are compared to the colours of the rainbow.

The city of Alakâ is, moreover, said to be unmatched for lovely girls, who learn to choose the flowers that suit them best.

> "The amaranth, bright glory of the spring:
> The lotus, gathered from the summer flood;
> Acacias, taught around their brows to cling;
> The jasmine's fragrant white, their locks to stud;
> And, bursting at thy rain, the young kadamba-bud"

The poet, speaking as the exiled Yaksha, dwells fondly on the loveliness of the fair angels of his native city, whose homes are

> "Too beautiful for tongues to tell;"

homes which

> "By night a starry radiance fills,
> Shot from the jewelled floors, where breathes the smell
> Of roses, . . . while melting music thrills."

His own dwelling he describes as having a jewelled archway, to the north of Kuvera's royal dome.

> "There, girt with emerald steps, a bright lake gleams,
> Where the gold lotus fires the lily's white:
> The swans that sail upon its silver streams
> Shall hail thy coming with renewed delight."

And, indeed, so gratified will the swans be at the arrival of a rain-cloud, that they will give up the idea of distant flight to mountain lakes. His mind dwells with fondness on a mount, around which is growing a plantain grove. This spot, he says, was loved by his young bride; and back to his soul comes fresh "the plantain's circling gold, the hillock's velvet green." He thinks of the "sweet, clustering trailers," and other fair flowers, which give grace and beauty to his lady's bower; the bright asoka, that asks the pressure of her foot," &c.; the pedestal crystal, with its golden column, where the blue-necked peacock drinks the evening air, &c. Led by these tokens, the Cloud will recognise the once bright dwelling . . . . . altered, since he has "been torn from all he loved away." On that loved home he bids the Cloud descend, but not to show himself in awful size or splendour, lest terror seize his "fair one." A few verses follow, in which his "lonely, weeping, miserable wife," is seen mourning for her mate, like a poor love-bird. "Her hanging tresses veil her drooping head." . . . . . "Like the cold moon is she,—sad, feeble, pale." . . . . . She weaves garlands with pious care twice every month; and she touches her lute, and pets her bird, and slowly counts, 'mid tears and deep-drawn sighs, "the long, long weary hours, that used to be like moments."

The Cloud is instructed to present itself when first "the sun-beams fire the eastern skies," and then, in deep-sounding tones, to express his "longing love and tender hope." He bids her not yield to dark despair.

> "Some friendly stars the moonless night illume;
> Some flowers of hope amid the desert bloom:
> Life has no perfect good, no endless ill,
> No constant brightness, no perpetual gloom;
> But, circling as a wheel, and never still,
> Now down, and now above, all must their fate fulfil."

Having given his message with all the force of which he was

capable, he says that, although it is received in silence, he knows that he does not pray in vain; for that when the rain-birds crave the cool shower, the Cloud cares not to speak in answer,—but sweet drops descend. This is pithily expressed in Wilson's translation:

> "To thee the thirsty Châtakas complain;
> Thy only answer is,—the falling rain."

The "airy envoy" faithfully carried the fond speech, by love made eloquent, and touched Kuvera's breast with soft compassion. He restored the exile to his home, and bade him "live with his love again with joy for evermore."

The Ritu-Sanhara, or the Seasons:

A lyric, much admired not only by the natives of India, but, with the exception of certain passages, by all students of Sanskrit literature. A very good translation in Latin and German was published in 1840, by Professor von Bohlen; and Mr. Griffith precedes his English translations by saying, that Sir William Jones spoke in rapturous terms of the beautiful and natural sketches with which it abounds; and after expressing his own admiration, adds, "it is much to be regretted that it is impossible to translate the whole." It is attributed, he says, to Kâlidâsa; "and it would be difficult to disprove the assertion by internal evidence."

The effects of the summer sun are very graphically described, not forgetting the tornadoes of dust, to which the hot season is subject.

For some extracts from this poem, we avail ourselves of Mr. Griffith's "Old Indian Poetry."

> "Now the burning summer sun
> Hath unchallenged empire won;
> And the scorching winds blow free,
> Blighting every herb and tree.

> Should the longing exile try,
> Watching with a lover's eye,
> Well remember'd scenes to trace,—
> Vainly would he scan the place:
> For the dust with shrouding veil
> Wraps it in a mantle pale."

The effect which fierce, continued heat, has upon the beasts of the forest, is given as by an eye-witness.

> "Lo! the lion,—forest king,—
> Through the wood is wandering:
> By the maddening thirst opprest,
> Ceaseless heaves his panting chest.
> Though the elephant pass by,
> Scarcely turns his languid eye:
> Bleeding mouth and failing limb,
> What is now his prey to him?"

And the elephants, on their part, give no heed to the lions' roar, but crash through the woods, vainly seeking for water. The serpent, faint with heat, crawls within the shadow of his ancient enemy, the peacock; whilst the gorgeous peacock, scorched by the red glow of the sun, closes his eye in agony. Frogs are driven from their parched homes, and come out in countless numbers; but the serpent heeds not even the frogs. But

> "Darting out his flickering tongue,
> Lifteth he his head on high,
> If some breeze may wander by."

A few more lines on the dried-up pools, and the consequent distress to animal life, may be given.

> "Where the sparkling lake before
> Fill'd its bed from shore to shore,
> Roots and twisting fibres wind,
> Dying fish in nets to bind,

> There the cranes in anguish seek
> Water with the thirsty boak.
>
> * * * * *
>
> "Elephants all mad with thirst,
> From the woods in fury burst;
> From their mountain-caverns, see!
> Buffaloes rush furiously;
> With hanging tongue and foam-fleck'd hide,
> Tossing high their nostrils wide;
> Eager still their sides to cool
> In the thick and shrunken pool."[1]

The rainy season is described with no less power.

> "Who is this that driveth near,
> Heralded by sounds of fear?
> Red his flag, the lightning's glare
> Flashing through the murky air.
> Pealing thunder for his drums,—
> Royally the monarch comes.
> See! he rides amid the crowd,
> On his elephant of cloud,
> Marshalling his kingly train:
> Welcome, O thou Lord of Rain.
> Gathered clouds, as black as night,
> Hide the face of heaven from sight;
> Sailing on their airy road,—
> Sinking with their watery load." . . . . .

The poet praises the emerald green of the buds and the beauty of the woods, "bursting with new life," and continues:

> "See the peacocks hail the rain,
> Spreading wide their jewelled train:
> They will revel, dance and play,
> In their wildest joy to-day."

[1] Specimens of Old Indian Poetry. R. T. H. Griffith. Summer: p. 68.

Ward gives a passage, which he says is from Kálidása's poem on the Seasons, which speaks of the streams formed in the valleys by the rains which have "become yellow, tinged with white, and carry on their surface worms, straw, and dust; they pursue their course in so serpentine a manner, that the frogs become affrighted at their approach."[1]

Hindus divide the year into six seasons. That which is called autumn, is marked by the return of the hansa birds,—swans, or, rather, flamingos,—and also by the flowering of jasmines and other white flowers.[2]

Autumn comes with a sound as of silver anklets, which is the song of the swans which accompany her.

> "Mark the glory of her face:
> 'Tis the lotus lends it grace.
> See the garb around her thrown:
> Look, and wonder at her zone.
> Robes of maize her limbs enfold,
> Girt with rice, like shining gold.
> Streams are white with silver wings
> Of the swans that autumn brings.
> Lakes are sweet with opening flowers,
> Gardens gay with jasmine bowers;
> While the woods, to charm the sight,
> Show their bloom of purest white."

The liveliness that characterised the rainy season is gone. No rainbows, now, in the sunlight glow of evening; no lightning's glare, flashing through gloom.

> "Nor the cranes in armies fly,
> Steering through the cloudy sky;
> Nor the peacocks lift the head:
> Love and joy for them are dead."

The most notable sound is the wild music of the hansas, which

---

[1] View of Hindus, vol. iv. p. 400. [2] Griffith's Idylls: Autumn.

sounds like the tinkling bells of a woman's zone, and "rings in mockery through the air," . . . . . for the youth "whom cruel fate keeps afar disconsolate."

GITA-GOVINDA.

"Thy lover, thy Krishna, is dancing in glee."

Jayadeva is supposed to have written as late as the twelfth century of our era. He is best known by the pastoral drama, entitled Gita-Govinda. Of this, Mr. Griffith has translated a few stanzas, but says "the exquisite melody of the verse can only be appreciated by those who can enjoy the original."

Krishna, the herdsman, loves Rádhá, the shepherdess, but has wandered from her to amuse himself with other maidens. Nanda, Krishna's foster-father, gives her warning, saying:

"Go, gentle Rádhá, seek thy fearful love;
Dusk are the woodlands,—black the sky above.
Bring thy dear wanderer home, and bid him rest
His weary head upon thy faithful breast."

Hearing these words, Rádhá made anxious search, pressing through tangled bushes, until a friend and attendant tells her in pity that Krishna will not be found in lonely forest shades; and sings to her as follows:

> "'In this love-tide of spring, when the amorous breeze
> Has kiss'd itself sweet on the beautiful trees;
> And the humming of numberless bees, as they throng
> To the blossoming shrubs, swells the kokila's song;—
> In this love-tide of spring, when the spirit is glad,
> And the parted,—yes, only the parted,—are sad;
> Thy lover, thy Krishna, is dancing in glee,
> With troops of young maidens, forgetful of thee'"

The description of spring, which follows, is very characteristic of India. The annual rains are over, and wives expect their absent husbands to return home.

> "The rich-laden stems of the vakul[1] bend low,
> 'Neath the clustering flowers, in the pride of their glow.
> In this love-tide of spring, when the spirit is glad,
> And the parted,—yes, only the parted,—are sad:
> Thy lover, thy Krishna, is dancing in glee,
> With troops of young maidens,—forgetful of thee.
> Dispensing rich odours, the sweet Mádhavi,[2]
> With its lover-like wreathings encircles the tree.
> And, oh! e'en a hermit must yield to the power,—
> The ravishing scent of the múliká[3] flower."

The damsel then sings a song, which describes Krishna

> "Wooing, caressing each young dancer's hand,
> With many a glance," and many a kiss.

---

[1] This is the rakula, or bakula-flower, the rich, oily scent of which makes it a favourite with women. The petals are undivided, and easily strung together in garlands.

[2] The mádhavi is the gærtnera racemosa. Roxburgh says: "The blossoms are uncommonly beautiful, and exceedingly fragrant." It is also called anti-mœcta and banisteria Bengalensis.

[3] The múliká seems to be a shrubby jasmine, which is peculiarly sweet in odour.

> "Saffron robes his body grace,
> Flowery wreaths his limbs entwine;
> There's a smile upon his face,
> And his ears with jewels shine.
> In that youthful company,
> Amorous felon! revels he;
> False to all,—most false to thee."

But although Krishna amused himself in this reckless fashion, "Rádhá's image" was "lingering in his breast;" and presently, by "woe opprest," he seeks her in the shady grove, and sings:

> "She is fled, she is gone! oh, how angry was she,
> When she saw the gay shepherd-girls dancing with me.
> Oh, Hari! vile Hari! lament thee and mourn:
> Thy lady has left thee,—has left thee in scorn.

> "How bright, in her anger, she seems to me now,
> With her scorn-flashing glance, and her passion-arched brow;
> And her proud, trembling eye, in my fancy I see,
> Like the lotus, that throbs 'neath the wing of the bee.
> Oh, Hari! vile Hari! lament thee and mourn:
> Thy lady has left thee,—has left thee in scorn."

Krishna entreats Rádhá to speak, and says:

> "E'en in wrath, thy cheek, love,
> Will shine away my fear."

He next praises her teeth, which sounds peculiar: "the flash of her teeth" is so bright that, as the moon dispels the night, it will dispel his dread. If she will not forgive him, he cannot live; but then he says:

> "Wilt thou have me slain, love?
> Then bite me, dear, to death;
> And life will come again, love,
> In the odour of thy breath."

After this the friendly attendant urges Rádhá to hasten to her beloved.

> "In love their voices raising, sweet birds around thee sing,
> And kokilas are praising the flower-darting king."[1]

Even the reeds, she says, are "bending low with pointed fingers," to show the way which she should go.

This Song of the divine herdsman is much prized in India. It is fully analysed by Lassen in his Latin edition, beautifully translated in German verse by Rückert, and has been dwelt upon with admiration by Sir William Jones, in his "Essay on the Mystical Poetry of the Hindus." The latter looks upon it as a specimen of "that figurative mode of expressing the fervour of devotion, or the ardent love of created spirits towards their beneficent Creator, which has prevailed from time immemorial in Asia." Mr. Griffith, from whom we borrow the above quotation, explains that, "As Krishna, faithless for a time, discovers the vanity of all other loves, and returns with sorrow and longing to his own darling Rádhá; so the human soul, after a brief and frantic attachment to objects of sense, burns to return to the God from whence it came."[2]

[1] Káma, whose darts were flowers.
[2] R. T. H. Griffith: Gíta-Govinda. Specimens Old Indian Poetry, p. 96.

Banyan. Ficus Indica.

CHAPTER XXXV.

PANCHATANTRA, FABLES IN FIVE SECTIONS.

It is well known that Hindus wrote no history, and that it is from their general literature that we must learn of their progress in the arts of civilised life,—of their customs,—or of superstitions prevailing at given periods. Under these circumstances, fables and popular fictions assume a degree of historical importance.

The ancient Hindu, and the modern Hindu, alike luxuriates in story-telling. The professional story-teller weaves for his own profit, and for the pleasure of his audience; whilst the philosopher makes fiction a medium for imparting important truth.

The subject of our present chapter will be "Fables,"—a form of fiction which has been thought to spring from the Hindu doctrine of transmigration. But Professor Wilson thinks, that the notion that birds and beasts might converse, is one readily suggested to the imagination; and that "an inventive fancy was quite as likely as a psychological dogma to have gifted mute creatures with intelligence and supplied them with a tongue."[1] He then reminds us that Homer makes horses speak, and that Hesiod allows the hawk to converse with the nightingale. But although the invention must not be claimed as exclusively a Hindu device, the "purposes to which Hindus directed it, and the mode in which they employed it, appear to have been peculiarly their own."[2] Each fable will be found to illustrate and exemplify some reflection on worldly vicissitudes, or some precept for human conduct; and instead of being aggregated promiscuously or without method, the stories are all strung together upon a connected thread and arranged in a framework of continuous narrative, out of which they successively spring; this being a sort of machinery to which there is no parallel in the fabling of Greece or Rome.

By fable the ancient Hindus taught niti, or polity, which means, a system of rules for the government of society in the "reciprocal duties of the members of an organized body, either in their private or public relations." Niti is therefore especially intended for the education of princes; and the celebrated work introduced to Persia and Europe as the fables of Bidpai, or Pilpay, have this niti character. The Hitopadesa is the collection of these fables which was first discovered by our Sanskrit scholars; but it is now well ascertained that the Panchatantra is the older

[1] H. H. Wilson, vol. iv. p. 83.   [2] Ibid, p. 85.

form of the work, and is the source from which the Hitopadesa and also the Arabic version is derived.

It would be useless labour to attempt to fix the period at which these fables were composed. But since the Panchatantra collection makes a quotation from the writings of Varáhamihira, who is also mentioned by name, the latter must have preceded it; whilst later than the sixth century it cannot be, because we find it translated into Pehlevi between the years A.D. 531 and 599. It appears that Núshírván, king of Persia, sent a physician to India in search of medical knowledge and books; and that this physician brought not only medical works, but the fables, which, being translated into Pehlevi, went forth to the world as the fables of Bidpai, or Pilpay. Several etymologies have been proposed of this word Bidpai, of which the most probable appears to be, that it is an attempt to give, in Pehlevi, the Sanskrit word vaidya, for physician, namely, baidya-i. More than a century after the Panchatantra had appeared in Persia it was translated from the Pehlevi into Arabic, by command of Almansur, second khalif at Baghdad;—the Arabic name given being Kalila wa Damna.

The Panchatantra and the Hitopadesa alike begin by stating, that a certain king was concerned at finding that his sons were growing up without knowledge. He called a council, at which the necessity of acquiring knowledge was discussed, and also the length of time required for the acquisition of such kinds of knowledge as were considered indispensable. The conclusion at which the councillors arrived was, that the king must be advised to entrust his sons to a Bráhman, named Vishnusarman, who undertook to teach them niti in six months. This being arranged, Vishnusarman took the young princes to his house, and composed for their benefit the series of fables which we are about to consider. We will begin with the Panchatantra, so called, from *pancha*,—five and *tantra*,—section; or Panchopákhyána,—five narratives.

The mode of teaching is not unlike that of Machiavelli. The world is exhibited as it appears from without. Rogues, if cunning and clever, succeed; fools and simpletons, though good and learned, fail. But good morals are allowed to be good in themselves, and to be preferred, where no failure is risked.

The framework of the stories may be thus described:—A merchant, living at a town in southern India, which some supposed to be St. Thome, desires to increase his wealth. He says many wise things about the means by which money may be acquired; but that no mode is so sure as that of carrying goods to a distance. By that means, wealth increases wealth, as a tame elephant attracts wild elephants. He buys two strong oxen, loads his waggon, and starts with bales of merchandize, in company with other merchants. When they arrive at the river Jumna an accident happens,—his fine ox Sanjívaka is disabled; and after some days, the caravan refusing to wait longer, the merchant is obliged to proceed, leaving his ox Sanjívaka to his fate. The poor beast was not long in recovering; and, refreshing himself with the water of the Jumna, he gave a loud bellow. This extraordinary noise frightened the lion, by name Pingalaka, who was king of the woods. At the moment, the lion was going towards the river to drink, but paralyzed by the awful sound, he stood stock still, with his attendant beasts all ranged around him. Then crept forth two jackals, named Damanaka and Karataka, who were the descendants of a king's minister who had lost his office, and who were watching and manœuvring to recover such hereditary dignity. The present seemed to them a fine opportunity. The lion-king was perplexed; and they might help him.

The second jackal, Karataka, is as eager to get into office as his companion, but he sees difficulties; because, interfering in other people's affairs often leads to trouble,—as happened, he says, to the ape, who drew out the wedge. How was that? says Damanaka? And Karataka tells that—

In the neighbourhood of a certain town a merchant was building a temple in the midst of a grove of trees. The workmen, and also the architect, went away at mid-day to have dinner in the town. Then came the apes, which had a settlement in that neighbourhood, to inspect what the workmen had been doing. They frolicked on the tops of the trees, and the points of the temple, and ran along the level beams. One beam of anjana-wood they found partly split; a wedge of khâdira-wood was inserted to keep it open, and a band placed round to keep the wedge in its place. An unfortunate ape, destined to speedy death, jumped into the opening, threw away the band, pulled out the wedge, and was killed.[1]

The jackals then consider the subject under many aspects, and quote wise sayings on the nature of kings, as—

A king attaches himself to whoever is nearest; for kings, women, and climbing plants, must have a support to cling to.

But, to retain the favour of a king, it is necessary that "his mother, his wife, his heir, his chief minister, his chamberlain, and even the guard at his gate," should be propitiated.

It is further observed, that "he who regards gambling as death's messenger, and wine as strong poison," is one who secures a king's favour. And amongst other rules, we find that a man who aims at being a favourite should enter first into a battle but last into a room, should never contradict, and never laugh in the presence of his king.[2]

The stories here become so discursive that we cannot afford time to show their connection. Some points may, however, be noted, from their bearing on other departments of literature. As for instance: a magician "personates Vishnu, and rides on a wooden representation of Garuda, guided by a pin."[3]

The jackals spend much time considering how to take advantage of the dismay which the bellow of the ox has caused the

[1] Benfey, vol. ii. p. 9. [2] Ibid, pp. 11—18. [3] Wilson's Works, vol. iv. p. 14.

lion, and then make a wrong move, by bringing them face to face. Instead of the jealousy and hate which they anticipated, the lion and the ox recognise in each other an honest, truthful nature, and become mutually attached. This does not suit the jackals; and occasion is therefore made, whilst the ox is absent, to make the lion suspicious of him. Stories are told of hasty friendships between opposite natures, which sooner or later end in grief, as—

A jackal strayed into a town, where he was worried by dogs, and only escaped by jumping into a vat of indigo. When he got out, the beasts all feared him as an unknown wonder. Leopards, tigers, and even the lions of the forest, did homage to him as their king; and he, on his part, ruled right royally, until one day a pack of jackals coming to the neighbourhood, set up their usual howl; and then, frantic with joy, and with tears in his eyes, he joined his howl with theirs. Instantly the assembled beasts discovered that their wonderful king was nothing but a jackal; and they killed him, even where they were, in the council hall.[1]

What the little birds who lived on the sea-shore had to do with these unequal friendships, does not much matter: but we will allude to it as characteristic of the country. A female bird wished to make her nest farther inland, because on the day of full moon the sea would be sweeping over the place where they were then abiding. But the male bird objected, believing that he was as strong as the sea, and that its waves would not venture to encroach upon his premises.[2] This story Professor Wilson considers as "one of the decisive proofs of the Indian origin" of the fables. The name of the bird in Arabic is *tītawí*, a word which cannot be resolved to any satisfactory Arabic root. "It is therefore probably only a transcript of the Sanskrit

[1] Benfey, vol. ii. p. 75. [2] Ibid, pp. 87—89.

tittibha, Bengali *titib*, and Hindi *titikri*,—the names throughout India for a kind of sandpiper, very numerous on the sandy banks and shores of rivers."[1] It is not unlike a snipe, but rather smaller, and from its strutting gait is regarded by the Hindus as the type of conceit; and it is even said, proverbially, that the sandpiper sleeps upon its back, with its legs held upwards, to prevent the sky from falling.

Much eloquence is exerted, and many tales are told, to convince the lion that friendship between him, who is a flesh-eater, and the ox, who is an eater of grass, is unsafe. And at last poor Pingalaka is convinced that his friend Sanjívaka is plotting his death, and that the only way to escape will be to take the very first opportunity of striking down the grass-eater.[2]

The wily jackal then seeks out the ox, and tells a series of stories to secure his presenting a hostile aspect to the lion, and so they meet in anger. The lion strikes down the ox, and the ox gores the lion, and the jackals tell each other stories, until the ox suddenly falls over quite dead. The book closes with more stories to the same effect, and one of these we will relate, because it refers to a Jaina ascetic.

A certain king who reigned at Ayodhyá, the capital of Kosala, sent his minister to subdue a rebellion amongst some of the rajahs in the hills. Whilst the minister was absent, a religious mendicant came to Kosala, "who, by his skill in divination, his knowledge of hours, omens, aspects, and ascensions, his dexterity in solving numbers, answering questions and detecting things covertly concealed, and his proficiency in all similar branches of knowledge, acquired such fame and influence, that it might be said he had purchased the country, and it was his own." The fame of this man at last reached the king, who sent for him, and found his conversation so agreeable, that he wanted him constantly beside him. One day, however, the mendicant did not

---

[1] Wilson, iv. pp. 18, 19.   [2] Ibid, p. 19.   [3] Benfey, vol. ii. p. 142.

appear, and when he next came, "he accounted for his absence by stating, that he had been upon a visit to Paradise; and that the deities sent their compliments to the king."[1] The king was simple enough to believe him, and was filled with astonishment and delight. His admiration of this marvellous faculty so engrossed his thought, that the duties of his state, and the pleasures of his palace, were equally neglected." But after a while his minister returned, having subdued the king's enemies in the hills, and is amazed and disgusted to find his king in close conference with a naked mendicant, instead of occupying himself as formerly with his appointed duties. He quickly ascertains the pretensions of the ascetic, and asks the king if what he had heard of the mendicant's celestial visit was true. "The king assured him that it was, and the ascetic offered to satisfy the general's apparent scepticism, by departing for Swarga in his presence. With this intent, the king and his courtiers accompanied the Sramanaka to his cell, which he entered, and closed the door." After some delay, the general asked the king when they would see him again. The king answered, "Have patience; on these occasions the sage quits his earthly body, and assumes an ethereal form, in which alone he can enter Indra's heaven."[2] If this be the case, said the general, let us burn his cell, and thus prevent his re-assuming his earthly body, your majesty will then have constantly an angelic person in your presence. To reconcile the king to this mode of proceeding, the general tells him a story which has reference to the serpent, or Nága tribes of ancient India. A Bráhman, named Devasarman, had no child, which denial made his wife miserable. At length, however, owing to "some mystic words," a son is promised, but what was the surprise of the mother, and the horror of the attendants, when the child so eagerly desired proved to be a snake. The assistants wished to destroy the monster, but ma-

---

[1] H. H. Wilson, iv., p. 30.   [2] Ibid, p. 21.

ternal affection prevailed, and the snake was reared with all possible care and affection. At the proper age, the mother entreated her husband to provide a suitable wife for their son. He said he would, if he could gain admission to Patála, where Vásuki, the Serpent king, reigns over the Nágas, and might grant such a request. But his wife was so distressed, that to divert her thoughts, he consented to travel. After some months, they arrived at a city in which a Bráhman offered his own beautiful daughter as a wife for the serpent. The girl consented to the marriage, and performed her duties admirably. After a time, her serpent-husband changed one night into a man, intending in the morning to re-assume his serpent-form; but the girl's father discovering that the snake body was abandoned, seized the deserted skin and threw it into the fire. The consequence of which was, that his son-in-law ever remained in the figure of a man, to the pride of his parents and the happiness of his wife. After hearing this narrative, the king no longer hesitated. The mendicant's cell was set on fire; the mendicant perished in the flames, and the king was, as his general desired, released from the thraldom of a cunning ascetic.[1]

The subject of the second book is the Acquisition of Friends. It commences by describing a splendid banyan tree which stands near the city of Meliapur, in the south of India. Its fruit fed many birds. In the crevices of its bark lived insects; bees hovered about its flowers, and wayfarers were refreshed by its shade. Here also dwelt a crow, or raven, named Laghupatanaka.[2] Going forth one day to seek food in the town, he met a strange figure of black complexion, with legs which turned outwards, hair standing up stiffly, in his hand he had a net, and he looked like the servant of Death, carrying the fatal noose.[3] The raven knew him to be a bird-catcher, and hastened back to his great tree

[1] H. H. Wilson, vol. iv., p. 25.
[2] Benfey, vol. ii., p. 156.
[3] H. H. Wilson, vol. iv., p. 28.

to warn its many inhabitants of the kind of danger with which they were threatened. Presently the fowler arrived, and spread his net, and scattered his grain; but the birds, warned by the raven, shunned the tempting grain as if it had been poison,— all except the pigeons, who, coming in a flock, would take no warning, but descended on the grain, and were caught. The story is then continued here, as in the Hitopadesa. Chitragríva, the king of the pigeons, bids his followers keep up their courage, and rising simultaneously, fly off with the net. And away they go, directed by their king, to the abode of his friend, Hiranyaka, a rat who lived to the north-east of Meliapur, in a house with a hundred doors. This and other stories with which it is grouped, teach the desirableness of alliance with friendly powers. The rat sets the pigeons free, and they fly off, but the raven who had kept them in sight becomes the best friend of the rat. Scarcity of food occurring in their district, the raven takes the rat on his back, and they go to a pond in a thick wood in the middle of the Dekkan, in which resides a friendly tortoise, named Manthara. The three enjoy each other's discourse, and the rat is persuaded to tell how he once had better fortune. It appears that the world went well with him, until getting into a Vihára, or convent of Jains, he found his way to the wallet of one of the monks. Here was a rich supply of food, but the monk who had stored it away, soon discovered the inroads made, and lay awake trying to catch the thief, and bemoaning his misfortune. Another monk coming to visit the Vihára, the two converse, but he whose food has been pilfered, gives but half attention, so intent is he on hitting the rat on the head with a bamboo pole; and his friend feels angry at being neglected. In the end, the covetous rat was defeated, and lost everything. The tortoise then tells stories, and says wise things to console him, as:—

There is no use in wealth unless it is enjoyed. "One must

acquire wealth in order to give it again, as one collects water in a tank in order to refresh the earth."

"The worst form of poverty is poverty of wisdom. If Siva possesses nothing but an ox, he is nevertheless the best endowed of all the gods."

Manthara, the tortoise, concludes with what is called "A verse of interesting resemblance."

"Dismiss all anxiety regarding your lost wealth, as it is said. 'He to whom the swan owes her white feathers, the parrot his green hue, and the peacock his variegated plumage, He will provide me sustenance.'"

The story of the elephant, liberated from his bonds by a rat, occurs in this portion of the Panchatantra. It is, of course, the same as that of the rat and the lion, with which Europe is familiar, and is a fitting illustration of friendship.

The third Tantra is entitled Inveterate Enmity, or war between crows and owls. In the Hitopadesa, the war is between peacocks and geese; but Professor Wilson believes the former to be the genuine title, "not only from the character of the work itself, but from its connection with a particular grammatical rule. "The Sûtras of Pânini afford a precept for the use of a particular affix, to form derivations from compound words." The rule being exemplified by the form Kâkolûkikâ : kâka, a crow, and ulûka, an owl, making a word which signifies the natural antipathy between the two, and it is inferred that as language precedes grammar, the rule was invented to explain a word, founded probably on a notion of great antiquity.

The introduction to this third Tantra gives a quotation from the Sabhâ Parvan of the Mahâbhârata enumerating the personages who surround a throne.

"Amongst officers to be distrusted are the minister, the priest, the general, the young prince, &c., &c. Amongst those

¹ Benfey, vol. ii., p. 200.

who are supposed to be attached to the cause of the king, are the queen-mother, the queen, the florist, the bed-maker, the astrologer or time-keeper, the physician, the cup-bearer, the betel-bearer, the preceptor, the captain of the body guard. Spies are important personages; the physician, the astrologer, and the preceptor, being the best spies to report to the king on the proceedings of his own party, whilst such men as exhibit snakes are the best spies upon the enemy. Some stories given in the Panchatantra are omitted in the Hitopadesa, as also in the Arabic version, and usually, it is observed, that a "much more decisive vein of satire, levelled particularly at princes and devotees, runs through the Panchatantra," as when the hare says of the cat, "Trust not in low persons, who exercise austerities for their own nefarious designs. Penitents are to be found at holy shrines, whose only piety is in their vaunts."[1]

We find here another story indicating the prevalence of snake worship.

A Bráhman, sleeping in the heat under the shade of a tree, dreamt that he beheld a large hooded snake coiled up upon an ant-hill at a little distance. Believing that this snake must be the tutelary deity of the spot, he bottled some milk so soon as he awoke, and, carrying it to the ant-hill, prayed to the snake as "lord of the soil," entreating forgiveness for having hitherto neglected his worship, and begging that this offering might be accepted. The next morning he found, in place of the milk, a dinar or gold piece.

This is followed by something very like a Buddhist legend, which we will give verbatim, from Wilson:—

A fowler caught a female dove, and being overtaken by a storm, happens to seek shelter from the tree in which the male dove was living. "Moved by the councils of his captive mate, and by his own estimate of the rites of hospitality, he not only gives the fowler shelter in the hollow trunk, but collects dry

[1] H. H. Wilson, vol. iv., p. 37.

leaves, and makes him a fire, and casts himself into the flames, to furnish his guest a meal. The bird-catcher liberates the dove, and she also throws herself into the fire; on which she and her lord assume celestial forms, and are conveyed to heaven in divine cars."[1]

The fowler becomes an ascetic, and voluntarily perishes in a burning forest.

Section four is entitled, "The Loss of that which has been gained." As it is less attractive than the other sections, we will pass on to section five, which is entitled "Inconsiderateness." "A man should never attempt a business which he has imperfectly seen or understood," says Vishnusarman, " or he will meet with such mischance as befel the imprudent barber." The young princes ask to what their tutor alludes, and Vishnusarman tells a story of Manibhadra, an eminent merchant or banker, who, without any fault of his own, was reduced to poverty. Having lost his wealth, he found himself neglected; then he became utterly despondent, and determined to end his days by abstaining from food. Having made this resolution, he fell asleep. In a dream, the spirit called Padmanidhi, or the "Lotus-Jewel," came to him, personified as a Jaina monk. "O merchant!" he said, "do not despair. I am the 'Lotus-Jewel,' which was acquired by you in a previous state of existence. In the morning I will come to your house in this same form. Then you must strike me on the head with a bludgeon, and I shall change for ever into gold. And so it happened. The seeming monk came, and was changed to gold, as had been promised. But it so happened that a barber, who had come to trim the nails of the banker's wife, witnessed the strange proceeding.

The banker charged the barber not to mention what he had seen, and the man promised secrecy, but kept pondering in his mind how to attract naked mendicants to his own premises and acquire gold by the same summary proceeding.

[1] H. H. Wilson, vol. iv. p. 41.

So next morning he went to the vihára, and, facing to the north, perambulated the Jaina object of worship three times. Then, going on his knees, and holding up his hands with reverence, he lifted the edge of the curtain, repeating in a high tone, "Glory to those Jainas who possess the only true knowledge, and are thus enabled to traverse the ocean of human passions." He then repaired to the chief of the convent, asked his blessing, and begged that some of the monks might be allowed to partake of food in his house. The chief of the vihára reproved him, and said that they were not *Bráhmans*, to be invited to dinner; and that when they went forth to gather alms they entered the mansions of those votaries only who were known to be of the approved faith. The cunning barber expressed reverence and obedience, and promised not to repeat the offence of inviting holy mendicants to partake of food in his unholy house; but he mentioned that he had a store of excellent cloths for covers for books, and materials for writing.[1] He then went home, provided himself with a bludgeon of hard mimosa-wood, and, watching near the door of the convent for the mendicants, who come out about four o'clock, he tempted them to his house, by talking of his wrappers for their books; and they being inconsiderate, followed the barber, and the barber being inconsiderate, knocked them on the head, and thought they would turn to gold. Several were killed, and the others struck up such a noise that the barber was quickly taken to the court of justice. He defended himself by saying, that he had only done the same as Manibhadra. Manibhadra was sent for; but after he had told his tale, the barber was reproved for rashness, and finally put to death for murder: whereas the banker was dismissed.[2]

This story is followed by that of the snake and the nakula, which is a mungoose or ichneumon, a small animal, noted for its enmity to snakes.[3]

[1] H. H. Wilson, vol. iv. p. 53.
[2] Benfey, vol. ii. p. 321.
[3] H. H. Wilson, vol. iv. p. 54.

This story has a special interest, as being the original of the beautiful ballad of Bethgellert. In India, dogs are not domestic animals, whereas the mungoose or ichneumon is often cherished as a family friend. The story is of a wretched, infirm child, the idol of its mother. She goes out to fetch water, and charges her husband to watch over their child during her absence. But he is a Brâhman devotee, in the habit of forgetting sublunary cares, and at a given time he goes forth to collect alms. Immediately a black snake crawled forth towards the bed whereon the infant lay. The mungoose sprung at him, and after a desperate struggle tore the snake to pieces. When the mother came back, the mangoose went joyfully to meet her, but his jaws and face were smeared with blood; and the poor woman, certain that he had killed her child, threw her water-jar at his head, and the animal died on the spot. Then she sees her child asleep, and the body of a venomous snake torn to pieces, beside him. She beats her breast and her face with grief; and, when her husband returns, reproaches him for having left the child to gather alms, and concludes with the oracular words: "The wheel whirls round his head, who evinced inordinate avarice." The husband asks how that happened; and she relates the history of four Brâhmans.

These four Brâhmans were intimate friends, and all equally in poverty. Poverty, they agreed, was intolerable. "Let a man," they say, "be brave, handsome, eloquent, learned; without wealth, he obtains not enjoyment. Better death than poverty. Better go to the cemetery and become a corpse, than live in poverty." They then enumerate the various modes by which wealth may be acquired, and say, as was said in the Introduction, that the only eligible mode is trade. Capital is multiplied twice or thrice over, in repeatedly buying and selling, by those who have knowledge, and travel to other lands. The idle and the weak alone are afraid of foreign countries. "Crows, deer, and dastards, die in their native place."[1]

[1] H. H. Wilson, vol. iv. pp. 55—57.

Having thus reflected, they commence their travels. Arriving at Ougein, they bathe in the river Siprâ, and worship in the temple to Siva, for which Ougein was celebrated. After this they meet with a Yogin, to whom they communicate the object of their search. The Yogin, who was a magician, gave them four balls, one to each, directing them to go to the mountains, where each would find treasure on the spot whereon his ball should fall.[1]

The first man found copper, and taking with him as much as he could carry, returned home. The second man found silver, and advised that each should take as much as he could carry, and that all should return: but this advice was ridiculed. The third ball indicated a vein of gold, on which the man to whom the ball belonged entreated the fourth Bráhman to remain there with him: but in vain. The fourth Bráhman went forward alone, expecting to find diamonds. Faint with thirst and scorched by the sun, he came at last to a place which was "whirling round." On it stood a man with a wheel on his head, whose body was covered with blood.

He approached, crying for water, and asking the man who he was, and why the wheel was placed upon his head. But scarcely had he spoken, when the wheel transferred itself to his own head, there to remain, perpetually whirling, he is told, until another man should come, as he had, with a magic ball. It is a law fixed by Kuvera, the god of wealth, for the protection of his riches.[2]

When the third Bráhman arrived, searching for his missing companion, he beheld him covered with blood, his head being cut by the sharp edges of the wheel. He learns from him the state of affairs, and says he should have taken his advice and stopped at the gold mine; but "your lack of sense prevented." Better sense than science, unless it improve by knowledge. Those

---

[1] H. H. Wilson, vol. iv. p. 59.   [2] The Siddhi-Nágas are referred to.

who want sense will as surely perish as did those who revived the lion."[1] The man with the wheel asked how that was; and his friend tells of four Bráhmans, residing in a village, who were friends. Three were men of great acquirements, but destitute of common sense. The fourth was acute, but had no learning. Being poor, they determined to go to some country in which learning was patronised, feeling certain that presents would speedily be sent them by the king. But suddenly it occurs to them that the fourth Bráhman is illiterate, and no king will send him rewards; and therefore, says the elder or first Bráhman, he must be left behind. But the others urged that they had been friends from infancy, and that he also should participate in whatever wealth they may acquire.

As they passed through a forest, they saw the scattered bones of a dead lion. "I have met," said one, "with an account of a method by which beings can be re-animated;—shall we try?" They agreed. The first undertook to put the bones together; the second, to supply the skin, flesh, blood, &c.; and the third, to communicate life. When the two first had performed their parts, the third was about to begin; but the fourth objected, exclaiming, that a lion, brought back to life, would eat them. The others calling him a blockhead, he took refuge by climbing up a tree; whilst the revived lion destroyed the three philosophers.

The last story is of an ass, who, during the day, carries the bundles of a washerman; but at night he enjoys himself, goes out with a jackal, breaks into cucumber fields, and feasts on the cucumbers. On one of these occasions he cried out to the jackal, "Nephew, is not this a heavenly night; I feel so happy, I must sing a song." And, notwithstanding wise warnings from the jackal, who says that silence becomes thieves, he commences to display his knowledge of seven notes, three scales, and twenty-

[1] H. H. Wilson, vol. iv. p. 60.

one intervals, &c. The gardener is awakened by the noise, beats the ass, and leaves him tied to a post, with a clog on his leg.[1]

After reading these stories for six months, the young princes were pronounced highly accomplished; and the five Tantras became famous throughout the world. "Whoever reads this work," says the Panchatantra, "acquires the whole Niti-Sástra, and will never be overthrown by Indra himself."[2]

[1] H. H. Wilson, vol. iv. pp. 66—67.   [2] Ibid, p. 9.

CHAPTER XXXVI.

HITOPADESA.

Fables, collected into Four Books.

This four-book form of Sanskrit fables is the counterpart of the Panchatantra, or work in five sections. But although essentially the same, it exhibits varieties, and is worthy of separate notice, inasmuch as it is the form in which the old Sanskrit fables became introduced into the literature of nearly every known language. The word Hitopadesa is formed, I understand, from the Sanskrit *hita*, good, and *upadesa*, advice. The framework is precisely similar to that of the Panchatantra. The king, who is distressed at the folly and ignorance of his sons, determines to entrust them to Vishnusarman, to be taught niti, or polity.

The reverend pandit accepts the charge, and says, whilst they all sit at ease upon the balcony of the palace,—

"Listen, princes:
"In the enjoyment of poetical works passes the time of the wise. But that of fools is spent in dissipation, slumber, or strife.

"For the amusement of your highnesses I will now, therefore, relate the admirable story of the crow, the tortoise, and the rat," &c.

Here, as in the Panchatantra, we find instruction never embittered by personal and dry rebuke. "Human weakness is illustrated for the most part by the history and proceedings of animals, which are represented as rational agents; and lessons of morality, propriety, and prudence, are thus delivered on what we may term neutral ground. And lest the attention of youths should flag, the author, in distributing his subject-matter over four books, in the manner familiar to us from the Arabian Nights, disposed his fables so artistically, that the curiosity of his hearers could not rest satisfied before reaching the end of each book. The fables themselves are written in prose; their morals, and the ideas they suggest, are conveyed in verse."[1] The fables and stories, probably, are little changed since the time when first they were collected; but the verses, which intersect or conclude the tales, appear to have been altered by successive owners and copyists;[2] "for it is obvious, that many of the verses were interpolated at various epochs of Sanskrit literature, and that a sound, critical edition of the text would probably have to go still farther than the distinguished scholars, Lassen and Schlegel, went, in lopping off the parasitical poetry, which overgrew the prose stem of the original work."[3]

[1] Hitopadesa. Translated by Prof. F. Johnson, p. 5.
[2] West. Review, Jan., 1863, p. 330.
[3] Westminster Review, Jan., 1863, pp. 330, 331.

The four books or chapters of the Hitopadesa are entitled: Acquisition of Friends; Separation of Friends; War; Peace. Some of the fables in the Panchatantra are omitted, the position of others is changed; and although a few new ones are introduced, it is shorter than the *Panchopákhyána*,[1] or five (collections of) stories, as the work is very commonly called in India. Sometimes merely the locality is altered, as the king whose sons required instruction lives at Patna. And again, the invocation, which in the Panchatantra, was to Saraswati, is here addressed to Siva, "on whose brow (shines) a digit of the moon, like a streak of the foam of Jahnavi."[2]

The first fable in the Hitopadesa is a short version of that in which the pigeons were snared by a fowler.

A flock of pigeons, hovering in the air, eagerly desire to pick up grains of rice, which they perceive on the way-side. The king of the pigeons demurs, thinking rice in a lonely forest suspicious: they might perish if they touched it, as the traveller perished through coveting a bracelet. "How was that?" said the pigeons. "One day," answered their king, "as I flew through a grove in the Dekkan, I saw an old tiger, who, having bathed and washed, with holy kusa grass in his paw, cried, 'Holloa, traveller; receive this, my golden bracelet!' Upon this, a traveller, eagerly desiring the bracelet, began to consider, and to question the tiger, who admitted that formerly, indeed, in the state of youth, he used to kill cows, Bráhmans, and men; but since that time his children had died, and also his wife, and he had become very religious. The tiger, moreover, quoted holy texts, as:

"'A gift, bestowed on the poor, is beneficial, O son of Pándu. Thou art distressed; therefore I am anxious to give to thee.'

"'Nourish the poor, O son of Kunti: bestow not wealth on the rich."[3]

---

[1] Wilson's Works, vol. iv. pp. 5—7.
[2] Hitopadesa. Johnson; ver. 1.
[3] Works, Sir W. Jones, vol. xiii. P. Johnson, Hitopadesa. Hertford, 1848.

These holy texts reassured the traveller, who went into the water, sunk into a quagmire, and was devoured by the tiger. The remainder of this section is not very different from what appears in the Panchatantra.

In the second section, "Separation of Friends," the jackals tell of a dog who allows a thief to carry off the property of his sleeping master. In the same court-yard with the dog was an ass, who urged the dog to do his duty, and give warning, but the dog bids the ass mind his own concerns, and says that their master has in fact been too long at ease, and has become remiss in supplying food.

"Without the appearance of something disquieting, masters are apt to become inattentive to their dependants."

The faithful ass was by no means satisfied by the dog's explanation of his conduct, but brayed out to his utmost, and the master, who was a washerman, waking up, vexed at the disturbance, beat the ass with a cudgel, whereupon the ass died.[1]

The third section commences by the young princes saying, "Worthy sir, we are the sons of a raja, therefore we have an eager desire to hear of war." Vishnusarman consents, and says, "Listen then to the narrative of a war, the first stanza of which is this: 'In a contest of geese (water fowl) with peacocks, in which the valour displayed was equal on either side, the geese (or water birds) were betrayed by crows, who lived in the mansion of their enemies.'"

The water fowl inhabited a lake in the lovely island of Karpūra. Their king was a flamingo, named Hiranyagarbha. Whilst sitting one day on a bed of lotus flowers, he perceived a crane, named Dirghamukha (long-bill), just arrived from some distant country. He enquired news, and was told that in *Jambudwipa* there is a mountain called Vindhya, whereon dwells a peacock, named Chitravarna (spotted-colour), the king of birds.

[1] Fable iii . F. Johnson, p. 41.

Whilst the crane was seeking food in a bare wood, the peacocks observed him, and inquired whence he came. The crane said he was a subject of the king of Karpûra, and was travelling for amusement. The peacocks then desired to know his opinion of their country, as compared with his own. But when the crane told them that the island of Karpûra was a paradise, and its king a lord of Paradise, and that they would do well to abandon their barren soil for such a home, the peacocks felt insulted. The crane thereupon observed,

"A sensible man may with advantage be admonished, but a blockhead, never; as may be seen by the birds who gave good advice to monkeys, and were, in consequence, driven from their nests."

"How happened that," said the peacocks?
"On the banks of the Narmadâ, or Nerbudda," replied the crane, stands a large simul or silk cotton tree,[1] in which certain birds had built their nests for years. Once, when the sky was dark as indigo, and rain fell in torrents, the birds observed shivering monkeys rushing to the tree for shelter. 'Hearken, monkeys!' said the birds, 'our warm nests are built with straws brought by us with our beaks. Why should you, who are furnished with hands and feet, sit despairing in the cold?'[2] But instead of profiting by these hints, the monkeys took offence, and so soon as the rain had ceased, they avenged their affronted self-importance by climbing up into the tree, destroying the nests, and throwing the eggs upon the ground." [3]

And so it happened that the peacocks flew into a rage at being told that their country was less luxuriant than that inhabited by the water-fowl, and they struck the crane with their beaks, and dragged him before their king, and cried out, "Vile crane, who made your flamingo a king?" The minister of the peacock king

---

[1] See ante, vol. i. pp. 68, 74.
[2] Sir W. Jones, vol. xiii., 119.
[3] Hitopadesa. Translated by Prof. Johnson, p. 72.

was a sensible and experienced vulture. Instead of being irritable and indignant, he asked who was minister to the king of the water-birds at Karpûra? "A Chakravâka" (Brâhmanî goose), said the crane. "A fit person," replied the vulture, "because he belongs to their race and country."[1] And then he quoted verses to the effect that a king should appoint as minister a man of his own nation, of good caste, "familiar with every science, not addicted to idle pleasures, free from loose habits; one who has read the body of laws, renowned; of an ancient family . . . . and an able financier."[2]

In this section, entitled War, with which we are at present occupied, we are constantly reminded that instruction in the arts of polity is the object, and that stories are here mediums. The stories, therefore, give place continually to make room for the introduction of familiar texts and ancient maxims. Thus, at the peacock council, the vulture calmly discourses on the qualifications desirable in a king's adviser. The parrot interrupts him, declaring that Karpûra, and all such islands, belong by right to the peacock king. The king having his covetousness thus excited, says in verse,

"A king, a madman, a child, a silly woman, and a purse-proud man, desire even what is unattainable,—how much more what is attainable."

At this, the crane gives way to anger, and says, that if mere assertion establishes a king's authority, his master, the king of the water-fowl, may lay claim to the whole of Jambudwipa, including the peacock territory. Being asked how that could be effected, he replies, by war. Whereupon the king of the peacocks said, smiling, "Go then and make preparation."

The crane desires that an ambassador from the peacocks be also sent. To which the peacock-king assents, but ponders as to who should be chosen for an ambassador; he should be—

---

[1] Code of Manu, ch. vii., v. 141.
[2] Johnson, p. 73.
[2] Sir W. Jones, vol. xiii., p. 119.

"Faithful, honest, pure, fortunate (or dexterous), patient; a Brâhman, knowing the thoughts of others, and extremely sagacious, exact in delivering his message," &c.

The parrot is finally fixed on as a fitting envoy. "As your majesty commands," said the parrot, "but with that crane I travel not;" and then tells stories to justify his refusal.

The crane had, therefore, to return alone; and, after he had finished relating his adventures to his king, and the assembled water-fowl, and had announced that he was closely followed by the parrot, the wise prime minister thus pronounced judgment: "This crane, this Dirghamukha (Longbill), having gone to a foreign country, has performed the king's business to the best of his ability, but such is ever the nature of fools."

"It is the opinion of a wise man, that one should give a hundred rather than quarrel. War, without necessity, is the part of a fool."

"Enough of reviling," said the king; "let the matter on hand be attended to." "Sire," said the minister, "I would speak with thee in private, for—

'Sagacious persons can interpret the inward thoughts by the colour, by sounds, by a change in the eye or mouth,'" &c.[1]

When alone with his king, the minister expressed freely his opinion that the whole affair was caused by the folly of the crane.

The king will not discuss the point; but says, "What ought to be done?" "Send a spy," says the minister, "then shall we know what is going on in that country—what may be its strength, and what its weakness."

A spy is the king's eye; whoever has no spy is blind. Thus it has been said—

[1] Johnson, p. 80.

"A king should maintain a correspondence with his emissaries, who wear the badge of ascetics, and under the pretext of acquiring learning, visit holy places, colleges and temples."

Whilst Hiranyagarbha, king of the water-fowl, and his minister, were still consulting in private, a chamberlain entered, and, after making obeisance, announced that a parrot from Jambudwipa was standing at the gate. The king looked at his minister, and the minister said, "Let a separate apartment be prepared for him. Afterwards he shall be presented." Many wise speeches are then made by the Chakravâka to check his master's eagerness to commence war. "Victory is ever doubtful," he is reminded; therefore

"By gentle means, by gifts, by sowing divisions; by all, combined or separately, he should strive to subdue his enemies."

"Fear, whilst the enemy is at a distance; heroism, when he is near,—is the quality of a great man."

"A prudent soldier, having betaken himself to his tortoise-like shelter, should sustain the shock of arms: but when he has found his opportunity, he should rise up like an enraged serpent."

"One skilled in expedients can be powerful against a strong foe, as against an insignificant; as the current of a river can uproot trees as well as grass. Then let this ambassador, the parrot, be detained here (he concludes) until the necessary fortifications are completed."

A verse from the Code of Manu is then introduced,

"One bowman, placed on a wall, is a match in war for a hundred enemies; and a hundred for ten thousand."

A fort must, therefore, be made. The next verse given is graphic, but not from Manu.

"A prince, stationed in his enemies' country without a fortress, ... is like a man fallen out of a ship."

Directions being rehearsed as to the battlements, provisions, water, wood, &c., required, the king concludes by inquiring to whom the preparation of such a fortress could be entrusted. The Indian crane, called Sárasa, is considered qualified, and the king appoints him. The Sárasa then bows to the king, and mentions a pool which has an island in its centre, which will meet the requirements, if well supplied with stores; and the stores, he says, must be of grain, for the brightest gems would not sustain life.

It is now announced that a crow has arrived, and desires to be admitted to the king and council. The king is willing, but his cautious minister reminds him that the crow is a land-bird, and says in verse,

"The blockhead who, after deserting his own party, attaches himself to the party of his opponents, will be destroyed by them, like the blue jackal."

After relating this story,[1] the clever, cautious Chakraváka allows that the parrot must be received, but reminds his king that Chánakya of old slew king Nanda, by employing a subtle messenger. At length, a council is assembled, to which it is resolved that the parrot, and also the crow, must be admitted. The parrot entered with his head a little raised, saying, "Hear, O Hiranyagarbha, what the glorious Chitravarna, the king of the peacocks, thus commands: If thou value life or fortune, come speedily and pay homage at our feet. If not, be assured of expulsion from thy territory." The king of the water-birds on hearing this, exclaimed in anger, "Can no one silence this parrot?" The newly-arrived crow said, "Let the king command, and I will put the base parrot to death." But the wise minister (Chakraváka) firmly interposed, saying,

"That is not a council where there are no elders; those are not

[1] Ante, p. 278.

elders who declare not the law. That is not law in which truth is not; and there is no truth where fear prevails."

The law, he says, requires that an ambassador never be slain, even though he should be a barbarian. An ambassador is a messenger who speaks as he is instructed. The parrot is, therefore, treated with courtesy, and dismissed with the usual compliments and ornaments of gold.

Arriving again at home in the peacock kingdom, on the Vindhya hills, king Jewel-Plume asks for his news. The parrot assures him that war must commence, for

The island of Karpûra, the home of the water-birds, is a province of Paradise. "How," he continues, "can I describe it?"

On hearing this, Chitravarna, the peacock-king, convened a council, and spoke thus:—"Now since war must be waged, advise what is to be done, for it is written

'Discontented priests and contented princes are alike ruined.'"[1]

His chief minister, a vulture, named Dûradarsin (far-seeing), then spoke,

"In distress, war is not to be waged;[2] . . . . . when the foe is unprepared, then war may be declared."

When the minister objects to the king's marching, because he has not yet ascertained the strength of the enemy, the king replies—

"Minister, do not on every occasion repress my energy; but instruct me how a prince, determined on conquest, must invade an enemy's territory."[3]

The minister consents to give the required advice, but adds, only when it is followed does it yield fruit.

---

[1] Johnson, p. 85. [2] Ibid, p. 85. [3] Sir W. Jones, vol. xiii., p. 142.

About twenty verses on how to conduct troops in an enemy's country are then given, until at length the king says, what need of so much talk? ..... Let an astrologer be called, and let him calculate an auspicious day for our expedition; and, at length, the peacock-king and peacock-troops all march forth. Shortly after, Hiranyagarbha received information through his messengers that the peacock force had already arrived on the top of the mountain Malaya. The messenger also intimated that some one within their fortress was an enemy in disguise, who certainly acted by the orders of the great vulture-minister of the advancing peacock. "O, king," said the Chakravâka, "that must be the crow." "That cannot be," said the king, "if it were so, would he have been so willing to kill the parrot?"[1]

But, nevertheless, the Chakravâka believes that the crow is betraying them, and tells the king stories to justify his suspicions. One of these stories is that of the beggar, who was changed into a pot of gold. It does not appear appropriate to this section, and is given without the graphic details of Jain customs, which make it interesting in the Panchatantra. The king gets impatient, and says, let the matter on hand be attended to. If Chitravarna and the peacock troops are actually encamped at the foot of the Malaya, what can be done?"

The Chakravâka says in reply, that he had heard from a spy that Chitravarna, the peacock, had been shewing disregard to the advice of his great minister, the vulture; that indiscreet prince may, therefore, be subdued, for "the avaricious, the cruel, the intractable, the liar, the careless, the timid, the unstable, the blockhead, the despiser of warriors, is an enemy easy to subdue." Therefore, whilst he has not yet invested our fortress, let the generals be directed to slay his forces in the rivers, on the mountains, in the forests, on the roads.

The Sârasa is in consequence sent forth with troops, and has

[1] Johnson, p. 88.   [2] Ibid, p. 92.

great success against the peacocks. The peacock-king is humbled and subdued; begs advice of his vulture minister, and is told to blockade the gates of the water-birds' fortress.

It is now king Hiranyagarbha's turn to become intractable; and, neglecting the advice of the wise Chakravâka, he listens to the treacherous crow, who advises the water-birds to march out, and whilst they are fighting at all the four gates, the crows set fire to every building in the fort. The Sârasa (Indian crane) is faithful to the last, and dies defending the fortress of which he had had command.

The section concludes with a wish or hope that the young princes may never themselves have occasion to fight with elephants, cavalry and infantry, but, says Vishnusarman, "may your enemies be overcome by the winds of prudent counsels, or flee for refuge to the caves of the mountains!"[1]

The section on Peace is a continuation of the same fable. When Hiranyagarbha discovered that the crow, who had departed, had been the cause of his defeat, he says:

"This is the fault of destiny, assuredly not of counsellors. A business, well planned, is destroyed through the influence of destiny."

But his minister subjoins:

"An ignorant man, when meeting with a rugged condition, reproaches destiny, comprehending not the errors of his own conduct."
"He who comprehends not the advice of well-wishing friends, will perish, like the foolish turtle that dropped from the stick."[1]

Stories which follow show, that neglect of good advice is followed by calamity; and soon afterwards Longbill, who had been out as a scout, returned, saying that the burning of the fortress had undoubtedly been effected by the crow, and that the crow

[1] Johnson, p. 99.　　　　[2] Ibid, p. 99.

had been under the direction of the vulture. The Raja sighed, and said:

"He, who on account of respect shown or assistance rendered, confides in enemies, is awakened from his delusion, like one fallen from the top of a tree in his sleep."[1]

Longbill then related what had been passing at the Peacock court, where the king, delighted with the crow for burning his enemies' fort, proposed to make him king of Karpûra. But the vulture exclaimed, that such a proceeding would be improper: the crow was a low person, and must not be placed in the station of the great.

"When a low person has obtained a high position, he seeks to cut off his master, as the mouse, having attained the form and force of a tiger, sought to kill the saint."[2]

The vulture tells this and other stories to enforce prudence and propriety; and at last the peacock said to his minister in private: "Father! advise me what to do."

The vulture replied:

"The guide of a king, lifted up with pride, like the driver of a restive elephant, incurs censure."

"Hearken, O king! was the castle demolished by my contrivance, or by thy strength?"

"By thy stratagem," answered the king.

So much being admitted, the minister urges the peacock to return to his own country, lest in the rainy season, which is now at hand, the water-birds should renew the attack, and retreat be then found difficult. "For the sake of our ease and credit, let us make peace and retire."

[1] Johnson, p. 108.   [2] Ibid, p. 105.

"A king has a helper in him, who, setting his duty before him, and disregarding his master's likings and dislikings, tells him unwelcome but wholesome things."[1]

"He should seek peace, even with an equal. In war, victory is doubtful. One should not do an uncertain thing: so saith Vrihaspati."

"What wise man would expose his friend, his army, his kingdom, himself and his reputation, to the uncertainties of war?"[2]

"Why," said the king, "was not this advice given before? Whereupon the vulture minister reminded the royal peacock that the war had not been commenced by his advice. The waterbird, Hiranyagarbha," he continues, "is of a peaceable disposition; and the poet says: "the true-speaking man, the virtuous man, &c., are declared to be the seven with whom peace should be made." Other verses are quoted, showing the difficulties of war and the advantages of peace; and the whole conversation is reported to Hiranyagarbha and his minister by their spy. Having a second time despatched the spy to the enemies' camp, the Chakravâka meanwhile diligently urges peace. Amongst other remarks, he makes the following:

"Power is triple; being formed of kings, of counsels, and of constant effort."[3]

"Fortune, which cannot be purchased, even at the price of life, although fickle, voluntarily seeks the palace of a king, who understands good morals."

At length the king fully perceives the desirableness of friendship with Jewel-Plume, the peacock king, whom they fear may be difficult to deal with. Under these circumstances, the Chakravâka proposes that a crane be despatched to their ally, the king of Ceylon, who appears to have been a stork; and that he be urged to excite an insurrection in Jambudwîpa. The king

[1] Johnson, p. 105. [2] Sir W. Jones, vol. xiii. p. 186. [3] Johnson, p. 106.

said, "Be it so;" and a crane set forth with a private letter.[1] At this time Longbill again returned, and reported that the vulture-minister had suggested that the crow, who had lived so long at the court of Hiranyagarbha, should be summoned to give testimony to the character of that king, and to that of his prime minister, the Chakraváka. "Please your Majesty," said the crow, "Hiranyagarbha speaks the truth as faithfully as Yudhishthira; and a minister equal to the Chakraváka is nowhere to be seen." "How, then," said Jewel-Plume, "was he deceived by thee?" To which the crow replied: "What dexterity is there in killing a child who has climbed into your lap and slumbers on your knee? Hear, O king: I was detected by that minister at the first glance; but Hiranyagarbha has great benignity, and was on that account imposed on."[2]

He who thinks a knave as honest as himself, is deceived by him, as the Bráhman was in the affair of the goat. Two stories are here told, of unsuspecting natures being easily deceived by the designing. "But, Night-cloud," said the peacock-king to the crow, "how couldst thou dwell so long among enemies and conciliate them?" "Sir," replied the crow, "what cannot be done by one seeking to promote his master's interests or his own private ends? People carry wood (respectfully) on their heads, although intending to burn it; and a river washes the roots of a tree, although at the same time it undermines them." The crow is then allowed to indulge in philosophical remarks and quotations, as:

"This body, wasting away every moment, is not perceived to decay, like a jar of unbaked clay standing in water: *its dissolution* is known when it has dissolved."

"Day by day death approaches nearer ..... as to a victim led step by step to the slaughter."

"As a plank of timber may meet *another* plank in the great waters, and after meeting may again separate; even such is the meeting of human beings."

[1] Sir W. Jones, vol. xiii. p. 86.   [2] Johnson, p. 100.

"What occasion is there for lamentation over a body composed of five elements?"[1]

But at length the crow applies the moral, and declares that, on every account, peace must be made. King peacock upbraids him with his bad judgment, and says that the water-fowl, being defeated, must either submit to live under vassalage or be further reduced by war. At this juncture a report arrives of the Singhalese invasion. This news puts king peacock in a fury; but his minister understands at once that it was a manœuvre of Chakravâka, the minister of Hiranyagarbha, and says within himself: "Excellent! O minister."[2]

Jewel-Plume declares he will march immediately and destroy the king of Ceylon. The vulture says, "Make not a thundering noise, for no purpose, like a cloud in autumn;" and ventures to remind his Majesty that if he departs without making peace, an attack will be made upon his rear. "A blockhead who, without knowing the true state of the case, becomes subject to anger, is tormented, as the Brâhman was on account of the weasel (or mungoose)."[3]

The story of the father who killed the mungoose, which had saved his child from a snake, is here introduced; and after sage reflections, the vulture-minister says that peace must be concluded. "Peace, grounded not on conciliation or cordial affection, is

"Like an earthen pot or a bad man, easily broken and cannot without difficulty be re-united; but a virtuous man, like a pot of gold, is broken with difficulty and easily repaired."[4]

At last king peacock gets tired of debate and desires the vulture to accomplish the object proposed.

The vulture then started on his mission. The crane, who

[1] Johnson, p. 113.
[2] Ibid, p. 116.
[3] Sir W. Jones, vol. xiii. p. 201.
[4] Johnson, p. 117.

acted as scout to the water-birds, gave warning of his approach. King Hiranyagarbha is alarmed lest he should be coming, like the crow, to work mischief. His minister, the Chakraváka, tells him there is no cause of fear, for Dûradarsin, the vulture, is a noble spirit. But so it is, he says, with dull-minded persons: one while they suspect no one, at another time everyone. When the vulture has been introduced, Chakraváka (the minister of Hiranyagarbha) says to him:

O great minister! enjoy this realm according to thy desire: it is at thy service. Even so, said the king. Be it so, said the vulture; but now an abundance of words will be useless. For,

"With money one should receive a covetous man; with hands joined in token of respect, a haughty man; with the humouring of his wishes, a blockhead; and with truth, a clever man."
"One should receive a friend with kindness; kinsmen with lively emotion; women and servants with gifts and honours; and other people with courtesy."[1]

Therefore, let us now make peace, and be gone. The different ways of making peace are then discussed,—the two ministers, the vulture, and the Chakraváka, repeating above twenty verses on the subject. At last king Hiranyagarbha ventures to observe, that they are both great scholars and must instruct him what to do. What says the poet? replied the vulture (from peacock-land).

"Who, verily, would commit injustice for the sake of a body, which to-day or to-morrow, may be destroyed by anxiety or disease?"
"The life of animals, verily, is tremulous, as the reflection of the moon in water."
"Viewing the world like the vapour of the desert, which passeth away in an instant, ... let a man seek the society of the virtuous."
"If a thousand sacrifices of a horse and truth were weighed in a balance, truth would outweigh the thousand sacrifices."[2]

---

[1] Johnson, p. 118.   [2] Ibid, p. 120.

"Wherefore, let the peace called golden be concluded, preceded by the oath named truth." "Be it so," said the Chakraváka. And then the vulture, having received gifts of jewels, vests, &c., went in great joy to his peacock-king, taking with him the Chakraváka. Peace was then ratified, and the Chakraváka sent back to Hiranyagarbha with great respect, and bearing many presents. Finally, the vulture said to king peacock:

"Our object is accomplished; let us return to our own home in the Vindhya mountains."

Each party then retired to his proper station, and enjoyed that which their hearts had longed for.[1]

[1] Sir W. Jones, vol. xiii. p. 308.

Gate at Barolli.
About the ninth century, a.d.

CHAPTER XXXVII.

FICTIONS.

Kathá-Sarit-Ságara, "Ocean of the Streams of Narrative;" collected about A.D. 1088.—*Allusion to the grammarians Pánini and Vararuchi.*

"THOSE who rank the highest among eastern nations for genius have," says Sir John Malcolm, "employed their talents in works of fiction, and have added to the moral lessons they desired to convey so much of grace and ornament, that their volumes have found currency in every nation of the world." The influx of these works into Europe, Sir John dates from the Crusades; and although at one time located in Persia, and appropriated as a portion of Persian literature, it has since been discovered that the Persians not only plundered the Hindus " of their real goods and chattels, but also of their works of imagination."

Sir J. Malcolm thus adds his testimony to the independence and originality of Sanskrit fiction in general; the " moral lessons" to which he alludes not being confined, we apprehend, to the fables which teach polity, but also extending to tales of domestic life, the direct object of which is diversion or amusement.

Tales of this description have been scattered broadcast over the length and breadth of India for countless centuries. From

age to age they have been repeated, with variations; and they
are so strictly indigenous that they appear coeval with the origin
and growth of the Hindus as a people. From time to time
floating tales were gathered into groups, some fanciful name
being given to the collection. The most popular of these books
are known by the following titles:

Kathá-Sarit-Ságara—ocean of the streams of narrative.
Vetála-Panchavinsati—twenty-five stories, told by a Vetâla.
Sinhásana-Dwátrinsati—thirty-two tales, told by the images
 which supported the throne of Vikramâditya.
Suka-Saptati—seventy-two tales of a parrot.[1]

With the first and second of the collections here mentioned
we will endeavour to make our readers somewhat acquainted.

The "Ocean" originated in the desire of a queen of Kashmir
to provide amusement and instruction for her grandson. Somadeva, the prime minister, produced in consequence these tales
in verse, "to enable the memory," he says, "more readily to
retain the complicated net of narrative invention." That verse
helps the memory, is admitted; but as "minuteness of detail is
the soul of all story-telling," Professor Wilson believes that the
older work, in prose,[2] would be found more animated and interesting than the versified compendium. In the Ocean Stream
of Stories we have fortunately a work, of which the date can be
fixed with some precision; for Harsha Deva was the son of
Kalasa, the son of Ananta, the son of Sangráma. And Sûrya-
vati, his grandmother, was the wife of Ananta, and mother of
Kalasa. Harsha himself reigned about A.D. 1125. According
to the Kashmir chronicle, his grandmother is supposed to have
burnt herself with the corpse of her husband Ananta, A.D. 1093.
Therefore, as the compilation certainly preceded that event, it is
thought safe to state A.D. 1088[3] as the most modern limit for

---

[1] Wilson, vol. iv. p. 106. [2] The Vrihat-Kathá. [3] Wilson, vol. iv. pp. 111—113.

any story it contains; whilst no limit can be fixed for their possible antiquity.

The work consists of eighteen books, divided into one hundred and twenty-four sections. The text has been published at Leipzig, by Professor Brockhaus, with a translation of the five first books, comprising twenty-six sections.

It commences thus:—

"On the summit of Kailâsa, a lofty peak of the Himalaya, resided the mighty deity, Maheswara, or Siva, attended by innumerable spirits and genii, and worshipped even by the superior deities." His wife was the daughter of the mountain monarch, of whom we read in the poem, called "Birth of the War-God." She "propitiated her lord by her celestial strains;" and he, in return, proffered her whatever boon she might request. In the poem, the name of this lovely wife was Umâ. She is here called Pârvatî, or Bhavânî. She says she has but one wish, and that is, to hear from her husband narrations as yet unknown. Siva then tells her of the worship offered him by Brahmâ and Vishnu in former ages, and of the favour obtained by Vishnu, on account of the service which he rendered to Siva. But when he proceeded to relate the story of Daksha's sacrifice, which caused the death of Sati, who was born again as the daughter of the mountain king, his wife felt annoyed, and wished him not to disclose such things. Siva then gave orders that no person should be admitted, and proceeded with narratives illustrating "the felicity of the gods, the troubles of mankind, and the intermediate and varying conditions of the spirits of earth and heaven." Now it so happened, that one of Siva's favourite attendants coming to the palace gate, was amazed at being refused admission, and rendering himself invisible, entered, overheard the marvellous stories, and retired, as he had entered, unobserved. But this demi-divine attendant, whose name was

---

[1] Wilson, vol. iii., p. 159.

Pushpadanta, was so imprudent as to communicate the narratives to his wife, and his wife equally unable to preserve silence, communicated them to her fellow attendants, and soon the affair became known to the goddess and her lord, both to Párvatí and Siva.

For this offence, Pushpadanta was condemned to a human birth, and "his friend Mályavat, who presumed to intercede for him, was sentenced to a like fate." In compassion for the distress of Pushpadanta's wife, a term was fixed to the period of degradation, as that when he should meet with a certain exile from the heavenly regions haunting the Vindhya mountains as a goblin, but remembering his original condition, "and shall repeat to him the tales, the curse shall no more prevail." This having been said, the two culprits, like a flash of lightning, blazed and disappeared.

After a due interval, the rash listener was born at the city of Kausámbí, and named Vararuchi. The first story in the collection gives his history as told by himself.

"I was born," he says, "at Kausámbí, the son of a Bráhman, named Somadatta, who died whilst I was a child, and left my mother in indigence, with the charge of my education. Whilst struggling with distress, it chanced that two Bráhmans stopped at our dwelling, and solicited hospitality for the night, as they were strangers, and weary with long travel. They were received. Whilst sitting together, we heard a drum, and my mother exclaimed in a tone of regret, 'Your father's friend, boy, the actor Navananda, holds some representation.' I replied, 'Do not be vexed, mother, I will go to see what is exhibited, and will bring every word to you.' This vaunt astonished our guests, who, to try my memory, recited the famous collection of phonetic rules, entitled the Prátisákhya, which I immediately repeated after them. They then accompanied me to the play, of which I re-

[1] Wilson, vol. iii., p. 100.

peated every speech to my mother on our return home." After this amazing exhibition of memory, one of the Bráhmans spoke to the mother of Vararuchi, saying that her son was the very person of whom they were in search.

This Bráhman, named Vyádi, was the author of a grammatical work, called Sangraha. He is sometimes called Dákshâyana, and is a descendant of Daksha and Dákshi. We know that the mother of the grammarian Pánini was named Dákshí, and that Vyádi was a near relative of Pánini, who "must have preceded him by at least two generations."[1]

The travelling Bráhmans, Vyádi, and his friend Indradatta, tell of a dream they had had, which commanded them to seek instruction from a learned man at Patna. But this learned man, by name Varsha, had disappointed them, for he was unable to communicate what he knew. He even appeared to them as an idiot, for he was under the peculiar condition of having nothing to say unless his pupil was a Bráhman, who could at once retain the whole. Vyádi and Indradatta had not this power, so they left their unsatisfactory teacher, and were in search of a Bráhman gifted with such retentive faculties as were possessed by the youthful Vararuchi.

On understanding the state of affairs, the mother consented to part with her son, who went with the Bráhman guests to Patna; and Varsha, released from embarrassment by Vararuchi's gift of memory, became a teacher of great repute.[2]

An anachronism here occurs, since the great Pánini is in this tale represented as contemporary with Vyádi and Vararuchi. As literary evidence of the age of Pánini, therefore, the passage is worthless; we will quote it, nevertheless, as indirect testimony to the importance attached to Pánini by his countrymen.

"Amongst the pupils of Varsha was a Bráhman, named Pánini, a fellow of remarkable dulness, and so incapable of

[1] Goldstücker's Pánini, p. 210 ff.   [2] Wilson, vol. iii., p. 163 ff.

learning, that he was at last expelled from the classes. Deeply sensible of this disgrace, he had recourse to devotion; and, setting off to the snow mountains, propitiated Siva by a course of severe austerities, in consequence of which the god communicated to him the system of grammar which bears his name."[1] When Pánini returned, he challenged Vararuchi to a public disputation. For seven days they argued on an equality; on the eighth day, the discussion was interrupted by a hideous noise, which so disconcerted Vararuchi, that he and his abettors abandoned the contest, and, from that time, Pánini's grammar has supplanted that of his rival. It was now Vararuchi's turn to go to the mountains and seek the favour of Siva. During his absence, he commissioned his lately married wife, Upasoká, to manage his affairs; and the history of her adventures, Professor Wilson says, is one of the best told stories in the book. During the absence of her husband, Upasoká became "the object of the addresses of the king's family-priest, the commander of the guards, the princes' tutor, and her husband's banker."

"She made appointments with them all to come to her house at different hours on the same night."

"At the expiration of the first watch of the night, the preceptor of the prince arrived. Upasoká affected to receive him with great delight; and, after some conversation, desired him to take a bath, which her hand-maidens had prepared." The preceptor made no objection; the bath was placed in a dark room, his own clothes were taken away, and in their place he was supplied with sheets, smeared with lamp-black oil and perfumes. When sufficiently rubbed, the women exclaimed, "Alas! here arrives our master's particular friend."[2] Thereupon they hurried the poor man into a basket, well fastened by a bolt outside; and, in the same way, they disposed of the priest and the commander of the guard. From the banker, Upasoká demanded

---

[1] Wilson, vol. iii. pp. 169, 170.   [2] Ibid. vol. iii., 171, 172.

her husband's money, and leading him near the closed basket, spoke aloud, and made him promise that she should have it. A bath was then proposed, but before it could be enjoyed, daylight appeared, and the banker was glad to depart.

Next day, Upasoká presented a petition to king Nanda, saying, that the banker sought to appropriate property entrusted to him by her absent husband, Vararuchi. The banker was then summoned into court, and Upasoká said that the household gods which her husband had left in baskets could give witness. The king having sent for the baskets, Upasoká said, "Speak, gods, and declare what you have overheard this banker say in our dwelling. If you are silent, I will unhouse you in this presence." The men in the baskets acknowledge that they had heard the banker admit that he possessed wealth belonging to the husband of Upasoká. The court was amazed, and the terrified banker promised restitution. The king now begged for a sight of these household gods, and out came the culprits like lumps of darkness; and, being recognised, they were not only exposed to ridicule, but banished as criminals from the kingdom, whilst Upasoká excited the admiration and esteem of the whole city.[1]

We here lose sight of Vararuchi, but may remember that in his heavenly state at Siva's court, he had a friend who was sentenced to be also born on earth, and in the history of this friend, we again stumble on philology or skill in various languages. "Gunádhya," we read, had a dispute with a rival Bráhman, which induced him to forego the use of Sanskrit, Prakrit, and Desya,[2] or vernacular languages. But he learns the Paisáchí, or language of the goblins, and this enables him to receive narrations told him by a metamorphosed Yaksha or Pisácha.

Having heard from the Pisácha seven hundred thousand stanzas, he wrote them with his blood, the forest not affording

[1] Wilson, vol. iii., p. 173. [2] Wilson, vol. iv., pp. 120—133.

ink. He then offered the work to a king, called Sâtavâhana, of Pratishthâna (supposed to be the king Sâlivâhana, who reigned about A.D. 78). This king at first rejected, but afterwards solicited the work, and translated it from the language of the Pisâchas.

Another story mentioned by Professor Wilson, as well known in Europe, but first met with in this collection, is that of a young husband who is obliged to leave his wife for a season. To assure them of each other's constancy, "a couple of divine lotus flowers of a red colour are obtained in a dream," the hues of which will fade should either prove untrue. The husband, Gúhasena, a young merchant, meets with companions, who learn the purport of his lotus, and set off to try the virtue of his wife. "They find an *old Buddhist priestess* willing to promote their designs." The conclusion is, that the young wife invites her wicked lovers to an entertainment, puts a narcotic in their wine, and when they are asleep brands them on the forehead, and is finally re-united in all trust and happiness to her husband.[1]

In the fifth book, which is the last translated by Dr. Brockhaus, a man being shipwrecked, is caught in a whirlpool, and escapes by jumping up and clinging to the branches of a fig-tree, apparently the banyan, Ficus Indica, celebrated for its pendulous roots.[2]

The later books of the Kathâ-Sarit-Sâgara appear to be much occupied with supernatural creatures, called Vidyâdharîs, who live in the island of the Golden City, and with magic, which enables men to desert one body and enter into another, and with Nâgas, who are "in their own persons serpents—demi-divine, but snakes nevertheless."[3]

---

[1] Wilson, vol. iv., pp. 122—126.
[2] Professor Wilson refers to the Odyssey xii., pp. 101—104, where Ulysses escapes from a whirlpool by jumping up and clinging to the branches of a fig-tree, probably, he says, the *Indian* fig-tree or banyan, the pendulous branches of which would be more within reach than those of the Sicilian fig ; and Homer, he thinks, may have borrowed the incident from some old Eastern fiction. See also, vol. iii., p. 257.
[3] Ibid, p. 133.

Branch of Pipal or Aswattha Tree (*ficus religiosa*).

CHAPTER XXXVIII.

THE VETALA-PANCHAVINSATI; OR TWENTY-FIVE TALES TOLD BY A VETAL.

VETALS appear to be the same creatures as those called Bhúts and Prets. Sometimes the spirit of a deceased person becomes a Vetál or Bhút, and enters the living body of some one else. But more frequently the Vetál is the spirit of a living person, which changes its abode, leaving its own body, and taking possession of a corpse. "A Bhût of the best class lives in his own house or in a pipal tree."[1]

The superstitions regarding Vetâla appear to be connected with the magic which prevailed in India about the fourth and fifth centuries.[2]

This series of twenty-five stories commences by introducing us to a Brâhman named Shantíl, who has given up the world, and is living in the woods as a hermit or ascetic. He had already become a magician by means of Yogi-practice. But magic, as usually attained, did not satisfy his ambition,—he coveted universal superhuman power; and for this he required the co-operation of an able pupil, carefully instructed, who should be qualified to assist in the sacrifice of a specially-indicated human being.[3]

Whilst Shantíl pursued his ascetic practice, and sat, cross-legged, Yogi-fashion, in his forest-dwelling, a severe famine occurred in the district of Delhi (or near the ancient city of Hastinapura.) The distressed inhabitants dispersed, in search of food; and a Brâhman, whose wife had died of hunger, wandered

---

[1] Bhûts usually haunt the place in which the body died, or in which it was burned, and live in trees, such as the mango, and different kinds of mimosa, and acacia. When a man, whose "Sapindí funeral ceremony has been performed," becomes "a Bhût, from over-anxious affection," .... he is said "to live in his own house," or in the sacred pipal tree.—Essay on Demonology of Gujerat, &c., by Dalpatram Daya, translated by A. K. Forbes, p. 8: Bombay, 1849.

[2] "The Vetâl Punchaviseey," translated from "the Sanskrit of Shewdass, by Crustnath Cassinathjee Prabhoo:" Bombay, 1825.

Another translation of this work was made in 1848, by Capt. W. Hollings, 47th regiment Bengal N.I.

The outlines given above are almost entirely taken from the first-mentioned work by Crustnath C. Prabhoo.

[3] Of the word Vetâl, I have been favoured with the following derivation: Veta, a dead (man), and âla, clinging to; that is, clinging to, or dwelling in, dead bodies. In one of our popular magazines, some stories were published as "Tales of a Vampire, adapted from the Sanskrit," and taken in a measure from the work before us. But Vetâls do not appear to be vampires. Vampire is, I am informed, a word of Slavonic origin, expressive of one who drinks off, drafts off, or taps, and meaning, in the case of vampires, that they are demons which drink blood. No such imputation rests upon the Vetâls of Sanskrit literature. They may have evil tendencies, but this is not a necessary condition of their being Vetâls, or ghosts; and the particular Vetâl, who tells the twenty-five stories of which an outline is here given, was undoubtedly an inoffensive being.

with his two sons, who had not yet attained to manhood, into what is called a foreign country. Afar off they perceived a "forest, surrounded by various trees, loaded with ripe fruits. . . . The symmetry, the neatness, and the admirable order of the trees, ... and the abundance and diversity of a thousand sorts of unknown fruits," were captivating. Presently they found themselves in front of an edifice, stately as a palace, although built with common materials. Within, sat the dreadful magician Shantil. To the weary wanderers he merely appeared as a holy ascetic, seated on the customary sacred darbha grass, and holding in his hand the usual string of holy beads, which consists of one hundred and eight of the beautifully-carved nuts or seed-vessels of the eleocarpus, here called in Sanskrit rudráksha. The travellers approached, prostrating themselves, and showing all imaginable reverence. Shantil returned their salutation, and inquired the object of their journey. Having heard their story, he turned to the father and said: "O Bráhman, be not afraid; I will take care of your sons until the famine has disappeared, ... but upon condition that you will then give one of these boys (whichever you like) to me."[1]

The father, feeling that he had no alternative, consented to this arrangement; and, after feasting on dainties for three days, he embraced his sons with many tears, and departed.

Shantil is described as a man skilled in all arts and sciences: nothing, indeed, was unknown to him. He lost no time in setting the boys tasks, to exercise their faculties and prepare them also for the acquisition of magic. He soon ascertained that the younger boy had the higher capacity; and of him he determined to possess himself: he never, therefore, allowed him to go out of his sight. He taught him "grammar, divinity, law, astronomy, philosophy, physiognomy, alchymy, geography, the power of transferring the soul to a dead body, the giving it

[1] "Vertal Panchaviseey," translated from "the Sanskrit of Shewdass, by Crustnath Cassinathjee Prabhoo." Bombay, 1835; p. 90 ff.

animation, and several other arts; amongst which was included
astrology, or the art of foretelling future events. In short, the
law which prescribes that a preceptor shall teach all that he
knows to his pupil (if he be wise and desirous of knowledge) was
fully obeyed." In this case, the diligent, accomplished preceptor was striving to secure an accomplice in a pupil. But, cunning as he was, he seems to have outwitted himself; for, wishing
that the father should prefer the elder lad, he fed him plentifully,
and clothed him handsomely, whilst he kept his younger and
more promising pupil half-starved and poorly clad.[1]

As might be expected, the younger pupil became, in consequence, anxious to escape; and being already "master of the
science which prognosticates future events," he perceived that
the famine had ceased, and that his father was coming to claim
one of his sons and carry him home. He knew also that his
father would be most attracted by his elder brother, who looked
fat, and was covered with jewels. Making use, therefore, of his
power of transporting himself to distant places, he went to his
father, and revealed to him the wicked character and intentions
of the Yogin, and obtained a solemn promise that his father would
choose him, and not his decorated brother, as the son to be
taken home. The father duly arrived at the hermitage; and
though he experienced much difficulty, he at length induced the
Yogin to part with his gifted pupil: and with him he departed.
But the father and son had not proceeded far before the son felt
certain that his tyrant was in pursuit; and, for protection, he
felt it necessary to change himself into a horse. At the same
time he charged his father to sell him at a neighbouring fair;
but for no consideration to part with him to any one in whose
presence he should neigh or paw the ground.

As the young man apprehended, so it happened: Shantil, the
Yogin, tracked them; and, discovering the disguise, presented
himself at the fair, and offered so large a sum that the father,

[1] Veytal Panchaviscey, pp. 93—94.

dazzled by the sight of an enormous heap of gold, sold his son to his dreaded enemy. Shantil then rides his captive back to his hermitage and places him under great restraint. After a few days the imprisoned horse is able to make himself known to his brother, who loosens his bonds,—and he bounds off. Again Shantil pursues; and again the fugitive escapes. On this occasion, assuming the form of a pigeon, he flies in at the open window of the king's palace, and is protected and concealed for a time by a lovely princess.

But Shantil was his master in the arts of magic, and every disguise was discovered. Upon his father he could not depend, for his father had sold him for gold. One refuge alone remained. Shantil had no power over Vetáls,—the spirits which animate dead bodies; and, despairing of other refuge, the young Bráhman Yogin rushed into a corpse which was hanging on a tree in a public cemetery.

This obliged Shantil to seek for a man of sufficient nerve and resolution to go alone to the cemetery, at night, cut down the body which contained the Vetál, into which his pupil had entered, and bring corpse and Vetál to an appointed shrine, at which he would await them.

The man of dauntless courage and resolution was found in king Vikrama,—whether Vikrama of Oujein, A.D. 65, or Harsha Vikrama, of A.D. 500, is not material; but the city is called Dhárá, to the south of the river Godavery.[1]

In Hindu poetry and fiction, Vikrama continually figures as the representative of victorious courage. In the work before us he is said to be handsome as the god of love, a devotee in religious worship, deferential to priests, hermits, or ascetics, and persons who, disgusted with worldliness and contumely of relatives, "had given themselves up to think on God."[2] He was

---

[1] "Bytal Prichoesee;" translated into English by Capt. W. Hollings, 47th regiment Bengal N.I. Calcutta, 1848.

[2] Veytal Punchavisewy; by Crustnath Cussinathjee. Bombay, 1825.

skilled in sacred sciences, warlike, though merciful, a cherisher of the poor, and a comforter of his subjects, whom he loved as if they were his children.

The palace of king Vikrama was large and magnificent. It contained the most splendid and costly articles, it was constantly sprinkled with aloes-water, and every article of furniture was adorned by precious stones.

One day, whilst Vikrama sat as usual on his throne, Shantil, the Yogin, presented himself; and so holy did he appear, that the king received him with the utmost reverence, and coming down from his throne, entreated his guest to take his seat. He then stood with clasped hands and paid him adoration. Shantil presented an artificial fruit, which he had brought, gave his benediction, and went away. For several successive days the same thing was repeated, until, on one occasion, the king happening to drop the fruit which had been presented to him, a pet monkey broke it open, and a splendid ruby was seen within. Thereupon the king desired to have all the other fruits, which the holy man had presented, brought into his presence; and each fruit, when opened, was found to contain rubies. These jewels were of the utmost rarity. Indeed, the smallest were of such value, that the largest could only be considered as beyond all price.

"Hermit" (or Yogin), said the king, "with what intention didst thou present me with such treasures; hast thou anything to ask of me?" Shantil did not at once acknowledge what it was that he wanted; but gradually revealed that he was engaged in rites for obtaining superhuman faculties, and that for their completion he required the personal assistance of the king. He had travelled over the greater part of the world, he said, vainly seeking such a person as would suit his enterprise. "At length," he continued, "I came to your court, and have found in your Majesty the physiognomy of a person fitted to act as assistant in the intended sacrifice." The king did not give him time to say more, but eagerly promised to do whatever was required. Shantil then explained, that a certain Vetâl must be captured and given into his possession. "On the 14th of Aswin, at midnight," he says, "your Majesty must go alone to the cemetery, on the banks of the Godavery, beyond the town. You must be clothed in black, and bear in your hand a naked sword."[1]

When the appointed day arrived, a certain tree was pointed out, from which he was to cut down the required corpse, and having thrown it across his shoulders, carry it in perfect silence to Shantil. Vikrama went, and found this burial ground filled with smoke from burning corpses, and resounding with piercing cries of devils, which were coming from all regions.

At length king Vikrama found the tree, and climbing into it, he cut the cord by which the corpse was suspended, and threw it to the ground; but just as he put out his hands to capture the Vetâl, it jumped up and suspended itself as before, high up on the tree. This happened more than once, until the king discovered that he must bind the corpse across his back before he came down.

But now the king encountered another difficulty; for the Vetâl within the corpse which he carried began telling stories, to beguile the fatigue of the journey he said, but in truth because he wanted to escape: and Vikrama could hold him only on condition of his being absolutely silent. The Vetâl's plan, was, therefore, to put the king off his guard, and just when his interest was excited to ask some pointed question. Five-and-twenty times did this succeed. So soon as the king spoke, the Vetâl flew back to his tree; and the whole process had to be repeated. The five-and-twenty tales, called the Vetâlapanchavinsati, are a record of the tales related on these occasions.

The first story is entitled "Prince Mukunda and Princess Padmâvati." The prince is son to a king of Vârânasi (Benares),

---

[1] Bombay translation, p. 5.

and is much attached to the son of his father's prime minister. The two youths delight in hunting; and, mounting their horses one morning, they go into the woods in quest of game. As the sun rises the heat becomes intense; and about noon, oppressed by thirst, they rush about frantically to find water. At length, at a little distance, they espy a lake and make towards it. On the bank of this lake grow several kinds of flowers, together with the sandal and other Indian trees, on which latter were perched birds, with their wings fluttering for joy, whose singing afforded a melodious harmony. On all four sides of the lake, ghats of brick had been built; and although the water was beautifully clear and cold, its surface could hardly be discerned, so numerous were the lotuses and water-lilies which grew thereon. Tortoises and gold-fish inhabited this delicious retreat; and the shells of the former resembled silver shields.[1]

The young men dismounted, quenched their thirst, and looking around, perceived a temple of Siva in a plantation. Thither they went; and after performing worship, said: "O Siva! who art existing in Pátál, on high in heaven, in the sky, on all mountains, in the ocean, in ashes, in fire, in timber, in iron, on the earth,—in short, who art omnipresent,—listen to our invocation to thee. That tongue is good and meritorious which moves in praise of god Siva; those hands are meritorious which are in readiness to serve and worship god Siva; that sight is of use which contemplates the god Siva. By prostrating once before Siva, with a contrite heart, men will be purified of all sins and offences whatsoever, and ascend to heaven. Thou, whose throat is blue, and on whose head shines Gangá (the river Ganges), and on whose thigh sits Girijá, his wife, and who has the skin of the tiger for a girdle,—may he save us from the misery of this mortal world."[2]

After this prayer, they came into the open air, reclined on

[1] Translation of Crustnath Cassinathjee, p. 7 ff [2] Ibid, pp. 8—9.

couches in the temple porch, and "viewed the prospect of the neighbouring wood." "At length, a handsome young lady, attended by female slaves, came to do homage to Siva." Her ravishing beauty struck the heart of the prince at first sight, and wounded it with five arrows. He and the young lady both swooned, and, after recovering, the lady made a series of signals to express her love. She then directed her steps homeward, and the prince again swooned, as if "she carried his life along with her." When he recovered, he asked his friend what she meant by all the signs she made. "His companion, who was more intelligent than the prince, and master of several arts (for it is generally the case that princes possess but little understanding, and can only govern through the counsel of their ministers, who are usually wise and prudent), then began to explain to his prince the meaning of all the signs the lady had made."[1]

The dull relation of intrigues with which this tale concludes, is not worth attention.

In the second story, the beautiful daughter of a Bráhman gathers flowers to present to the images in her father's house. Unhappily, she trod upon the tail of a venomous serpent, was bitten, and shortly expired. By magical incantations, contained in a book, she is restored to life.

The fifth story is of the daughter of a king of Ougein. She begs her father to let her marry a man possessed of universal excellence. Her father seeks for such a husband for her, and three Bráhmans present themselves.

The first understands all knowledge and science.

The second has made a chariot, which conveys its possessor in a second to whatever place he desires to reach.

The third could hit with an arrow not only what was seen, but what was heard.

---

[1] Translation of Crestuath Cassinathjee, pp. 10, 11.

Whilst the king was pondering and considering to which of these Bráhmans he should give his daughter, she disappeared. The king took council of the three lovers.

The first reflected for about fifteen minutes, and then announced that a demon had taken her to the top of a mountain.

The second said he would shoot the demon.

The third said, "mount my carriage, and having killed the demon, bring her here."

Having narrated so much, the Vetál asks whose wife she would become. Vikrama declares she would be the wife of him who slew the demon; and the Vetál, so soon as the king spoke, flew back to his tree.

The sixth story borders on the humorous; it tells of a young prince who promises to sacrifice himself to Deví, if that goddess permits him to marry a girl with whom he has fallen in love. He is married, as he desires, and a few years afterwards remembering his promise, he presents himself at Deví's shrine and cuts off his head; his friend coming to look for him, sees his headless trunk, and follows his example. Next comes the young wife, and she in despair proposes to die also, but the goddess holds her hand, and offers a boon. "Give life to these two persons," says the princess. "I give it," replies the goddess; "you need only join the heads to the respective bodies." But unluckily the princess is so confused with hope and joy, that she joins the prince's head to his friend's body, and so forth. No sooner had she done so, than they come to life. And here the Vetál pauses and asks king Vikrama which of these persons should be considered the husband of the princess? The king answers he who had her husband's head, and the Vetál as usual flies off.

In the eighth story, a king separates from his retinue, and loses his way in a forest, whilst out hunting. A young prince from another country rides up to him and offers his services; the king says he is hungry; the prince fetches fruits, and conducts the king safely to his royal city. The king rewards him with robes of honour, and engages his services. One day, the king having sent this new attendant to a distant place on the sea-shore, he fell in love with a most wonderful young damsel, who was about to offer worship in a temple of Devî. She bids him bathe in a neighbouring pool or tank. No sooner is he in the water, than he finds himself transported to the city whence he came. He tells all the circumstances to the king, who then accompanies him to the tank, and sees the wonderful damsel, and also falls in love. But too generous to supersede one who depended upon him, the king commands the young lady to marry the prince.[1]

The tenth story tells of a king in Burdwan, who was converted to the Jaina religion by his minister, and who forthwith prohibited the worship of Siva and Vishnu, gifts of cows, land, balls of rice, gambling and wine, and would not allow any one to carry away bones to the Ganges.

When this king died, he was succeeded by a son, named Dharm Dhwaja, who, preserving the original religion, caused the Jaina minister to be seized, seven plaits of hair to be placed on his head, his face to be blackened, and mounted on a jackass, to be led round the town to the beat of the drum. This king was, however, visited by afflictions. Strolling one day in a garden, in the season of spring, accompanied by his wives, he was in the act of presenting a lotus flower to his queen, when the flower escaped from his hand, fell upon her foot and broke it. The second wife sitting on the balcony by moonlight, was blistered by the lunar rays. And the third wife suffered acute pain in her head from the sound of a wooden pestle pounding rice in her neighbour's premises.

The fifteenth tale is the story of Jimûtavâhan and Garuda, which refers apparently to the "Tree and Serpent Worship,"

---

[1] Translation of Crustnath Cassinathjee, p. 46.

lately explained to us by Mr. Fergusson. A king in the Himalaya mountains supplicated a celestial tree for a son. A son was granted; and, according to custom, so soon as the son attained the proper age, the father abdicated the throne in his favour. The new king, on his ascension, "compelled all the people to pay regard to their respective religions. . . . . . Sûdras were ordered to observe charity; Dwijas to perform sacrifice; gluttons and libertines were left to sensual enjoyments. There were no conspiracies at home, nor apprehensions of war with foreign potentates. All was peace and tranquillity. The rain fell in the city seasonably, and the earth produced all grains in abundance. The cows yielded plenty of milk; the trees were fruitful —the women faithful."

This king prayed to the celestial tree to make all the people in the empire opulent, and the result was, that poor wretches heretofore living in woods came out and concerted means for seizing the kingdom. Rather than shed blood, the old king and his queen and their son retired to a holy mountain.

One day, the young king perceived in a certain part of this mountain a white heap, near an angura tree,[1] he asks what it is, and is told that it is "a heap of serpents' bones, left there by Garuda, who comes daily to feed on serpents." On hearing this, the king goes towards a temple, but is arrested by the cry of a woman, who says, to-day my son will be eaten by Garuda. She and her people were serpents in human shape. The king was moved with pity, and told the woman not to fear, for that he would expose himself to be eaten in the place of her son.

The king accordingly placed himself as a victim upon the appointed flat stone, and was seized by Garuda; but before Garuda had time to fly off, the intended serpent victim came forward, and cried to Garuda to stop, for that the king was not a serpent. Garuda is amazed, and remonstrates with the king, and being at length convinced of his generosity, says "Ask what you like." The king says, "Henceforth do not feed upon serpents, and

[1] Mimosa Sirisa.

(pointing to the heap of bones) be pleased to reanimate the serpents to whom those bones belonged."

The story ends by the Vetâl asking the king which was the more generous, the king or the serpent. The king cannot resist saying that the serpent was the more generous, and then, as usual, the Vetâl escapes, and once more hangs himself on his tree.

The twenty-fifth, and concluding tale, is of an unfortunate Raja, whose city was attacked by another Raja. For many days he continued fighting, but his army deserted to the enemy, and then reduced to despair, he went forth at night to the jungle, taking his wife and daughter with him. When they had travelled far into the forest, day dawned, and a village appeared in sight, and the Raja left his wife and daughter, and went towards the village to procure food. Presently he found himself surrounded by Bheels, with whom he fought for three hours, but at length he was killed. The queen and his daughter wept, striking their breasts, and being too weary to travel further, they sat down to indulge in grief. Now it so happened that a certain king and his son, who were hunting in that jungle, saw the marks of the two women's feet. The son said to his father that some queen with her daughter must have passed that way. "The large steps may be those of the mother, and the small those of the daughter." "Well then," replied the father, "you may take the small-footed one (supposing it the daughter), and I will take for myself the large footed: we will marry them."

The traces guided them to the hiding place of the women. As it happened that the large-footed female was the daughter, and the small-footed her mother, the king said to his son, "Son, you must now change." "No, father, I will not, for an honest man does not alter the word which he has once uttered."

In short, the king married the daughter, and the prince married her mother.

In due time children were born—a son and a daughter, who again married each other, and had children. At this point the

Vetâl broke off, and desired the king to tell him "the relationship of that generation." But king Vikrama seems at last to have learned wisdom, for he smiled in silence, and the Vetâl said, Raja, I have been delighted with your firmness and resolution, and will therefore warn you of a great danger with which you are threatened. A man has come into your city, the hairs of whose body are like thorns, and his body like wood. His name is Shantil; he is sitting at a shrine performing incantations, waiting for you to bring me to him." The Vetâl further explains that Shantil intends to offer king Vikrama in sacrifice, and then himself to reap the fruit of such sacrifice. In order to avert this catastrophe, the Vetâl gives careful directions. "When he shall have finished his prayers, he will say to you, 'Raja, make a prostration, so that the eight parts of your body may touch the ground.'" Whereupon Vikrama must reply, "I am the Raja of all Rajas, and all Rajas come and make salutation to me. I have not made salutation to any one, be pleased to shew me how to do it."

The Vetâl then abandoned the corpse, which he bid Vikrama carry to Shantil. At night he did so, and Shantil was pleased, and greatly extolled him. Having pronounced some incantations, and awakened the dead man, and being seated towards the south, he offered up the different ingredients of the oblation he had made ready, and having given pawn, flowers, perfumes, lamps and consecrated food, and repeated prayers, he bid Vikrama walk around the altar, and then prostrate himself, so that the eight principal parts of his body should touch the ground. The king following the Vetâl's instructions, said, " O hermit, I know not how to do this thing unless you shew me." The hermit (Yogin) accordingly walked round, and the king followed him sword in hand, and so soon as Shantil fell prostrate, Vikrama gave him a blow with his sword which instantly severed his head from his body. Then were heard celestial voices shouting, Victory—victory to king Vikrama.

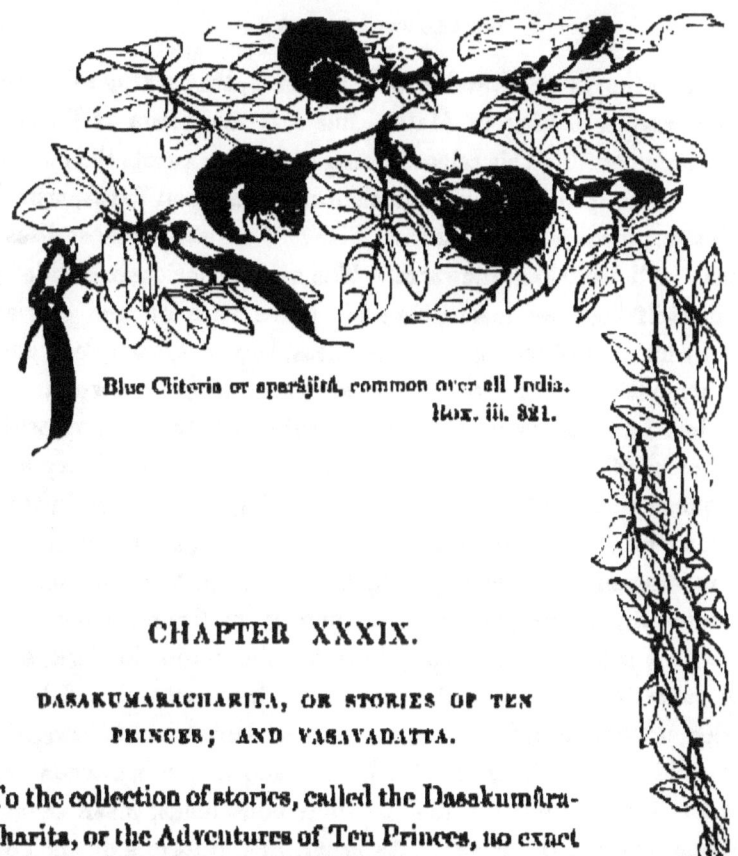

Blue Cliteria or aparájitá, common over all India.
Rox. iii. 321.

CHAPTER XXXIX.

DASAKUMARACHARITA, OR STORIES OF TEN PRINCES; AND VASAVADATTA.

To the collection of stories, called the Dasakumāracharita, or the Adventures of Ten Princes, no exact date can be assigned. They are stories of common life, relating the adventures of a lively set of people, who kill, cheat, and rob, as it were for diversion;—something, indeed, after the fashion of pantomimes and farces, which are still popular in Europe. But, in addition to their diverting power, these stories possess considerable interest for those who care to study the manners and customs of India under varieties of aspect.[1]

[1] H. H. Wilson. Works, vol. iv. Reprinted from Quarterly Oriental Magazine, from 1826 to 1828.

The outline of the Dasakumáracharita is, that a king of Patna takes prisoner a king of Malwa, but sets him again at liberty. Most ungenerously this released king of Malwa awaits the opportunity of the spring festival, and then marches upon Patna, armed with a magic mace, obtained from Siva. The result is most disastrous. All are taken unawares. The king's charioteer is killed; he himself becomes insensible; his horse runs off and carries him in his chariot to the forest fastness, to which the queen and her attendants had retired. The king's ministers are wounded, and left for dead upon the battle-field; but they revive with the breeze of morning, and also hasten to the forest. They tell the queen that the king is missing, and she, feeling certain that he must be dead, is eager to die also, from which the ministers try to dissuade her; but she steals away from her companions at midnight, and prepares to hang herself, by fastening her garment to a banyan tree. Fortunately, although in the dark, she had come to the very spot upon which her husband had been hurled, unconscious, from his chariot. At her arrival he revived; and gradually the king and the queen, and all their attendants, and the king's ministers, and all their households, make themselves a home in the forest. As usual, in the forests of ancient India, a Rishi (a sage or holy hermit) has taken up his abode within its precincts, and is ready to give counsel. The Rishi on this occasion was Vâmadeva; and his advice to the king was, to live tranquilly where he was, awaiting the birth and growth of a promised son, who was to repair his broken fortunes. This advice is followed, and the child is born. At the same time the wives of the king's ministers give birth to sons, destined to be the companions of the young prince; and a few stray infants being gathered in, the little band is augmented to the number of ten.

The histories of the stray infants are, like the rest of the story, very characteristic of the country; as when, after a defeat, a king's twin infants are carried to the woods, one of the nurses, frightened by a tiger, drops the child. The child scrambles under the dead body of a cow. The tiger seizes the carcase, an arrow from a forester kills the tiger, the forester carries the infant to his home; and a few days afterwards the nurse discovers her nursling in the midst of a crowd of the forest population, who are anxious to kill the beautiful child, and present it as an offering to their forest goddess. These people are called *Sararas*. Another story tells of an infant born in a wood, owing to its mother having been shipwrecked in a voyage from Ceylon. Whilst the mother lay senseless beside a pool, the nurse, who was an elderly person, went with the infant in her arms to seek assistance. A wild elephant sprung out upon her; she dropped the child and ran away. The elephant picked up the infant with its trunk, but being attacked by a lion, it cast the child into a tree, where it was caught by a monkey; and ultimately was reared as one of the princes. Thus we have a picture of elephants, lions, tigers, apes, of wild tribes which sacrifice human beings to a goddess, and of a Rishi living in a kind of secular forest-convent or settlement of learned men. The ten young princes grew up under favourable circumstances. "They were taught to write and to speak various tongues; they were taught the holy sciences,—as policy, rhetoric, history, and sacred records (Purânas); also metaphysics, astrology, law, and the morals of princes." To these acquirements were added music, medicine, and magic; how to manage the horse, the elephant, and the car; to use various weapons; and to excel in thieving, gaming, and other similar accomplishments. But at length the wise Vâmadeva advised the king that the time had arrived when his son should go forth "to conquest;" and accordingly Râjavâhana and his nine companions "go forth," and meet with the varied adventures recorded in the popular work entitled Dasakumâracharita.

One of these youths, arriving at a place called Champá, on the Ganges, sees a Bauddha mendicant seated under an asoka tree, near the entrance to a vihâra (or Bauddha convent). The mendicant gives an account of himself, telling that he was the son of a rich banker, but that having had an unhappy experience he was now hiding his griefs in a convent.

The experience of the mendicant does not act as a warning to the young prince Apahâravarman, for he proceeds to the city, to "encounter the tricks and frauds of the rogues, with which Champâ notoriously abounds."[1]

"I entered," he says, "the gambling houses, was associated with the gamesters, and was never tired of watching those who were skilled in the twenty-five sorts of games, knowing how to cog dice and shift cards, &c., unperceived." He delighted, also, to engage in affrays, ... to wheedle the resolute, and to bully the timid. . . . . . After he had become thoroughly acquainted with the city he went out, "on a night as dark as the throat of Siva, putting on a black jacket, and with a sword under his arm, a scoop, a whistle, tongs, a sham head, magic powder, a magic light, a measuring thread, a wrench, a rope, a lamp, and a beetle in a box, to the house of a celebrated usurer," &c.[2] In the course of the story this man marries, and gives up thieving; but he says, "Man, however ingenious, cannot avoid his fate."[3] So one day he got drunk; "and, as intoxicated people follow the practices to which they are naturally or customarily addicted,"[4] he went out thieving again, and was taken prisoner, &c. When in love, he drew or painted a portrait of his beloved,—a practice often followed in these tales, and one which we previously observed in a drama of Bhavabhûti.

This story is followed by that of a twin-brother of the previous narrator. Their father's kingdom of Mithilâ was possessed by strangers. The narrator goes there without making himself known. The queen, he finds, dislikes her husband, with whom she says she is as ill-matched as a lovely Mâdhavi-flower twined

[1] Wilson, p. 196. [2] Ibid, p. 196. [3] Ibid, p. 204. [4] Ibid, p. 208.

around a bitter Nimba tree.[1] The story is not interesting, but abounds in allusions to the trees and plants of India. A man, who enters a garden by night, crosses the ditch by a bamboo ladder; ..... he passes slowly a bakula bower, and an avenue of champas; ..... he turns to the north by the bignonias; and having leapt over the canal that runs to the palace, proceeds on a gravel walk bordered by red asoka trees and jasmines. In the summing-up of the tale, the usurping king is killed and the widow married to the twin who recovered his father's throne.[2]

Next come the adventures of Arthapála, in Benares. To the south of the city he meets "a man of stout, robust make, tightly girded, and his eyes red with incessant weeping." Arthapála sits down with him under an oleander tree, and listens to his tale, which began as follows:—" I am the son of a man of property, and my name is Púrnabhadra. I was accustomed always to follow my own inclinations; and in spite of my father's cares addicted myself, as I grew up, to the profession of a thief."[3] Being detected, the wilful youth had been sentenced to death, and was led forth in front of the palace gate, where, in the presence of the chief minister, a wild elephant was let loose upon him, and approached amid the clamour of the multitude, clattering his bells and curling up his trunk. But Púrnabhadra had no fear, and struck the elephant with the logs in which his arms were wedged. Three times the animal retreated, and was again forced forward. At length the driver could do no more; and the minister, who was presiding, said: "The elephant you have discomfited has been hitherto as irresistible as death: so much valour merits not so vile a fate." And forthwith he attached Púrnabhadra to his service. He treated him with perfect confidence, and told him passages of his own history; as, that when a young man, he had come by chance to this city of Kási (or Benares), and had fallen in love with the king's daughter, by

---

[1] Wilson, p. 214. [2] Ibid, p. 216. [3] Ibid, p. 222.

2—22

seeing her play at ball with her attendants.[1] The story is not worth pursuing; but in the course of it we find some lovely princesses imprisoned in a cave by a tyrannical old king, and tended by an aged woman, who resembled a "tuft of white-headed kās."[2]

The narrator rescued the imprisoned damsels by darting upon the old king at midnight, "as an eagle pounces on a snake." Another of the ten companions describes a festival in a grove, at which he had accidentally been present. Crowds of people had assembled, and whilst wondering what it might be that was going on, he observed a young man sitting apart in a bower of atimukta flowers, and playing on the vinā. The young man tells him that the king has a daughter, who was granted to him by the goddess, with the condition that on a certain day each month she should play at ball in public, and that she should be allowed to marry any one whom she should choose. This festival was now commencing. The princess was seated in an open pavilion of great splendour. "She rose gracefully, and touched with the tips of her lovely fingers the footstool of the goddess. She then took the ball, red like the eye of love when moved to wrath; she first let it gently strike the ground, and as it slowly rose, beat it down with her open hand, till at last catching it at the rebound on the back of her hand, she threw it up as high as she could, caught it in its descent, and threw it up again. As long as it kept good time, she struck it gently, but when it slackened, she reiterated the blows without mercy; occasionally she kept it fluttering in the air like a bird, hitting it up alternately with either hand, in a straight line above her, whilst at others, when it descended obliquely, she sprang forwards and sideways to catch it. Thus sporting gracefully, she attracted the gaze and applause of the people collected around the pavilion."

[1] Wilson, p. 223.
[2] Ibid, p. 231. Banisteria saccharum spontaneum, grows on the banks of rivers, in hedges, and on moist, uncultivated land. "The immense quantity of long, bright, silver-coloured wool gives this species a most conspicuous appearance."—Rox., i. 236.

The next story worth noticing, is of a young merchant of considerable wealth, named Saktikumára, who, considering that there was no real happiness in a single life, and also that felicity in wedlock depended upon the wife's character, determined to go forth in search of a spouse. For this purpose, he adopted the character of a fortune-teller, and carrying with him some rice bound up in his cloth, proceeded on his travels. Being a fortune-teller, girls were everywhere brought to him by their mothers to have their fortunes told. His plan was, when a girl pleased him, to terminate his prognostications by asking her, as a favour, to shew him how well she could cook his rice. Some laughed, and some were angry, but all sent him away without complying, until, arriving at a town of the Sivis, on the southern side of the river Kaveri, a damsel was brought out by her nurse, whose parents were both deceased. He looked at her, and observed that she was perfect; limbs neither too long nor too short, too slight nor too stout, hands marked with all the lucky signs, as the fish, lotus, vase, &c., &c. Her eyes were of the darkest jet, rolling in the purest white. The young merchant was enchanted, and with an agitated bosom, proposed his ordinary test. She smiled as she looked archly at her attendant, and taking the rice, desired the guest to sit at the threshold, whilst she washed his feet. The guest, we must remember, was not appearing as a rich merchant, but as a fortune-teller, and the girl, who was apparently very poor, was acting from simple-hearted goodness. She steeped the grains a little in water, dried them in the sun, and rubbing them gently in the ground, removed the awn without breaking the grain. She then said to the nurse, "This bran will be acceptable to the goldsmiths to clean their jewellery; go, sell it to them, and purchase with the price fuel, an earthen boiler and two platters." Her whole cooking is performed on the same œconomical principle. When she has finished, she directs her nurse to desire Saktikumára to bathe. He then rubs himself with the oil and myrobalan which she had prepared, sits down on a part of the floor well swept and levelled, eats two spoonfuls of rice with ghee, and the rest with spices, curds and milk, drinks cool water, fragrant in a new jug, perfumed with agallochum; feels the highest satisfaction, seeks no further, but marries the damsel, and takes her along with him. She unexpectedly finds herself a woman of wealth and consequence, but continues to worship her husband, and to pay the most assiduous attention to his household affairs. "In this way she acquired the entire confidence of her spouse, who, leaving all his domestic concerns to her care, tasted in his corporeal form the joys of Paradise."

The next tale is of a girl, whose husband takes a dislike to her; she consults an aged female devotee, and it is contrived that her husband shall see her splendidly drest, playing at ball in public on the terrace of a friend's house, and shall fall in love with her, taking her to be another person. This is the third occasion on which young girls bewitch beholders by playing at ball in public. The bride in this case is the daughter of a ship-owner, at Valabhi in Guzerat, named Grihagupta.

Another of the ten princes, named Mantragupta, tells of his adventures in Ceylon, in which place he fell in love. "The vernal season had set in, and the air was scented with the breezes of Malaya, and musical with the song of the koil," the king of Kalinga, with all his household and attendants, were passing a fortnight on the sea-shore, where the wind, cooled by the spray of the ocean, attempered the fierceness of the solar rays; but, whilst engaged "in every kind of elegant diversion," the king and his suite were suddenly surprised, and carried away captive by the king of Andhra, on the Ganges, who had suddenly landed "from the flotilla, with which he scoured the coasts." Mantragupta followed the party to Andhra, on the Ganges, and took up his abode in a grove on the edge of a

---

¹ Wilson, p. 265.

spacious lake, lovely with lotus flowers, and lively with flocks of wild geese." He had disguised himself in the dress of an old conjuror, and collecting a few followers, kept them in good humour with presents obtained from villagers in return for the tricks which he practised on their credulity.

The concluding story is that of Visruta. The scene is in the Vindhya Mountains. By the side of a well a boy weeps bitterly, and cries for help. His aged guardian has fallen into the well. Visruta arrives in time to rescue the old man, drawing him out by the help of long trailing plants. He then knocks down with stones fruit from some tall likucha trees, draws water in a bamboo, and sits down with his new friends to enjoy this little repast. He then persuades the old man to tell what brought him and the boy to so secluded a spot. The boy, it appears, is rightful heir to a kingdom, of which the king has been dethroned, and has been sent into the forest for safety. The story differs from the others of the series, inasmuch as it touches little on intrigue, and much on the necessity of good government.

A certain wise king of Vidarbha died, and was succeeded by a son, who was graced by every excellence, but little esteemed the science of politics. A faithful preceptor, who was also a minister, warns and reproves his youthful Raja, and says, he who allows his mind to be almost wholly engrossed by the "trivial amusements of music, drawing, painting and poetry," whilst his intellect is not exercised in worthy studies, is "like gold that has not been refined in the fire." A prince, whose understanding is uncultivated, is unable to "judge of the objects to be effected, or the means by which they are to be attained." And he further shews that the judgment of such a prince not being good, his orders are disregarded, and general demoralisation ensues. "Abandon, therefore," he concludes, "mere external accomplishments, and study those sciences by which your

---

¹ Wilson, pp. 270—271.

authority will be respected, and your power extended throughout the sea-encircled world."

The young Raja, not relishing this advice, tells it to a minister of totally different character, a man "well skilled in singing, dancing and playing; thoroughly acquainted with the town, of witty fancy, &c.; one who had a peculiar tact in finding out a person's weak side, could excite laughter, &c.; a pandit in craft—a pilot in vice—a professor of all vicious arts." This dangerous counsellor delighted the prince by throwing ridicule on the good old Vasurakshaka. If a man is prosperous, he says, some one always comes forward to tease him; to bid him place his hopes on the goods of the life to come; shave his head; wear a girdle of straw; smear his body with butter; go to bed without his supper; and there are some, indeed, who would do worse, and persuade him "to relinquish children, wives, and even life." Or if advice of this description fails, they will promise to convert a gross of cowries into a heap of gold; to destroy enemies without weapons; to give universal dominion, &c.; and when asked by what means, they will reply, there are four branches of royal knowledge, of which the most important is Dandaniti (or policy), as recently composed by the learned Vishnugupta, in six thousand stanzas, for the use of the Maurya king. So the king sets to work, and reads and listens till he grows old, and when he has finished, what (continues the caricaturist) has he learnt? The first lesson is, never trust to wife or child. The next is, so much water is required to boil so much rice, and so much fuel to heat that water. Then, when the king has risen and washed his mouth, he has to examine his receipts and expenditure. Not a handful, nor a half-handful must escape him, yet even whilst he is listening the superintendent will cheat him. In a quizzing fashion, the king's occupations throughout the four-and-twenty hours are described as:—after eating, he lives in dread of poison until his food is digested. In the fifth watch, he is plagued with the schemes of his counsellors, who misstate the reports of spies, &c. In the evening, he must receive his secret emissaries, and appoint their work of fire, sword and poison. At length, he is allowed a three hours' slumber, if his poor thought-labouring brain will allow him to repose. Then come agents and emissaries, and men relating dreams and omens.

"But," says this 'Pandit in craft,' "if mistrust of all is to be entertained, what is the prosperity of a state?" And so he advises his willing listener to abandon all restraint, and give himself up to idle pastimes.

Hunting strengthens the constitution, improves the appetite, punishes the deer and wild cattle for injuring crops, and makes the roads safe by destroying wolves and tigers. The pleasure of traversing mountains, or of beholding various countries, are also reasons for hunting; whilst gambling is good, because it teaches persons not to be elated with success or depressed by ill-luck; to acquire the power of confining their thoughts to a fixed object, and to exercise determined perseverance and unremitting acuteness. By gambling, also, a man learns disregard for personal perils, and a noble disdain of individual danger. Love is advocated, as a school for eloquence and ingenuity; wine, as a medicament for various diseases; and the dissipater of care, highly serviceable in war, and as rendering man insensible to fear and pain. The young king who followed this advice had, however, but a very short reign, and was universally despised. Neighbouring Rajas made war upon him; and although his own false friend for a time outwitted them, he soon secured the throne for himself. The boy crying beside the well, at the commencement of the story, was the heir-apparent, and is ultimately placed upon his rightful throne.[1]

The series of tales concludes with the following wise thoughts:

"Government is an arduous matter; it has three principles:

[1] Wilson, p. 279.

council, authority, and activity. These, mutually assisting each other, dispatch all affairs. Council determines objects, Authority commences, and Activity effects their attainment. Policy is a tree, of which Council is the root, Authority the stem, and Activity the main branch; the seventy-two Prakritis are the leaves, the six qualities of royalty the blossoms, power and success the flowers and the fruit. Let this shade protect the king."[1]

Vasavadatta.

This is a love-story, but we cannot call it a novel, according to the modern acceptation of the word; for the author cared more for ingenuity of diction than for the working out of emotions, events, and characters. Dr. Fitzedward Hall has looked at the subject critically, and he thinks it must have been written not more than twelve hundred years,—not until the fine taste and feeling of Kâlidâsa and the better poets and dramatists had given way to bombast and quibble. He quotes the following sentence from the author's account of himself:—"Subandhu, an intimate of none but the virtuous, and a fund of dexterity in framing discourse made up of equivoques in every syllable."

Puns are common in all Sanskrit compositions, from even the earliest periods; but Subandhu's work is described as a volume of puns, and honoured with the denomination of poem, not so much by reason of the sustained elevation of its diction, as on account of its clever alliteration and the elaborate ambiguity of its phrases. So to choose and to dispose his diction as "to render it susceptible of a diversity of interpretation," was the distinct aim of the author; and consequently he is, as might be expected, sometimes unintelligible. Perturbations of grief and despair, the terrible, and the revolting, are well described; but the author does not appear to have so well understood real tenderness or

---

[1] Works by H. H. Wilson, vol. iv. p. 288.

deep affection. The plot is peculiar. A king, who lived somewhere on the Ganges, was a follower of Siva, and ruled his kingdom so admirably that impiety was unknown, proof by ordeal never needed, and violence never practised. This king had a son, who was the delight of all who sought his protection. His sagacity secured him from deception. His religious feeling was shown by marked devotion to cows, and to Brâhmans; and being comely as the god of love, he was admired by all maidens, far and near. The extraordinary fact was, however, that the maiden with whom alone he fell in love was one that appeared to him in a dream. He longed to dream again, but the fervour of his emotion prevented sleep. He shut himself up in solitude, and refused nourishment. Then a faithful friend persuaded him that travelling might bring relief. They pursued their way to the Vindhya Hills; the sun was about to set as they entered a wilderness. The friend collected roots and fruits, and the young prince fell asleep on a couch, made up of branches from the trees. But not for long; for he was awoke by the conversation of two birds, who nestled in the jambu tree above him. The female bird was reproaching the male for coming home so late, fearing that he must have been dangling after some other *sârikâ*. The male bird replies, solemnly, that he has been attending to a transaction most unprecedented. He then relates, that in the city of Kusumapura (probably the same as Patna), there is a lovely princess, named Vâsavadattâ. Being of full age, the king, her father, invited "the high-born heirs of many principalities," that she might choose a husband. The suitors came, and the damsel took her place upon a dais to survey them; but no one pleased her: and she and they withdrew in disappointment. At night, the young prince who had fallen in love with her in a dream, appeared to her in a vision; and she felt at once that he was her destined husband. The vision made known his name, which was Kandarpaketu; but she suffers torments of love and grief from not knowing how to meet with him. Under these circumstances her confidante volunteers go to search for him; and, says the bird, she arrived here when I did, and is at this moment beneath our tree. The love-sick prince no sooner heard this welcome intelligence than he introduced himself to the confidante, talked with her for twenty-four hours, and then went with her to Kusumapura. Here he found the lovely Vásavadattá in a gardenhouse of ivory. On seeing each other they faint for joy, and then rehearse their past sufferings. The confidante speaks for the princess, and says, that "if the heavens were a tablet, the sea an inkstand, the longævous Brahma the amanuensis, and the king of Serpents the narrator,—only a trifling part of those agonies could be told," and so forth. They next resolve on what we should call a "runaway-match;" and this they effect by mounting a magic steed, which carries them to the Vindhya forests in the twinkling of an eye. They sleep soundly in a bower of flowery creepers; but when the sun is at meridian height the prince awakes, and finds Vásavadattá missing. He bitterly laments, and wonders what can have caused so dreadful an affliction. "Had he not accomplished himself in the sciences?" "Had he not adored the fires?" "Had he affronted Bráhmans?" "Had he neglected to make devout circuits around milch kine?"

Ultimately his Vásavadattá is restored to him, and they live in happiness at her father's court. Her disappearance was caused by her having been struck, on waking, by the emaciated appearance of her husband; and leaving him asleep, she went in search of fruits for his refreshment. She is alarmed at seeing a general and troops in pursuit of game; and meets with other adventures.

"Let the king establish rules for the sale and purchase of all marketable things; having duly considered whence they came, if imported, whither they must be sent if exported."—CODE OF MANU, Book viii. v. 401.

CHAPTER XL.

COMMERCE AND MANUFACTURES.

Ancient Hindus a commercial people.—Products and Manufactures early obtained in Western Countries.—Ancient Hindu Laws treating on Commerce.—Merchants in Old Literature.—Trade with India of present importance to Europe.—Success depends upon knowledge of Hindu Habits and Antecedents.—Indigo, Cotton, Wool, Iron.—Perfection of Hindu Manufacture.

It is said in the Rig-Veda that "merchants desirous of gain crowd the great waters with their ships." And the activity in trade, thus early noted, has continued ever since to be characteristic of the country. Professor Lassen[1] considers it remarkable that Hindus themselves discovered the rich, luxurious character of India's products. Many of the same beasts, birds, and fragrant oils, are produced in other countries, but remain unnoticed until sought for by foreigners; whereas the most ancient of the Hindus had a keen enjoyment in articles of taste or luxury. Rajas and other rich people delighted in sagacious

[1] Lassen, Indische Alterthumskunde, vol. i. (2nd ed.), p. 342.

elephants, swift horses, splendid peacocks, golden decorations, exquisite perfumes, pungent peppers, ivory, pearls, gems, &c.; and, consequently, caravans were in constant requisition to carry these, and innumerable other matters, between the north and the south, and the east and the west, of their vast and varied country. These caravans, it is conjectured, were met at border stations, and at out-ports, by western caravans or ships bound to or from Tyre and Egypt, or to or from the Persian Gulf and the Red Sea.

To the appearance of India goods in Greece, Professor Lassen attributes the Greek invasion of India. The cupidity of conquerors was excited by the sight of such treasures, and the courage and endurance of their followers was sustained by the prospect of such spoil. And for hints of India's products in Asiatic caravans, we may refer to the Book of Genesis, where we read that Joseph was sold by his brethren to "Ishmaelites come from Gilead with their camels bearing spicery, balm, and myrrh, going to carry it down to Egypt."[1] Here, Dr. Vincent observes, we find "a caravan of camels loaded with the spices of India and the balsam and myrrh of Hadramaut." And this transaction, he observes, notwithstanding its antiquity, "has all the genuine features of a caravan crossing the desert at the present hour."[2]

Dr. Vincent's idea is, that even before the call of Abraham caravans traversed Asia from Bussorah to Medina, and thence through Petra to Tyre, keeping up extensive communication between Egypt and India. Neither Hindus nor Egyptians are supposed to have made long sea-voyages, although they made much use of their magnificent rivers.

"Spicery," which the Ishmaelites were carrying to Egypt, would seem to be the term used in trade for pepper,[3] cardo-

---

[1] Genesis, chap. xxvii. v. 25.
[2] Periplus, part 2, book iii. p. 328.
[3] Pepper still bears its India name.

—Lassen, Alter. vol. i. (2nd ed.) p. 326.

mums, and probably ginger, all found in abundance and in perfection on the coast of Malabar. Balm and myrrh may or may not have come from India; for although these perfumed gums exude from a tree called Balsomadendron, which grows well in India, the same trees are now found also on the borders of Arabia Felix and in Abyssinia. It is, however, noteworthy that Pliny could not discover from whence Egypt obtained balm and myrrh; the Egyptians said that it came from the country of the Troglodytæ, and the late Dr. Royle observed that myrrh is called *bal* by the Egyptians, whilst throughout India it is known by the Sanskrit name of *bola*.[1]

We again feel ourselves to be amongst products from India when reading of king Hiram's trade with Ophir.

"1 Kings, Ch. ix. 11. Now Hiram, the king of Tyre, had furnished Solomon with cedar-trees, and fir-trees, and with gold. . . . .

"Ch. ix. 26. And king Solomon made a navy of ships in Eziongeber, which is beside Eloth, on the shore of the Red Sea, in the land of Edom.

"Ch. ix. 27. And Hiram sent in the navy his servants, shipmen that had knowledge of the sea, with the servants of Solomon.

"Ch. ix. 28. And they came to Ophir, and fetched from thence gold. . . . .

"Ch. x. 11. And . . . . great plenty of almug trees and precious stones. . . . .

"Ch. x. 18. Moreover the king made a great throne of ivory, and overlaid it with the best gold.

"Ch. x. 21. And all king Solomon's drinking-vessels were of gold, and all the vessels of the house of the forest of Lebanon were of pure gold; none were of silver; it was nothing accounted of in the days of Solomon.

"Ch. x. 22. For the king had at sea a navy of Tharshish with the navy of Hiram; once in three years came the navy of Tharshish, bringing gold, and silver, ivory, and apes, and peacocks."

[1] Royle, Ant. Hindu Med. pp. 119—121. Smith's Dictionary of the Bible, s. v. Myrrh.

So also in the Book of Chronicles, "the servants of Hiram and the servants of Solomon, which brought gold from Ophir, brought almug-trees and precious stones." A great hunt has been made after "Ophir." The learned Professor Lassen suggested its being a sea-port on the south-west coast of India. Writers in Smith's Dictionary of the Bible and some others prefer to find it in Africa. Into so critical an inquiry we dare not enter; but we venture to think that Hiram's ships were laden with just those objects which Hindus of king Solomon's time would have considered best worth sending.

To begin with peacocks. India is emphatically the home of peacocks. No traveller writes of Upper India without mentioning flocks of peacocks; and every Sanskrit poem alludes lovingly to these splendid birds. "Peacocks unfolding in glittering glory all their green and gold." "Peacocks dancing in wild glee at the approach of rain." Peacocks around palaces "glittering on the garden wall," are expressions of frequent occurrence. Ancient sculpture shows the same delight in peacocks, as may be seen, for instance, in graceful bas-reliefs on the gates of Sanchi,[1] or on the panels of an ancient palace in Central India, figured in Tod's Rajasthan.[2] Whether peacocks were so early observed and cared for in any other country we do not know; but there is some evidence that Hiram procured his peacocks from India in the name by which they were received in the Holy Land. The word for peacock in Hebrew is universally admitted to be foreign; and Gesenius, Sir Emerson Tennent, and Professor Max Müller, appear to agree with Professor Lassen[3] in holding that this word, as written in Kings and Chronicles, is derived from Sanskrit.

Aristophanes called peacocks "Persian birds," and to Persia they were introduced from India or Ceylon. Aristotle was acquainted with them, for he says, "Some animals are jealous

---

[1] Fergusson, Illus. Hind. Archi.
[2] See p. 405 of this work.
[3] Ind. Alterth., vol. i. (2nd ed.), p. 353.

and vain like the peacock."[1] It was not, however, till after the Indian campaign of Alexander the Great that peacocks became general in Egypt, Greece, and Rome. The Romans are then noted for having spent immense sums of money on maintaining large flocks of peacocks. Not only the tongues but the flesh was cooked and prized at the tables of the old Roman epicures, whilst the live birds adorned their gardens, and of their tail feathers they made splendid fans.

We are not proposing to touch upon each item of Hiram's cargo, but ivory cannot be omitted, for of ivory King Solomon made a "great throne;"[2] and as ivory was largely used, not only in ancient India and the Holy Land, but in Assyria, Greece, Egypt, and Rome, its name and its history have acquired a special significance. Elephants are indigenous (or aboriginal) alike in Africa as in India, but it is observed that they were scarcely known to the ancient Egyptians; for although some sort of figure, intended for an elephant, has been discovered in the old hieroglyphics, Champollion calls it a very indistinct representation; and from this, and other considerations, Lassen decides that elephants were neither used nor tamed in ancient Egypt.[3]

But in India, on the other hand, elephants were the cherished friends of the household; and a passage from the Rig-Veda is cited,[4] in which a man places his elephant side by side with his son, as an object to be prayed for. "Who importunes Indra for his son, his elephant, his property, himself, or his people."

The affection with which the ancient Hindus regarded the elephant is also shown, by the variety of names used in Sanskrit.[5] Habits and peculiarities are noted. He is called *hastin* and *karin*, because his trunk serves the purpose of a hand. He is

---

[1] Dictionary of the Bible, article "Peacock."—Lassen, Alterthumskunde, vol. i. (2nd ed.) p. 353.
[2] 2 Chronicles, xi. 17.
[3] Alterthumskunde, vol. i. (2nd ed.) p. 354.
[4] R. V. i. 84, 17; Wilson's trans., vol. i. p. 218.
[5] Alterthumskunde, vol. i. p. 863.

dwipa, "the twice-drinking," because he first sucks up water with his trunk and then pours it into his throat. He is *pindapáda*, heavy-footed. And many other apellations he has, as *nága*, meaning that he is a native of mountain tracts; and *cárana*, one that bears and protects the king, because the king rode into battle on an elephant. The word, however, by which the domestic elephant is called is *ibha*. This name appears never to be used in Sanskrit for an elephant, merely as an animal, but is reserved for elephants belonging to the household. The same word, *ibha*, is the name by which the elephant's tusks are and were sold in the bazaars of India; and it is believed that by this name, or by words derived from it, ivory must have been introduced to Egypt and Greece, although by what process *ibha* was converted into the Greek, *elephas*, is not satisfactorily explained. Homer speaks of ivory as largely used; but elephants were unknown to Greeks until they came face to face with these huge beasts in the battle of Arbela. Darius was, on that occasion, aided by fifteen war-elephants with managers or drivers from India.[1]

The Greeks at once recognised these new antagonists, as armed with the ivory tusks familiar to them in commerce, and they called the animal elephas, that being the name already in use for ivory; and by this name Aristotle made elephants known to Europe. Herodotus also described the ἐλέφας, and ever since, the name of the animal bearing tusks of *elephas* has been elephant. In Egypt, ivory was known as *ebu*; and Professor Lassen thinks that the appearance of words so much alike as *ibha* and *ebu*, in languages so unlike as Sanskrit and the Ancient Egyptian, can only be accounted for by common origin, and that the Sanskrit name, *ibha*, might easily have reached Egypt through Tyre.

Hindu appreciation of elephants is also shown in their mythology, as: their ancient god, Indra, has a favourite elephant, called

---

[1] Alterthumskunde, vol. i. (2nd ed.) pp. 365, 365 ff.

Airávata; and their modern god, Ganesa, who symbolises wisdom, is represented with an elephant's trunk.

Without going farther into the subject, it seems most probable that ivory from India first made the product known in Greece, and perhaps even in Jerusalem and Egypt. In saying this we by no means imply that after ivory came into use it was not supplied from Ethiopia. Indeed, it is believed that Hindus were too much attached to their elephants to have killed them for the sake of their tusks; and when they needed more ivory than came to them from elephants which died by the way of nature, ivory from Ethiopia was imported into India.[1]

Nard, or spikenard, cassia, calamus, and what appears to be the bdellium of Scripture, may all be traced to India, where scents were very early valued and carefully prepared. Sugar bears a name derived from Sanskrit; and the oldest Sanskrit literature alludes to sugar, and to kinds of food concocted from sugar, which are good to "chew and to suck." It was in India that the Greeks first became acquainted with sugar, and to that period the first importations of this article into Europe are referred. With the sugar travelled its Sanskrit name into Arabia and Persia, and thence became established in the languages of Europe.[2]

The indirect evidence afforded by the presence of India's products in other ancient countries, coincides with the direct testimony of Sanskrit literature, to establish the fact that ancient Hindus were a commercial people. The code of Manu requires the king to determine the prices of commodities, and also the trustworthiness of the weights and measures used. And that the transactions contemplated were not restricted to local products is evident from reference to the charges for freight for articles in river boats, and the undetermined and larger charges to which sea-borne goods were liable. The account of King

---

[1] Lassen, Ind. Alb., vol. i. (2nd ed.) p. 306, and ibid. p. 302, *note.*

[2] Lassen, l. l., p. 318.

Yudhishthira's coronation in the Mahábhárata affords an instance of precious articles from distant lands brought into India. So also in the Rámáyana, we read that when Ráma and his brothers were married, the brides were clad in silk from China. The drama of Sakuntalá, again, affords testimony of the importance attached to trade. A case, written on a leaf, is presented at the footstool of the king. It states that a merchant, who had extensive commerce, had been lost at sea, and had left a fortune of many millions.

We might speak also of the caravan of merchants in the well-known story of Nala and Damayantí; but not to multiply instances, we will merely observe that merchants are constantly being introduced into Sanskrit fiction, and equally often into Buddhist legend. They seem to have been always at hand to give variety and movement to the monotony of daily life. We observe, however, that whilst in Sanskrit story merchants are usually represented as rude people, outside Hindu "society," they appear in Buddhist tales as religious men, whose rank is determined by attainment in holiness, not by birth.

Enough has now been said to show that Hindus have ever been a commercial people, and here we ought to leave the subject, if we would strictly confine ourselves to "Ancient India." But the past affects the present; and commerce with India has become a gigantic power, influencing national prosperity. Hindus cannot now, as formerly, quietly indulge their taste in imports and manufactures, undisturbed. The whole world has become connected by magnetic currents and bands of steam-power; and India and Europe are alike under obligations to wake up to the consciousness, that whether this new rapidity of commercial intercourse shall cause incalculable torment or incalculable profit, must depend upon the knowledge and wisdom of those by whom it is conducted. Under these circumstances, we feel that knowledge of its chief staples, such as indigo, cotton, wool, and iron, has peculiar importance; and that it is essential to view them in connection with Hindu history, tastes, habits, and requirements.

We will begin with a few words on indigo, which is mentioned in the code of Manu. It is manufactured from the bluish-green juice of a trefoil plant which grows wild in the north-east provinces of India, on the eastern Ghats, in Ceylon, and in other parts of India. The plant thrives best in the Tirhut province of Bengal, whilst the seed attains its highest perfection in the rocky soil of central India. Bancroft, in his work on colours, gives the "natives of India" much praise for having "so many thousand years ago discovered means by which the colourable matter of the plant might be extracted, oxygenated, and precipitated from all other matters combined with it." This valuable dye bears the name of its father land,[1] and by this name has certainly been known in Europe since the time of Pliny, who says: "Cast the right Indico upon live coals, it yieldeth a flame of most excellent purple." In India it is called nil, or nili, that being the Sanskrit for blue.

Indigo tinctoria, which is the species most generally cultivated, is a half-shrubby plant, two to three feet high, with pinnate leaves, and racemes of pale red flowers. Bengal alone produces about nine millions of pounds of indigo in the year; and the sum which Europe pays annually for indigo is estimated at eight or ten millions of pounds sterling.[2]

It may prove instructive to bear in mind, that although indigo distinctly belongs to India, it is possible to produce it in other countries; and that whilst its manufacture was, for a time, neglected in Hindostan, the West Indies, about the year A.D. 1747, succeeded in securing the indigo trade to themselves. This was, however, soon corrected.

John Prinsep, the father of seven Mr. Prinseps who have since been more or less known to fame in India, was then a

---

[1] Lassen, vol. i. (2nd ed.) p. 325 f. 1. [2] Chambers' Encyclopædia, s.v., p. 558.

merchant in Calcutta; and in 1779 his exertions restored this remunerative branch of commerce to its original birth-place.

Yet more important to the commercial relations of India and Great Britain is the product to which next we would draw attention. We refer to cotton, which does not appear amongst Solomon's imports, but is thought to have reached Europe in the time of the Crusades through the medium of the Arabs, the Arab word *kutn* becoming our cotton.[1] Cotton trees and cotton shrubs grow freely in many parts of India. The trees are very beautiful; but with them we are not at present much concerned, because the silky cotton, bursting from their pods, is wanting in the lateral roughness of fibre necessary for spinning these fibres into thread; and, consequently, *simal*, or the silky cotton of the simal-tree is, and has been, only used for padding armour or stuffing beds and pillows. The valuable properties of the cotton-wool produced from the cotton-shrub (Gossypium herbaceum) were early discovered. And we read in Rig-Veda hymns of "Day and Night," like "two famous female weavers"[2] intertwining the extended thread. We read also of "The fathers who wove, and placed the warp and woof,"[3] or that night enwraps the world "like a woman weaving a garment," or, again, of a singer consumed by cares, as "rats consume a weaver's threads."[4] Cotton, in its manufactured state, was new to the Greeks who accompanied Alexander the Great to India. They describe Hindus as clothed in garments made from wool which grows on trees. One cloth, they say, reaches to the middle of the leg, whilst another is folded around the shoulders.[5]

Hindus still dress in the fashion thus described, which is also alluded to in old Sanskrit literature. In the frescoes on the

---

[1] See also Dr. Royle's observations on the door-curtains or hangings in the Book of Esther, [6. Results of Great Exhibition of 1851, p. 187.
[2] Rig-Veda, ii. 3; Wilson's trans., vol. ii. p. 218.
[3] Rig-Veda, x. 130; Colebrooke's Essays, vol. i. p. 34.
[4] Wilson's trans., vol. i. p. 97.
[5] Nearchus, quoted by Royle, Culture of Cotton, p. 110.

Caves of Ajanta this costume is carefully represented. The copies from these pictures, which we once possessed, were, unfortunately, destroyed by fire in the Crystal Palace at Sydenham; but a few wood-cuts had happily been made from them, and to the importance of these, "as a record of costume," reference is made in the Edinburgh Review for January, 1868.[1]

The cloth which Nearchus speaks of as reaching to the middle of the leg is the dhotí. It is from 2¼ to 3½ yards long by 2 to 3 feet broad. In the picture which represents the Conquest of Ceylon,[2] the king sits on a stool or chair ready to be inaugurated. He is crowned with a tiara, is naked from throat to waist, but from the waist appears the dhotí. The attendants wear dhotís around their waists, a scarf across the chest. The figure behind, with a long straight sword, wears a dhotí, folds hanging in front, one end over the right shoulder. Persons with presents, groups of soldiers, bands of musicians, all alike wear dhotís.

The article under consideration next calls attention to the two

---

[1] In an article reviewing Textile Manufactures, by Dr. Forbes Watson, and written, we are assured, by Captain Meadows Taylor, well known for his accurate knowledge of Hindu history and Hindu habits.

[2] See p. 893 of the first volume of this work.

persons conversing, who are naked to the waist, and who "wear the ordinary dhotí."[1]

Other pictures, and also sculptures, give the same testimony; so that from the first or second century of our era, if not sooner, it would appear that for kings or commoners, and with or without necklaces and ornaments, the dhotí has been the invariable costume. And so it continues to the present day; for even if a Hindu wear drawers or trowsers, "he will have a dhotí, large or small, underneath." Dhotís are usually worn in pairs, the second sheet being thrown over the head and shoulders, or passed across the chest. It is a costume much resembling that of a Greek statue, and the only change observable within 3,000 years is, "that the dhotí may now be somewhat broader and longer." "Anything more perfectly convenient," it is observed, "to walk, to sit, or to lie in, it would be impossible to invent."[2]

We are thus particular in describing Hindu garments, because from century to century they have not changed; and it will be more possible for British manufacturers to conform to Hindu customs than for Hindus to adopt deviations made by British manufacturers. The dress of women in India also consists of one long piece of cloth, often called a *chudder*, or sheet; but the correct name is *Sári*. For poor people, about three yards of calico is made to suffice; but occasionally the *Sári* is eighteen yards long and a yard in width. "The texture varies from the finest and most open character of muslin, in Bengal and in the South of India, to the still fine but close texture of the Deccan, Central India, and Guzerat."[3] *Sáris* are of all qualities, to suit all ranks, whether peasant or princess. Hindus, male and female, appear to have been weaving and wearing such

---

[1] Native Sepoys march thirty or forty miles a day in dhotís without fatigue.—Edinburgh Review, January, 1868, p. 186.
[2] Hindu bearers, who pull pankahs for British residents in India, wear at all times a small dhotí, adding a second sheet when in the presence of ladies.
[3] Forbes Watson, Textile Manufactures, Intro. 2.

garments ever since they settled in India; and it would appear that, some centuries before our era, they produced muslins of that exquisite texture which even our nineteenth century machinery cannot surpass.

A Buddhist book, translated by Csoma de Körös, devotes some sections to the subject of discipline, and gives careful directions regarding the dress permitted for persons adopting the religious life, and living as members of a convent or Vihára. Luxury in dress is discountenanced, but to go without dress is absolutely immoral. From the frequency of such denunciations it would appear that to wear no clothes was, at that time, regarded by some classes as a token of piety and religious austerity; and we mention the circumstance here because it has reference to the fineness of the muslin then manufactured.

The following is the passage:

"Leaf 272. The king of Kalinga sends to Gsal-rgzal, the king of Kosala, a piece of fine linen cloth as a present. It comes afterwards into the hands of Gsug-Dgah-mo" (who is said to be a woman of loose character, although living in a Vihára). "She puts it on, and appears in public; but, from its thin texture, seems to be naked." Sákya (or Buddha) thenceforth forbids religious women to accept or wear such thin garments."[1]

The same testimony to the fineness of Hindu manufacture is given in an anecdote recorded by Mr. Bott in his work on the "Cotton Manufactures of Dacca." The Emperor Aurungzeb reproved his daughter for showing her skin through her clothes. The daughter justifies herself by asserting that she had on *seven* suits or *jamahs*.

The very names which Hindus have given to their muslins are evidence of the interest taken in these exquisite productions. One, which is regarded as third in quality, is called "Evening

---

[1] Analysis of Dulva, which is a portion of the Kah-Gyur.—Asiatic Researches, vol. xx. p. 85.

Dew,"[1] and when spread upon the grass can scarcely be distinguished from the dew. The second quality is Abravan, or "Running Water;" and it is related that in the time of Nabob Allavardy Khan, a weaver was turned out of Dacca for his neglect in not preventing his cow from eating up a piece of this muslin, which he had carelessly left upon the grass. The first quality of Dacca muslin is known as "Woven Air," and all goods of these three qualities appear to go under the name of *Mulmul Khas*, or king's muslins. £1 per yard is a usual price.

Hindus consider the Jam, or loom-figured, to be their *chef-d'œuvre* in muslins. £81 is said to have been the price of that manufactured for the emperor Aurungzeb; whilst, in 1776, these muslins reached the extravagant price of £56 per piece.[2] Comparing these fabrics with those manufactured in Great Britain, Dr. Watson finds the yarn finer than any yet produced in Europe, whilst the *twisting* given to it by the Hindu hand makes it more durable than any machine-made fabric. And thus the strange-looking spinning-wheel exhibited here, in 1851, with its "richly-carved wood bound round by unsightly threads," proves to have powers not to be obtained by any other means.[3]

Dacca is not the only place in India capable of manufacturing fine muslins, although its position in the moist climate of the Sunderbunds is doubtless very advantageous. Some intelligent residents venture to deny the influence of climate, and attribute the pre-eminence of Dacca manufacture entirely to skill; but skill without moisture will not suffice; and where the air is naturally dry, artificial moisture is secured. In Chundeyree, for instance, which is cited as "an old seat of native manufacture," weaving is performed in underground workshops. So also in the dry air of the table lands of the Deccan yarn is spun in closed cellars, the floors of which are continually watered.

[1] As quoted by Dr. Forbes Watson in Textile Manufactures, p. 76.
[2] Textile Manufactures, p. 79.
[3] Professor Cooper. Report on Great Exhibition of 1851.

Dryness of air prevents the filaments from elongating; and, therefore, even in Dacca spinners only work from early dawn to nine or ten A.M., and again from three or four P.M. till near sunset.[1]

For spinning, women are preferred to men; and the finest thread is given to women under thirty years of age. It is a favourite occupation with women of all classes in India; "even the highest amuse themselves with the spinning-wheel." The remuneration is, however, incredibly small; for a spinner who devotes all the available hours of the day to this work makes in a *month* thread to the value of 16s., or 8 rupees.[2]

It appears that the short fibres of Dacca cotton are not well adapted to machinery; whilst, on the other hand, "the long cylindrico-spiral, and more elastic fibres of American cotton ... cannot be made into fine yarn by or with the primitive spindle of the Hindu."[3] It is further remarked, that the Dacca yarn is softer than mule twist, ... "but that fabrics made of it are more durable than those manufactured by machinery." Native weavers judge the quality of cotton by its tendency to expand from moisture. The cotton which swells the least on bleaching is considered the best, and their common remark is that English yarn swells, but that Dacca-spun thread shrinks and becomes stronger.[4] Much that has been said of spinning applies equally to weaving in India, for which also warm moist atmosphere is needed; and the finest goods are in consequence produced only between the middle of May and the middle of August. The perfection of such goods depends also on the skill and experience of a workman, who must bestow five or six months in accomplishing a half piece of *Malmal Khas*, or *Circar*

---

[1] Forbes Watson, Textile Manufactures, p. 42. Edinburgh Review, Jan., 1808, p. 145.
[2] Forbes Watson, Textile Manufactures, p. 89.
[3] Descriptive and Historical Account of Cotton Manufacture in Dacca, by a former Resident, J. Mortimer, 1851, as quoted by Dr. F. Watson, Textile Manufactures, p. 64.
[4] Ibid, p. 70.

all, the cost of which is from 70 to 80 rupees, or £7 or £8 of British money.

Calicoes and muslins made by the hand and the foot of the Hindu are better than any produced by machinery, but the process is slow and ill-remunerated. Exquisite muslins will be reserved for palaces and museums, whilst domestic industry will give way to steam-power.

But it is evident that slow operations and minute gains will not suit the India of the present day. If the millions of natives in India are to have garments at all, they must, Dr. Forbes Watson observes, make use of the looms of Great Britain; and since India is thus in a position to become "a magnificent customer," it is for no trifling result that our merchants are advised to study the "characteristics of Asiatic costume and manufacture."[1]

Wool is less characteristic of Hindostan than cotton, but its value was early perceived; and amongst the merchandise on which it was the custom to raise money we read in the Code of Manu, of "wool and hair." And, again, at what one feels tempted to call the "Great Exhibition," held on occasion of king Yudhishthira's coronation, we find "shawls of goat's hair" and "cloths of wool" figuring amongst the rich offerings brought from northern mountains.

Woollen coverings have, in fact, always been prized even in the sunny lands of India; and we understand that, throughout a great portion of the country, "suffering from cold during certain seasons, and particularly at night, is as great as in Europe, and as prolific a source of disease and death."[2] This is especially owing to the sudden changes of the temperature, a thermometer which showed ninety degrees of heat during the day often descending to sixty degrees during the night. It would be interesting to touch on the varieties of wool, and hair,

[1] J. Forbes Watson, Textile Manufactures and Costume of India, p. 125.
[2] Dr. F. Watson, Lecture, Society of Arts, February 5th, 1868.

and down, of which shawls, and chogas, and rugs, and carpets are made in India; but we must forbear, and only say a very few words upon shawls and carpets.

Shawls, like *dhotis*, are made in pairs, and a pair of shawls of fine quality cannot be manufactured in less than twelve or eighteen months. Shawls, we must remember, are a national institution. Fine shawls are royal robes, worn at state ceremonials, and so much prized that natives are, or have been, unwilling to let them be purchased by strangers. The Lahore Committee, for 1862, states that "a woven shawl, made at Kashmir, of the best materials, and weighing seven pounds, will cost in Kashmir as much as £300. Of this amount, the cost of the material, including thread, is £30, the wages of labour £100, and the duty £70.

Shawls, made in Kashmir, are still unrivalled; for, although Kashmir weavers have been settled in the Punjab since about the year 1830, when a terrible famine visited their native Valley, the shawls of Umritsur do not attain the *highest* excellence, because there is a chemical peculiarity in the waters of Kashmir favourable to the process of dyeing; and also because the finest kinds of wool are not allowed to leave the Valley.

Carpets are made at Masulipatam, and at some other places, with unrivalled Hindu taste. Carpets have also been made, in later days, in Government prisons, under British superintendence. The result proves that we must not attempt to teach art to India. The mingling of forms and colours in rugs or carpets, made according to ancient Hindu custom, is ill-replaced by brilliant roses and gaudy daffodils. It is well remarked, that if we desire to foster art in India, it must be by making Hindus more fully and generally acquainted with their own original productions. We quote the following important observations from the discussion at the Society of Arts, February 5th, 1868:—"The distribution throughout India of the best specimens of her manufactures could not fail to have an important influence."[1] These speci-

[1] See Journal of Society of Arts, February 7th, 1868.

mens are to be exhibited in Government schools. Their superiority and perfection will be intuitively perceived; and when the Hindu student finds that we also realise this fact, "it will give that impulse and encouragement which hitherto have been wanting. Once show the native student that we, the rulers of the land, respect his art," and he will be proof against the deteriorating influences of the love for glaring colours.

An account of Ancient India's manufactures must include iron, although at present it is, unfortunately, of little importance to India, politically; for the supply is too small, and the cost of working too great, to permit of competition with iron from Europe. But if we look back, it seems probable that "Ancient India" possessed iron more than sufficient for her wants; and that the Phœnicians fetched iron, with other merchandise, from India. In the lament of the prophet Ezekiel over Tyre, at chapter xxvii., we read in—

Ver. 12. "Tarshish was thy merchant by reason of the multitude of all kind of riches; with silver, iron, tin and lead, they traded in thy fairs."

Ver 19. "Dan, also, and Javan, going to and fro occupied in thy fairs: bright iron, cassia, and calamus, were in thy market."

At all events, we know that architectural details were firmly executed in India at very remote periods. The monoliths and rock-cut temples, described in our chapter on architecture, give evidence of this several centuries before our era; and they were probably executed with the few rough and simple tools which at the present day are all that is necessary to a Hindu workman. M. Petrie, an engineer, says a carpenter will have a chisel and a plane, and a tool of a wedge-like shape, sharp at one end and broad at the other, which he will use for a variety of purposes. With the wedge, the chisel, and the plane, *all* their work was managed. The now-silent quarries of Bijanagger still bear marks of the chisel. This grandest of Hindu cities was constructed entirely of granite: its walls, pillars, arches, and even flat roofs and beams, were all made of granite, some blocks being fifteen feet in breadth. The highly-tempered, pencil-shaped chisels, were of steel; the wedges of iron from two to three and a-half inches long. The hammers were sometimes of wood; but if iron hammers were used, the Hindu made a hollow in the striking-face of his hammer, which he filled with lead or soft iron, to diminish vibration and save the edge of the chisel.[1]

The superior quality of Hindu steel has long been known, and it is worthy of record, that the celebrated Damascus blades have been traced to the workshops of western India. The figuring of these swords is found to depend upon a mode of crystallization, called *wootz*, which is the name given in India to manufactured steel. The ore is beaten with a stone hammer into a bar, then cut into small pieces and placed in crucibles, with green berries and dry wood. Much importance is attached to the kind of wood used, as this influences the kind of steel produced. Steel, manufactured in Cutch, enjoys at the present day a reputation not inferior to that of the steel made at Glasgow and Sheffield; and in the ancient days,[2] thirty pounds of steel was a precious gift, deemed by King Porus worthy of presentation to Alexander the Great. Another sign that Ancient India was celebrated for steel is given by the Persian phrase,—to give an "Indian answer;" meaning, "a cut with an Indian sword."[3] Splendid specimens of daggers, and other warlike weapons, were sent by the Rajahs of India to the International Exhibitions of 1851 and 1862. But, beautiful as the jewelled arms of India are, it is still for the intrinsic merit of their steel that they are most highly prized. The swords of the Sikhs are said to bear bending and crumpling, and yet be fine and sharp as the scimitar of

---

[1] J. R. A. S., No. xiii. Paper read 15th January, 1842: Hindu Modes of Quarrying Granite. By Lieut. Newbold, Madras Army.

[2] Heath, J. R. A. S., Feb. 16, 1839.
[3] Royle Lecture: Art Man. of India, p. 466.

Suliman, made famous by the graphic description of Sir Walter Scott.

How much more plentiful iron may have been in former days we cannot accurately ascertain. But we know, that in centuries not far from our era it was the custom to put iron roofs on large buildings, supported by one thousand columns; whereas at present, iron cannot be found in sufficient quantity to be available for any public works. We read of iron mines in Kattywar as "mere circular pits, sunk into the ground to the depth of from five to twenty feet," worked with a pick-axe and a shovel. A shed is raised to shelter the workmen, the ground is scooped out in the centre, and a furnace is placed at each end. The workmen gain but a miserable subsistence; and the whole amount of iron fabricated at six such foundries is not more than one hundred and fifty tons in a year.[1]

The practical bearing of this history of commerce and manufacture seems to be, that India can make calico, muslins, shawls, carpets, steel in perfection; but that as she cannot make fast enough for the newly-awakened needs of the five hundred millions of her population, Great Britain must supply goods for the masses; whilst Dacca, Kutch, Kashmere, Masulipatam, &c., produce prize specimens for the rich and luxurious. But it is not only in the manufacture of expensive and important goods that the Hindu excels; and Dr. Forbes Watson most justly observes, that the study of Indian art might in numberless ways improve the character of the every-day articles around us. Hindus make these things now as they have made them from time immemorial; but nevertheless, a certain perfection of taste is seen "in everything which the artizan has touched, from the fan with which he cools himself to the vessel with which he drinks."

---

[1] Report on the Iron of Kattywar. By Captain Legrand Jacob. J. R. A. S., No. xiii., p. 98. May, 1842.

[2] Dr. J. Forbes Watson: Lecture, Society of Arts.

POSTSCRIPT.

It is with reluctance that I bring these volumes to an end. I would rather work on, striving to make them more complete, but I feel that the most fitting duty for me at this moment, is to let my work go forth, trusting that it will be received with kind indulgence.

If it prove useful to students, I shall be glad; but much greater will be my satisfaction if it should induce some of those who live in India to make themselves more fully acquainted with the people and the literature of the land in which they seek a temporary home.

LONDON:
LEWIS AND SON, PRINTERS, SWAN BUILDINGS, MOORGATE STREET.

INDEX.

abhāva, i. 182.
abhidhānaratnamālā, i. 389.
abhimanyu, ii. 59.
abhishēka, i. 97 f. 102; ii. 48.
achāra, i. 276, 304.
āchārya, i. 297; ii. 14.
achyuta, i. 251.
adharma, i. 199.
adhibhūta, i. 128.
adhidaiva, i. 128.
adhikārin, i. 207.
adhishṭhāna, i. 415.
adhyayna, i. 128.
adhwaryu, i. 36, 76, 78, 88, 91, 95, 97, 109.
adhyātman, i. 128, 228.
aditi, i. 2 f. 6, 26, 30.
ādityas, i. 5, 26, 29 f. 111 f. 120 f. 104, 209.
ādilya-purāṇa, i. 286.
agastya, i. 30, 24 f. 61, 77; ii. 19, 85.
agni, 7, 12 ff. 26 f. 30, 32 f. 36, 42, 46, 49, 52, 55 f. 61, 63, 82, 89, 91 ff. 112, 120, 126, 133, 249, 262, 336, 342; ii. 25, 63.
agnidhra, i. 88, 90.
agnidhriya, i. 90, 141.
agnihotra, i. 86 f. 130 f. 209.
agnimindha, i. 28.
agni-purāṇa, i. 244, 251.
agnishṭoma, i. 87.
agnivarṇa, ii. 97.
agnivēsa, i. 342.
ahankāra, i. 156, 187, 242.
āhavanīya, i. 90 f. 98, 114, 141, 145.
ahi, i. 18 f. 24, 36.
airāvata, ii. 353.
aiśwarm, i. 156.
aitareya-āraṇyaka, i. 123.
aitareya-brāhmaṇa, i. 85 f. 324, 360; ii. 47, 152.
aja, ii. 96 ff.

ajanta, i. 109, 392 ff. 434; ii. 357.
ajigarta, i. 96 ff.
ākānkshā, i. 109.
ākāsa, i. 156, 206.
ākhyāna, ii. 29.
ākrunchana, i. 166.
aloka, ii. 258 f. 262 ff.
albirūnī, i. 370.
amarakosha, i. 380.
amarasinha, i. 399.
ambashṭhas, i. 283.
āmra, i. 215.
amṛita, ii. 75.
anāddyavidyā, i. 211.
ananta (king), ii. 312.
anuntu, i. 251, 339; ii. 75 ff.
andhra, ii. 240.
anga, ii. 35.
angiras, i. 77, 305.
angirasa, i. 65 f. 98.
angirn, ii. 330.
anjahcara, i. 98.
anāhāryapachana, i. 145.
anṛumbhaṭṭa, i. 187, 200.
anmalā, i. 404.
ansa, ii. 153 f.
ananmati, i. 66.
antarāla, i. 416.
anusubas, i. 194.
anusṭubh, i. 194.
anurādhapura, i. 399, 418.
anupasankāri, i. 195 f.
anunyayatireki, i. 194.
anyonyābhāva, i. 200.
apalāsatarman, ii. 336.
apakshepaṇa, i. 199.
aparājita, ii. 333.
apaurush, ii. 125.
upastambha, i. 305.
apagā, i. 52.
apratiyogitwa, i. 197.
aprī, i. 97.

24

apsaras, i. 61; ii. 192 ff.
āruṇyaka, i. 122 ff. 153, 301.
arāhamaalapa, i. 410 f.
arishṭaka, i. 341.
arjuna, i. 218 ff.; ii. 31, 33 ff. 132.
artha, i. 171.
arthapāla, ii. 337.
arupa, i. 120.
arupi, i. 145.
ārya, i. 56, 66 f. 82 ff. 116 f. 274, 396; ii. 37, 44, 65.
āryabhaṭa, i. 364 ff.
aryaman, i. 2, 7, 26 f.
aryaka, ii. 169 f.
āryāshṭaçata, i. 306.
ṇadhāraṇa, i. 195 f.
āvana, i. 168 f.
avaṅga, i. 66.
açoka, i. 397 f.
açoka (tree), ii. 164, 196, 229, 331, 335.
āçrama, i. 249, 277, 392.
āçrayāsiddha, i. 196.
astika, ii. 73 f.
āsuri, i. 103.
asura, i. 34 f. 51, 65, 90, 139, 237, 274, 333; ii. 87.
açvalāyana, ii. 95.
açvamedha, i. 27, 29; ii. 3.
açvapati, ii. 87.
açvattha, i. 102, 217, 336; ii. 48.
açvins, i. 8 ff. 33, 56, 58, 97, 102, 112, 336 f.; ii. 52, 60.
atharva veda, i. 31, 37, 42 f. 60, 78 f. 83, 308.
atimukta, ii. 338.
atirātra, i. 76.
ātmabodha, i. 210 ff.
ātman, i. 148, 171, 182 f. 211 ff.
atri, i. 35, 62, 77, 168, 205, 336, 339.
ātreya, i. 339 ff.
atyantābhāva, i. 197, 200.
ālyaniti, i. 104.
auraca, i. 336.
avanti, ii. 155.
avayūj, i. 28.
avarava, i. 175.
avāpya, i. 97.
ayodhyā, i. 324, 392, 395; ii. 3 f. 18, 22, 25 ff. 90 f. 98, 111 f. 108, 270.
ayodhyā-kāṇḍa, ii. 18.
āyur-veda, i. 339 ff.
āyus, ii. 206.

B.

bālarāyaṇa, i. 303, 305.
bodhita, i. 197.

bahu-vadha, ii. 79.
bakri, i. 337.
bala, i. 19.
bāla-gopāla, i. 286.
bālabhaṭṭa, ii. 140.
barolli, i. 428 ff.
bauddhas, i. 414, 421; ii. 143, 168, 170, 221 ff. 285.
bhāngaradgītā, i. 216 ff. 250; ii. 56, 79.
bhagavat, i. 253 ff.
bhāgavata-purāṇa, i. 244, 253 ff. 267.
bhairava, i. 270.
bhakti, i. 290, 250, 255, 268 f.
bharadvāja, i. 51, 61, 77; ii. 17.
bharata, i. 72 ff. 103 f.; ii. 6 ff. 15 ff. 25, 30 f. 95, 190.
bhāravi, ii. 133.
bhartṛihari, ii. 137.
bhāshāparichheda, i. 183 f. 187.
bhāskara āchārya, i. 373, 376.
bhaṭṭikāvya, ii. 137.
bhavabhūti, ii. 159, 207, 230, 336.
bhāvanā, i. 199.
bhavishya-purāṇa, i. 244.
bhīma, ii. 31, 33 ff. 50 ff. 60 ff. 85 ff.
bhikshus, 45, 50, 56, 60 ff.
bhoja, ii. 218.
bhojadeva, i. 189.
bhojas, i. 66.
bhṛigu, i. 77; ii. 72.
bhṛigus, i. 10.
bhūmi-khaṇḍa, i. 247.
bhūriprayoga, i. 389.
bhūta, ii. 319 f.
bhuvaneçwara, i. 245, 201, 425 f.
bidpai, ii. 275.
bodha, i. 212.
brahmā, i. 95, 97, 130, 142, 231, 246, 248, 251, 265, 274, 307, 314, 330, 414; ii. 75, 78, 120 ff. 253.
brahmaçāriṇ, i. 143 ff.
brahmagupta, i. 364, 372, 376.
brahman (n.), i. 42, 69, 114, 120, 123, 127 ff. 130 ff. 142 ff. 146 ff. 153, 205 ff. 218, 225, 235, 240; ii. 150, 205, 242 ff.
brāhmaṇa, i. 69, 79, 85, 119, 153, 201, 277, 360 f.
brahmaṇaspati, i. 69.
brahmāṇḍa-purāṇa, i. 244.
brāhmans, i. 40 f. 52, 66 f. 69 ff. 121, 145, 228 f. 263, 286, 273 ff. 301 ff. 320 f.; ii. 3, 30, 41, 62, 143, 207, 246.
brahma-purāṇa, i. 244 f.
brahmasūtra, i. 205.
brahmavaivarta-purāṇa, i. 241, 251.
brahmāvarta, i. 74, 280.

bṛihad-āraṇyaka, i. 123 ff.
bṛihaspati, i. 7, 148, 272, 306, 320, 330;
ii. 304.
bṛihat-saṃhitā, i. 306 ff.
buddha, i. 315, 380, 401 ff.; ii. 168 f.
buddhi, i. 156, 183, 209, 211 f.

C.

chaitanya, i. 368 f.
chaitya, i. 396 ff. 406 ff.
chakra, i. 189 f.
chakravāka, ii. 296, 298, 300.
champā, ii. 335 f.
champa, ii. 337.
chāmuṇḍā, ii. 212, 214.
chāṇakya, ii. 220 ff. 290.
chandana dāsa, ii. 220, 227.
chandragupta, ii. 219 f.
chāṇḍālas, i. 145.
charaka, i. 342 ff.
charaṇa, i. 79, 260, 273.
chārudatta, ii. 156 ff.
chārvākas, 271; ii. 249 f.
chāṭvāla, i. 91.
chauri, i. 322.
chedi, ii. 89 f. 134.
cherial, ii. 74.
chhandoga, i. 138.
chhāndogya-upanishad, i. 138 ff.
chikitsā, i. 339, 342.
chikitsitasthāna, i. 344.
chintāmaṇi, i. 517.
chitragriva, ii. 382.
chitrakūṭa, ii. 17, 24, 108; ii. 260.
chitrasena, i. 250.
chitravarṇa, ii. 294, 299 f.
chittore, i. 428 ff.
chūḍābuddha, ii. 157.
chyavana, ii. 204.

D.

dadhīti, i. 65.
dadhikrā, i. 30.
dāsa, i. 269.
dādūpanthis, i. 269.
dagoba, i. 390 ff.
daitya, i. 247; ii. 52.
daksha, i. 3, 245, 305, 334; ii. 313, 315.
dākshāyaṇa, ii. 316.
dākshi, ii. 315.
dakshī, i. 334; ii. 315.
damanaka, ii. 276 ff.
damayanti, i. 395; ii. 85 ff. 136, 138, 354.

dāmara, i. 18, 34; ii. 194 f.
daṇḍaka, ii. 18, 21 f.
daṇḍanīti, ii. 342.
daṇḍī, i. 290.
daṇḍin, i. 270.
daṇḍiśā, i. 414.
darbha, i. 91.
darpaṇas, i. 161, 204, 243.
darpapūrṇamdas, i. 109.
daśagītiśāstra, i. 366.
daśaratha, ii. 2 f. 140.
daśārṇa, ii. 260.
daśakumāracharita, ii. 333 ff.
daśapuraṇaku, ii. 148, 146.
daśamīā, i. 270.
dasyus, i. 20, 56, 64 ff. 88, 116 f.; ii. 195.
dātiaka, i. 326 f.
dāyabhāga, i. 317, 329 ff.
deṇya, ii. 317.
devarāla, i. 98.
devas, i. 139, 237.
dronparvan, ii. 260.
devi, ii. 328.
devi-māhātmya, i. 257.
dhanamitra, ii. 189.
dhanvantari, i. 338 f.
dhārā, ii. 323.
dhāraṇā, i. 166.
dharma, i. 199, 202, 270, 309; ii. 52, 251.
dharmadhwaja, ii. 329.
dharmaśāstra, i. 276, 304 f.
dharmasūtra, i. 275.
dhrīti, i. 320, 383 f. 386, 389.
dhātupārāyaṇa, i. 386.
dhātupāṭha, i. 382, 389.
dhanurveda, ii. 47, 51 ff.
dhishṇyas, i. 90.
dhodi, ii. 357 ff.
dhṛishṭadyumna, ii. 41, 45, 55.
dhṛitarāshṭra, i. 331; ii. 31, 49.
dhyāna, i. 166.
digambaras, ii. 363.
dikshā, i. 91, 260.
dikshaṇīya ishṭi, i. 91.
dilīpa, i. 249 f.; ii. 97 ff.
dīpaka, ii. 137.
dīrghamukha, ii. 294 ff.
dīrghatamas, i. 29.
divodāsa, i. 10, 64.
draupadi, ii. 33, 43 ff. 85, 92.
dravya, i. 181.
drishadvati, i. 52.
dṛishṭānta, i. 172.
droṇa, ii. 32 ff. 38 ff. 50 ff. 85, 96.
droṇa-kalaṣa, i. 98.
drupada, ii. 32, 38 ff. 55 ff. 96.
duḥsama, ii. 40 ff.

duḥkha, i. 199.
dūradarçin, ii. 300, 307.
durgā, i. 250.
durgālāsa, i. 336.
durgāpūjā, i. 272.
durvāsas, ii. 180.
duryodhana, ii. 31, 35 ff. 49 ff.
dushyanta, i. 108 ; ii. 62 ff. 172 ff.
dwāraka, i. 210, 247, 261 ; ii. 44, 47, 85, 154 f.
daçaka, i. 199.
dwijas, ii. 12, 330.
dwīpas, i. 240.
dyaus, i. 2.

E.

ekachakrā, ii. 37 f. 70.
ekāmrakānana, i. 245.
elephanta, i. 422.
ellora, i. 420 ff.
svayamvarī, i. 28.

G.

yamuna, i. 109.
gandharva, i. 29, 37 ; ii. 93, 195.
gāndhārī, ii. 57.
gāṇḍīva, ii. 57, 63.
gaṇeça, i. 272 ; ii. 353.
ganyā, i. 50, 52 ; ii. 4, 73 f. 118 f. 262, 326.
garbhagṛiha, i. 416.
gargya, i. 129.
gārhapatya, i. 87, 90, 92, 142, 145.
garuḍa, ii. 277, 329 f.
garuḍa-purāṇa, i. 244.
gauḍapāda, i. 153.
gautama, i. 77, 134, 144.
gautamī, ii. 184.
gāyatrī, i. 3, 34, 42, 280, 207.
ghaṭakarpara, ii. 180.
girijā, ii. 328.
giriagoriśnī, ii. 209 ff.
gokulasthas, i. 266 f.
gomatī, i. 53, 62.
gopāla, ii. 343 f.
gopura, i. 417 f.
gosain, i. 367.
gotama, i. 33, 151 f. 170 ff. 181, 305, 313.
gotra, i. 77.
griha, ii. 153.
grāvagrābha, i. 28.
grihagupta, ii. 340.
grihyasūtras, i. 275 f. 297.

gritsamada, i. 6, 24, 337.
gūhasena, ii. 318.
gulma, i. 343, 345.
guṇa, i. 156, 181, 227.
guṇāḍhya, ii. 317.
guñjā, i. 287.
guru, i. 80, 127, 142 f.

H.

haimakosha, i. 389.
halāyudha, i. 380.
hansa, i. 30, 138.
hansapadikā, ii. 184.
hanumat, i. 264, ii. 23 ff. 127, 168.
hari, i. 230, 252, 265.
haritaki, i. 4.
harichandra, i. 98 ff. 324.
hārīta, i. 305, 340.
harsha, ii. 220.
harshadeva, ii. 312.
harsha-charita, ii. 323.
hastināpura, i. 31, 33, 37, ff. 69, f. 2, 172, 180, 184.
havirdhānas, i. 30, 93.
hemachandra, i. 380, 389.
heramba, ii. 216.
hetu, i. 175.
hiḍimba, ii. 37.
himālaya, ii. 118 ff.
hiraṇyagarbha, i. 209, 254, ii. 204, 208 ff.
hiraṇyaksha, ii. 282.
hitopadeça, ii. 275 f. 391 f.
horā, i. 300.
hotṛi, i. 28, 78, 87, 90, 97 ff.

I.

ikha, ii. 252.
ibn asnība, i. 353.
ichhā, i. 199.
ikshwāku, i. 224, ii. 3, 26.
ilāsha, i. 94.
indra, i. 16 ff. 29, 32 f. 35, 36, 42, 48 f. 51, 58, 61, 64 ff. 71 ff. 82 f. 94, 96, 100, 108, 112, 116 f. 125, 133, 205 f. 227, 240, ii. 3, 14, 46, 52, 63 ff. 69 ff. 120 ff. 154, 189, 290.
indradatta, i. 315.
indraprastha, i. 46, 52, 131 f.
indra-sabhā, i. 421 f.
indriya, i. 171.
ingudi, ii. 17, 174.
indriyānādau, i. 344.
ira, ii. 173.

INDEX.

īçvara, i. 164 ff. 219, 254.
īçvara kriahna, i. 158, 164.
itihāsa, i. 141, 146.

J.

jabālā, i. 145 f.
jagannātha, i. 308, 425, 427.
jahnavī, ii. 293.
jaimini, i. 151, 204.
jaiminīya-nyāyamālāvistara, i. 205.
jainas, i. 414, 421, ii. 286, 301, 329.
jīvātman, i. 171.
jalandhara, i. 251.
jamadagni, i. 77.
jambu, ii. 201.
jambudvīpa, ii. 294, 304.
janaka, i. 119 ff. 124, 233, ii. 5 ff.
janamejaya, i. 108, ii. 69 f. 72.
jātaçruti, i. 142 f.
jauma, i. 369.
jarāsandha, i. 47.
jātaka, i. 360.
jātaveda, i. 133.
jayadeva, ii. 154, 369.
jīmūtavāhana, i. 317, ii. 329.
jīvagoçha, ii. 223.
jīva, i. 212.
jīvātā, i. 214.
jīvanmukta, i. 214.
jnāna, i. 210.
jyotisha, i. 362.

K.

kabīr, i. 266 f.
kabīr chaura, i. 260.
kabīrpanthīs, i. 269.
kadalī, i. 312.
kādambarī, ii. 140.
kaibeyi, ii. 6 ff. 21.
kailāsa, i. 420, 422, ii. 5, 813.
kālavilūkikā, ii. 263.
kakshivat, i. 58, 336.
kaliapa, ii. 312.
kali, ii. 87, f. 136.
kālidāsa, ii. 92, 97 f. 103 f. 115 f. 133, 138 f. 143, 150, 171 f. 191, 220, 257, 265, 344.
kalila wa damna, ii. 275.
kalinga, ii. 340, 350.
kalinyga, i. 96, 251, 326.
kalpa, i. 227.
kalpasthāna, i. 345, 355.
kalpasūtra, i. 275 f.
kāma, i. 44, ii. 122 ff. 208 ff. 251, 244.

kāmandaki, ii. 210.
kamboja, ii. 8.
kāmpilya, ii. 46.
kanāda, i. 151, 152, 180 ff.
kandarpaketu, ii. 245.
kanva, i. 50, 251, 336, ii. 93, 172, 174 f. 190 ff.
kāçyapa, i. 66.
kapālika, ii. 263 ff.
kapi, i. 120.
kapila, i. 151 f. 164.
kapinjala, i. 34.
kāpya, i. 120.
karajaka, ii. 276 ff.
kararira, ii. 169.
karli, i. 406 ff. 424.
karmaa, i. 181, ii. 241.
karya, ii. 35 f. 60 ff.
karpūra, i. 294 ff.
kāla, ii. 339.
kāçikhirritti, i. 365.
kaçyapa, i. 77, 111, ii. 190, 207.
kathāsaritsāgara, ii. 311 ff.
katha-upanishad, i. 133 ff.
kātyāyana, i. 110, 123, 305, 308 f.
kātyāyanī, i. 124.
kuvera, i. 219 ff. ii. 30 ff.
kauçalyā, ii. 7, 9 f. 15.
kauçambī, ii. 360, 314.
kauçītaki-brāhmaṇa, i. 305.
kauçika, 72 ff. ii. 175.
kaustubha, i. 336, ii. 78.
kautilya, ii. 221.
kavacha, i. 94, 103.
kavirāja, ii. 140.
kāvya, ii. 2, 115, 140.
kāvyaprakāça, ii. 144.
kena-upanishad, i. 131 ff.
keçava, ii. 174.
keçaki, ii. 214.
kevaladvaayi, i. 194.
kevalanyativeti, i. 194.
khāṇḍava, i. 98, 300, ii. 277.
khāṇḍavaprastha, ii. 46.
khara, i. 92.
khela, i. 58.
khetaka, i. 66, 83.
kinçuka, ii. 60.
kirātārjuniya, ii. 133 f.
kīrtivarman, ii. 243 f.
koçala, ii. 2, 236 f. 279, 350.
koçka, i. 211, 280.
kripa, ii. 35.
kripā, ii. 49.
kripāna, i. 34.
krishna, i. 85 ff. 219 ff. 251 ff. 359, 365 ff. ii. 44 ff. 96, 184 ff. 260.
krishṇā, ii. 46.

kriśāpa-miçra, ii. 242 ff.
kṛit, i. 382.
kṛidayuga, i. 96.
krama, i. 53.
kṛkaṭa-kśīrṣa, i. 345.
kshatriya, i. 71, 97, 99 ff. 134, 145, 222, 238 f. 273 f. 295, ii. 17, 36, 44, 92, 95.
kshatra, i. 233 ff.
kshatrajña, i. 238 ff.
kubhā, i. 53.
kuladharmas, i. 275.
kulika, i. 329.
kumāra-sambhava, ii. 115 ff.
kumārila-swāmin, i. 205.
kumbhaka, i. 167.
kunjara, i. 348.
kundī, i. 222, ii. 35 ff. 45.
kūrma, i. 171.
kūrma-purāṇa, i. 244.
kuru, i. 219, ii. 30 ff.
kurukshetra, i. 94, 112 ff. 392, ii. 57 f. 68, 262.
kurwaka, ii. 196.
kuça, i. 88, 92, 296.
kuçika, i. 71.
kusumapura, ii. 345 f.
kutas, i. 14, 36, 55, 68.
kuvera, ii. 258, 263, 265, 289.

L.

laghupatanaka, ii. 281.
lakshmaṇa, i. 264, ii. 4 ff. 17, 19.
lakshmī, i. 338.
lalita indra, i. 245, 426.
laṅkā, ii. 19 ff. 168.
laṅkārdhwa, i. 399.
lauhika, i. 189.
lavaṇa, ii. 216.
lavangikā, ii. 214.
likhita, i. 305, 319.
likucha, ii. 341.
līlāvatī, i. 373.
liṅga, i. 194.
liṅga-purāṇa, i. 244.
liṅgapurāṇarpa, i. 194.
lohamahāpaya, i. 418.
lohaprāsāda, i. 418.
lokāloka, i. 249.
lokapālas, i. 300.

M.

mādhava, ii. 207 ff.
mādhavāchārya, i. 205.

mādharī (flower), ii. 234, 270, 336.
madhumati, ii. 216.
madra, ii. 57.
mādrī, ii. 31.
magadha, ii. 47.
māgadhas, i. 283.
maghā, ii. 134.
mahābhārata, i. 67, 117, 217, 219, 248 f. 258 f. 260, 334, 338, 392, 395, ii. 1 f. 15, 39—96, 136, 156, 283, 354.
mahākāryas, ii. 133 ff.
mahāmudopa, i. 417.
mahant, i. 265.
mahat, i. 155, 246.
mahātmyas i. 257.
mahāwellipore, i. 448 f.
maheçwara, i. 248, 290.
maitreya, ii. 156 ff.
maitryī, i. 124.
maheroda, ii. 209 ff.
mālati, ii. 207 ff.
mālatimādhava, ii. 207 ff.
malaya, ii. 300, 340.
mālikā, ii. 270.
mālyavat, ii. ii. 314.
manas, i. 155, 170, 182, 209, 211 ff.
mānasa, ii. 5, 260.
mānasāra, i. 413 f. 416, 426, 431.
mānava, ii. 195 ff.
mānaras, 276 f. 279 f. ii. 92.
mandara, i. 338, ii. 75 ff.
maṇibhadra, ii. 285 f.
maṇikyala, i. 400.
manka, i. 368.
mantapa, i. 422, 436 f.
manthara, ii. 262 f.
mantharī, ii. 6.
mantra, i. 119, 124, 309, 379.
mantragupta, ii. 340.
manu, i. 3, 62, 100, 115 ff. 142, 234, 246, 263, 270, 273 f. 304 ff. 325 ff. 338, 352, ii. 12, 72 f. 92, 95 f. 296, 353, 355, 362.
mārjāli, i. 90.
mārkaṇḍeya, i. 247.
mārkaṇḍeya-purāṇa, i. 244, 247.
marudeviddhā, ii. 52 f.
maruts, i. 21 ff. 27, 32, 68, 62 f. 309, 337.
māsha, i. 310.
mashpāra, i. 102.
matali, i. 268.
matharya, ii. 176 ff.
matharṣa, i. 389.
matsya, i. 57.
matsya-purāṇa, i. 244.
maurya, ii. 343.
māyā, i. 209, 224, 227, 250, ii. 343 ff.

INDEX. 375

madhâtithi, i. 325.
meghadûta, ii. 133, 138, 257 f.
menâ, ii. 118 f.
menakâ, ii. 96, 171 f. 175.
meru, ii. 62, 75, 79, 99.
mimânsâ, i. 201, 305.
mitâkshara, i. 351, 317, 320 ff. 329 ff.
mithilâ, i. 304, 332, ii. 5 f. 26, 336.
mitra, i. 2 f. 6 f. 14, 26 f. 30, 35, 47.
moha, ii. 242.
mrichchhakati, ii. 155 ff.
mudrârâkshasa, ii. 219 ff.
mûjavat, i. 59.
mukunda, ii. 325.
mulmul khas, ii. 360 f.
munis, i. 304, 313 ff. 358.
munja, i. 100.
mura, ii. 136.

N.

nâbhi, i. 23.
nachiketas, i. 133 ff.
nâgas, ii. 46, 68 f. 72, 85, 93, 250 f. 318.
nâgojibhatta, i. 168.
naishadhiya, ii. 133, 136.
naiyâyika, i. 176, 204.
nakshatras, i. 361, 363.
nakula, ii. 31, 66, 236.
nala, i. 295, ii. 85 ff. 136, 138, 354.
nalodaya, ii. 138 f.
namuchi, i. 253.
nânak shâh, i. 269.
nanda, ii. 220 ff. 269, 299, 317.
nandana, ii. 211 ff.
nandini, ii. 101.
nârada, i. 96, 146, 240, 326, ii. 119, 184, 205.
nâradîya-purâna, i. 244.
nârâyana, i. 247, 255.
narsinha deo, i. 427.
nâtaka, ii. 144.
nâtya, ii. 144.
naubandhana, ii. 74.
navananda, ii. 314.
nayathya, ii. 173.
nicha, i. 66.
niddanathâna, i. 342.
nigamana, i. 175.
nighantu, i. 389.
nimba, ii. 337.
nirukta, i. 9, 27, 381 f. 389.
nishâdas, i. 54, 396, ii. 16.
nishadha, ii. 85 ff.
nishka, i. 58.
niti, ii. 274, 290 f.
niyama, i. 186.

nrishoda, i. 356.
nritta, ii. 144.
nritya, ii. 144, 151.
nûshîrwân, ii. 275.
nyâsa, ii. 153.
nyâya, i. 151 ff. 170 ff. 185 ff. 203, 305, ii. 252.
nyagrodha, i. 102, 145 f.
nyuhja, 94.

O.

om, i. 80, 136, 139, 164, 238.
ophir, ii. 349 f.

P.

pada, i. 164, 160, 198.
padârtha, i. 181.
padmakalpa, i. 247.
padmaudbhadatta, i. 369.
padmanidhi, ii. 235.
padma-purâna, i. 244 ff.
padmâvati, ii. 208, 215 f. 325.
paipêrhi, ii. 317.
paksha, i. 195.
pala, i. 307.
palâsa, i. 96, 106, 109 f. ii. 46, 90, 123.
papa, i. 306.
panchâla, i. 144, ii. 31 ff. 36 ff. 85, 253.
panchasikha, i. 163.
panchatantra, ii. 273 ff. 293.
panchavinsa-brâhmana, i. 202.
panchopâkhyâna, ii. 275, 293.
pândava, i. 219; ii. 30 ff.
pându, i. 219, ii. 30 ff. 140.
pânini, i. 2, 106, 110, 123, 130, 251, 330, 364 f. ii. 33, 137, 289, 315 f.
panis, i. 13.
pârs, ii. 215.
parama-brahma, i. 261.
parâpara, i. 305, 316.
paramâtman, i. 148, 153, 206, 255.
parâtman, i. 212.
parishad, i. 81.
parjanya, i. 17.
poruahni, i. 22, 52.
pârvati, i. 432, ii. 313.
patâla, i. 249, ii. 281, 326.
patâla-khanda, i. 249.
patanjali, i. 151 f. 164 ff. 364.
pâtaliputra, ii. 219.
patni, i. 329 ff.
paulisa-siddhânta, i. 369.
pâundra, ii. 58.
paura, i. 55.

INDEX.

pauṇâgṇa, ii. 70 ff.
pedu, i. 10.
piṅgala, i. 251.
piṅgalaka, ii. 276 ff.
pippalâda, i. 127 ff.
piśâcha, i. 250, ii. 317 ff.
pitâmaha, i. 309 f.
pitṛimedha, i. 108.
pitṛis, i. 34, 88, 134, 146, 229, 312.
plakaha, i. 102.
prabodhachandrodaya, i. 273, ii. 242 ff.
pradhâna, i. 155, 161, 246.
pradhwaṅri, i. 200.
prâgabhâva, i. 200.
prahlâda, i. 247.
prajâpati, i. 39, 42, 45, 100, 110 ff. 123, 127 ff. 140 ff. 361.
prâkṛita, ii. 147 ff. 230, 317.
prakṛiti, i. 156, 157, 234, 226, ii. 344.
pramâ, i. 191.
pramâṇa, i. 170, 180.
prameya, i. 170.
prâṇa, i. 189, 206 f. 213.
prâṇâyâma, i. 166 f.
prapathas, i. 58.
prâsâraṇa, i. 199.
prasna-upanishad, i. 123 ff.
prastotṛi, i. 90, 92.
pratardana, i. 206 f.
pratihartṛi, i. 92.
pratijnâ, i. 175.
prâtiṡâkhya, i. 385, ii. 314.
pratishṭhâna, ii. 318.
pradyâdhâra, i. 160.
prasarṅya, i. 92.
prayôga, ii. 193, 196, 203.
prayatna, i. 199.
prâyaṡchitta, i. 276, 304.
prayoga, i. 88.
prem-ságar, i. 367.
preta, ii. 319.
pṛithâ, i. 223, ii. 31, 43.
pṛithiri, i. 2.
punarabhisheka, i. 99, 102.
purâṇas, i. 108, 142, 146, 242 ff. 260, 305, 314, ii. 75, 352.
puri, i. 245, 425, 427.
purnabhadra, ii. 337.
puroḍâṡa, i. 91.
purohita, i. 70 f. 103 ff. ii. 69.
purusha, i. 40 ff. 110 f. 129 f. 148, 156, 164, 237, 248, 354, 343 f. ii. 266.
purushamedha, i. 108.
purusha-sûkta, i. 40 f.
purûravas, ii. 192 ff.
purushottama, i. 330, ii. 250.
pûrva-mimânsâ, i. 151, 153, 201 ff.
pûshan, i. 7, 35.

pushkara, i. 246 f.
pushpadanta, ii. 314.
pushpapura, ii. 224.
pattra, i. 338.

R.

râdhâ, i. 266, ii. 269 ff.
râgavibodha, ii. 152, 154.
râghavapâṇḍavîya, ii. 140.
raghu, ii. 12 f. 97 f.
raghuvaṁṡa, i. 240, ii. 97 ff.
râhu, i. 370 f.
râjasûya, i. 40 f. 70, 83, 121.
râjarshi, i. 71.
rajas, i. 234.
râjasûya, i. 97, 102.
râjavidhana, ii. 335 f.
râkshasa, ii. 330 ff.
râkshasas, i. 10, 17, 88, 90, 337, ii. 3, 19, 23 ff. 37.
raktikâ, i. 363.
rukmya, i. 143.
râma, i. 259 f. 263 f. 266, 269, 396, ii. 2, 4, 6 ff. 47, 97 ff. 108 ff. 137, 140, 354.
râmachandra, i. 264, 268.
râmagiri, ii. 19, 159.
râmakṛishṇa-tîrtha, i. 307.
râmâṇandî, i. 264 ff.
râmâṇuja, i. 263, ii. 242.
râmâṇujas, i. 263 ff. ii. 242.
râmâyaṇa, i. 240, 253, 269 f. 261, 323, 392, ii. 1—30, 47, 72, 192, 354.
raṅi, i. 53.
raṅa, i. 342.
ratheṡtiti, i. 63.
rati, ii. 123, 125, 245.
ratnâvali, ii. 229 ff.
rûvapa, ii. 19 ff. 137.
reṇâ, ii. 260.
rhases, i. 352.
ṛibhus, i. 27.
ṛig-veda, i. 1, 3, 107, 114, 117, 148, 229, 259, 368, 397, 360 f. 392, ii. 4, 347.
ṛijîswana, i. 65 f.
ṛishiku, i. 53.
ṛishis, i. 14, 22, 35, 40 ff. 53, 62, 85, 69, 77, 94 f. 110, 118, 146, 225, 231, 247, 249, 253, 255, 260, 314, 368, ii. 72 ff. 334.
ṛitaparṇa, ii. 91.
ṛitasaṁhâra, ii. 265 ff.
ṛitvij, i. 87.
rohiṇi, i. 361, ii. 196.
rohita, i. 96 f.

rudra, i. 14 ff. 22, 141, 262, 287, ii. 192.
rūpa, ii. 144.
rūpaka, ii. 144.

S.

çabara-swāmin, i. 205.
sadāchāra, i. 249.
sadānanda, i. 207.
sādhanācyāpakatwa, i. 197.
sādhyaz, i. 40 f.
sādhyacyāpakatwa, i. 197.
sāgariká, ii. 332 ff.
sahadeva, ii. 31, 48, 66.
saivas, i. 209 ff.
çakaṭa-dāsa, li. 222.
çaktikumāra, ii. 339.
çakuni, ii. 49.
çakuntalā, ii. 92 ff. 139, 141 f. 171 ff. 354.
çākya-muni, i. 215, 321, 308; ii. 359.
çāla, i. 309.
śālagrāma, i. 250, 254, 396.
śālagrāma-kshetra, i. 247.
çālākya, i. 345.
sālātura, i. 364.
çalya, i. 345; ii. 57.
samādhi, i. 108.
samāsiddhikarana, i. 107.
sāmānya, i. 131, 199.
samavega, i. 191.
sāma-veda, i. 34, 42, 78, 86, 106 ff. 117, 138, 144, 220 f. 308.
sāmayāchārika-sūtraz, i. 275.
sambandha, i. 207.
sambara, i. 64.
samūha, i. 263, ii. 156.
sami, ii. 48.
samsara, ii. 237.
samvarta, i. 305.
samyama, i. 107 f.
sanatkumāra, i. 145 f.
sandhi, i. 94.
sandilas, i. 51.
sāndilya, i. 142, 149.
sangita, ii. 151.
sangita-dāmodara, ii 152.
sangita-nārāyaṇa, ii. 152 f.
sangita-ratnākara, ii. 152.
sangraha, ii. 312.
sangrāma, ii. 312.
sanhitā, i. 307 f.
sanjīvaka, ii. 276 ff.
sankara-āchārya, i. 131, 210, 270. f. ii. 241.
sankara-miçra, i. 186.

sankha, i. 305, 319.
sānkhya, i. 151 f. 155 ff. 208, 210, 218, 225, 244, 246, 254, 313.
sānkhyakāriká, i. 158 ff.
sānkhyapravachana, i. 152, 154.
sanniddhi, i. 198.
sanyāsin, i. 266, 270, 300, 302.
sançaya, i. 172, 198.
sanskāra, i. 199, 207.
santri, i. 28.
sapaḍma, i. 196.
sapiṇḍa, i. 322.
saptasindhu, i. 50.
saramā, i. 11 f. ii. 68.
sārameya, ii. 68.
saranyū, i. 37.
sārasa, ii. 209.
saraswati, i. 50 ff. 66, 69, 94 f. 271, ii. 26, 190, 245, 252, 254, 293.
sarayū, ii. 22, 20, 98.
sāri, ii. 358.
sārika, ii. 233, 235, 345.
sarira, i. 171.
sariraasthāna, i. 344.
sarvamedha, i. 100.
sastra, i. 346.
sat, i. 238.
satadrū, i. 52.
satapatha-brāhmaṇa, i. 44, 110 ff. 124, ii. 73, 193.
sātātapa, i. 305.
sātavāhana, ii. 318.
sati, ii. 318.
satpratipaksha, i. 196.
sattwa, i. 156.
satyakāma, i. 144.
sātyaki, ii. 48, 135.
sālyarat, ii. 82 ff.
saudāmini, ii. 215 ff.
sauraçūlas, i. 3, 272.
sauvaras, ii. 335.
savitri, i. 2 f. 6. 27, 60, 100, 101, 300.
sāvitrī, ii. 82 ff.
savyabhichāra, i. 196.
sāyaṇa, i. 71, 107.
sacha, i. 248 f.
sehanāga, ii. 220.
shantil (sāṇḍilya), ii. 320 ff.
siddhānta, i. 172.
siddhānta-muktāvali, i. 187.
siddhisthāna, i. 346.
pitaka, i. 330, 335.
çilpaçāstra, i. 413 f. 416, 431.
simai, i. 68, 74; ii. 350.
sindhu, i. 50, 58; ii. 215.
sinhāsana-dwātrimçati, ii. 312.
pippaji, i. 300.
sipra, ii. 288.

pippala, ii. 124 f.
pippalavrudha, ii. 124, 154.
sitā, i. 264; ii. 6, 9, 18 f. 108 ff.
piva, i. 108, 244 ff. 259 ff. 432; ii. 69,
  96, 118 ff. 145, 156, 168, 212 ff. 343,
  252, 299. 313 f.
piva-purāṇa, i. 344.
piri, i. 249; ii. 339.
skambha, i. 42 f.
skanda-purāṇa, i. 244.
ślokasthāna, i. 343.
smṛiti, i. 305, 306.
smṛitichandrikā, i. 317, 319, 320, 330 f.
soma, i. 18 ff. 29, 32 ff. 69, 71, 70, 63,
  86 ff. 95, 100 ff. 112, 140 ff. 227, 309,
  335 f. 361.
soma, (mun.), ii. 152 ff.
somadeva, ii. 312.
somaprovāka, i. 87.
somatīrtha, ii. 174.
somayāga, i. 87.
soshā, i. 344.
sphujidhwaja, i. 369.
sraddhā, i. 322 f.; ii. 15.
sramana, ii. 168, 170.
sri, ii. 2, 78, 214.
sriharsha, ii. 183, 136.
srikantha, ii. 207.
srotriya, i. 86 f.
sruti, i. 213, 305.
sthitisthāpaka, i. 199.
stridhana, i. 333.
stūpa, i. 390.
subandhu, ii. 140, 344.
subodhinī, i. 330.
sudās, i. 66, 69, 71 ff. 83, 109.
suddhātman, i. 212.
śūdra, i. 40 f. 98, 229, 238 f. 273 ff.;
  ii. 330.
śūdraka, ii. 156.
sugrīva, ii. 23 ff.
suksaptati, ii. 312.
sukha, i. 199.
sushecpa, i. 95 ff.
sunandā, ii. 102.
suparṇakā, ii. 25.
sūrya, i. 4 f. 9, 18, 27, 35, 129.
sūryapati, i. 272.
sūryasiddhānta, i. 362 ff.
sūryavatī, ii. 312.
sushupti, ii. 233, 235.
sushmna, i. 104.
sushna, i. 18 f. 36, 65.
suvrata, i. 251, 339.
sita, i. 347 f. 253 ff. 353.
sūtras, i. 88, 151, 154, 305, 314.
śvagavas, i. 96.
swadhā, i. 43.

swarbhāṇu, i. 34 f.
swaryasthanda, i. 249.
swarūpasiddha, i. 196.
swātman, i. 212.
swayamvara, ii. 38 ff. 86, 90, 92, 101.
svasta, i. 247.
syeti, i. 53.
syetakoṭu, i. 145.

T.

taddhita, i. 331.
taittiriya-brāhmaṇa, i. 274.
taittiriya-sauhitā, i. 107 f.
takshaka, ii. 46, 71 f. 219.
talavakāra-upanishad, i. 131 ff.
tamas, i. 156.
tantras, i. 267.
tapas, i. 42, 44.
tāraka, ii. 120 ff.
tarka, i. 198.
tarka-sangraha, i. 187 ff.
tat, i. 233.
tatwa, i. 155, 164.
tilaka, i. 309.
tirthas, i. 243.
tittibha, ii. 273.
traividyā, i. 114; ii. 305.
traivarṇa, i. 237.
traidyuga, i. 90.
trigarta, ii. 53.
trimūrti, i. 432.
trikāṇḍa-sesha, i. 339.
triphala, i. 351.
trishṭomā, i. 53.
trishṭubh, i. 34.
trita, i. 29.
tribhus, i. 73.
tulasī, i. 241, 251 f. 264, 366.
tura, i. 103.
tukārāma, i. 269.
turvasu, i. 66.
twashṭri, i. 29.

U.

udāharaṇa, i. 175.
udasruja, i. 64.
udayana, ii. 233.
udayagiri, i. 401.
udgātri, i. 34, 78, 87, 90, 95, 97, 139.
udgītha, i. 139 f.
udūlaka, i. 120, 142.
udumbara, i. 90 f. 100, 102; ii. 48.
ujjayinī, ii. 287.
umā, ii. 110 ff. 313.

upâdhi, i. 218 f.
upamāna, i. 197.
upanaya, i. 175.
upamiti, i. 197.
upanishads, i. 126 ff. 149 ff. 158, 201, 254, 271, 277, 297, 300.
upasaṃhti, ii. 316 f.
upaveda, ii. 252.
urvasi, ii. 191 ff.
ushas, i. 10 ff. 63, 97.
ushnas, i. 305.
ushasti, i. 139 f.
utanka, ii. 70 ff.
utkala, i. 245.
utkshepana, i. 193.
uttara-khaṇḍa, i. 240.
uttararāma-charitra, ii. 25.
uttaradaru, i. 101.
uttara-mīmānsā, i. 151, 153.
uttara-vedi, i. 90 ff. 98.

V.

vâchaspati miçra, i. 160.
vāgbhaṭa, i. 345, 358.
vaidika, i. 105.
vairāgin, i. 268, 270.
vaiçeshika, i. 151, 153, 176, 180 ff.
vaishṇavas, i. 263 ff. ; ii. 241.
vaiçya, i. 40 f. 145, 228, 238 f. 272 ff.
vaitālīya, ii. 135.
vairasvata, i. 134.
rājasrava, i. 134.
vājasaneyi-sanhitā, i. 118.
vaka, ii. 38. See baka.
vakula, ii. 270, 337.
valabhi, ii. 340.
vallabhāchāryas, i. 267.
vallabha-swāmin, i. 266 ff.
vālmiki, ii. 2, 27, 30.
vāmadeva, i. 30, 33, 70 ; ii. 334 f.
vāmana-jayāditya, i. 385.
vāmana-purāṇa, i. 244.
vāmarputi, i. 31, 309.
van astha, ii. 336.
vāraha-purāṇa, i. 214.
vārāhmihira, i. 368 ff. ; ii. 275.
vārayāvata, ii. 36.
vararuchi, i. 315 ff.
varṇa, i. 274 f.
varaha, ii. 315.
varuṇa, i. 2 f. 6 f. 14, 29 f. 35, 46 f. 59, 68, 82 f. 95 ff. 141, 307, 360 ; ii. 63.
vasantaka, ii. 234.
vasantasenā, ii. 159 ff.
vāsavadattā, ii. 140, 288, 310, 311 ff.

vasishṭha, i. 69, 72 ff. 82, 97 f. 108 ; ii. 16 f. 90, 99 f.
vasishṭha (law), i. 305.
vasabhūti, ii. 297.
vāsudeva, i. 227, 235, 252 ; ii. 46.
vāsuki, i. 246, 338 ; ii. 73, 76, 237.
vaswati, ii. 185, 189.
vasvakshaka, ii. 342.
vasu, i. 29 f. 136, 141, 309.
vata, i. 31.
vatsa, ii. 290 ff.
vātsyāyana, i. 248.
vāyu, i. 21, 27, 126, 138. 141 ; ii. 53.
veda, 3 ff. 237, 241, 252, 259 f. 262, 272, 275 f. 291 ff. 305, 314, 380 ;
ii. 3, 12, 26, 33, 69, 73, 83, 252. See Rig-Veda.
vedāngas, i. 305, 380 ff. 389 ; ii. 2, 75, 252.
vedānta, i. 133, 151, 153, 205 ff. 218, 244, 271, 313 ; ii. 193, 241 f.
vedānta-sāra, i. 207, 216.
vedi, i. 90, 98, 100.
vena, i. 189.
vetāla, ii. 319 ff.
vetālapanchaviṃçati, ii. 312, 319 ff.
vibhidaka, i. 50.
vibhishaṇa, ii. 23 ff.
viderbha, ii. 85 ff. 341.
videhas, i. 119.
vidura, ii. 46, 40 ff.
vidūshaka, ii. 149, 158.
vidyādhari, ii. 318.
vihāra, i. 245, 401 ff. 434 ; ii. 282, 336, 385 f. 359.
vīja, ii. 145.
vijayapita, i. 376.
vindus-bhikshu, i. 169.
vijñānesvara, i. 317.
vikrama, ii. 191 ff. 323 ff.
vikramabāhu, ii. 240.
vikramorvaṣi, i. 432 ; ii. 191 ff.
vimāna, i. 245, 416 f. 422, 425 ff.
vimānasthāna, i. 314.
viṇā, ii. 153.
vipakaha, i. 195.
viparyaya, i. 198.
viçada, i. 52 f. 62 ; ii. 14.
viruddha, ii. 222 ff.
viriji, i. 40.
viruta, ii. 52 ff.
viruddha, i. 196.
viçākhadatta, ii. 219.
viveka, i. 157 f. 199.
vishaya, i. 307.
vishṇu, i. 7 f. 23, 27, 55, 91, 112 f. 224, 227, 231, 233, 244 ff. 259 ff. 324 ;
ii. 26, 75 ff. 123, 243, 252, 813.

vishṇu (law), i. 305, 331.
vishṇugupta, ii. 343.
vishṇu-purāṇa, i. 344, 351 f.
vishṇudharmma, ii. 275, 291 ff.
vishṇuswāmin, i. 268.
vispalā, i. 58.
visruta, ii. 341.
viswaka, i. 65.
viswakarman, i. 89 f. 148, 411.
viswāmitra, i. 30, 31, 60, 69, 71 ff. 82,
    97 ff.; ii. 4 ff. 17, 93, 96, 171, 175.
viswanātha panchānana, i. 148 ff.
viswaprakāsa, i. 390.
viswadevas, i. 141.
viswapwara, i. 342.
viṭa, ii. 149.
vrāḍha, i. 309.
vīvara, ii. 337.
vīnavaṭī, i. 37, 284.
vopadeva, i. 253, 386; ii. 137.
vrata, i. 240.
vṛitra, i. 76 ff. 86, 72, 259.
vyāḍi, ii. 315.
vyāḳaraṇa, i. 380 ff.
vyakta, i. 283.
vyāpaka, i. 175.
vyāpti, i. 174.
vyāsa, i. 151, 169, 205 f. 250; ii. 80,
    37, 45, 46.
vyūha (law), i. 306, 331.
vyavahāra, i. 276, 304.
vyavahāra-mayūkha, i. 308, 317.

Y.

yādavas, i. 66 f. 252.
yadu, i. 66, 332, 361.
yajamāna, i. 87.
yajas, i. 114, 144.
yājñawalkya, i. 106, 110, 118 ff. 124 f.
    201, 304 ff. 320 f. 329.
yajur-veda, i. 44, 78, 107 ff. 118, 229,
    273.
yaksha, i. 257; ii. 258, 263, 317.
yama, i. 29, 36 ff. 133 ff. 166, 302;
    ii. 66, 88 f.
yama (law), i. 305.
yami, i. 37.
yamunā, i. 50, 52; ii. 303.
yāska, i. 9, 27, 39, 63, 71, 389.
yātra, i. 369.
yatus, i. 88.
yachana, i. 364 f.; ii. 176.
yayāti, i. 248.
yogāli kepari, i. 245.
yoga, i. 151 f. 164 ff. 218, 222, 225,
    238, 249, 271; ii. 58, 148, 156, 253.
yogin, i. 168, 214, 252, 270, 304; ii. 283,
    322 ff.
yogini, ii. 215.
yogyatā, i. 198.
yudhishṭhira, ii. 31 ff. 92, 134 f. 140,
    354, 362.
yūpa, i. 90, 98, 309.
yuvarāja, ii. 36.

www.ingramcontent.com/pod-product-compliance
Lightning Source LLC
Chambersburg PA
CBHW032030220426
43664CB00006B/426